Caribbean Life in New York City:

Sociocultural Dimensions

Caribbean Life in New York City:

Sociocultural Dimensions

Edited by
Constance R. Sutton
and
Elsa M. Chaney

1994
Center for Migration Studies of New York, Inc.

CARIBBEAN LIFE IN NEW YORK CITY:
SOCIOCULTURAL DIMENSIONS

First Edition

Copyright © 1987, reprint 1992, 1994 by

The Center for Migration Studies of New York, Inc.
209 Flagg Place
Staten Island, New York 10304–1199

Library of Congress Cataloging-in-Publication Data

Caribbean Life in New York City:
Sociocultural Dimensions

Bibliography: p.
Includes index.
1. Caribbean Americans—New York (N.Y.)—Social Conditions.
2. New York (N.Y.)—Social Conditions.
3. New York (N.Y.)—Social life and customs.
I. Sutton, Constance R.   II. Chaney, Elsa.
F128.9.C27C37 1986   305.8'68729'07471   85-47915

ISBN 0-913256-88-9 (Hardcover)
ISBN 0-913256-92-7 (Paperback)

The Editors dedicate this book

to

SAMUEL SUTTON

(1921–1986)

"all o' we is one"

ACKNOWLEDGMENTS

The concept for the issue of the *INTERNATIONAL MIGRATION REVIEW* (Volume 13, No. 2) that provides 6 of the 20 articles in this collection, emerged from several papers presented at a panel on Afro-Caribbean and Hispanic migration to the United States, organized by Chaney and Sutton at the joint meetings of the Latin American Studies Association and the African Studies Association in Houston in 1977. The co-editors wish to express their gratitude to the original contributors, who reexamined and, in some cases, updated their original work.

We owe a special debt to the new contributors, many of whom wrote their articles specifically for this volume (Basch; Georges; Glick-Schiller, *et al.*; Gregory; Kasinitz and Freidenberg-Herbstein; Reimers, and Soto).

We want to thank the following for permission to use material that appeared, sometimes in longer form, elsewhere: the Conference of Latin Americanist Geographers (CLAG) for the article by Conway and Bigby from *CONTEMPORARY ISSUES IN LATIN AMERICAN GEOGRAPHY*, B. Zentrek, editor (Munchie, Indiana: CLAG, Ball State University, 1983); Roy S. Bryce-Laporte for Marshall's article from *FEMALE IMMIGRANTS TO THE UNITED STATES: CARIBBEAN, LATIN AMERICAN, AND AFRICAN EXPERIENCES*, Delores M. Mortimer and Roy S. Bryce-Laporte, editors (Washington, D.C.: Research Institute on Immigration and Ethnic Studies, The Smithsonian Institution, 1981); Mouton Publishers for a version of Sutton and Makiesky-Barrow's contribution, which appeared originally in the volume *MIGRATION AND DEVELOPMENT: IMPLICATIONS FOR ETHNIC IDENTITY AND POLITICAL CONFLICT*, Helen I. Safa and Brian M. du Toit, editors (The Hague: Mouton, 1975); *DAEDULUS*, for an adaptation of an article by Flores, Attinasi, and Pedraza that appeared in Volume 110, No. 2 (Spring, 1981); and to Aaron L. Segal and Linda Marston for permission to use the map on page 6.

Finally, acknowledgment is made to the Ford Foundation's Caribbean Migration Program which funded the traveling expenses of the Caribbean participants to the original panel in Houston, and to LASA for a seed grant for planning the original panel. Most of the grant was used for an annotated "state-of-the-art" bibliography by Christine Davidson and Hubert Charles that appeared in *CARIBBEAN IMMIGRATION TO THE UNITED STATES*, Roy S. Bryce-Laporte and Delores M. Mortimer, editors (Washington, D.C.: Research Institute on Immigration and Ethnic Studies, The Smithsonian Institution, 1976, RIIES Occasional Papers No. 1). We also thank the Faculty of Arts and Science of New York University for a grant to assist in preparing this book for publication.

TABLE OF CONTENTS

INTRODUCTION

THE CONTEXT
OF CARIBBEAN MIGRATION

ELSA M. CHANEY
Georgetown University

Caribbean life in New York City is the product of the continuous circular movements of people, cash, material goods, culture and lifestyles, and ideas to and from New York City and the islands and mainland territories of the English- and Spanish-speaking Caribbean and, in recent times, the island of Haiti. As other immigrant groups, the first Caribbean migrants preserved strong familial and cultural links to their homelands; unlike them, these links have not been severed over time, but continue to be reenforced by the geographical closeness between the Caribbean and New York City.

Cheap airfares facilitate frequent comings and goings of island peoples and goods to an extent never dreamed of by immigrants of earlier times. On Sundays and holidays, international telephone circuits are clogged with the relatively inexpensive direct-dial service to and from Area Code 809. That particular "space" in New York City where each Caribbean group first established its center becomes like a distant province of the homeland, part of the same social and, in some cases (where migrants are encouraged to vote in their home country elections), political system.

Even if they prosper and move away from the original enclave, migrants return to encounter the foods, music, newspapers, and latest gossip of the homeland. Thus, an inventory of business and other concerns in Chapinerito, the area in Queens where Colombians settled in the years after World War II (named for a middle-class barrio, Chapinero, in Bogotá), reveals travel agents who offer round-trip excursion fares to Colombia at holiday times; real estate agencies with Colombian representatives who sell houses both in Jackson Heights and in Colombia; booksellers who vend Colombian newspapers and magazines; the headquarters of the many regional sports clubs. Chapinerito is the place to eat Colombian food or to buy the ingredients from the small ethnic grocery stores in the neighborhood. There is even a bakery specializing in Colombian pastries (Chaney, 1983).

Most Caribbean migrants do not appear to leave their homelands definitively, even though they may never return except for visits. Their insertion in New York City retains a provisional quality. Migration scholars talk of the "myth" or "ideology" of return as a strong feature of the Caribbean migrant experience, differentiating it sharply from that of early pioneer or "settler" migrants who never contemplated returning to their homelands. As Dominguez had noted (1975:59),

> Caribbean migrants to the United States are unlike European immigrants searching for the New Land and the New Frontier. Psychologically, Caribbean migrants are more like the inhabitants of a European colony, trying to reap as much benefit as possible by residing in the colonial power.

And Segal (1987) points out

> The Caribbean exodus is distinctive because its migrants have been so quick to seek integration abroad and to reject assimilation, (that is), the Caribbean Diaspora has insisted upon full civic, political and economic rights and opportunities (in the host societies), at the same time that it has resisted assimilation and sought to retain homeland ties and cultural identities.

Because of the continued strong ties to the homeland, a full understanding of Caribbean life in New York City demands some knowledge of contemporary conditions in the Caribbean, and of the demographic, economic, and psychological determinants of migration. One of the most obvious reasons for the increasing Caribbean presence is the dependent status of most Caribbean countries and territories on the United States and Canada, as well as several European metropolitan powers. In the introduction to the original volume that was the start of this collection, we explained Caribbean migration in the context of the world economy as "directly related to the disparity in growth between developed and developing countries," and as also related to the nature of growth in the industrialized nations "that apparently rests to an unacceptable degree on the availability of imported laboring hands" (Chaney, 1979:204, 207).

These arguments now are so familiar and well established that it is possible to take as "givens" a whole range of issues related to the unequal nature of global relationships. Instead of focusing on the dynamics of this global labor reserve, we can take a closer look by way of introduction at what is going on in relation to migration within the Caribbean region.

Mintz (1974:21–22) defines the Caribbean as including the more than 50 inhabited islands stretching from Trinidad, Aruba, Bonaire, Curaçao, Margarita, and others off the coast of Venezuela in the South, to Jamaica, Cuba, Hispaniola (Haiti and the Dominican Republic), and Puerto Rico—the Greater Antilles—in the North. The Caribbean includes all those islands that stretch in an arc nearly 2,000 miles long between Trinidad and western Cuba, and encompassing a few outlying islands such as Providencia and San

Andrés to the South. Because of their historical identification with the islands, and their similar histories under British and Dutch rule, the mainland territories of Guyana, Surinam, French Guiana, and Belize are often considered as belonging to the Caribbean region. It was this area, says Mintz (*ibid.*:22), that became

> . . . the first sphere of western colonization outside Europe itself, the site of the first important overseas capitalist experiments, and the starting place for tropical estate agriculture, the plantation system, and the large-scale New World enslavement of African peoples.

In 1980, the populations of these nations and territories totaled about 31 million persons, ranging from some 11,000 people in Montserrat to around 10 million in Cuba. If the Atlantic littoral of mainland countries whose shores are touched by the Caribbean—Colombia and Venezuela—is included, as some scholars suggest, the numbers would be considerably greater. The largest territory in terms of geographic size, Guyana, has 83,000 square miles, and the smallest, again Monserrat, only 38. Chart 1 plots the relative size, as well as the population densities, of the major entities.

Populations of African origin are numerically the most important in the English-speaking West Indies, although East Indian people comprise about two fifths of the population of Trinidad and one half that of Guyana (Commonwealth Caribbean 1970; the 1980 census figures have not yet been released). In the Hispanic and French Caribbean, persons of African origin are preponderant only in Haiti, Martinique, and Guadeloupe, although substantial numbers also reside in Puerto Rico, the Dominican Republic, and Cuba. According to Mintz (*ibid*:24), they make up at least 75 percent of the total Caribbean population—depending upon the local norms of perception. While the importance and meaning of racial identity varies significantly from one society to another, Mintz *(ibid.)* says that "the fact remains that the Caribbean region is a core area of contemporary Afro-America."

If there is one strong common, and reiterated theme among migration researchers of the Caribbean, it is the awareness that movements to and from the region are not a new phenomenon. Bach (1982:6) quotes Lewis' "tenth commandment" for understanding the ethnic and colonial heritage of the area: "Caribbean peoples have always been, and still are, a massively uprooted people." This is one of the features of Caribbean migration that distinguishes it from that of other regions in the Hemisphere, where extensive outmigration is fairly recent.

Of course, Caribbean peoples share with some South American populations the fact that their ancestors were transplanted from other continents. Although Amerindian peoples also originated on another continent, they are considered the true indigenous populations of the New World, including the

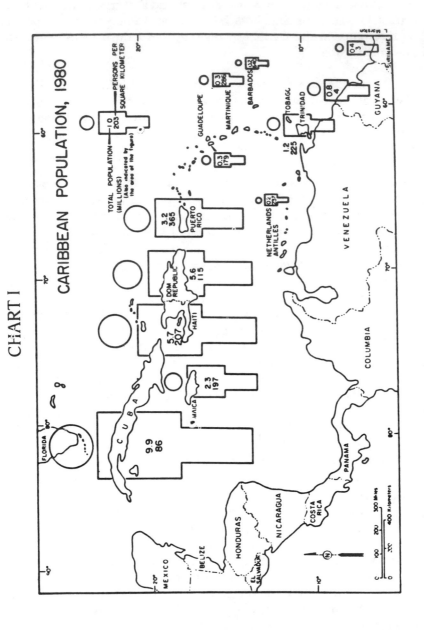

CHART I

CARIBBEAN POPULATION, 1980

Source: Caribbean Review, 11, 1 (Winter, 1982): 52. Used with permission.

Caribbean to which various groups of Amerindians had migrated beginning some 2500 years before the Spanish arrived. However, in the 16th century when the Spanish first colonized the region, large numbers of Amerindians were either deliberately exterminated, died of disease and malnutrition, or were absorbed into the population through intermixture with the Spaniards. In the following two centuries, mortality rates were high and fertility low because of the initial low female/male sex ratios among the slaves and the harsh conditions of the slave regimes. As Harewood (1981:40) notes, population growth at that time was largely synonymous with immigration, voluntary but in the main involuntary.

During the period before slavery ended on islands colonized by the English, planters did migrate with their slaves to other islands and to the U.S. South. The large-scale emigration of Blacks came only after Emancipation in 1834. As Thomas-Hope (forthcoming:1) notes,

> Migration was one of the few means open to former West Indian slaves whereby they could demonstrate their newly gained freedom and their abhorrence of a system that had bound them for so long to one place.

The principal historians of Caribbean migration divide the movements into essentially four stages: interterritorial migration of English-speaking islanders in the years immediately following Emancipation, particularly to British Guiana and Trinidad; an overlapping movement of the English-speaking islanders toward Panama and other destinations in the Hispanic Caribbean to work on the Panama Railroad and Canal, on the sugar in Cuba, on banana plantations in Costa Rica and, later, on the plantations of the American (later United) Fruit Company; a period during World War I and the Great Depression of little outward movement and many returnees; and the period from World War II to 1962–1965 when large-scale emigration to the United Kingdom took place. (See, Marshall, 1982 and 1983; Mintz, 1974; and Roberts, 1974).

From the U.S. perspective, Bryce-Laporte (see, article in this volume) and others add a fifth period, from the mid-1960s onward when, because of exclusionary legislation in Britain and adjustments in U.S. laws, large numbers of "new immigrants" began entering the U.S. from both the English- and Spanish-speaking Caribbean.

In the Dominican Republic, stagnating agriculture and industrial development that did not contribute to expanded employment in the post-Trujillo years sent some 150,000 migrants to the U.S. between 1966–77, a tenfold increase over any period prior to the assassination of Trujillo in 1961 (Grasmuck, 1985:148–49). In Colombia, the introduction of modern agricultural methods and machinery tended to exclude from the market all those who could not afford the new technology, while the agrarian reform program of the 1960s affected relatively few of Colombia's peasants. There was an ever-accelerating movement of people toward the cities and, beginning in the early 1960s, toward the U.S. (Chaney 1976:108–09). Four Caribbean countries—Cuba, the Dominican Republic, Jamaica and Colombia, in that order—along with Mexico accounted for nearly three quarters of Western Hemisphere Migration to the United States in the two decades from 1961 through 1979 (U.S. Bureau of the Census 1984: Table 131:90). Table 1 shows crude emigration rates from selected Caribbean countries over a ten-year period. This table demonstrates that emigration is not necessarily correlated with the degree of economic development as measured by Gross Domestic Product: several more developed countries registered emigration rates as high as those from the less developed, and some less developed countries had lower emigration rates than many of the better-off islands and territories.

Today Caribbean migration is directed overwhelmingly toward Canada and the United States. The proportions are large, both as percentages of the donor populations, as well as of total international migration. Segal (1975, 1987) was a pioneer in drawing attention to the dimensions of the Caribbean exodus in recent times. He estimates that Caribbean net emigration since 1950 constitutes approximately 20 percent of all voluntary international migration, legal and illegal. Between 1950 and 1980, about 4 million persons left the Caribbean to establish permanent residence elsewhere, principally in Europe and North America. This number represents 5 to 10 percent of the total population of nearly every Caribbean society, a higher proportion than for any other world area (ibid.:2; Cross, 1976:69–70). For some countries the proportion is much higher: in the mid-1970s, according to United Nations estimates (1979: Table 29:44), 16 percent of the total population of Jamaica, and 25 percent of the populations of Puerto Rico and Surinam, were living abroad.

For the region as a whole, intercensal growth rates declined in 1960–1970 to less than 1.5 percent per year, and similar low growth rates have continued during the past decade. These low growth rates were achieved not only in the face of continued high, although declining, fertility in most countries, but also in spite of marked improvements in life expectancy.

What are we to make of this phenomenon which, at present, shows no signs of abating? Metropolitan scholars tend to see migration in terms of the problems of the receiving societies. From a Caribbean perspective, however, emigration is not conceived as a problem to be solved, but as Basch (1982:11) aptly puts it, "as a deeply institutionalized strategy for economic subsistence and betterment." Marshall (1984:1) thinks the tendency to view migration positively explains why relatively few Caribbean scholars have displayed interest in migration studies.

This attitude may explain why most Caribbean governments have evinced only intermittent interest in framing policies either to encourage migration or to stem the flow, although as Segal (1987) notes, some governments of the

TABLE 1

CRUDE EMIGRATION RATES (CERs) FROM SELECTED CARIBBEAN COUNTRIES TO THE U.S. AND CANADA, 1966–1975 (AS PERCENT OF POPULATION AT 1970)

Sending Country	Native-Born Pop. 1970 (000s)	CERs U.S.	CERs Canada	Combined CERs
More Developed English-speaking Countries/GDP more than U.S. $2,500				
Trinidad/Tobago	869	6.1	4.3	10.4
Cayman Islands	10*	4.7	0.7	5.4
Bahamas	138	3.8	0.9	4.7
Barbados	222	6.7	3.8	10.5
Less Developed English-speaking Countries/GDP less than $2,500				
British Virgin Is.**	7	36.2	1.7	37.9
Montserrat**	10	10.7	3.0	13.7
St. Lucia	101	1.6	1.0	2.6
Jamaica	1,764	6.7	3.0	9.7
Antigua-Barbuda	58	5.5	2.5	8.0
St. Kitts-Nevis**	64*	7.0	1.8	8.8
Guyana**	687	2.7	3.5	6.2
Dominica**	71*	2.5	1.4	3.9
St. Vincent**	87	2.2	3.4	5.6
Grenada	94	2.8	2.4	5.2
More Developed Other Caribbean Countries/GDP more than $2,500				
Martinique	338	0.1	0.0	0.1
Guadeloupe	327	0.2	0.1	0.3
Less Developed Other Caribbean Countries/GDP less than $2,500				
Surinam**	371	0.2	na	0.02
French Guiana	51	0.1	0.0	0.1
Dominican Republic**	3,974	3.2	0.0	3.2

Source: Kritz 1981:220–21; Pastor 1985:5.

*Total population used because latest census conducted in year other than 1970.

**GNP. Years for measures vary.

region "discreetly promote emigration," and a few advertise abroad for the return of their skilled professionals. However, doubts about large-scale emigration, expressed in the Sudan, Tunisia, Egypt, and elsewhere, he says (*ibid.*), "are still latent in the Caribbean."

Exceptions in recent times are Cuba, which has closely regulated emigration, and Barbados and Trinidad, which have taken strong measures against illegal migration into their territories (United Nations, 1982:73). Barbados at several periods also took an interest in openly sponsoring the emigration of its nationals. In the late 19th century, the government arranged for the migration of both men and women to Panama (Thomas-Hope, 1978:74). During World War II and its aftermath, Barbados also gave official encouragement, training and financial assistance to nurses and hospital orderlies wishing to work in Britain, as well as to 4,000 men who were trained as bus drivers and hired by the London Transport Board (Davison, 1962:27–28). The Barbadian government also sponsored for a time a migration scheme for domestic servants to Canada.

So far as the causes of Caribbean migration are concerned, recent studies demonstrate skepticism of conventional explanations. Earlier scholars—primarily population demographers and geographers—stressed the demographic determinants and consequences; they talked of the "push" factors of rapidly-growing populations living on small, overcrowded islands, the "safety valve" of emigration with its dramatic effects on population growth and distribution. After that, the discussion widened as development economists began to emphasize that emigration was a response to the lagging economic development of the Caribbean, with its high unemployment rates and wage differentials between the islands and the metropolitan countries.

These explanations, in turn, have been questioned on several grounds. First, when all the islands and territories are taken into account, it can be shown that there are no necessary correlations or neat rank orderings of emigration rates with population growth rates and densities, with degree of economic development, with unemployment rates, or any other variable (Bach, 1982:7–9; see, also Table 1). Nor is Caribbean outmigration adequately explained by employment differentials between home country and the metropolis. As Thomas-Hope (1983:46) notes,

> The irony is that white collar workers migrate in large numbers from the Caribbean despite the deficits created in the labor market at home . . . pointing to the fact that it is not a simple reflection of supply and demand in the labor market in the countries of the periphery and the center.

More recently, migration has been viewed in terms of how the Caribbean is inserted into a global capitalist economy with an international division of labor that keeps small Caribbean islands dependent for their economic growth on the fluctuating world market for their agricultural products; their mineral exports, if they have them; and on an international tourist trade. Adopting this global, structural approach, Bach (1983:142) writes,

> . . . migration is viewed as part of the interlocking relationships that form a single regional economic system. Developed and underdeveloped countries are not separate entities but politically

and administratively bound parts of a unified economic division of labor. As origins and destinations of migratory flows, these states are not isolated points, but are partners in an integral pattern of economic development.

Nevertheless, as Thomas-Hope (1983:46) suggests, this macro-structural approach should not be viewed as providing a total explanation, but only as a framework within which to consider other factors at other levels of specificity, such as the effect on migration of local class, ethnic, and political conflicts or the manner in which household structure and family, kinship, and gender roles and relationships influence the nature of the migratory flow. In some cases, the desire to reunite families contributes to the movement of people to and from the islands, while in other cases a strong "migrant ideology" may be decisive, as foreign travel comes "to be regarded as a necessity in order to 'become a man,' to know the world and to understand life . . . a social imperative" (Thomas-Hope 1978:77).

All these aberrations and exceptions point to the complexities of establishing any unicausal explanation for migration. All have an element of truth, but have to be viewed in the context of the strong ideological and historical tradition of migration from the Caribbean.

Lately, migration scholars have been turning to questions of the effects on Caribbean societies of the migratory movements. The long history of out-migration from the region has, of course, had profound effects on the societies (these are treated at length in a state-of-the-arts paper on what we know about the consequences of migration for sending countries [Chaney, 1985]). The impacts can be most clearly seen, perhaps, in remittances and migrants returning home.

The major issues related to remittances concern their magnitude, and whether they are put to productive uses to further development in the home islands. The questions related to returnees revolve around the degree to which they contribute, through new skills and innovative approaches, to changes in the administrative and occupational structures—and the degree to which they invest their savings in productive ways.

Theories about these sets of questions often have suggested positive answers. In the Caribbean, however, the impacts are far from clear. In a review of the literature, Rubenstein (1983) finds that despite the large sums remitted to the Caribbean, and their importance for individual well-being, there is no positive contribution to rural economic rejuvenation. Rather, remittances and the larger export-labor phenomena of which they are a part are products of overarching political and economic forces that lie outside the West Indies; it is the already-developed world that is the real beneficiary of Caribbean migration, he says (ibid.:245).

While returned migrants apparently are accorded a new status in most home communities, scholars are almost unanimous in pointing out that

Caribbean returnees do not have so much influence on their home societies as had been assumed. The question is not so much difficulty in readapting, but that those left behind do not accept the returnees (Bovenkerk 1974:200ff.). Daniel (1976:162) and Gmelch (1980:151) both note the critical attitude return- ees bring, which provokes reciprocal criticism. In any case, those migrants with little education to begin with most likely spent their time abroad in tasks requiring little skill or training (Myers, 1976:445; Gmelch, 1980:147); thus they have neither much cash to bring back, nor many innovations to offer.

These are only a few of the issues that could be raised in relation to migrants' impact on the countries of origin. The impact of the Caribbean diaspora on the receiving society, in this case on the City of New York, where so many of the Caribbean's people come to live and work, is discussed in the next chapter and, indeed forms the major concern of this book.

BIBLIOGRAPHY

Bach, R.L.
1983 "Emigration from the English-speaking Caribbean." In U.S. Immigration and Refugee Policy: Global and Domestic Issues. M.M. Kritz, ed. Lexington, MA: Lexington Books. Pp.133–53.

_____
1982 "Caribbean Migration: Causes and Consequences," Migration Today 10(5):6–13.

Basch, L.
1982 Population Movements in the English-speaking Caribbean: An Overview. New York: United Nations Institute for Training and Research. Mimeographed.

Chaney, E.M.
1985 Migration from the Caribbean Region: Determinants and Effects of Current Movements. Washington, DC: Georgetown University, Center for Immigration Policy and Refugee Assistance.

_____
1983 "Colombian Outpost in New York City." In Awakening Minorities: Continuity and Change. J.R Howard, ed. New Brunswick NJ: Transaction Books. Second edition, Pp.67–76.

_____
1976 "Colombian Migration to the United States." In The Dynamics of Migration, Part 2. ICP Work Agreements. Washington, DC: Smithsonian Institution, Interdisciplinary Communication Program. Pp. 87–141.

Cross, M.
1979 Urbanization and Growth in the Caribbean. New York: Cambridge University Press.

Davison, R.B.
1962 West Indian Migrants: Social and Economic Facts of Migration from the West Indies. London: Oxford University Press for the Institute of Race Relations.

Dominguez, V.R.
1975 From Neighbor to Stranger. The Dilemma of Caribbean Peoples in the United States. New Haven: Yale University, Antilles Research Program. Occasional Papers No. 5.

Grasmuck, S.
1985 "The Consequences of Dominican Urban Outmigration for National Development: the

Case of Santiago." In *The Americas in the New International Division of Labor*. S. Sanderson, ed. New York: Holmes and Meier. Pp. 145–76.

Harewood, J.
1981 "Introduction to Population and Migration Section." In *Contemporary Caribbean: A Sociological Reader*. S. Craig, ed. Port-of-Spain, Trinidad: The College Press, Maracas, Pp.39–48.

Kritz, M.M.
1981 "International Migration Patterns in the Caribbean Basin: an Overview." In *Global Trends in Migration: Theory and Research on International Population Movements*. M.M. Kritz, C.B. Keely and S.M. Tomasi, eds. Staten Island, NY: Center for Migration Studies. Pp. 208–83.

Marshall, D.I.
1984 "The Impact of Migration in the Eastern Caribbean." Paper presented at the Regional Awareness Conference, CARICOM Population and Development Projects, St. Lucia.

_____
1983 "Toward an Understanding of Caribbean Migration." In *U.S. Immigration and Refugee Policy: Global and Domestic Issues*. M.M. Kritz, ed. Lexington, MA: Lexington Books. Pp. 113–31.

_____
1982 "The History of Caribbean Migrations: the Case of the West Indies," *Caribbean Review* 111:6–9; 52–53. Winter.

Mintz, S.W.
1974 *Caribbean Transformations*. Chicago: Aldine.

Pastor, R.A.
1985 "Introduction: The Policy Challenge." In *Migration and Development in the Caribbean: The Unexplored Connection*. R.A. Pastor, ed. Boulder, CO: Westview Press. Pp. 1–39.

Roberts, G.W.
1974 *Recent Population Movements in the Caribbean, Jamaica, Kingston*. The Herald, Ltd., for Committee for International Coordination of National Research In Demography (CICRED).

Segal, A.L.
1987 "The Caribbean Exodus in a Context: Comparative Migration Experience." In B. B. Levine, ed. *The Caribbean Exodus*. New York: Praeger.

_____
1975 *Population Policies in the Caribbean*. Lexington, MA: D.C. Heath and Company.

Thomas-Hope, E.M.
Forth-   "Caribbean Diaspora—the Inheritance of Slavery: Migration from the Commonwealth
coming Caribbean." In *Legacies of Slavery*. C. Brock, ed. London: Frank Cass.

_____
1983 "Off the Island: Population Mobility Among the Caribbean Middle Class." In *White Collar Migrants in the Americas, the Caribbean*. A.F. Marks and H.M.C. Vessuri, eds. Leiden, Netherlands: Royal Institute of Linguistics and Anthropology, Department of Latin American Studies. Pp. 39–59.

_____
1978 "The Establishment of a Migration Tradition: British West Indian Movements to the Hispanic Caribbean in the Century After Emancipation." In *Caribbean Social Relations*. C.G. Clarke, ed. Liverpool: University of Liverpool, Center for Latin American Studies. Monograph Series No. 8. Pp. 66–81.

United Nations, Department of Economic and Social Affairs
1982 *International Migration Policies and Programs: A World Survey*. New York: United Nations. Population Studies No. 80. ST/ESA/SER.A/80.

1979   *Trends and Characteristics of International Migration Since 1950.* New York: United Nations. Demographic Studies No. 64 ST/ESA/SER.A/64.

United States
1984   Statistical Abstract of the United States, 1982–83.

THE CARIBBEANIZATION OF NEW YORK CITY AND THE EMERGENCE OF A TRANSNATIONAL SOCIOCULTURAL SYSTEM

CONSTANCE R. SUTTON[1]
New York University

In the mid-1980s, New York has again become a city of immigrants. With over a third of its population now estimated to be foreign born,[2] the proportion of the city's newcomers has climbed to a high last recorded in 1900. Arriving mainly after 1965, this massive influx of new peoples coming primarily from Asia, Latin America, and the Caribbean has changed both the composition and culture of the city.[3] It has infused New York with a new energy, effervescence, and volatility and has further internationalized its famous ethnic and racial heterogeneity. New York is now a truly global city. Its third world outreach in the domain of corporate business, finance, and politics is mirrored in the presence of its large third world work force. These two phenomena, local expressions of the international circulation of capital and peoples that took off after World War II (see, Bonilla, 1986; Sassen-Koob, 1981), form interconnected parts of a single transnational system.

The impact of this system on New York City raises a number of important anthropological questions. What changes in the life of the city have resulted from the restructuring of its economy and the transformation of its popula-

---

[1] I wish to thank Antonio Lauría for sharing his knowledge about Puerto Ricans, and Eleanor Leacock and Louise Meriwether for their editorial suggestions.

[2] This estimate includes both documented and undocumented immigrants, political refugees (see, Bogen, 1985), and Puerto Ricans, who as U.S. citizens are not considered "immigrants."

[3] Figures on the size of each of these groups residing in New York City vary considerably. The higher mid-1980s estimates put the size of the Asian population at around 500,000; Hispanics at about one and a half million (of whom 60 percent are Puerto Rican, with Dominicans the next largest group, followed by Colombians and other Latin Americans); and West Indians—English-speaking and Haitian-Creole speaking—at about 1 million (half of whom are Jamaicans). West Indians, referred to as "Afro-Caribbeans," and Puerto Ricans and Dominicans, referred to as "Hispanic-Caribbeans," constitute the population with which this book is concerned. They now number over 2 million of New York City's 7 million people.

tion? How have the different migrant streams been positioned within the city's economy and in its class, ethnic, and racial structures? How have the newcomers gone about reconstituting and remolding their cultural heritages? And, what effect has all this had on the city's cultural and political landscape?

The volume of articles supply partial answers to these questions for the largest stream of third world migrants to New York City, the Caribbeans. Although they have emigrated from virtually all the large and small islands in the Caribbean archipelago, it is the Puerto Ricans and Dominicans from the Hispanic Caribbean and the Jamaicans, Haitians, and Trinidadian/Tobagonians from the Afro-Caribbean regions[4] that form the largest and hence most visible Caribbeans.

But it is not just the magnitude of this Caribbean presence that is noteworthy. Caribbeans constitute a crucial case for considering how a past colonial history and contemporary U.S. political and economic domination of a region combine to structure the immigrant experience. Coming from the most intensely colonized of all third world regions, Caribbeans migrate to the metropoles to which their countries remain linked today by ties of inexorable economic and political dependency. The cultural penetration that is part of the domination of the region causes Caribbeans to have a foreknowledge of the culture they encounter as migrants as well as an ambivalence about their own heritages, which were denigrated under colonialism. They also bring the knowledge that comes from operating in steeply sloped class hierarchies, still partly based on race and color. Thus it is not surprising to find that issues of culture and politics inform how Caribbean migrants represent themselves in the country which today dominates their region.

One might expect then that the immigrant experiences of Caribbeans will differ in a number of ways from that of their European predecessors. For example, what effect does their African (or mixed African/European) ancestry have on the identities imposed on them and their placement in New York City's racial/ethnic hierarchies? How are their cultural traditions perceived

---

[4] The term "Afro-Caribbean" is used instead of "West Indian" or "non-Hispanic Caribbean" to create a parallel to the accepted term of "Hispanic Caribbean." Afro-Caribbean refers to the Anglophone, Francophone and Dutch-speaking regions of the Caribbean which share important similarities as islands whose historic baselines were the slave plantation economy and whose populations, overwhelmingly of African descent, created a submerged Afro-creolized folk culture distinct from the hegemonic Euro-creole forms maintained by their English, French, and Dutch colonial masters. This contrasts with the Hispanic Caribbean—Cuba, Dominican Republic, and Puerto Rico—where the historic baselines established by Spanish colonizing involved a more diversified settler economy onto which plantation slavery was later grafted. In these latter colonies there was greater mixing of peoples of Indian, African, and Spanish ancestry and a blending of their distinct traditions within a more culturally unitary though stratified social system in which peoples of Spanish descent and a creolized Spanish tradition were dominant. This does not mean that Afro-Caribbean cultural forms are not present and indeed celebrated in the Hispanic Caribbean. But the acknowledged African and Amerindian heritages are synthesized in a dominant Hispanic-Antillean cultural tradition rather than forming an identifiable creole folk culture practiced by the nonelite masses in the Afro-Caribbean region.

by New Yorkers and how do they view the city? What influence does their past experience as colonized peoples have on the identities they affirm? And of central importance to our current notions of immigrant assimilation and acculturation, how do their strong ties to their homelands influence the transfer and transformation of their cultural heritages?

In relation to these issues, four general points can be made concerning the new Caribbean presence in New York City."[5]

THE CARIBBEANIZATION OF NEW YORK CITY

New York City is being Caribbeanized in a number of areas. In the city's economy, the labor power of Caribbean people has been critical to the complex restructuring and polarization of wealth that has been taking place since the 1970s (see, Bonilla and Campos, 1986; Freedman, 1979; Rodriguez, 1984; Sassen-Koob, 1985). Indeed, by offering themselves as a relatively low wage and flexible labor force, Caribbean migrants have made capital investment in the metropole attractive and profitable once more. Puerto Rican and now Dominican women have kept the garment industry from completely moving elsewhere. Afro-Caribbean women working as child caretakers and domestics have facilitated the pursuit of professional careers for a growing number of middle and upper class White women (see, Colen, 1986), thus filling the gap created by Black American women leaving this type of work. Caribbean women and men have provided much of the labor power for the expanded restaurant and taxi industries, as well as for the smaller sweatshops and home industries that have recently reemerged. The large growth in the service sector, particularly in the health care industries, has been made possible because of the relatively low wages Caribbean women will accept. And, along with Black Americans, Caribbeans are found concentrated in the city's federal, state, and municipal agencies—largest employers of "minority" people since the late 1960s. In addition, Caribbeans have expanded the informal sector of the economy, both licit and illicit, creating employment for themselves as they produce goods and services for their communities and the wider metropole, and participating in the international traffic in drugs and stolen car parts. Moreover, by using their labor and financial resources to engage in low-cost housing rehabilitation (see, Marshall, 1985; van Capelleveen, ms.), they have helped to maintain and restore the social and physical infrastructure in many areas of the city. Thus, in the midst of sharpened economic inequality, Caribbean migrants have been both critical

---

[5] Prior to World War II, New York City had a sizable Caribbean population, the result of earlier migrations which began around the turn of the century. By the 1930s, West Indians constituted between a fifth to a quarter of New York's Black population and Puerto Ricans numbered about 60,000 prior to World War II. But a new "critical mass" has been reached in the 1980s as a result of the size and scale of the post World War II migrations.

to the city's economy and successful in increasing their incomes beyond what they would earn in their home countries.

Caribbeanization of New York City is also manifest in the richness introduced into the city's life styles: new languages and public speech forms (*e.g.*, the widespread use of Spanish in public advertising and of Spanish, "Spanglish," and West Indian creoles in public places and plays); new Afro-Caribbean religious practices; new community and city-wide organizational activities; new mass media contents, public performances, use of public facilities and spaces; new programs and content in schools, museums, and public theaters; new popular arts, foods, music and dance; and finally, the new political struggles and issues being addressed—concerning bilingualism, community control of resources, educational content of school curricula, redlining and gentrification, welfare policies, and U.S. economic and political activity in the Caribbean.

Caribbean peoples have also brought with them the vivacity, color, rhythms, noises, and sociality that characterize island life. Despite secret cults and an often hidden quality to aspects of its folk culture, most of Caribbean social life is played out in public, not private, arenas. The transposition of this island heritage has meant that both the street life of local neighborhoods as well as the many public spaces of the city are being infused with Caribbean popular culture. A proliferation of Caribbean cultural forms has appeared throughout the city, from Reggae and Salsa concerts, Rastas and domino street players, graffiti and politicized street mural arts, to productions of the Caribbean Cultural Center, Joseph Papp's month-long summer Latino/Caribbean performances, and a growing number of Hispanic and Afro-Caribbean dance and theater groups.[6]

But it is not only New York City's popular culture that is being Caribbeanized. Caribbean peoples have also begun to make themselves felt in the city's institutions of "high" culture. Public and private universities have increasingly become centers where peoples of Caribbean origin—Hispanic and Afro-Caribbean—are producing new bodies of formal knowledge as they examine, codify, and theorize about their experiences and struggles.[7] In

---

[6] There is an upbeat quality to the profusion of Caribbean cultural forms that is occurring, paradoxically, as inequality in the city's economic and social structure has increased. While perhaps this is part of the ethnic diversity now being celebrated, it seems to illustrate the point Frank Bonilla has made about the need of capitalism as it internationalizes to identify "with the language and culture of those who people its market rather than with the ethnic attributes of its owners" (1986:79).

[7] In addition to the research being carried out within university departments and in the special programs devoted to Afro-American and Puerto Rican studies that have been introduced into higher education following the protests of Black and Puerto Rican students during the late 1960s, there now exist a number of university centers, such as the Centro de Estudios Puertorriquenos at Hunter College, the Caribbean Research Center at Medgar Evers College, and the Center for Latin American and Caribbean Studies at New York University, where interdisciplinary research directed toward Caribbean communities and public policy is being conducted. The CUNY (City University of New York) Association of Caribbean Studies, which in 1985 began to publish the journal

this process a Caribbean presence is beginning to be asserted in the discourses of the city's overlapping elites.

NEW YORK CITY AS A CARIBBEAN CROSS-ROAD

New York City has become the Caribbean cross-roads of the world. It contains the largest concentration and most diverse commingling of its people. With a Caribbean population of two million (this figure includes Puerto Ricans), New York forms the largest Caribbean city in the world, ahead of Kingston, Jamaica, San Juan, Puerto Rico, and Port-of-Spain, Trinidad, combined. It is in New York that the different islanders "cross-roads," learning about one another in their various encounters at work, in the streets, in schools and communities, at public affairs, and through the media. It is here that they have begun to build social bridges and alliances as they confront similar problems in their neighborhoods, the schools their children attend, their places of work, and the city at large. And it is in New York City that particular island identities become fused into broader ethnic identities: West Indian, pan-Caribbean, third world, Hispanic and Afro-American. These fused identities, often produced through ethnic mobilization for the staging of power politics, are expressed most clearly in cultural activities. The wider identities point to a growing consciousness of unifying perspectives and goals, and mark a sense of new possibilities in a struggle for cultural and political empowerment.

THE CARIBBEAN TRANSNATIONAL CULTURAL SYSTEM

New York is a Caribbean cross-roads in yet another important sense, one that involves the transposition and production of cultural forms and ideology. Both Hispanics and Afro-Caribbeans reconstitute their lives in New York City by means of a "cross-roads" process created by the mutual interaction of happenings in New York and the Caribbean. In general contrast with the situation of European immigrants, New York's Caribbean population is exposed to a more continuous and intense bidirectional flow of peoples, ideas, practices, and ideologies between the Caribbean region and New York City. These bidirectional exchanges and interactions have generated what can be called a transnational sociocultural system, a distinctly unitary though not unified transmission belt that reworks and further creolizes Caribbean culture and identities, both in New York and the Caribbean.

Cimarron, further testifies to the enormous expansion of scholarly interest in Caribbean life in the city and on the islands.

It is the emergence of this transnational sociocultural system which suggests that the model of immigrant/ethnic incorporation into a "culturally pluralistic" American society is not the destiny of migrant Caribbeans. For unlike most European immigrant/ethnic groups whose heritages became confined to their private, personal lives as they became incorporated into the economy and policy of U.S. society, the cultures and identities of Caribbean migrants are public, politicized issues. Moreover, Caribbean cultures are being replenished by the transnational system created by the continuing inflow of Caribbean peoples and by circular migration. This provides grounds for affirming a separate cultural identity. It is perhaps ironic that in the U.S. this affirmation of a separate Caribbean identity, especially among Puerto Ricans, is equated with a puzzling resistance to the process of becoming "Americanized,"[8] whereas in the Caribbean region there is concern with a loss of their distinctive Caribbean identities as the region has become increasingly "Americanized" both economically and culturally.

If the transnational system is influential in shaping Caribbean cultures and identities in New York City, so too is New York's race/class hierarchy into which Caribbeans are incorporated. We turn now to this significant factor in the immigrant experience.

CARIBBEANS IN NEW YORK CITY'S RACE/ETHNIC HIERARCHY

An important aspect of the Caribbean presence is its relation to and impact on the city's racial/ethnic hierarchy. Unlike European immigrants who are ethnically differentiated by their national origins and secondarily by religious affiliation, Caribbean migrants are placed within one or the other of the city's two principal minority status categories—"Blacks" and "Hispanics."[9] Within these two categories, Black Americans and Puerto Ricans—the two groups whose earlier presence gave rise to these categories and who today form the largest percent of each category—have experienced the longest and most thorough process of being Americanized. Furthermore, for Black Americans and Puerto Ricans this process represents a reversal of the European immigrant experience. Instead of joining an American mainstream through gaining socioeconomic mobility, Black Americans and Puerto Ricans have experienced over time more downward than upward economic mobility, a general deskilling, cultural denigration, and continued separation from

---

[8] *See*, Safa, 1983 for discussion of the latter issue, and Prager, 1982 for an analysis of the resilient symbolic role of racist conceptions in American thought and as countercurrent to the dominant American cultural ideology.

[9] For discussions of the difference between racial and ethnic identities and their significance in U.S. society, *see* Mullings (1978); Sudarkasa (1983); and Sutton (1975). The issue is related to what some analysts have seen as a replication of colonial relations when formerly colonized populations migrate to the metropoles of Europe and the U.S.

the resources and rewards of "mainstream" society (Mullings, 1978; Rodriguez, 1984). Today, as in the past, they possess the lowest incomes and the highest school drop-out and unemployment rates in the city. Hence for Caribbeans, who are compared to and compare themselves to Black Americans and Puerto Ricans, there are few incentives to become Americanized into either of these low-status categories. Possessing both higher average incomes and higher social statuses than the two more Americanized populations with which they are associated, Caribbean peoples in New York City are not readily induced to shed their cultural heritages or separate island-based identities as they seek to further their socioeconomic status in New York.

On the other hand, the recent Afro-Caribbean and Hispanic immigrants have contributed in substantial ways to diversifying the U.S. racial/ethnic hierarchy as well as to U.S.-perceived images of Black and Hispanic peoples. Moreover, though the newer groups have benefited from distinguishing themselves from Black Americans and Puerto Ricans, they also know that they have benefited from the political struggles carried out by these two peoples whose insistent claims to equality and justice have strongly influenced, and sometimes radicalized, Caribbean immigrants. The struggles of Black Americans and Puerto Ricans have changed how Caribbeans think about their positions in U.S. society and their own countries, and about the value of the non-Western components of their creolized cultural heritages.

Thus, Caribbeans experience contradictory pressures in relation to their identities as Black and Hispanic peoples. This causes them to oscillate between particularistic island/ethnic identities and definitions of interests, and more generalized political/racial alliances in which joint demands are made on the municipal, state, and federal governments. What this implies for the future—politically, economically, and culturally—is a question of strategic significance not only to New York City, but also to the federal government and the Caribbean region.

SOCIOCULTURAL DIMENSIONS OF CARIBBEAN LIFE IN NEW YORK CITY: TOWARD A COMPARATIVE ANALYSIS

The preceding discussion notes both the impact of the Caribbean presence on New York and the wider context affecting the incorporation of Caribbeans in the city—namely, U.S.-Caribbean relations plus the compelling structure of New York City's racial/ethnic hierarchy. The dual-place orientations and identities resulting from the active ties Caribbeans maintain to their homelands while becoming New Yorkers has resulted in a transnational sociocultural system coming into being. How this system operates concretely with respect to the diverse groups of Caribbean immigrants in New York is examined in the eighteen other essays in this volume written by 30 authors most of whom are anthropologists,[10] some of whom are of Caribbean origin or ancestry, and many of whom have conducted research in the archipelago. With a focus on sociocultural dimensions of Caribbean life in New York, the book addresses a topic that has been relatively neglected in the many recent studies of Caribbean immigrants. These studies which have examined the demographic characteristics, the sectors of the economy into which Caribbeans are incorporated, and their patterns of ethnic mobility, schooling and political participation, have been mainly concerned with assessing how well and in what ways Caribbean immigrants are integrating themselves into U.S. society. By contrast, the essays presented here analyze the culture of Caribbeans in New York City and its relation to life on the islands. Moreover, the essays address the experience of both Hispanic Caribbean and Afro-Caribbean groups in order to underwrite a Pan-Caribbean conceptual unity and to invite systematic comparisons of the diversities and commonalities found between and among peoples from the two major Caribbean historical, cultural regions.

The essay material is richly informative. The introductory section offers a general context for the specific case studies that follow. Chaney sketches the Caribbean background to the recent migrations. She notes that extensive outmigration in search of new economic frontiers is not a recent phenomenon but an institutionalized strategy, especially in the Afro-Caribbean region where outmigration has been a desired goal for over a century. Integral to this ideology is the expectation that migrants retain strong ties to their home countries, regarded as places they would prefer to live if economic conditions and/or the political situation were more favorable. A case in point are the Garifuna discussed by Gonzalez, a population of approximately 200,000 living along the central coastline of Belize, Nicaragua, Honduras, and Guatemala. Some 10,000 have recently migrated to New York City and Gonzalez underscores the fact that their long history of temporary and recurrent migration has both helped maintain the Garifuna sociocultural system at home and "pre-adapted" Garifuna migrants to the experience of living among other peoples while retaining their own cultural identity. Sutton and Makiesky-Barrow report a similar positive orientation toward migration among Barbadians, adding that their outmigration not only helps sustain their home society but may serve also as a channel for repatriating change-inducing ideologies, in this case the Black Power ideology.

Reimers gives a brief synoptic history of New York City and its major migrant populations, describing the initial positioning of each group within the city's changing class/ethnic divisions and biracial social structure and how the immigrants have contributed to the growth of the city and its

---

[10] Studies by anthropologists of Caribbean life in New York City are part of a larger trend in today's practice of urban anthropology which teaches that "the field" (of study) is not elsewhere but everywhere.

institutions. He raises the question of where the new Third World immigrants fit into the city's race/class hierarchies and how they may alter it. Bryce-Laporte discusses related issues and the multiple linkages involved in recent Caribbean immigration to New York City. He notes the ethnic invisibility of Afro-Caribbeans, regarded by White Americans as Black, and the often ambivalent attitudes toward the new immigrants within the ranks of the two minority categories with whom they are identified. Stressing the point that "New York City must be seen as a major point of international convergence," Bryce-Laporte's examples support the contention that between the Caribbean and New York City a transnational sociocultural system has come into being.

Conway and Bigby conclude the introductory section with an examination of Caribbean residential patterns in New York City. They find that the English-speaking Afro-Caribbeans and the French-speaking Haitians live in relatively close residential proximity to each other but are residentially more separated from the Spanish-speaking Dominicans and Cubans than Black Americans are from Puerto Ricans. Thus cultural differences between Afro- and Hispanic Caribbeans are replicated sociospatially in New York City, while Black Americans and Puerto Ricans are sociospatially closer. Conway and Bigby's analysis underscores diversity and raises interesting questions about future patterns of intergroup association and separation.

The Afro-Caribbean case studies begin with a discussion by novelist Paule Marshall of an earlier group of West Indian immigrants—the Barbadian women who came to New York after World War I and whom she knew while growing up in Brooklyn. Employed as day-work domestics to "scrub floors" in White America, they came together after work to recreate a separate West Indian "yard life" as they sat around the kitchen table "hold[ing] onto the memories that define[d] them," and distinguished them from Black Americans. They saw Black Americans as lacking a racial pride and militance they possessed because "Be Jesus Christ, in this white man world you got to take your mouth and make a gun." Marshall is among the first to discuss the perceptions of immigrant women and to describe the style of discourse in which they dissected experiences and articulated a political consciousness (a style that has been recorded and analyzed for West Indian and Black American men but seldom for women). Marshall strikes two themes that are explored further in the following essays: the position of Afro-Caribbeans in relation to Black and White America, and the nature of the female half of the immigrant experience.

Barbadians are also discussed in Sutton and Makiesky-Barrow's essay on changing racial and political consciousness of West Indian migrants in New York City and London. Traveling different routes to a converging consciousness of being "Black People in a White world," both groups of Barbadians became receptive to the 1960s Black Power Movement's challenge to structures of inequality and to its assertions of pride in race and culture. The authors examine the impact of this new racial/political consciousness in Barbados. They point to the transnational content of the newly acquired consciousness, attributing it to the bidirectional exchanges between Caribbean islands and the metropoles.

West Indians in New York and London are also compared in Foner's study of Jamaican migrants. Although relatively successful in both cities, their success is greater in New York than in London. Foner argues that a critical factor is the different racial contexts in the two societies. In the absence of a large native Black population, Jamaicans in London become a visible racial minority, compared unfavorably to a White majority. Moreover, in London they lack a Black constituency to support their entrepreneurial, professional, and political endeavors.Elsewhere, Foner (1985) compares the identities Jamaicans acquire in London and New York City. Again she finds that the existence of a large native Black American population in New York is advantageous to Jamaicans, cushioning the racial discrimination and prejudice encountered by Jamaicans in London, where they are defined in racial terms as Black Britons rather than in ethnic terms as West Indians. By the second generation they occupy a position in London's racial hierarchy similar to that of Black Americans in the U.S. (*see*, Arnold, 1984). Given the colonial dimension of Britain's relation to West Indians and the semicolonial nature of the U.S. relation to its Black American population, the New York/London comparisons support the view that the positioning of immigrants in their host society's racial/ethnic hierarchy is strongly influenced by existing power relations between host and home societies.

Soto's paper on West Indian child fostering and Garrison and Weiss's study of Dominican family networks both demonstrate the ways in which Caribbean kin structures and practices are being internationalized by migrants. Soto's focus on children as an integral part of Afro-Caribbean circular migration adds a new dimension to the study of migrant ties to their home societies. She shows how child fostering maintains links between dispersed female members of the international migrant community and thereby helps build women's wealth and power. Internationalized child fostering, the work of women, is an important component in sustaining a historical and cultural continuity between home and host societies. Its role in generating and regenerating the Caribbean transnational cultural system needs to be noted.

Internationalized child fostering has emerged as part of the new female-initiated migration found among women coming from the Afro-Caribbean region. These women are responding to U.S. labor market conditions and possess family forms which support the independent migration of women who have children. Soto compares Puerto Rican versions of internationalized child fostering to those she describes for West Indians. Given a different family structure and different gender roles, she questions whether the institution plays a similar role among Puerto Ricans. Hopefully, the question will stimulate the comparative research needed for an answer.

Garrison and Weiss describe the internationalizing of Dominican kin networks and the strategies that members of a patrifocal Dominican family adopt in order to become reunited in New York City. They point out that because the U.S. family reunification law is based on a too restricted concept of family, Dominicans are compelled to resort to illegal as well as legal means in order to reconstitute themselves as a corporate family group in New York. The family structure described in this case study differs not only from the U.S. definition of family but also, and in different ways, from Afro-Caribbean family forms. However, what is common to both Caribbean groups is the not inconsiderable movement of individuals trying to maintain "patterns of reciprocal family obligations [that] persist among kin dispersed between New York and" the island societies.

Pessar provides another perspective on Dominican family ideology and loyalties. She examines how the waged employment of Dominican women working in the garment industry improves their status in their culturally ascribed "domestic sphere." Although most of the women work at "dead end" jobs, the majority of those interviewed regard themselves as middle class rather than working class. Pessar imputes this to the power of Dominican family/household ideology. The women she interviewed tended to define themselves by the consumption power of their households rather than by their status in the work place. Hence, while there is a high rate of labor force participation among Dominican women, what counts for them is that their wages have increased their decision-making power in the allocation of household resources and contributed to the purchase of household prestige goods that have become markers of modernity and mobility. Thus because of women's strong identification with their households, the improvement in the status of the household is seen as an enhancement of women's status. While Pessar concludes by questioning whether this pattern will persist into the second generation, her study points to the need for comparative analysis of the female immigrant experience, currently a subject of considerable scholarly interest (see, for example, Basch and Lerner, 1986; Ewen, 1985; Morokvasic, 1984; Mortimer and Bryce-Laporte, 1981; Simon and Brettell, 1986).

The articles by Buchanan-Stafford on Haitians and by Flores, Attinasi, and Pedraza on Puerto Ricans take up the issue of language as a marker of identity. For both groups, conflicts over language encapsulate conflicts over the political, cultural, and/or class orientation immigrants assume. These conflicts have their origin in the home countries and become transposed and often magnified in New York. Among Haitians, the conflict is internal to the community, centering on whether Haitian Creole, language of the Haitian masses, or French, language of Haiti's past colonial and present elite, is to be privileged as the marker of Haitian identity. Among Puerto Ricans, the language issue is not only an internal community issue, but also a city-wide contentious public issue. In Puerto Rico, the struggle waged to maintain Spanish as the national language in the face of U.S. hegemony caused language to become identified with Puerto Rico's political conflicts over its relation to the U.S. In New York, the Puerto Rican struggle for a bilingual approach to education in the city's public schools, where over a third of the children are of Hispanic origins, has also become identified as a status issue—in this case the status of the Puerto Rican migrant community.

Compared to other immigrant groups, Puerto Ricans are seen as actively resisting cultural and linguistic assimilation by refusing to abandon their distinctive ethnic markers. But in their study of the actual linguistic practices of Puerto Ricans living in working-class El Barrio in East Harlem, Flores, Attinasi, and Pedraza found a dynamic bilingual code switching between Puerto Rican Spanish and urban varieties of American English. This resulted in a speech form referred to as "Spanglish." As in the case of West Indian creoles and Black English, the code switching linguistic practices have expanded communicative skills. As Spanglish becomes incorporated into popular culture, it becomes "a new amalgam of human expression," and a resource for challenging politically dominant views and traditions.

Challenge to the imposition of dominant views and traditions is also an aspect of the growing participation in *Santería*. Santería is an Afro-Caribbean religion (derived from Yoruba beliefs and practices) which Cubans brought to New York. As Gregory states in his essay, it has drawn considerable numbers of Hispanics, Black Americans, and some West Indians, and has attracted many of the college-educated, second generation Caribbeans who have become interested in African culture. Gregory writes that joining Santería "houses" provides an "inter-ethnic sense of identity, grounded in both African culture and New World social history, [that] has emerged from the encounter of Caribbean peoples and Black Americans in New York City." Santería in New York is another example of the conscious effort of Caribbeans to reproduce aspects of their heritage that had been denigrated, and to resist the destruction of their distinctive cultural identities.

Ethnic organizing—regarded as identity-creating culturally reproducing, supportive, and politicizing among immigrants—is discussed in papers dealing with both Afro-Caribbeans and Hispanics. Sassen-Koob compares the incidence of different types of ethnic associations found in New York's Dominican and Colombian communities, noting that their differences cannot be explained in terms of a shared Hispanic culture. She proposes instead that the class status of immigrants and the disparity between their places of origin and destination better account for their modes of articulation, *i.e.*, more internally-oriented, expressive activities among Dominicans, more outwardly-oriented, instrumental organizations among Colombians. In a useful exchange, Georges amends this formulation. With data from her recent research on Dominicans, she questions the implicit linear view of the devel-

opment of ethnic organizing Sassen-Koob presents. Georges suggests that
the nature of ethnic organizing can be better understood in terms of the
specific "political-economic context of both sending and receiving societies
at the moments under scrutiny." Sassen-Koob's response to Georges' comment further clarifies the issues involved in understanding forms of ethnic
organizing. She ends by noting that "Georges' findings on the continuing
importance of home country politics is an important variable underscoring
the distinctiveness of today's immigrant mobilization." Both of these latter
points are borne out in the two articles on the politics of ethnic organizing
among Afro-Caribbeans. Basch describes how the political activities linking
Grenadians and Vincentians to their home countries strengthen rather than
detract from their mobilizing activities around political issues in New York.
Moreover, homeland ties have heightened their sense of being ethnic groups
with distinct political interests while remaining within the orbit of Black
American politics. This conscious coming out as an ethnic group within Black
America is a new phenomenon for West Indians. It is further analyzed by
Kasinitz (1987), who sees it as evidence of the new cultural and political
awareness of New York's Caribbean community. Basch's assertion that more
active West Indian involvement in the political life of both their home and
host societies has created "a single field of action comprised of a diverse yet
unitary set of interests" is also well documented in the article by Schiller, *et
al.* Charting the course of Haitian organizing activity in New York from 1957
to the present their historical overview calls attention to the multiple identities around which Haitians have organized. The authors further show how
changes over time have been determined by changes in the political relations
between the U.S. and Haiti. Their analysis leads to the view that Haitian
identities and organizations are transnational in content and orientation.

The book concludes with a comparison of two annual Caribbean celebrations in the streets of New York City. Kasinitz and Freidenberg-Herbstein
analyze the Puerto Rican parade and West Indian Carnival as two collective
rituals. They compare how they are organized and staged, the images of
Puerto Ricans and West Indians that are projected, the political messages
conveyed, and the goals that are dramatized. For each case, it is shown how
the ritual drama that is played out in the street represents an intermeshing
of the culture and politics of both home and host societies.

While not all aspects of contemporary Caribbean sociocultural life are
covered in this collection, the essays point to a similar transnational cultural
and political dynamic underlying the changes and continuities examined.
Hence, the case studies refer to a wider sociopolitical field than heretofore
considered relevant in most immigrant studies. This indicates that the ways
in which Caribbeans are reconstituting their lives in New York City represents something beyond new additions to New York's famed ethnic diversity. Their presence challenges older notions of immigrant assimilation and

acculturation and aspects of the ideology by which the U.S. has come to view itself as a nation of ex-immigrants.

BIBLIOGRAPHY

Arnold, F.
1984 "West Indians and London's Hierarchy of Discrimination." *Ethnic Groups*, v.6, pp. 47–64.

Basch, L. and G. Lemer (eds.)
1986 "The Spirit of Nairobi and the UN Decade for Women." Special issue of *Migration Review;* 14(1–2).

Bogen, E.
1985 *Caribbean Immigrants in New York City, A Demographic Summary, October, 1985.* New York Department of City Planning, Office of Immigrant Affairs.

Bonilla, F.
1986 "Ethnic Orbits: The Circulation of Capitals and Peoples." In *Industry and Idleness.* F. Bonilla and R. Campos. NY: Centro de Estudios Puertorriquenos, Hunter College, CUNY. Pp. 61–85.

_____ and R.Campos
1986 *Industry and Idleness.* NY: Centro de Estudios Puertorriquenos, Hunter College, CUNY.

Colen, S.
1986 "With Respect and Feelings: Voices of West Indian Child Care and Domestic Workers in New York City." In *All American Women: Lines that Divide, Ties that Bind. J.B. Cole, ed. New York: Free Press. Pp. 46–70.*

Foner, N.
1985 "Race and Color: Jamaican Migrants in London and New York City." *IMR* 6(4):708–727.

Freedman, M.
1979 "The Labor Market for Immigrants in New York City," *New York Affairs*, (7)4:94–111.

Kasinitz, P.
1987 "New York Equalize You: The Political Economy of New York's West Indian Community." Forthcoming in January issue of *New York Affairs.*

Marshall, P.
1985 "Rising Islanders of Bed-Stuy: The West Indian Zest to 'Buy House' Rejuvenates a Community." In *The New York Times Magazine*, Nov. 3. Pp. 67.

Morokvasic, M. (ed.)
1984 *Women in Migration.* Special issue of *IMR*, 18(4).

Mortimer, D.M. and R.S. Bryce-Laporte (eds.),
1981 *Female Immigrants to the United States: Caribbean, Latin American, and African Experiences.* Washington, D.C.: Smithsonian Institution, RIIES Occasional Paper No. 2.

Mullings, L.
1976 "Ethnicity and Stratification in the Urban United States." In *Annals of the New York Academy of Sciences*, 318:10–22.

Prager, J.
1982 "American Racial Ideology as Collective Representation." *Ethnic and Racial Studies*, 5(1):99–119.

Rodriguez, C.
1984 "Economic Survival in New York City." In *The Puerto Rican Struggle: Essays on Survival in*

the U.S.C. Rodriguez, V. Sanchez Korrol, J.O. Alers, eds. Maplewood, NJ: Waterfront Press. Pp.31–46.

Safa, H.
1983 "Caribbean Migration to the United States: Cultural Identity and the Process of Assimilation." In *Different People: Studies in Ethnicity and Education.* E. Gumbert, ed. Atlanta, GA.: Center for Cross-Cultural Education, Georgia State University. Pp. 47–73.

Sassen-Koob, S.
1985 "Changing Composition and Labor Market Location of Hispanic Immigrants in New York City, 1960–1980." In *Hispanics in the U.S. Economy.* G. Borgas and M. Tienda, eds. Orlando, FL: Academic Press.

_____
1981 *Exporting Capital and Importing Labor: The Role of Caribbean Immigrants to New York City.* NY: Center for Latin American and Caribbean Studies, New York University Research Program in Inter-American Affairs. Occasional Paper 28.

Simon, R. and C. Brettell
1986 *International Migration: The Female Experience.* Totowa, NJ: Rowman and Allanheld.

Sudarkasa, N.
1983 "Race, Ethnicity and Identity: Some Conceptual Issues in Defining the Black Population in the United States." Paper delivered at Conference on Immigration and the Changing Black Population in the U.S., Ann Arbor, May 18–21.

Sutton, C.
1975 "Comments on Immigrants and Forms of Group Identity." In *Migration and Development: Implications for Ethnic Identity and Political Conflict.* H.I. Safa and B.M. DuToit, eds. The Hague: Mouton Publishers.

van Capelleveen, R.
ms. "Caribbean Immigrants in New York City and the Transformation of the Metropolitan Economy." On file at Center for Latin American and Caribbean Studies, New York University.

NEW YORK CITY AND ITS PEOPLE:
An Historical Perspective Up to World War II

DAVID M. REIMERS
New York University

Because so many different people entered the United States through New York, from its earliest day the City was noted for both racial and ethnic diversity. During its first era of slow, then rapid growth as a trading center (1624 to the 1820s), Dutch, French and English settlers, and African slaves constituted the principal groups of which it was comprised. From the 1820s until the late nineteenth century, when the City with its present five boroughs was created, New York City reigned as the United States' major port. During this second era of development, the so-called Old Immigrants from Northern and Western Europe (especially the Irish and Germans) accounted for most of the newcomers. During the third era of the city's growth, from the 1880s to the Great Depression, immigrants from Southern and Eastern Europe (mostly Jews and Italians) poured in. About the same time, and especially after 1910, southern Blacks arrived in large numbers.

This chapter concentrates on the main migrant groups settling in the City, noting their cultural heritages, how their experiences were similar or different, the economic and population growth of the City, and how the immigrants related to and changed the City. This history provides the background for the post-World War II arrival of "new immigrants" from the Caribbean, the subject of this book.

THE DUTCH

New York grew slowly both under Dutch rule (1624 to 1664), and under the British. In the seventeenth century, New York was essentially the tip of Manhattan, with a population of only 1,500 (1664). There was at the time a smaller settlement in Brooklyn, and scattered farms in Staten Island and Long Island. Under eighteenth century British rule, the City gradually became an important colonial port, second in size to Philadelphia. From the American Revolution to the 1820s, New York expanded more rapidly.

The Dutch who founded the City in 1624—then called New Amsterdam— developed a lucrative fur trade with the American Indians, but the City did not prosper as hoped. The Dutch never invested large amounts of capital in New Amsterdam, and only a few sought their fortunes in the New World. In addition to the Dutch, in the early years there were English, French-speaking Walloons from Belgium, and a variety of other Europeans. In 1643, Father Isaac Jogues, a French Jesuit, reported in a famous remark that among the approximately 500 settlers in New Amsterdam one could hear eighteen languages spoken (Archdeacon, 1983:11).

During the 1650s, the first Jews, Sephardics fleeing the Portuguese conquerors of Brazil, arrived in New Amsterdam. The General Director of the colony, Peter Stuyvesant, believed Jews to be usurers and wanted them deported. However, the West India Company had Jewish backers and told Stuyvesant that the Jews must be allowed to remain (Marcus, 1970:215–48). While the Dutch disliked both Jews and Roman Catholics and denied them full civil rights, they also disliked members of the Society of Friends, who frequently aroused hostility when they entered colonies such as Massachusetts and New York.

Apart from Europeans, there were the Indians who had originally inhabited Manhattan, although few actually resided within the bounds of the walled City after the Dutch arrived, and Africans imported as slave laborers. One historian has estimated that African slaves made up about 4 percent of the colony's population near the end of Dutch rule (McManus, 1966:11). Thus, New Amsterdam began as a city of both free and slave workers, and despite less harsh treatment of slaves under the Dutch, the racist ideology of European superiority was present from the earliest times.

THE BRITISH

Substitution of English rule for Dutch brought, of course, increasing use of the English language, as well as imposition of English forms of government and laws, and hegemony of English culture. By the time of the American Revolution, the English were the principal group, and people of Dutch origin probably accounted for only one sixth of the city's population. With a variety of other European nationalities and religious groups migrating to New York between 1664 and 1776, there was a growing toleration that received a further boost during the Revolution when New Yorkers disestablished the Anglican Church (Klein, 1976:61–62; Dolan, 1975:11). Contributing to the City's growth and diversity during the 18th century were French Huguenots escaping persecution in France, followed by German and Scot-Irish immigrants (Butler, 1983: ch.5).

The relative proportion of the Black to White population and the economic roles they filled changed over the eighteenth century. In the first half of the 1700s, slaves increased at a faster rate than did free laborers. By the mid-century in Manhattan, about one person in five was an African slave. Across the East River in Brooklyn, the proportion of the Black population was even higher (Connolly, 1977:3–6). In the second half of the 1700s, the numbers of free laborers grew at a more rapid pace. The improved economy of New York attracted White laborers, and slaves could be sold at higher prices in the southern colonies than they could in New York. During the massive European immigration of the nineteenth century, the proportion of Blacks fell even further, and did not again reach the levels of the mid-eighteenth century until after World War II.

Slaves engaged in a variety of occupations, including work on fortifications, agriculture, and as skilled craftsmen (where they were resented by White artisans). As their proportion of the population dropped and the slave trade declined, many became household slaves. Working as domestic servants set a future pattern for Blacks, who were excluded from better paying jobs, a pattern extending to the present day as West Indian migrant women, along with American Blacks, continue to dominate this occupation (Colen, forthcoming).

Whatever their occupation, the status of Blacks deteriorated following seizure of control by the British. Until New York State began to abolish slavery in 1799, a series of laws tightened the grip of slavery. Following an unsuccessful slave rebellion in 1712, the city's Whites panicked. Of the 27 slaves charged in the plot, 21 were convicted, though the evidence was sparse in some cases. Some of the convicted were burned alive. Only the intervention of the governor saved others (McManus, 1966:122–23). Another panic occurred in 1741, with consequent rumors, convictions and deaths of both accused Whites and Blacks. In addition to these bloody reprisals, White New Yorkers piled new restrictions on their slaves (*ibid.:*126–27 and ch. 5).

POST-REVOLUTIONARY DEVELOPMENT

By the 1820s, New York City had become the nation's largest urban center, overtaking Philadelphia. As ships visited the harbor in growing numbers, most of the new nation's imports came through New York, and a considerable amount of the exports, too. New York merchants served as credit agents for southern planters, and the opening of the Erie Canal gave New York a central role in trade to the old Northwest as well. Foreign and domestic trade stimulated construction in the City and jobs were readily available (Albion, 1984:6–15).

During this era of New York City's rapid expansion, the dimensions of immigration to the City and to the rest of the nation were small. The federal government did not begin to collect data on immigration until after 1819, and the first reports indicate that only a few thousand entered the United States yearly during the 1820s. Among the post-Revolution newcomers were exiles from the French Revolution and the Irish who fled after the British crushed the United Irishmen movement around 1800. Other immigrants came for economic reasons. It was hard for Irish peasants to make a living as it was for the German farmers who came. Artisans from England, Scotland and Wales also migrated in small numbers prior to 1840.

Because immigration was relatively low compared to the 1840–1920 period, the era of Great Migrations, New York was less a "foreign" city than perhaps at any time in its history. The City grew by natural increase and internal migration rather than by massive immigration. Of the City's 166,000 residents in 1820 only 18,000 were unnaturalized foreigners; perhaps an equal number were foreign-born citizens (Rosenwaike, 1972:38–40). The English language began to replace Dutch and German in their last strongholds, the churches. Older groups like the French Huguenots largely disappeared as a distinct ethnic group (Butler, 1983:176–98).

Yet the City retained its diverse international flavor. In 1835, German immigrant and scholar Francis Lieber noted that among the languages heard in New York were:

> English, German, French, and Spanish, which, with the addition of Italian, you may hear almost any day on Broadway at the hours when it is most frequented (Ernst, 1979:22).

A few years later the people of New York were listed as including:

> free Negroes, or as they are called, people of color . . . Germans and Dutch . . . Irish . . . French, Danes, Swiss, Welsh, English, Scotch, Italians, Turks, Chinese, Swedes, Russians, Norwegians, Poles, Hungarians, Spaniards, Sicilians, Africans, and in short, a few of all the nations upon the earth (ibid.:23).

Freedom but not equality came for Blacks during this era. After long debates, New York in 1799 finally enacted a gradual manumission law. The legislature freed remaining slaves in 1827. Although they obtained their freedom, Black New Yorkers remained second-class citizens. Segregated by law and custom in schools, churches, and public facilities, and limited politically and legally, most Blacks continued in unskilled jobs (McManus, 1966: chs. 9–10; Curry, 1981:20, 21, 26, 53, 83, 138, 152–53). Thus the pattern was set early for the residential, social and economic segregation that Afro-Caribbean migrants would experience in their turn, even after the legal barriers had disappeared.

GATEWAY FOR IMMIGRANTS

Just as it had led the nation in imports and exports between 1830 and the 1880s, New York City also became the chief port of entry for immigrants. Whereas Philadelphia, and to a lesser extent Boston, competed successfully in the colonial era for immigrants, by the mid-nineteenth century between two-thirds to three-quarters entered through New York City. The federal government gradually took over the regulation of immigration. Castle Garden at the tip of Manhattan served as the reception center for these immigrants before the opening of Ellis Island in the 1890s. Most remained only a few days in the City and moved west by rail or canal to find employment in other cities or on farms.

Yet, many settled permanently in the growing City. The swelling number of immigrants largely explains the City's rapid growth. From a population of about 200,000 in 1830, Manhattan claimed over 800,000 at the time of the Civil War. When the five boroughs combined near the turn of the century, the City had a population of over 3 million. This population became increasingly foreign. Of Manhattan's 813,000 inhabitants in 1860, nearly one-half were foreign born, compared to less than one-quarter in 1820. By 1860, the foreign born and their children made up a majority of the population. Of Brooklyn's inhabitants that year, about 40 percent had been born outside the United States. These large proportions—about double those in the 1820s—grew even larger after the Civil War. By the turn of the century, the majority of New Yorkers were foreigners or the children of one or two foreign parents. Not until Congress drastically restricted immigration in the 1920s would the proportion of the population that was foreign born begin to decline.

THE IRISH AND THE GERMANS

The era between the 1830s and 1880s was that of the Old Immigrants , those from Western and Northern Europe. These included English, Scots and Welsh from the British Isles, and scattered groups of Norwegians, Swedes, Belgians, Danes, and others. The majority were either Irish or German.

Conditions in Ireland were already miserable when disaster struck in 1845. As the Irish population grew, competition for land became intense, and Irish peasants scratched a meager living from their tiny plots. Their diet consisted largely of the potato. Before 1840 most Irish migrants headed for English or Scottish towns in search of work, but some migrated to America. This exodus did not suffice to avoid disaster. The potato crop rotted in 1845, followed by five desperate years of the Great Famine (Coleman, 1973).

From 1845 to 1854 about 1.5 million Irish went to the United States, while a similar number starved to death. The numbers dropped during the disruptions of the Civil War, but afterwards the movement resumed again. From 1870 to 1920, about 50,000 Irish each year found their way to the United States.

Though conditions in Ireland improved after 1860, periodic agricultural blight and political difficulties prompted many to emigrate. Only in the late nineteenth century did this movement of millions slow.

Most Irish arriving during the Great Famine were poverty-stricken, often illiterate, peasants; about one-third did not speak English. Because of educational improvements in Ireland in the late nineteenth century, however, the later immigrants, while still unskilled and largely rural, were literate in English and better able to cope in the New World (McCaffrey, 1976:60–62; 70–74).

Next to the Irish in numbers of immigrants were the Germans. In the German states, land division, overpopulation and crop failures stimulated emigration. As did the Irish, Germans sought employment in nearby cities and overseas (Dinnerstein and Reimers, 1982:14). German immigrants included a variety of religious groups: Lutherans, Catholics, and Calvinists. A few fled after the failure of the 1848 Revolutions, and many more left because of religious persecution. Among the German migrants of the nineteenth century were some 250,000 Jews, of whom 80,000 had settled in New York City by the turn of the century. Jews migrated in part because of religious reasons. Unlike so many other Germans who were peasants or unskilled or semiskilled workers, Jews were urban in origin, frequently skilled or with small business backgrounds. German immigration fell during the Civil War, then rose again, outstripping the Irish in the late nineteenth century, and in numbers rivaling the Irish in New York City (Archdeacon, 1983:67).

FIRST EMPLOYMENTS

The expanding American economy attracted immigrants who, even if they had few skills and knew little or no English, felt they could find jobs in the United States. Railroads and state bureaus actively recruited them, offering them land at cheap prices. For a brief period during and after the Civil War it was legal for employers to contract laborers abroad. Encouraged by families and friends who had come to America, prospective immigrants sometimes received letters from the U.S. containing money or prepaid tickets. As was the case after World War II when Caribbean immigrants began migrating to the City, these immigrant networks were important in bringing friends and relatives to New York City. Immigrants generally settled near other immigrants from their home places, making the City a composite of urban ethnic "villages."

Because immigrants faced prejudice, had few skills, lacked education and money and often did not speak English well, they had to take what jobs were available. Most rural Irish did unskilled labor in urban New York. Although some American households feared the alleged evil influences of Irish Catholics upon their children, many others hired young Irish women as domestics. Others worked in the needle trades (Ernst, 1979:66–68). Irish men did most of New York's heavy labor, as dockworkers and porters (*ibid.*:69-72). The Irish also worked in the building and clothing trades. It was not uncommon for employers to advertise "No Irish Need Apply." Old stock New Yorkers were characteristically hostile to immigrants, but no group was so hated as the Irish not only because they were poor but also because they were Roman Catholic (*ibid.*:67).

While Germans also did heavy unskilled labor, some from urban areas had skills that gave them advantages over the Irish. Germans became important in furniture and piano-making as well as other skilled jobs, and they dominated the growing brewery industry (Nadel, 1981:128–50). They became the center of the developing labor movement among immigrants.

LIVING CONDITIONS

Low wages doomed the majority of immigrants to living in appalling conditions. Even before the heavy immigration, poverty and squalor were hardly new in American cities (Mohl, 1971:24–25). However, as immigrants poured into nineteenth century New York City, landlords subdivided housing into small rental units, and builders erected tenements to accommodate the rapidly growing population. Boarding houses for single persons were jammed, and immigrant families commonly took in lodgers to make ends meet—not unlike conditions today, when single men among West Indian migrants may live four or five to a room.

The Lower East Side, which had become the center of German and Irish communities, expanded northward as thousands more arrived. In addition to overcrowding, immigrants faced periodic epidemics—cholera in 1832 and 1849, typhoid in 1837, and typhus in 1842 (Ernst, 1979:ch.5; Smith-Rosenberg, 1971:32–36). Sewage and garbage disposal, though aided by hungry and roaming hogs and dogs, were not effectively dealt with until later in the nineteenth century when the city moved to improve public sanitation.

Before the Civil War, Manhattan's most notorious immigrant slum was the Five Points District, near the site of the present City Hall and Chinatown. It had a well-earned reputation for unsanitary conditions, disease, crime and prostitution until late in the nineteenth century (Smith-Rosenberg, 1971:35).

ETHNIC AND RELIGIOUS HOSTILITY

Not the least of the problems encountered by New York City's nineteenth century immigrants were ethnic and religious hostility. Many White Americans believed that the newcomers (especially the Irish) brought disease, were degenerate, lazy, rowdy, and a public burden. They pointed to the City's almshouse, disproportionately filled with immigrants, as evidence of their inferiority (Ernst, 1979:56).

As noted, the Irish as did many Germans aroused opposition because they were ᵔoman Catholics. Because of the close church-state association in Catholic countries, Protestant New Yorkers condemned Irish Catholics as a menace to liberty and religious freedom. Nativist movements and conflicts, including pitched battles in the streets, erupted in the 1830s and again after the Civil War (Headley, 1970:289–306). In New York City, the Protestant Public School Society, received public funds. In 1840, Archbishop John Hughes asked that Roman Catholic schools also be subsidized, setting off a storm of controversy. Eventually the state ended the Public School Society's subsidy, but for many years Protestants controlled the board of education and maintained the Protestant orientation of the public schools (Archdeacon, 1983:79).

Immigrants also competed with one another for jobs, and the Irish found themselves in sharp competition with Blacks for low-skilled employment (Ernst, 1979:104–105). Black-Irish antagonism was so great that it led to open violence during the Civil War. Resentful, Irish feared that they would be drafted, and that New York's Blacks or those coming from the South would take their jobs. This ugly mood led to a week of street violence in 1863 when Irish immigrants burned a Black orphanage in Manhattan and terrorized and lynched other Blacks (Headley, 1970:148–70, 207–209, 213–14, 242, 274–77).

IMMIGRANT ASSISTANCE

Immigrants arriving in the nineteenth century did not encounter the modern bureaucratic state so characteristic of post-1940 America. Yet the City provided some minimal aid to the destitute among the newcomers. During times of unemployment, local poor relief was available, usually food and firewood. For the absolutely destitute, the almshouse was the last resort. The City also ran an insane asylum that, like the almshouse, claimed immigrants disproportionately among its inmates. These wretched facilities had a well-earned reputation as places to be avoided. The immigrant poor without families and friends had no other place to go.

Private charity also offered some aid to the immigrant, though meager, irregular and meant only for those whom the White Protestant managers of private philanthropy called the "deserving poor." Those who consumed alcohol were considered improvident and immoral, undeserving of assistance. Some voluntary organizations concentrated on the moral and spiritual, not physical, needs and stressed religious conversion, temperance and moral uplift. Largely the work of Protestant reformers, these paternalistic organizations were scarcely adequate to deal with jobs, discrimination, and the housing needs of the poor. The largest such organization was the New York Association for Improving the Condition of the Poor, founded after the depression of the 1830s by the City Tract Society. This Association did turn its attention to the living conditions of the immigrant poor. Whatever its limitations, the Association and other similar groups were the forerunners of later progressive agencies such as the settlement houses that worked with immigrants (Smith-Rosenberg, 1971).

Immigrants also had their own organizations. The immigrant aid societies, founded in the late eighteenth and early nineteenth centuries, met people at the boats, provided information and helped the newcomers learn about their new country (Mohl, 1971:154–55; Ernst, 1979:32–35). They lacked funds and adequate staffs, and hence they could scarcely help all the immigrants, though often they were the only friendly groups meeting the immigrants. Immigrant churches also developed social programs and schools for their followers. Historian Jay Dolan (1975:ch.7) has argued persuasively that an important role was played by the Catholic Church in serving the Irish and German Catholics in the City, especially when public institutions and other private organizations were so inadequate. Like the churches, Jewish synagogues aided the newcomers, but they did not directly sponsor elaborate institutions as the Catholic Church did. Ethnic newspapers also provided useful information for the immigrants. The New York *Irish American*, founded in 1849, claimed a circulation of 40,000 in 1861, and the German press which had been dying before 1830, began to revive (Jones, 1960:140–41).

Once established, immigrants went on to form new organizations and publish newspapers. Some—such as the parochial schools—were religious and educational in nature, while others—for example, the voluntary fire departments—were both social and public. Still others—like the German Verein—combined a variety of functions (Nadel, 1981:228-50). These organizations supplemented the work of the immigrant aid societies, assisting the immigrants and helping to maintain their ethnic cultural traditions.

UPWARD MOBILITY

After an initial period of adjustment, immigrants found better jobs and housing. All were eager to leave behind their slum environment, and some moved uptown or out of the City. The process of upward social mobility was slow, and rags-to-riches stories were few in the first generation. Often several generations were required to rise in income, occupation and status. The second generation usually improved incomes and jobs, while the third acquired higher education and became professionals.

German Jews turned their hands to business. Although many had been small tradesmen in Europe, because they lacked capital they began as peddlers. From this base, they opened small shops. The most successful would later found many of the City's large department stores. The elite of German Jews entered the world of finance and laid the basis for the large Jewish banking and investment firms that emerged in the late nineteenth century. On the whole, New York's German Jews rose rapidly, and they were well established when the mass immigration of Jews from Eastern Europe began in the 1880s.

For the Irish poor progress was slow. Gradually they moved out of laboring jobs to semiskilled and skilled positions, leaving the newer post-1880 Southern and Eastern European immigrants to take the lower level working-class jobs.

Two factors were crucial to the Irish New York experience: the church and politics, which were closely tied to everyday life and gave them both an identity and, for some, a path out of poverty. The Irish had arrived at a propitious time. By the late 1830s the City had universal White male suffrage, and the Irish utilized the ballot to rise in politics. Building on the Church, saloon and voluntary organizations like the fire companies, the Irish quickly moved to political prominence. Tammany Hall, founded in 1789, recruited the Irish, and the Irish in turn dominated Tammany. No doubt their experience in politics in Ireland gave them an advantage. In 1880, when they elected the city's first Irish Roman Catholic mayor, William Grace, voters began to replace the old-stock English mayors. Thus began a new Irish "boss" rule that lasted until after World War II (McCaffrey, 1976:139–40; Glazer and Moynihan, 1963:221–29).

The mayoralty was not the only prize. As the City expanded in education, fire and police protection, public health and the civil service, the Irish were in disproportionate share of positions in these activities (McCaffrey, 1976:80).

Also important was the Irish American Church, which had served as a bulwark for the Irish against the English. Faced with American hostility to Catholicism, the Irish found in the Church a source of ethnic cohesion. In Ireland, the Church was parish-oriented and it became similarly organized in the United States (Dolan, 1975:45–46). The Irish quickly took over leadership of New York City's Catholicism, replacing the French domination. By the mid-nineteenth century, the Irish accounted for the majority of priests and membership (ibid.: 21–22). The Church provided social mobility for both men and women. Men became priests, bishops and archbishops; women became nuns who worked in the Church's schools and hospitals.

German Catholics expressed displeasure with Irish domination. They wanted their own parishes with German-speaking priests. The resulting conflict lasted well into the twentieth century. In theory, the Church rejected "nationality" parishes, but in practice it accepted them (ibid.:68–71 and ch.5).

Better jobs and higher incomes changed settlement patterns. With more money, immigrants moved to healthier, less crowded, neighborhoods. In 1820, most New Yorkers lived below 14th street, but the population rapidly expanded as new transit lines encouraged the uptown movement of business and people. Few of the original neighborhoods had been ghettos composed solely of one ethnic group. They were mixtures of people, although each group had its own cultural institutions. Population turned over rapidly even in the worst areas.

THE "AMERICAN WAY OF LIFE"

The completion of bridge, and later subway, links between Manhattan and Brooklyn made rapid growth possible in the latter borough. After 1900, Queens and the Bronx acquired better transportation, and this, in turn, encouraged high population growth there. Of course, some of the more successful children and grandchildren of the nineteenth century Northern and Western European immigrants left the City entirely, seeking still better conditions in the suburbs, a movement that became even more pronounced after World War II (Rosenwaike, 1972: chs. 5,6). Away from original immigrant neighborhoods, many became involved in creating a distinct "American way of life." Ethnicity lessened in significance or changed in content. The immigrants watched their children acquire fluency in English, attend the public schools, find jobs outside the ethnic businesses and neighborhoods, read the American rather than the ethnic press, and move into less-crowded and less ethnically-concentrated neighborhoods. There were, however, differences in this process of acculturation and assimilation.

While the Irish continued to build their lives around the Church, politics and local neighborhood, and persisted in their ethnicity well into the twentieth century, German Jews quickly acculturated. Their religious expression was Reformed Judiasm, akin to middle-class American Protestantism, and its spokesman, Stephen Wise, believed America to be the land of freedom and opportunity. He wanted rabbis to be trained in America, not Europe, and Judiasm to be closely allied to American culture (Glazer, 1957:36–42).

Yet assimilation was elusive. Even the elite German Jews discovered themselves barred from (or permitted only limited access to) clubs , resorts, universities, and employment. Not until after World War II would some of these barriers fall, and Jewish-Christian intermarriage rates rise.

Acculturation and assimilation among non-Jewish Germans was also pronounced. Many aspects of German American culture declined under the pressures of World War I when German American organizations were attacked as being disloyal. As these organizations disintegrated during the war, there was a dramatic drop in the use of the German language in churches, stores, and homes and a similar decline in German newspapers and magazines, once the nation's largest foreign-language press (Luebke, 1974). Second generation German Americans found much to accept in the emerging American way of life.

Although World War II was not nearly so dramatic for German Americans, it further accelerated the decline. By the 1980s, New York had no German American culture of any prominence (Nadel, 1981:275–76). German Jewish refugees of the 1930s and 1940s had moved into Washington Heights in Manhattan, but after 1970 that community was small and declining and was being replaced by immigrants from the Hispanic Caribbean. A few reminders of the German presence—in the form of signs and buildings—can be found in the Lower East Side and Yorkville. But by the early 1960s when Glazer and Moynihan published their study of the persistence of ethnicity in *Beyond the Melting Pot*, they omitted the Germans.

THE SOUTHERN AND EASTERN EUROPEANS

From the 1880s to World War II, New York City experienced dramatic economic growth and rapid neighborhood changes. The City maintained its position as the nation's largest port, although West Coast ports gained after 1900. Growing banking and commerce were closely allied to the City's trading role; few immigrants, however, found employment in these institutions. More important for them was the sensational growth of light industry, especially in garment manufacturing. While the city continued its expansion to upper Manhattan, it was the new bridge, tunnel, elevated car, and subway construction that opened the way for building booms in Brooklyn, the Bronx and Queens, with Staten Island growing more slowly during this period.

Two major population movements occurred during this era. First came the immigrants from Southern and Eastern Europe who entered through Ellis Island. Often they stayed for only a day or so before moving west to join family and friends. among them were Greeks, Poles, Russians, and peoples from the many regions of the Austro-Hungarian Empire. In this migration two groups stood out in both numbers and their impact on the city: Jews from Eastern Europe—mainly Poland, Latvia, Russia, and Lithuania—and Italians. The second movement was of rural, southern Blacks. This internal migration began in the 1880s and became pronounced after 1910.

Jews fled the vicious antisemitism of Europe and the pogroms of Russia, which intensified in the late nineteenth century. Jews emigrated mainly as families, and once in New York or the United States, had little desire to return to Europe. Compared to other new immigrants, the Eastern European Jews were more apt to be literate, urban in background, and skilled workers. (Ricschin, 1964: ch.2). Since many of the men had worked as tailors before arriving in New York, these skills may have aided them in gaining a foothold in the city's rapidly expanding clothing industry (despite the fact most of the jobs in the garment industry required little skill). Because Jewish immigrants, whether skilled or not, arrived with practically no money, many simply took these readily available sweatshop jobs (*ibid.*:ch.3; Kessner, 1977: chs.2–3). Those working-class Jews who did not move out of the sweatshops became active in the city's growing trade unions, especially the International Ladies Garment Workers and the Amalgamated Clothing Workers (*ibid.*: ch.2 and pp. 86–93). Now these jobs have been taken over, in great part, by Caribbean migrants, sometimes under a renewal of sweatshop and "putting out" conditions not so different from former times.

Like the German Jews before them, many began as peddlers in the famed Lower East Side. Still others opened stores—butcher shops and bakeries—to serve their fellow ethnics. Cigar making, bookbinding and other similar occupations also attracted some of these immigrants. Some took in boarders to make ends meet or they worked on garments at home (*ibid.*:99–100). Few of the first generation were professionals or white-collar workers (*ibid.*:59–70).

The congested tenements of the Lower East Side became the first home for the bulk of these new immigrants. There, a variety of churches , newspapers, theaters, coffee shops, schools, political parties, saloons, and charities supported the newcomers in their adjustment to New York. No other immigrant group seemed to approach Jews in building so many of their own institutions, apparently a pattern developed under the segregated conditions in which Jews had lived in Poland and Russia.

For the new Jewish immigrants from Eastern Europe, the presence of older jewish groups made their adjustment easier. Established Sephardic and especially German Jews gave of their time and money to aid the Russian and Polish Jews. Yet this aid from the Germans did not come easily, and, at first, friction existed between the older and newer groups. The Germans, largely assimilated, prosperous and Reformed, did not understand or appreciate the Russian Jews' orthodoxy or their radical politics. To the Germans, the Russians appeared uncouth and vulgar. Gradually the frictions eased and German Jews assisted the Russians with a variety of educational and philanthropic institutions. If the efforts of the "Uptowners" were not enough, the Russians from "downtown" established their own institutions of self-help (Rischin, 1964:103–111; Goren, 1970).

Possessing a cultural heritage that stressed education, Jews emphasized the importance of acquiring a formal education. In America, it became the route that they used to escape the poverty of their immigrant neighborhoods. Jewish youth flocked to the public schools, and then to the City's free colleges. Many of the second, and especially the third, generation found white-collar employment, including the professions of law, medicine, and teaching. As the public schools expanded to educate the growing number of immigrant children, the Jews replaced the Irish as the source of new teachers and eventually of administrators as well. By the 1920s and 1930s the schools had introduced a Jewish component in the curriculum to counter the anti-semitic bias in education (Moore, 1981:97–121). During the presidency of Franklin Roosevelt and the mayoralty of Fiorello La Guardia, Jews also became more prominent in the Democratic Party and found employment in the city's government (Bayor, 1978:24–27).

As Jewish immigrants found better jobs, they moved from the Lower East Side, which reached its peak density around 1910. Indeed, some new immigrants after 1900 did not even settle initially in Manhattan. A few German Jews had settled in Harlem just after the Civil War, and their small numbers were augmented in the late nineteenth century by a growing number of Eastern European Jews (Gurock, 1979:7–14). Along with this movement came

Jewish institutions, synagogues, schools, political clubs, and cultural forums (*ibid.*: chs.2–3). The Bronx—especially along the Grand Concourse—along with Brooklyn's Williamsburg and Brownsville also attracted the upwardly mobile Jews (Moore, 1981:22–39). Jewish institutional life, both secular and religious, flourished in these new surroundings (*ibid.*: chs.3–5). These movements were the prelude to the post-World War II migrations of Jews to the city's suburbs when the Jewish population of the city declined after decades of steady growth.

THE ITALIANS

Italians—mostly from southern Italy and Sicily—came to New York to escape wretched poverty. Largely from peasant background and frequently illiterate and unskilled, they often intended to work for only a few months or years and then return to Italy. Unlike Jews, these immigrants were commonly young males who did not arrive with their families. Many, working in New York and elsewhere, did return home and then migrate again to the New World (Kessner, 1977:26–31; Gambino, 1975:42–76). In time, however, many men began to marry in the United States, or returned home to find a spouse or, if married, sent for their families to settle in the United States.

In New York, lacking education and training, Italians worked at unskilled jobs. As did Jewish immigrants, some entered the expanding garment trade or found jobs in similar industries. Yet Italians were more apt to do heavy, manual, and unskilled labor, such as in subway construction or on the docks. As the Jews, Italians also became active in trade unions. They also opened businesses and worked in service industries such as barber shops (Kessner, 1977:51–59; Gambino, 1975:77–127). Second, and even first, generation Italians generally improved their lot, although they did not progress so far in the occupational hierarchy as did Jews. Some moved within the ranks of the working class; others prospered by operating ethnic businesses and still others through organized crime. As Jewish, Irish and other immigrant gangsters, Italians found opportunities in crime that were not readily available elsewhere (Nadel, 1981:174–81; Nelli, 1976; Ianni, 1972; Joselit, 1983).

A major consideration in the relative lack of Italian socioeconomic mobility was education. Southern Italians came from a society that offered little formal education, regarding education as a threat to family oriented traditions. Moreover, the Protestant orientation of New York's public schools was viewed with suspicion by Italians as well as other Catholic immigrants. Italians frequently dropped out of school, thus remaining working class for a much longer period than did Jewish immigrants (Kessner, 1977:77–86; Gambino, 1975:91–92 and 245–73; Cohen, 1982:443–66).

As other immigrants, Italians clustered in ethnic enclaves, such as Mulberry Bend in lower Manhattan. As they moved out of their original neighborhoods, they sought out other Italians in Manhattan's East Harlem or the

City's growing boroughs of Brooklyn, the Bronx and Queens (Gurock, 1979:49–50; Glazer and Moynihan, 1963:186–90). Some scholars believe that Italians did not think of themselves as Italians before they came to America, but rather as members of small villages and communities in Italy. Large-scale organizations to help them adjust to the New World did not exist as they did among the Jews. Nor did the Irish dominated Catholic Church necessarily offer comfort to these immigrants (Gambino, 1975:229–41). Perhaps because they lacked strong ties to the Church or were not supported by a host of organizations, Italians remained closer to their families and local neighborhoods and took longer to become active in the City's politics (Glazer and Moynihan, 1963:208–210). Although La Guardia, the City's first Italian American mayor, was elected in 1933, the real rise of Italians in New York City's politics came after World War II (Mann, 1957). Then Italian Americans began attending public high schools and colleges in large numbers and leaving behind older neighborhoods to be settled by newer immigrants.

SOUTHERN BLACKS

Black migration from the rural South was the last major movement of people to New York City in the period from 1880 to World War II. In the century following the American Revolution as millions of Europeans poured into the city, few Blacks had migrated to New York, and the Black proportion of the city's population fell. By 1900, there were only 60,666 Blacks out of almost 3.5 million people—less than two percent of the total. Most lived in Manhattan (Rosenwaike, 1972:75–77).

Little changed for Black New Yorkers during the nineteenth century. In Manhattan they often lived in White or mixed neighborhoods, but they worked at the poorest paying, menial jobs and suffered the worst health standards. City blocks heavily populated by Blacks were characterized by overcrowding and poor conditions. Black women, more often than White, were apt to work so that their families could survive. Only a small Black middle class existed. While Blacks obtained the ballot after the Civil War and the state abolished some of the official forms of racial segregation, Blacks remained virtually excluded from the city's political life and social institutions (Osofsky, 1965: ch.1; Scheiner, 1986: chs.1–3).

Nor was violence unknown. A riot in 1900 revealed the depth of racial prejudice. During that August riot Irish policemen actually encouraged the White rioters rather than enforcing the law. While some criticized the police, few demonstrated much sympathy for the dead or injured Blacks, and newspaper comment at that time demonstrates how widespread racial stereotypes were among Whites (Osofsky, 1965:46–52).

In the late nineteenth century, amid deteriorating conditions following the end of Reconstruction, a growing number of southern Blacks headed north in search of a better life. When World War I and the immigration restrictions acts of the 1920s sharply curtailed European immigration, the movement of Black southerners rapidly increased. By 1930, over 300,000 Blacks lived in New York City. They found few places to live except in the emerging ghetto of Harlem. There, older German, Jewish, and Italian communities began moving out as Harlem became a racially segregated slum. A similar pattern developed in Brooklyn (*ibid.*: chs.6–8; Connolly, 1977: ch.3).

In keeping with U.S. patterns of racial discrimination and segregation, New York City did not offer Blacks the employment opportunities that it offered European immigrants. Thus, the southern Blacks found job opportunities little different from those available to New York City's Black population in the nineteenth century. Moreover, the housing available to them was segregated and deteriorating, and they also were largely excluded from the city's mainstream religious, social, and political life. Black schools were overcrowded and ill equipped to help southern Black children who had received meager schooling prior to their migration to New York. One historian noted that the typical Harlem school of the 1920s ran double or triple sessions and that classes were of 40 to 50 students (Osofsky, 1965:148). Yet even if Blacks managed to survive the educational system, employers would not hire them for skilled or better-paying jobs.

While Blacks were the poorest of New York's ethnic groups, an important middle class emerged, consisting of ministers, teachers and other professionals, artists, and small businessmen. Black New York, like Jewish New York, also developed its own cultural and institutional life. Established churches such as St. Philip's Protestant Episcopal Church developed social programs. Adam Clayton Powell, who in the 1940s was elected as the first Black congressman from New York, began his career as minister of the large Abyssinian Baptist Church. Many of Harlem's residents found solace in the store-front churches. Black protest groups like the National Urban League and the National Association for the Advancement of Colored People flourished in Harlem. When Marcus Garvey searched for an American base for his movement, he chose New York. During the 1920s, Harlem had the reputation for being the Black capital of the United States, the center of a cultural renaissance. It was a maturing, creative period in the history of Black music, art, poetry and literature (Huggins, 1971).

Although Afro-Americans and Europeans and their descendants made up the vast majority of New York's population on the eve of World War II, people from what we now call the Third World did migrate to New York City before 1940. In that year, about 60,000, or one sixth, of New York's Black population were foreign-born, mostly West Indians from English-speaking colonies in the Caribbean (Osofsky, 1965:131–35).

The largest number of Spanish-speaking people in New York City before 1940 were Puerto Ricans. By virtue of becoming American citizens following the U.S. conquest of Puerto Rico, they had free immigration to the United States. By the time of the Great Depression they numbered about 45,000

(Glazer and Moynihan, 1963:91–93). Small numbers of Central and South Americans, in addition to some Hispanics from the Caribbean, had emigrated to New York during the nineteenth century. Even before the Spanish American War, a few Cuban exiles from Spanish colonialism made their home in New York City.

Smaller numbers of immigrants from Asia had also settled in the city prior to World War II. The Chinese, who first appeared in New York City in 1850, were the largest group. By 1890, the city had 2,559 Chinese located in present-day Chinatown. Yet that population grew slowly and was largely a bachelor society on the eve of World War II (Wong, 1982:5–8).

These Third World peoples were vastly outnumbered by Black Americans, Europeans, and their descendants. Following World War II, they have grown in importance and visibility as larger numbers of peoples from the Third World have emigrated to New York City as a consequence of changes in the world's social and economic conditions and in U.S. immigration policy.

Two streams have dominated the post-World War II immigration to New York. Largest in numbers has been the Caribbean migration, the subject of this book. Puerto Ricans currently make up about sixty percent of the city's nearly one and one half million Hispanics. Their migration was heaviest during the 1940s and 1950s. Next to Puerto Ricans among the City's recent Hispanics have been Dominicans from the Caribbean and Colombians from South America. Yet Spanish-speaking immigrants have entered from all Latin American countries .

In addition to Hispanics, many English-speaking and Haitian Creole-speaking peoples from the Caribbean have migrated in growing numbers. Almost half of Jamaican immigrants to the United States have settled in New York City and its surrounding area. The precise number of Haitians is unknown because many are undocumented and missed by the census takers.

The second stream of recent immigration has been from Asia. The 1980 census reported 230,000 Asians in New York, but many observers believe that to be an undercount. They have continued to arrive in substantial numbers since 1980, so the figure today is certainly higher than 230,000. Chinese make up the largest number of new Asians, but the City has witnessed the growth of its Asian Indian, Korean, Filipino and even Indochinese refugee population since 1965. The city's Chinatown is now larger than that of San Francisco.

As a result of these new migrations, the city's foreign population has grown substantially. The 1980 census reported one in four of New York's residents was foreign-born. While precise data for the 1980s is lacking, the proportion is higher than one in four today. The borough of Queens claims the largest number of these immigrants, with Brooklyn closely behind and then Manhattan and the Bronx. Few immigrants live in Staten Island.

While immigrants can be found in all boroughs and occupations, certain patterns stand out. Brooklyn is the home for large numbers of West Indians and Haitians. Queens is an especially polyglot borough with sizable numbers of Colombians, Koreans, Chinese and peoples from all over the globe. Upper Manhattan is the center of the city's Dominicans.

Asian Indians are often medical professionals or the owners and managers of city newsstands. Koreans, also highly educated, run about eighty percent of the greengrocers. Chinese are associated with restaurants and the low-paid garment industry, which has been expanding recently. English-speaking West Indians are often skilled or professional workers, while Haitians and Dominicans have usually been confined to low-paid service sectors of the economy.

This new immigration has renewed New York City's historic role as a city of immigrants. These "newcomers" from the Caribbean and other Third World regions have not only added to New York City's racial and ethnic diversity but have also internationalized the heterogeneity of its population to a far greater degree than heretofore. It can now be said that New York has indeed become a "global" urban center. And what this implies, both for its changing character as a city and for how the "new immigrants" fare, has become a matter of great interest and concern. For while it is clear that the "new immigrants" share with the immigrant groups from Europe many common experiences, it is also clear that the important ways in which they differ from the "old immigrants" go beyond the differences of either "old immigrant" experiences noted in this article or "new immigrant" experiences described in articles in this volume. Thus, there are parallels in the economic and political conditions that have prompted the large-scale emigrations, in the motivations of those who actually migrate, in the willingness of immigrants to take up the "unwanted jobs," at least temporarily, in their forming communities with self-help organizations, in their maintaining some ties with and interest in their countries of origin, and in their mobilizing along ethnic lines to form political interest groups. There are also differences that stem from the fact that the "new immigrants" are "colonial" immigrants, coming from countries that have been colonized in the past and that today may be dependent on those very centers to which they migrate. This means that the "new immigrants" enter New York City with the experience in their own country of some combination of a racial, class, and ethnic hierarchy, bolstered by the cultural hegemony of a colonial or neocolonial power. They encounter in New York City a biracial system which, along with its great ethnic diversity and class divisions, took root at the inception of the City in the early seventeenth century.

While today New York City has the largest Black population in the U.S., it is evident that the experience of southern Black migrants differed from that of the European immigrants. Black Americans were (and are) prevented from climbing the same "ladder of success" due to institutionalized racism. The question then is where do the "new immigrants" fit into this pattern? Is it likely that in becoming incorporated into the City's economic, social and political life, they will follow the course set by New York's European immigrants or will they be subjected to experiences which parallel those of the U.S.'s southern Blacks? More likely, they may alter the two-category racial system.

The evidence is not all in. However, it is clear that New York City's racial hierarchy is of central importance to how peoples from the Caribbean, and other Third World regions, make out in the economic and social life of the City, to how effective they will be in their political mobilizations, and to the nature of the ethnic leadership that develops. It is also clear that these newcomers will surely diversify the racial categories and attributions with which the City has operated in the past, as well as give a new political meaning to the ethnic assertions in which they engage. The internationalization of New York City, which their presence represents, is bound to be reflected in the political consciousness of the City.

BIBLIOGRAPHY

Albion, R.G.
1984 *The Rise of New York Port (1815–1860)*. Boston: Northeastern University Press.

Archdeacon, T.
1983 *Becoming American*. New York: The Free Press.

Bayor, R.
1978 *Neighbors in Conflict: The Irish, Germans, Jews, and Italians of New York City, 1929–1941*. Baltimore: The Johns Hopkins Press.

Butler, J.
1983 *The Huguenots in America: A Refugee People in New World Society*. Cambridge: Harvard University Press.

Cohen, M.
1982 "Changing Education Strategies Among Immigrant Generations: New York Italians in Comparative Perspective." *Journal of Social History*, 15(3):443–466. Spring.

Coleman, T.
1973 *Going to America*. Garden City: Anchor Books.

Colen, S.
In "Just a Little Respect: West Indian Domestic Workers in New York City." In *Enough is*
Press *Enough: Domestic Service in Latin America and the Caribbean*. Elsa M. Chaney and Mary Garcia Castro, eds.

Connolly, H.X.
1977 *A Ghetto Grows in Brooklyn*. New York: New York University Pre ss.

Curry, L.P.
1981 *The Free Black in Urban America, 1800–1850*. Chicago: University of Chicago Press.

Dinnerstein, L. and D.M. Reimers
1982 *Ethnic Americans: A History of Immigration and Assimilation*. New York: Harper and Row. Second Edition.

Dolan, J.
1975 *The Immigrant Church: New York's Irish and German Catholics, 1815–1865*. Baltimore: The Johns Hopkins Press.

Ernst, R.
1979   *Immigrant Life in New York City: 1825–1863.* New York: Octagon Books.

Gambino, R.
1975   *Blood of My Blood: The Dilemma of Italian Americans.* Garden City: Doubleday.

Glazer, N.
1957   *American Judaism.* Chicago: University of Chicago Press.

Glazer, N. and D.P. Moynihan
1963   *Beyond the Melting Pot: The Negroes, Puerto Ricans, Jews, Italians, and Irish of New York City.* Cambridge, Massachusetts: The M.I.T. Press. Second edition.

Goren, A.A.
1970   *New York's Jews and the Quest for Community: The Kehillah Experiment, 1880–1922.* New York: Colombia University Press.

Gurock, J.S.
1979   *When Harlem Was Jewish, 1870–1930.* New York: Columbia University Press.

Headley, J.T.
1970   *The Great Riots of New York, 1712–1873.* Indianapolis: Bobbs-Merrill.

Huggins, N.
1971   *The Harlem Renaissance.* New York: Oxford University Press.

Ianni, F.A.J.
1972   *A Family Business: Kinship and Social Control in Organized Crime.* New York: Russell Sage Foundation.

Jones, M.
1960   *American Immigration.* Chicago: University of Chicago Press.

Joselit, J.W.
1983   *Our Gang. Jewish Crime and the New York Jewish Community, 1900–1940.* Bloomington: Indiana University Press.

Kessner, T.
1977   *The Golden Door: Italian and Jewish Immigrant Mobility in New York City, 1880–1915.* New York: Oxford University Press.

Klein, M., ed.
1976   *New York: The Centennial Years, 1876–1976.* Port Washington, New York: Kennikat Press.

Luebke, F.
1974   *Bonds of Loyalty.* DeKalb: Northern Illinois University Press.

Mann, A.
1965   *La Guardia Comes to Power: 1933.* Philadelphia: J.B. Lippincott.

Marcus, J.R.
1970   *The Colonial American Jew, 1492–1776.* Vol. 1. Detroit: Wayne State University Press.

McCaffrey, L.J.
1976   *The Irish Diaspora in America.* Bloomington: Indiana University Press.

McManus, E.J.
1966   *A History of Negro Slavery in New York.* Syracuse: Syracuse University Press.

Mohl, R.
1971   *Poverty in New York, 1783–1825.* New York: Oxford University Press.

Moore, D.D.
1981   *At Home in America: Second Generation New York Jews.* New York : Columbia University Press.

Nadel, S.
1981   "Kleindeutschland: New York City's Germans, 1845–1880." Unpublished Ph.D. dissertation, Columbia University.

Nelli, H.S.
1976   *The Business of Crime: Italians and Syndicate Crime in the United States.* New York: Oxford University Press.

Osofsky, G.
1965   *Harlem: The Making of a Ghetto, 1890–1930.* New York: Harper and Row.

Rischin, M.
1964   *The Promised City: New York's Jews, 1870–1914.* New York: Corinth Books.

Rosenwaike, I.
1972   *Population History of New York City.* Syracuse: Syracuse University Press.

Scheiner, S.M.
1965   *Negro Mecca: A History of the Negro in New York City, 1865–1920.* New York: New York University Press.

Smith-Rosenberg, C.
1971   *Religion and the Rise of the American City: The New York City Mission Movement, 1812–1870.* Ithaca: Cornell University Press.

Wong, B.P.
1982   *Chinatown: Economic Adaptation and Ethnic Identity of the Chinese.* New York: Holt, Rinehart and Winston.

NEW YORK CITY AND THE NEW CARIBBEAN IMMIGRATION:
A Contextual Statement [1]

ROY SIMÓN BRYCE-LAPORTE
College of Staten Island, City University of New York

As it once represented for many European and other North Atlantic immigrants, New York City continues to represent the ultimate urban frontier (or conduit) for many Caribbean and other South Atlantic immigrants. Ellis Island, Idlewild (now J.F. Kennedy Airport) and the Statue of Liberty are only a few of the most visible symbols of this historic role.

The inscription on the Statue of Liberty continues to hold meaning for peoples from many parts of the world. No longer, however, is it reflective of the compassion and intention once imputed to the peoples of the United States. Once it was conventional wisdom to view the United States as a willing attractive, recipient or "pull" force in world immigration. Today it is more appropriate to view this country as a responsible, active "push" agent operating through certain forces in a system to displace, induce and direct people from their own lands to enter U.S. ports and cross U.S. boundaries by almost any means possible. As a result of certain group interests and government practices, the U.S. performs the responsibilities implied in its new character only with a measure of difficulty and an apparent ambivalence. Since the middle of the 19th century, the United States has been undergoing categorical if not evolutionary changes in its developmental needs, international role, and structural complexity, all of which have registered in its changing policies toward immigration and immigrants; such changes have manifested themselves perhaps most dramatically in New York City (Sandis, 1979).

New York City still stands as the financial center of the (capitalist) world economic system. It is the primary target of world labor, profit, and consumer capital, and is a principal source of investment capital, technological knowl-

[1] This article is dedicated to Ira de Augustine Reid, pioneer in the study of Caribbean immigration (1901–1970), posthumous recipient of the 1978 DuBois-Johnson-Frazier award, American Sociological Association, San Francisco. Reid is the author of *The Negro Immigrant*, a classic reference in the field. The author wishes to acknowledge the assistance of Camila Bryce-Laporte and Marian Holness-Gault, but holds himself soley responsible for the contents of this article.

edge, and popular style. With Washington, D.C., New York City also constitutes the political and economic power base of today's capitalist system in which the Caribbean, by and large, is but a subordinate, dependent, and less developed component. As an objective locality, New York City represents a contextual extreme in scale, structure, and even life style to the local ambience from which many Caribbean immigrants come, although not uniformly so. As a subjective reality, it probably holds a special meaning and curious utility for the Caribbean immigrant as well. In this sense, it is the maximal representation of the international inequality to which Caribbean immigrants often respond, even though they tend to do so with exaggerated expectations of opportunity and modernity or with simplistic images of racism and crime; it is the arena in which they are "seasoned" and are "struggling" with the American way-of-life; it is hell; it is heaven. It is the new stage on which West Indians play out their history of what Barbadian born Elliot D. Parris would call their "sweetness" and "sufferings."

Even conceding the unique geographical and transportational functions of Miami relative to the Caribbean region, New York remains the leading target and *entrepôt* (port of entry) for Caribbean peoples to the United States. There are other large North American cities in which sizable numbers of immigrants from individual Caribbean countries can be found; *e.g.*, Haitians in Chicago and Boston; Trinidadians in Washington, D.C. and Boston; Colombians in Washington, D.C. and Miami; Cubans and Bahamians who cluster in Miami and the greater Dade County of Florida; and Puerto Ricans in almost all the major cities of the Northeast. Despite these exceptions, however, there is no other metropolitan area in which one would find a greater number of West Indians of any country and so many groups of West Indians from various countries congregating in such large numbers as in the New York metropolitan area.

Long before even thinking of migrating or visiting the United States, most people of the Caribbean region would at least know of New York City. Some would have conceived of it as equivalent, if not interchangeable, with the United States as a whole. Increasingly, others come to know it to be distinct from the South and for other reasons, distinct from Hollywood, Miami, and Washington, D.C. as well. These latter distinctions have developed as literacy, personal correspondence, local gossip, education, mass media, promotional propaganda, news from "America," overseas travel opportunities, and credit or chartered systems have become more available.

Traditionally, New York City has been conceived as the mecca of Caribbean-United States migration and tourism. Increasingly, depending on the class of people or the time period involved, this distinction may be redirected instead to a specific borough or satellite suburb of New York City, *e.g.*, Harlem, Brooklyn, Bronx, Queens, Long Island, Yonkers, "Jersey," or "Connecticut." Even those West Indians who enter or first settle in other parts of the country or in Canada are driven by a special curiosity and determination to get to New York City eventually. No visit or residence in the United States is felt to be complete without at least one New York City experience. In the folklore, gossip, and even geography lessons of the peoples of the region the image of the City is pregnant with marvel, mystery, and myth. Therefore, an ultimate arrival in New York City for many Caribbean people is partly due to: 1) a much nurtured need to fulfill the dream, curiosity, sense of achievement, and drive for adventure which are tied up with the City as a special object in the immigrant ethos of the Caribbean; 2) an actual desire to establish acquaintances and reestablish linkage with transplanted kinsmen, neighbors, and compatriots; and 3) an impulse or inducement to emigrate from their less developed, generally dependent, and sometimes politically repressed countries to what they have learned to be the most free, liberal, cosmopolitan, urban, and opportunity-employment gilded metropolis in their larger concept of the world.

THE "NEW" IMMIGRATION

The history of the United States is, indeed, a history of immigration; so too is the history of New York City. Despite the fact that since colonization there has been no complete cessation of immigration (and for that reason emigration), the movement of alien peoples into the United States is often presented by historians in terms of discrete waves which may be characterized by way of magnitude, sources, conditions, contributions, and various qualitative features of the particular aggregate of immigrants involved.

Presently, this country is experiencing a new wave of immigrants which began in the late 1960s. Although its anticipation may have triggered an internal adjustment of status among certain segments of the alien population, the major dateline commencing the new immigration was 1965, in which was passed a comprehensive legislation on immigration by Congress. Distinct from the much more exclusionary, selective, and racist character of preceding legislation from 1882 through 1952, the Immigration and Nationality Act of 1965 replaced the national quota system with hemispheric ceilings. The Act also increased the quota of immigrants from (non-North American colonies in the Western Hemisphere, provided a set of preferences, and required job certification with the intent to facilitate the reunification of families on one level while seeking to protect domestic labor on the other. In 1975, President Gerald Ford introduced adjustments to bring about some equity between hemispheres and amended the preference system, but for all purposes retained the orientation of the Act of 1965. Since then, there have been several significant legislative and executive actions, critical judicial decisions and diplomatic agreements on the federal level as well as controversial positions taken by local authorities and jurisdictions on the entry, recategorization and treatment of refugees and illegal aliens coming especially from countries of the Caribbean Basin into the U.S.

Comparing the eleven years of pre- and post-1965 legal immigration to the United States, the following observations may be made:

a) An increase of about 1 million (35%) on the world level;

b) A general leadership of the Eastern over Western Hemisphere as a source of legal immigration;

c) The significant reduction of the gap between Europe and Asia as leading continental sources, and Asia overtaking Europe as the principal source as of 1970;

d) An increased West Indian output so that now the region produces almost as many immigrants in number and proportion to the United States as the North American countries of Mexico and Canada; and

e) The accompaniment of Cuba by the Dominican Republic among the top ten leading source countries in the mid to late 1970s, other Caribbean countries which are highly ranked since 1965, being Jamaica, Haiti, and Trinidad-Tobago (Bryce-Laporte, 1978).

Also associated with this new movement is the fact-and-fiction of a sizable component of illegal or undocumented aliens, which is further supplemented by refugees from Haiti, Cuba, East Africa, and Indochina and the "internal" movement of people from the United States overseas territories, *i.e.*, Puerto Rico, Marianas, Samoa, Guam, Virgin Islands, etc., to the mainland. The exact figures for illegal immigrants to the United States are often speculative and believed to be gravely exaggerated for political and special interest reasons. Nevertheless, based on the number reported to be apprehended (or asked to depart if not deported), three Caribbean countries—Dominican Republic, Haiti, and Jamaica—are among the alleged top fourteen sources of such movements (Bryce Laporte, 1977:18–69; Portes, 1977:31–37; and U.S. Department of Justice, 1976a).

The new immigration, therefore, may be characterized by an increase in volume of legal *imigrés*, a drop in the output from the traditional European and Canadian sources and marked increases from Asia, the Caribbean and some parts of South America. Due to legal regulations a larger number of aliens enter as nonimmigrants, which includes refugees, students, and tourists. Three categories, when added to legal dependents, represent the areas in which migrants are most likely to register status changes in the direction of legal or illegal "permanent residents." Due to labor regulations there are certain categories and configurations of occupations available to immigrants and in which, therefore, these immigrant groups tend to be clustered. Even then, many changes seem to occur once residence is fully established, depending on the job market.

THE MIGRANT FLOW

With respect to the Caribbean, the new immigration can be characterized as a conflux of changes in political status or orientation in some of the most populous nations of the region; the closing of traditional European or Canadian targets; decreases in the movement of people from Puerto Rico and the Virgin Islands, which are, however, complicated by these territories then becoming targets and conduits for illegal and legal migration from the rest of the Caribbean and Latin America; shifts in the base of labor recruitment for certain United States industries; increased imbalance between population growth and economic growth; and unequal distribution of wealth, goods, services, or opportunities. From these countries, a large body of persons come to the United States and by overstaying or other maneuvers or violations, become illegal workers. In this latter measure, Caribbean illegals, with the exception perhaps of Haitian "refugees," differ from Mexicans or other aliens who tend to cross the border illegally or fraudulently from the outset and who are also more likely to repeat entry at short intervals.

With respect to New York City proper, the New Immigration reveals some interesting observations:

1) Since 1821, over 31 million immigrants have entered through the Port of New York equalling about 62 percent of the total immigration into the United States since that year (Griffin, 1976);

2) From 1956 to 1965, a total of 674,413 aliens declared New York City as their intended place of residence, averaging about 77.3 percent of the declaration of the State; from 1966 to 1975, a total of 716,079 declared the same, averaging 78.9 percent of the declaration for residence in the State (Griffin, 1976);

3) The Immigration and Naturalization Service data on leading sources of the United States immigrants for 1965 indicated that 3,778 of 19,760 Cubans (19.1%) settled in New York City, while 16,503 Jamaicans entered the United States, of whom 11,302 (68.5%) settled in New York; and of 3,801 Haitians entering the United States, 2,824 (74.3%) settled in New York City. In 1976, ten years after the law, 29,233 Cubans entered the United States and 2,897 (9.9%) settled in New York City; 12,526 Dominicans of whom 8,505 (67.9%) settled there; 5,410 Haitians entered and 3,585 settled there (66.3%); and of 9,026 Jamaicans who entered 4,812 (53.3%) settled there. These data reinforce the aforementioned statement

of New York City as the prime destination of the majority of Caribbean immigrants with the exception of Cubans whose flow seems to be directed elsewhere (U.S . Department of Justice, INS *Annual Reports*, 1966 and 1976a);

4) According to 1970 United States Census figures, New York City has a total of 3,305,012 persons of foreign stock of whom 324,786 (9.8%) came from the Caribbean islands; and of these, 226,166 (69.9%) are foreign born and the remaining 68,620 are of mixed or foreign parentage. Of the total Caribbean population in New York City, about 82.5 percent are nonwhite. With reference to citizenship only 33 percent of the Cubans residing in New York City are naturalized, while the remaining groups of the Caribbean may be too small to register. The Caribbean shows a higher percentage of foreign born than the other groups in the City (43.5%) reflecting, among other things, the recency or continuity of immigration; the region shows a significantly higher percentage of nonwhite than the percentage of foreign born in the entire City (10.7%), reflecting then on the phenotypically ethnic and perhaps sociocultural visibility of Caribbean immigrants (U.S. Bureau of the Census, 1973—New York Tables, 138, 141–144);

5) Bearing in mind that census officials acknowledge an undercount of Blacks, Hispanic Americans, and Asians in this country, United States Census data reveal that the number of Puerto Ricans in New York City increased from 612,524 in 1960 to 817,712 in 1970, compared to 1,391,463 Puerto Ricans in the country and 878,000 of them in the State of New York. The increase of 25 percent of all Puerto Ricans in New York City between 1960 and 1970, and the concentration of 58.7 percent of United States Puerto Ricans in that City in 1970, show that the movement is oriented toward urban New York. This configuration is impressive when it is noted that in many years of the latter decade, Puerto Rico has received more migrants than it has sent, indicating a strong returned migration to the Island (U.S. Commission on Civil Rights, 1976:19–41); and

6) Figures on the illegal immigrant flow and population in New York City are not known with any degree of accuracy or reliability. Between 1959 and 1974, about 5,000 illegals were deported from New York City; 55,000 left "voluntarily," and 48,000 were asked to leave according to the Scheuer Report. This Report shows estimates of from 500,000 to 1,500,000 illegals in the City (Scheuer, 1978).

Although a major characteristic of the "new" immigration is the saliency of its Caribbean components, Caribbean immigration to the United States is not a new phenomenon per se. Some of the earliest Spanish expeditions and settlements on the North American mainland included free and slave Blacks from the Caribbean islands. A significant number of the early slaves were "seasoned" in the Caribbean islands before reaching the North American markets and plantations. In fact, much of the slave population of the Carolinas and Louisana came from the wholesale transfer of West Indian planters and their slaves. The 1850 Federal Census showed a foreign born "colored" population of 4,669, exclusive of oriental and "civilized" Indians. By 1930, there were 199,606 such persons recorded by the Census. Previous to 1870, only 16 percent of the foreign black population came from the West Indies; since then however, the majority has been of West Indian stock (Reid, 1939:85–92).

The Caribbean immigration to the United States has been predominantly urban for some time, even though there has been a smaller rural migratory component as well (Foner and Napoli, 1978:491–503; and DeWind, 1977). Free West Indians were present in New York City even during the early period of slavery and some individuals among them were active in the city during the War of Independence. Early West Indian concentrations, which according to Ira Reid, parallel the great migration of United States Blacks from the South, were found in such cities as Tampa, Miami, Cambridge, Boston, Philadelphia, Chicago, New Orleans and, of course, New York. Some of the urban concentrations were subethnic-specific; others showed an overlap among Spanish-speaking, English-speaking and French-speaking peoples from the Caribbean. Additionally, there was the possibility of internal or intercity movements among the migrants. However, in 1930, New York City already was the place of settlement of 60 percent of the country's foreign black population (Reid, 1939:85–92). This could be explained by such factors as: 1) its role as the major port of entry for Atlantic immigration; 2) access to relatively convenient interregional travel or communications facilities; and 3) various levels of job availability and opportunity for mobility or self-improvement compared to the economies of the undeveloped Caribbean. There was also the City's image as a relatively less hostile milieu for Blacks and other "colored" people; its reputation as a center of popular culture, modern life style and social excitement; and the self-generating pull of an ever-increasing presence of a West Indian community where many persons in the homeland had some kin or neighborly connections with New York City.

The concentration of West Indian people in urban centers, especially New York City, is not peculiar, un-American, or wholly negative—any more than are the experiences or the reactions to their presence. There are intellectual and popular biases in the United States which tend to tie immigration to a westward movement from urban to rural, and to claim for it such exclusive or superior virtues as opening, settling, exploiting, and developing the frontier; participating in democratic government; and exposure to healthy, more open and economically less dependent or alienating ways of life.

The sociological version of the myth of the frontier puts the city in opposition to all that is ideally good about the "open" countryside and by extension, the "organized" suburb. Beneath the seemingly contradictory stereotypes of the sophisticated ambience of good life, high society, *haute-couture* or *avant-garde* movements of the City, the myth really treats it as a disorganized, degenerate, depressed, draining and therefore, detestable place. It views those people who (must) inhabit the City, particularly New York City, with suspicion, regret, disdain, disregard, awe or envy. The historical version of the myth declares the frontier dead, meaning by that the unavailability of much more rural terrain. The myth conceptualizes the City as closed and occupied rather than open space. It contends that within the City there is no mode of accommodating massive migration or providing economic activities and political ambience for the kind of experimentation and growth which generally accompanied such movements in the rural frontier.

Both versions of the myth are faulty and, therefore, incomplete as they ignore certain crucial realities. From another intellectual orientation the city can also be viewed as a complement to the countryside or the suburb; it is generally the hub of economic, cultural if not political activities for the surrounding hinterland; and is a partner or peak rather than the only and total locus of urbanization or development in the larger society. Depending on the stage or pattern of development of the economy, the city represents a reservoir, source, or conduit for certain key elements in that process. In the United States, certain powerful classes, some of the traditional or new ethnic groups (of recent immigrant status) and smaller social entities have settled or invested in the City. They treat it and its various sectors, institutions, sections, and symbolic-cultural subsystems as their frontier.

As such, the City becomes an arena of contest, where special interest groups struggle to dominate it, direct its policies and priorities, claim its space and properties, move up its socioeconomic and stat us structure, and benefit from its advantages (Bryce-Laporte 1971:257–84). Although these special interest groups may be ethnic or class specific, often they can also represent what Milton Gordon calls "ethclasses"; that is, they can also represent coalitions or cross-sections of selected sections of certain ethnic groups who belong to or represent specific classes or their kinds of class orientation and interest.

The Jewish, Irish, and Italian immigrants are among the older groups now termed "white ethnics" that have been concentrated basically in the urban areas and have utilized and regarded the City (and in later years the suburbs as well) as a place to advance, protect themselves and later to try to dominate and negotiate the political structures. Occupationally, these groups were originally industrial and construction laborers, service or domestic workers, small merchants and professionals who served and survived on the urban working classes. In New York City they were the forces behind the early urban development of the City, recipients of many kinds of exploitation, discrimination and prejudices, and also the contributors to urban protest, labor agitation, and political radicalization.

Today, some of these groups have extended their presence and power higher, deeper, wider, and with greater strength into the spectrum of socio-economic, political, and cultural domains of the City. They have risen in the service institutions and, in some cases, varying numbers among them have moved out of the city proper into the nearby suburbs. This outward move-ment was followed by the continued urban immigration of southern Blacks, Mexicans, Puerto Ricans, and other early Caribbean immigrants. Buttressed by recent refugees as well as the legal and illegal components of the new immigration (of which Caribbean people comprise a major component), this movement has resulted in an increasing number of cities with actual or projected non-White majorities at the same time experience shifts in control, sources of revenue, capital investment flow, and labor intensive industries from the City to suburb (or from the industrial North to the "industrializing" Sun Belt).

The urban character of Caribbean immigration is not peculiar per se but falls into the same category as most of the white groups mentioned above. What is peculiar to it, however, is shaped, in part, by its relationship, size, and alikeness vis-à-vis other visible ethnic groups; most specifically, the U.S. Blacks. Considering that it is an old movement of a distinct people in its own right, it is unfortunate that West Indian Blacks are so often viewed only vis-à-vis or as a part of the larger group of native-rooted American Blacks and sometimes national Latin American minorities. Consequently, their distinct problems and unique proclivities are generally overlooked or sublimated vis-à-vis the large non-White native minorities of the country, and they tend to be viewed and treated with the same disregard and discrimination which the native Blacks or Hispanics suffer as visible minorities. Paradoxically, they suffer multiple "invisibility" and "minoritization" of status because of their commonly shared visibility with their native peers. As observed with the Black native minority of the U.S., differences among or within new immi-grant groups are overlooked (sometimes purposely so) in the eyes of the majority group and its institutions because of what is perceived as a common-ality of race, language, culture, or region of origin: e.g., Hispanic-Caribbean peoples (Allende, 1975:135; Dominguez, 1973; and Sutton and Makiesky-Bar-row, this volume), thus facilitating their control and treatment in public situations. The broader socioeconomic status of the U.S.-Caribbean residents, relative to other American ethnic or immigrant groups has not been clearly established (Palmer, 1976; Sowell, 1981). Therefore, two questions can be asked: Given their ambition, Protestant ethic, and European-colonial accul-turation, what would have been their progress, status, and power in the

United States were they not Black or Brown and of neo-colonial background? Do these particular, non-White immigrants represent a special prism of American racism or its open mobility structure? (Bryce-Laporte, 1972:29–56; and 1973:44–61).

Some would hold that as part of an ongoing process of immigration the new immigrants have entered the city and will follow patterns of movement and assimilation quite similar or replicative of those who came during the great European migration at the turn of the century, through the post-World War II period.

Others would concede to the new Caribbean immigrants similarity only insofar as both movements came principally as sources of labor. However, the visibility of the new immigrants, their countries of origin as well as the period of time of their arrival, account for significant differences. In addition, those stereotyped as laboring classes moved into low marginal rather than mobile jobs and industries. Many of these European immigrants who came were laboring or peasant classes, even though there was an appendage of small businessmen, professionals, intellectuals, and artists among them. They came from economically devastated countries but which, while distant and isolated from the United States, were independent and had positive ties, statuses, and akinness to this country. They came at a point in the development of capitalism and of the political, economic, and social structure of the United States when New York City and the rest of the country were still viewed internally and internationally as frontiers; lands of opportunity with the need and place for ambitious, hard-working aliens (some of whom were non-Europeans and included Caribbean peoples).

Many would concede to the new Caribbean immigrants only that they, too, came as poor ambitious peoples, and providers of labor with their middle-class appendages. The Caribbean peoples are, of course, from countries where ties with the United States are not so prestigious, their culture not often viewed as superior and coveted, and their populations are by phenotype and other characteristics quite likely to be held in prejudice by the North American majority. Additionally, they come from countries not generally devastated by war or prolonged drought, although political repression and revolution, and economic stagnation and occasional natural disasters are recurrent realities of the region. Rather, most of the countries of the Caribbean are emergent. They are economically, politically, and increasingly culturally dominated by the United States or one of the Western counterparts. They are locked into delicate but unquestionable situations of dependence and even subordination to the United States which are veiled by euphemistic categorization more aptly applied to Europe, Japan, and Canada. Thus, compared to their European predecessors who may immigrate to the United States or specifically to New York City to seek relief from temporarily devastated, static, objectively dull, or restricting milieu, the new Caribbean immigrants come from small, powerless, and often poor or less-developed emerging nations, caught in the path of lingering racism and ethnocentrism, legacies of colonialism, and the caprices and contradictions of world capitalism.

The situation of the Caribbean immigrants is complicated. Too often their reasons for departure are expressed or interpreted to be either romantic, emotional, pragmatic aspirations, or mere frustration with a corrupt misguided, incompetent stagnant political and economic system or leadership. On a deeper structural basis, their dissatisfaction and problems really emerge from painful contradiction as they and their countries aspire at this point in history to become developed, sovereign, independent nation states, symbols of progress, and promised lands of equality. Nevertheless, they are still catalogued as smaller, subordinate, exploitable and needy parts of larger political-economic orders. They are, therefore, parts of international systems which tend to "progress" even as the vast inequality between their major and minor partners and their core and peripheral members is being perpetuated. As this order has assumed a more transnational character (of which the New Immigration is but a mobile and systemic expression), the aspirations for independence and sovereignty of particular Caribbean states have remained adversely affected and the socioeconomic lag between them and the more developed metropolitan countries has persisted in manner and has compounded in magnitude.

The new Caribbean immigrants have entered the U.S. at a different point, in the development of world capitalism, witnessing both the fluctuating political economy of the United States, and political transition of the nation's cities. Compared to the earlier European and even older Caribbean immigrants who arrived as late as the 1950s, the new Caribbean *imigrés'* entry was accompanied, or soon followed some of the most vexing urban economic crises of the century: the abrupt and disgraceful ending of the Vietnamese debacle and the resulting depression in urban and national employment potential associated with the decline of a war economy; the return of veterans and entry of refugees with no economic structure to absorb them satisfactorily; the shift in ethnic balances and spread of minority activism in urban centers; the subsequent political manifestation in government; school desegregation, housing; increased use of automation; the shift of sites of intensive labor to the suburbs, the South, and overseas; the significant unemployment in the cities especially among youth, women, and visible minorities; and the skyrocketing of prices and rising inflation.

THE IMPACT IN THE CITY

In New York City itself these setbacks and tensions have been highlighted by its economic bankruptcy in the mid 1970s which required special federal intervention and new revenue sharing formulas. Consequently, there emerged a climate of heightened antagonism and even violence among the different ethnic groups or socioeconomic classes of the City, expressed on the one hand by frustrations of those visible, low-status minorities who developed high expectations in response to anticipated projects, programs, and legislation; and on the other hand by the traditional non-White ethnics who developed a sense of envy, threat, and resentment toward the first set. In addition, there had been various antiurban expressions in the larger country, highlighted by the insensitivity and reluctance of politicians from rural sections of this country (and some suburbs) to respond with assistance and sympathy to New York City's financial crisis. Rather, they charged the City with gross mismanagement particularly with reference to its massive social and welfare services, which attracted large numbers of poor, unemployed and migrant ethnic minorities. In so doing they also chose to overlook that the City itself has historically served as a safety-valve source of remittances in an earlier period, and now provides the country with skilled and professional members of a new middle class or urban trained descendants of earlier immigrants who are essential to their own industrial progress (Evans, 1978:25–26; and Paris, 1977a, b).

The new Caribbean immigrants, then, entered New York City at a point of marked structural and attitudinal adversity. This was in part because of a revival and fusion of antiurban and antiminority trends in the larger country. Additionally, the voting American population, already rendered hypersensitive to such issues as overpopulation, environmental abuse, and the inflation/unemployment syndrome, continued to be bombarded with anti-immigration propaganda. Using a system which either capitalizes on law and order, nationalism and racial superiority, or which appeals to the liberal preoccupation with human rights, under-class formation, and labor and minority problems, neo-exclusionary forces have been trying desperately to escalate the case of the new immigrants and isolate the least defensive among them—the illegals—to have them seen as causes (scapegoats) rather than victims and symptoms of the larger process of the economic-political imbalance which confronts this society as a whole (and the larger part of the world system which it dominates as well).

In historic perspective the situation of the new immigrant is perhaps more reminiscent of the experience of the early Chinese and Mexican laborers on the West Coast. In both cases these peoples immigrated in response to U.S. legislated inducement or negotiated recruitment projects designed to acquire labor forces to meet the needs of the economic sector. Later, they were economically exploited, victimized by discrimination, suffered adjustment problems, and became the subject of intense debate which eventually led to exclusionary legislation and anti-immigrant social policies (Hume, 1977).

The ambivalence toward the new immigrants is registered even in the ranks of the visible minorities themselves. In the case of Caribbean immigrants in New York it is expressed not only among native-rooted Blacks, but also Puerto Ricans and even other non-Whites of Caribbean ancestry. There are some indications of significant behavioral and objective class differences between earlier and more recent Caribbean immigrants (Gordon, 1979; and Johnson, 1977). Yet, for reasons such as strong kinship, geographical or ethnic identity, and some ideological awareness that problems arise out of structural limitation rather than contained labor competition per se, tensions between native and immigrant minorities, old and new immigrants, visible majority citizens and legal immigrants have not crystallized into fixed adverse struggles or violent confrontations.

Although there may be subethnic enclaves, as well as status or regional differences among them, in general the new immigrants (even the illegals) tend to be part of a larger ethnic or class ghetto of which the members attend many of the same institutions and share many of the same limited resources and acute problems (Alers, 1978; Bonnett, 1980; Chaney, 1977:60–64; Forsythe, 1976; Hendricks, 1974; Henry, 1973; Holder, 1977; Walter, 1977). It is unlikely that the new Caribbean (legal) immigrants are entrenched in any significant number in either extreme of the socioeconomic structure or cultural lifestyle of the City. The larger majority is caught in the pathways and treadmills of mobility, such as coping, working hard, raising a family, saving, spending, studying, praying, etc. They contain or entertain themselves in family, fraternal, real, and popular lifestyles of the City or in provincial rather than cosmopolitan circles. While there can be no doubt that poverty, linguistic limitations, and illegality may suppress the degree of community or nature of community politics in which new immigrants may engage, their relative invisibility should not lead us to believe that as a subgrouping they do not have distinctive features and, therefore, problems and proclivities, or that these differences do not have consequences on the cities, communities, subsocieties, and classes of which they are part. Insofar as the new immigrants, by definition, are the last to come from their country of origin, they represent the continuing linkage between the new communities and the old country, and the changing but still different cultures, social mores and languages. Some bring with them expertise and other resources; still others become the wards, proteges, beneficiaries, and *raison d'etre* of the jobs or activities among the more successful middle class. Some are links to roots people wish to rediscover, while others are bearers of problems that people can hardly forget.

Thus, the new immigration, particularly in the Caribbean-United States aspect, dramatizes the growing sense that classified definitions of nations and states are being blurred and nation-specific policies are being comprehended in the emergent world system, because of the diffusion of multi- and transnational arrangements and the concomitant flow, linkage, and formation of classes within the status and culture groups across the nations. Thus, immigration today is more a consequence and expression of the larger order or imbalance in national and international political-economic relations than a reflection of simple increases in individual motivation, ordinary push-pull operations, or even increased accessibility to more capable transportation media.

The new immigrants everywhere, but particularly in their cities of concentration such as New York, dramatize the growing necessity for conscious interlinking of local, national, international (and global) policies. In New York City, as their presence becomes more consequential it suggests that, as a city New York extends beyond definition which distinguishes it in form and function from countryside or suburb. New York City must be seen as a major point of international convergence of labor and capital and also of exchange of culture, art, academic thought, interests, folklore, ideology, identity, religion, life-styles, and technologies or technical methods. With regard to the Caribbean immigrants, it may well be that New York City is now a northern frontier, or at least a pole in a circular migratory stream not only of bodies, but of their objects, ideas, and sentiments as well. There are signs that New York functions as a site of significant cultural and political contacts in which there occurs a coalescence, structural reformation, and fusi/on of Caribbean peoples of various persuasions, cultures, classes, and subregions who were apart, antagonistic, and even ignorant of each other at home. A Pan-Caribbean spirit is emerging in New York City, to some extent in Washington, D.C. and in many other Eastern seaboard cities. One Hispanic example is a Puerto Rican group-sponsored exhibit and seminar on Cuban Santería and Haitian Vodun as part of the collective African heritage they want to retain and protect (See, Vega, 1978). The emergence of even broader cross-identification can be observed in the celebration of the West Indian Carnival and *Dia de la Raza* (Columbus Day) as well as the institution of Caribbean studies programs, the proliferation of Third World radio stations and political philosophizing in New York City. Whether *shango* or *soucouyant*, *sancocho* or *souse*, *sankey* or *son*, *susu* or *se-se*, *"sonny boy"* or *sa-u-dila*—Afro-Caribbean sounds, terms, and traits abound in New York City.

More important is the possibility that because of a greater access to finance, institutional space, and technological managerial know-how, it is this urban, Caribbean, overseas community which may eventually be intervening in behalf of and impacting on certain lines of radical restructuring and reorientation of the Caribbean region itself. Even more the City may well be the object of Caribbean transplantation (or transformation) in both the cultural and neo-colonial senses of the word. While most Caribbean social structures have not yet begun to duplicate the socioeconomic structure of the new North American metropolis so much as is claimed for Puerto Rico (Campos, 1980) New York City has begun to assume a role not at all unlike London and Paris as a reluctant place of refuge for the surplus or displaced and exploitable labor from the periphery of outlying satellites and colonial states (Katznelson, 1973). New York-based Orde Combs, the late Vincentian writer and television commentator prophesied a "Caribbeanization" of Manhattan Island with Brooklyn and Queens as rimland by the year 2000! One may ponder in turn to what extent there would be a similar New Yorkization of the entire Caribbean Basin in perhaps a lesser period of time.

NEW PERSPECTIVES

It was earlier stated that objectively, visible as they are, Caribbean immigrants suffer multiple levels of Elisonian-like invisibility. Part of the special invisibility of Caribbean immigrants (and immigration) in the United States is, of course, reflected and perhaps caused by the dearth of studies or course materials on it as a subject. It is only recently (some years after my own appeal) that serious academic work has begun to be pursued on this population (Bryce-Laporte, 1972, 1973). First published in 1939, *The Negro Immigrant*, by Ira Reid, a Black sociologist, continues to be the *magnum opus* of the field. Although artists, creative writers, journalists and immigrants themselves have done a bit better, there is still no classic treatise on American society or New York City from a Caribbean point of view. Nor has there been significant research on the contributions, lives, and roles of Caribbean immigrants in this country or this city, from a socioscientific or an historical perspective.

As sociologists, we would want to codify their insight and criticism into such conceptual categories as culture shock, reality reconstruction; definition of situation or self and so on. We have not, however, said it all. There are many questions which remain unasked. We, as social scientists, must complement our objective concerns with the structure and context by conducting empirical fieldwork and in-depth probing of the new Caribbean immigrants not only as a category or condition but as persons and groups who behave, react, and act upon their settings; who bring and develop meanings for their settings, and who, therefore, must be studied and listened to as such. This is a challenge not only for scholars but also for policy-makers and the native population. New York City is a moving, busy city where ethnicity never really melts away and where class and generation differences remain visible. Many outsiders would say, "it is a place to visit but not to live. It is a place to be from." Many of its former dwellers now find the city dirty, dangerous, and their neighborhoods "not like before," "everything changed" since, of course, it has been taken over by minority and/or migrants. Indeed, New York City—old, immense, heavily populated, heterogeneous, complex and dynamic as it is—has different meanings for all. As an "older" immigrant to the city, Antiguan-born poet Louchland Henry (1974:13) states:

> New York is anonymous
> Among millions as he strolls.
>
> New York City is a story
> That will never be told.

Not only are more comprehensive studies needed about the new Caribbean immigrants of New York City, but no sensible understanding of the city itself can be made without being sensitive to their presence and participation. How much have they changed the city? How much has it changed them? Lourdes Casals (1981:52), the late Cuban social scientist and poet leaves with us a telling, memorable response:

> And despite it all, New York is my home.
> I feel fiercely loyal to this acquired homeland.
> Because of New York I am a foreigner in whatever other place . . .
>
> But New York City is not the city of my infancy . . .
> Because of that I will always remain on the margin, a stranger between these rocks . . .
>
> Then, now and forever, I will always remain a foreigner
> Even when I return to the city of my infancy.
>
> I will always carry this marginality . . .
> too *habanera* to be New Yorker
> too New Yorker to be
> . . . ever to become again . . .
> anything else.[2]

As new Caribbean immigrants will now start to pose their own questions, hopefully informed scholars among them will strive to provide answers. Like their artists, these Caribbean immigrant scholars must take the initiative and be encouraged to do their own studies, make their own statements and give their own policy advice. Caribbean immigrants—residents and citizens, business people and politicians, artists and scholars—must begin to exercise and enjoy a right they share with all other American ethnic groups: to participate in a respectable way in determining the visibility they want to have in their city of settlement, to shape the kind of city they want to live in, and to influence the relations of that city with their region and in respect to their countries of origin.

BIBLIOGRAPHY

Allende, C.H.
1976 "Organizations Servicing Puerto Ricans and Virgin Islanders i n New York City: A Report." In *Exploratory Fieldwork on Latin Migrants and Indochinese Refugees*. R.S. Bryce-Laporte and

---

[2] Excerpts translated by R.S. Bryce-Laporte.

S.R. Couch, eds. Washington, DC: Smithsonian Institution, Research Institute on Immigration and Ethnic Studies. RIIES Research Notes No.1. Pp.135–137.

Alers, Jr., O.
1978   *Puerto Ricans and Health.* New York: Fordham University, Hispanic Research Center.

Bonnett, A.W.
1980   "An Examination of Rotating Credit Associations among Black West Indian Immigrants in Brooklyn." In *Sourcebook on the New Immigration: Implications for the United States and the International Community.* R.S. Bryce-Laporte, ed. New Brunswick, NJ: Transaction Books. Pp. 271–283.

Bryce-Laporte, R.S.
1971   "The Slave Plantation: Background to Present Conditions of Urban Blacks." In *Race, Change and Urban Society.* P. Orleans and W.R. Ellis, Jr. eds. Beverly Hills, CA: Sage Publications, Urban Affairs Annual Reviews 5. Pp. 257–284.

——
1978   "The New Immigration and Its Caribbean Component—an Overview." Hearings before the Select Committee on Population, House of Representatives, 95th Congress, 2nd Session, April 4–7. Washington , DC: Government Printing Office. Pp. 355–378.

—— ed.
1977   "The New Immigrant Wave." *Society*, 14(6):18–69. Sept./Oct. (Special Issue).

——
1973   "Black Immigrants." In *Through Different Eyes: Black and White Perspectives on American Race Relations.* P.I. Rose, S. Rothman and W.J. Wilson, eds. NY: Oxford University Press. Pp. 44–61.

——
1972   "Black Immigrants: The Experience of Invisibility and Inequality," *Journal of Black Studies*, 3(1):29–56. Sept.

Campos, E.
1980   "The Process of Migration and the Social Structure of Puerto Rican Society." In *Sourcebook on the New Immigration: Implications for the United States and the International Community.* R.S. Bryce-Laporte, ed. New Brunswick, NJ: Transaction Books. Pp. 99–108.

Casals, L.
1981   "Para Ana Velfort," *Areito*, 3(1):52. Summer. (Translated by R .S. Bryce-Laporte).

Chaney, F.M.
1977   "Colombian Outpost in New York City," *Society*, 14(6):60–64. Sept./Oct.

DeWind, J., T.Seidl and J. Shenk
1977   "Caribbean Migration: Contract Labor in U.S. Agriculture," *NACLA: Report on the Americas*, 11(8):4–37. Nov./Dec.

Dominguez, V.
1973   "The Spanish-Speaking Caribbeans in New York City: The Middle Race," *Revista Review Interamericana* 3(2):135–42. Summer.

Evans, E.
1978   "The City, South and Caribbean, I and II," *The New York Times.* June 25, 26.

Foner, N. and R. Napoli
1978   "Jamaican and Black American Migrant Farm Workers: A Comparative Analysis," *Social Problems*, 25(6):491–503. June.

Forsythe, D.
1976   "Black Immigrants and the American Ethos: Theories and Observations." In *Caribbean Immigration to the United States.* R.S . Bryce-Laporte and D.M. Mortimer, eds. Washington, DC: Smithsonian Institution, Research on Immigration and Ethnic Studies, RIIES Occasional Papers, No. 1. Pp. 55–82.

Gordon, M.H.
1979   "Identification and Adaptation: The Study of Two Groups of Jamaican Immigrants in New
       York City." Ph.D. dissertation, City University of New York.

Griffin, J.J.
1976   "America's Gateway—Immigration through the Port of New York , 1821–1975," *New York
       City Perspective*, 3(2):1–7. April.

Hendricks, G.L.
1974   *The Dominican Diaspora: From the Dominican Republic to New York City—Villagers in Transi-
       tion*. New York: Columbia University, Teachers' College Press.

Henry, K.S.A.
1973   "The Place of the Culture of Migrant Commonwealth Afro-West Indians in the Political
       Life of Black New York, 1918–1966." Ph.D. dissertation, University of Toronto.

Henry, L.A.
1974   *Touch Me Inside*. Scarsdale, NY: High Publications, Inc.

Holder. C.
1977   "The Rise of the West Indian in Politics in New York City, *Afro-Americans in New York's
       Life History*.

Hune, S.
1977   *Pacific Migration to the United States: Trends and Themes in Historical and Sociological Litera-
       ture*. Washington, DC: Smithsonian Institution, Research Institute on Immigration and
       Ethnic Studies. RIIES Bibliographic Studies, No. 2.

Johnson, A.
1977   "The Perception and Social Characteristics Related to Occupational Mobility of Black
       Women and Interracial Assimilation of Blacks in America." Ph.D. dissertation, New School
       for Social Research.

Katznelson, I.
1973   *Black Men, White Cites: Race, Politics and Migration to the United States,1900–1930, and Britain,
       1948–1968*. London: Oxford University Press.

Palmer, R.W.
1976   "Migration from the Caribbean to the United States: the Economic Status of the Immi-
       grants." In *Caribbean Immigration to the United States*. R.S. Bryce-Laport and D.M. Mortimer,
       eds. Washington, DC: Smithsonian Institution, Research Institute on Immigration and
       Ethnic Studies. RIIES Occasional Papers, No. 1. Pp. 44–54.

Paris, A.
1977a "New York City Fiscal Crisis: Hidden Diversions." Paper presented at the American
       Sociological Association Meetings, Chicago.

1977b "New Immigration: The Circum-Caribbean." Paper presented at the Society for the Study
       of Social Problems, San Francisco.

Portes, A.
1977   "Labor Functions of Illegal Aliens," *Society*, 14(6):31–37. Sept./Oct.

Reid, I. de A.
1939   *The Negro Immigrant: His Background, Characteristics and Social Adjustment. 1899–1937*. New
       York: Columbia University Press. Republished by Arno in 1969.

Sandis, E.E.
1979   "Ethnic Group Trends in New York." In *New Ethnics: the Case of the East Indians*. New York:
       Praeger Publishers.

Scheuer, J.M.
1978   "Illegal Immigration—Problems and Prospects," *City Almanac*, 12(6):1–15. April.

Sowell
1981 *Ethnic America.* New York: Basic Books.

United States Bureau of the Census
1973 *Puerto Ricans in the Continental United States: An Uncertain Future.* Washington, DC: U.S. Commission on Civil Rights.

United States Department of Justice, Immigration and Naturalization Service
1966 *Annual Reports,* 1965–1975. Washington, DC: Government Printing Office.

1976a *Annual Report* Washington, DC: Government Printing Office.

1976b *Preliminary Report on Illegal Immigrants.* Washington, DC: Domestic Council Committee on Illegal Aliens.

Vega, M.M., ed.
1978 *Caribe,* 1(3):2–7. Dec.

Walter, J.C.
1977 "West Indian Radical Politics in New York." *Western Journal of Black Studies,* 1(2):131–141. June.

WHERE CARIBBEAN PEOPLES LIVE IN NEW YORK CITY

DENNIS CONWAY and UALTHAN BIGBY
Indiana University, Bloomington

In spite of the acclaimed presence of West Indians as part of the Black minority in New York City, little is known about the residential adjustment of this extremely varied *mélange* of Caribbean immigrant groups, and how the groups have fared *vis-à-vis* each other. Particular ethnic subgroups have been identified with general areas within the city. Notably, Puerto Rican residential patterns have been documented (Boswell, 1976) and Dominicans in New York City have been treated as a special case (Hendricks, 1974; Lowenthal, 1976). However, among the English-speaking West Indian groups Jamaicans have received the most attention (Dominguez, 1975; Kessner and Caroli, 1981), and generalization about Caribbean residential patterns have rarely been anything more than occasional asides in discussions on occupational mobility (Foner, this volume).

The focus of this chapter is on this neglected aspect of New York City's socio-spatial structure, namely a comparative analysis of the contemporary residential patterns of the various immigrant subgroups which comprise the Caribbean presence. It distinguishes among the Dominican, Cuban, and Haitian subgroups and compares the residential patterns of these Spanish and "Creole (French)-speaking" immigrant groups with those of the Jamaican, Trinidadian, Barbadian, Guyanese, and "other island" subgroups among the English-speaking immigrants.

A modified index of residential segregation (Burnley, 1975; Stimson, 1975) will be used to determine the relative degrees of residential separation and association among these subgroups.[1]

It is expected that far from being a homogeneous entity, the subgroups within this overlooked minority will display selective residential clustering within the New York metropolitan area. The Spanish-speaking group will exhibit a distinctive separation from the English-speaking immigrant coun-

---

[1] Fortunately, the United States Immigration and Naturalization Service (INS), which collects information on resident aliens, has compiled a listing of nationalities by zip code areas for a few major metropolitan areas, including New York City. The 1980 data tape used in this study comprised 203,617 cases of Caribbean immigrants in New York City and categorizes them by current address (zip code area), date of entry to the United States, country of birth, country of previous residence, if different from birthplace, sex, and present occupational status.

terpart, and the "Creole (French)-speaking" Haitian subgroup will have a singular and distinct residential pattern which will differentiate it from the other two cultural groups. Different degrees of residential separation are to be expected within the English-speaking West Indian group in accordance with nationalistic and cultural perceptions and stereotypes these islanders hold of one another and of Black and White Americans.

In general, the experience of the various Caribbean immigrant groups in New York City rests on the characteristics of their island homes and their concomitant cultural backgrounds, on the persistence of ties between these immigrant sojourners and their island communities, and on their "nonwhiteness." While they are likely to experience discrimination in employment, education, and housing along with their American minority counterparts, at the same time being "outsiders" may provide them with a somewhat unique identity and potential for leverage over the native minorities which are their competition in the urban arena. In this chapter we focus on immigrant residential patterns as indicators of nonassimilation, not merely as an independent dimension but rather as one manifestation of the pluralism which continues to prosper in New York City, the nation's major *entrepôt*.

COMPARISON OF RESIDENTIAL PATTERNS IN NEW YORK CITY

According to the 1980 INS data, approximately 200,000 Caribbean immigrants are on record as residents in 173 zip code areas in Manhattan, Bronx, Queens, and Brooklyn.[2] Dominicans are the dominant immigrant group (43%), and

---

To determine the relative degrees of residential separation and association between the Caribbean immigrants, the following modified index of residential segregation (I_s) is used (Burnley, 1975):

$$I_s = \frac{\frac{1}{2} \sum\limits_{i=1}^{k} |X_i - Y_i|}{\frac{1 - \Sigma X_{ai}}{\Sigma Y_{ai}}}$$

where I_s is the Index of Residential Separation (Segregation), X_i is the percentage of the reference population (other national group or cultural group) in a zip code area, ΣX_{ai} is the total number of an immigrant group in the metropolitan area. ΣY_{ai} is the total number of the reference population in the metropolitan area, and k is the number of zip code areas in the metropolitan area.

[2] Bryce-Laporte estimates there were 324,786 Caribbean immigrants in New York City counted by the 1970 U.S. Census, so these INS data are clearly an undercount (*see,* p. 56 in this volume).

Despite this qualification, a comparison between Cuban patterns in the INS data and in the 1980 U.S. census reveal considerable similarities between data sets. Hence we have assumed that the INS data provide sufficient coverage to assess the 1980 residential patterns of the various Caribbean immigrant groups in the four major areas of New York City; Manhattan, Bronx, Brooklyn, and Queens.

TABLE 1

CARIBBEAN[a] IMMIGRANTS RESIDENT IN NEW YORK CITY
IN 1980 ACCORDING TO INS RECORDS

Rank Order	Caribbean Country of Origin	Total No. Cases	Percent Caribbean
1.	Dominican Republic	87,811	43.1
2.	Jamaica	37,336	18.3
3.	Cuba	18,535	9.1
4.	Trinidad and Tobago	17,035	8.4
5.	Guyana	14,813	7.3
6.	Haiti	12,189	6.0
7.	Barbados	9,168	4.5
8.	"Other Commonwealth Caribbean Islands"	6,730	7.3
	Total	203,617	100.0
	Total No. of Immigrants in New York State	228,849	

Note: [a] This excludes Puerto Rican migrants.

although Jamaicans constitute the second largest group (18%), appreciable numbers (in excess of 10,000) of other West Indian nationalities are recorded, Cubans (9%), Trinidadians (8.4%), Guyanese (7.3%), and Haitians (6%) (Table 1). Although use is made of zip code areas to describe the residential patterns of these immigrant groups, it is recognized that this subarea unit in no way represents a homogeneous neighborhood. This problem also has been noted when using census tracts to investigate segregation in New York City (Cowgill and Cowgill, 1951.) To provide a general frame of reference for the first descriptive phase of this analysis, certain neighborhood identities have been superimposed on the map of zip code areas (Figure I).

When note is taken of the proportional representation of the various immigrant Caribbean groups throughout New York City (Figures II through V) in relation to the neighborhood identities in Figure I, certain general features emerge. Crown Heights, Bedford Stuyvesant, and East New York in Brooklyn emerge as a Commonwealth Caribbean "core district" where many of the English-speaking West Indian nationalities are highly concentrated. Elsewhere in South Queens in the neighborhoods of Jamaica, South Jamaica, Hillside, and Cambria Heights, other concentrations of English-speaking immigrants are observed. Relatively few English-speaking West Indians live in Manhattan; few live in the northern part of Queens, and although the Bronx is another area where English-speaking West Indians reside, there is little evidence of large concentrations in any one of its neighborhoods (Figures III, IV, and V).

Spanish-speaking Caribbeans do, however, concentrate in Manhattan. There is a distinctive Dominican "core district" in the neighborhoods of Spanish Harlem, the Upper West Side, and Washington Heights in Manhat-

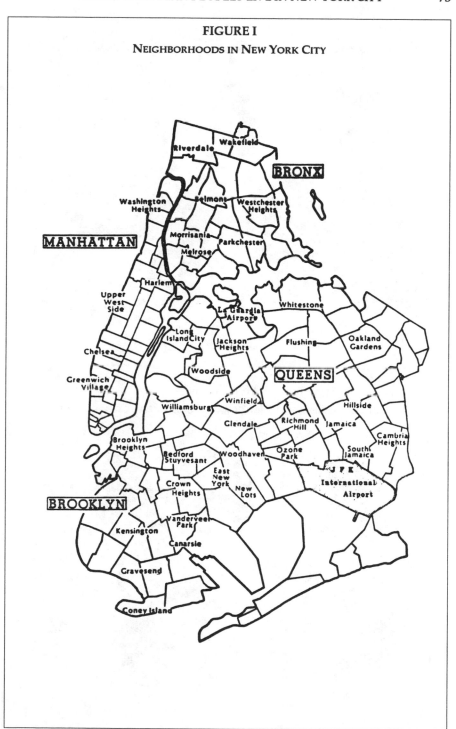

FIGURE I

NEIGHBORHOODS IN NEW YORK CITY

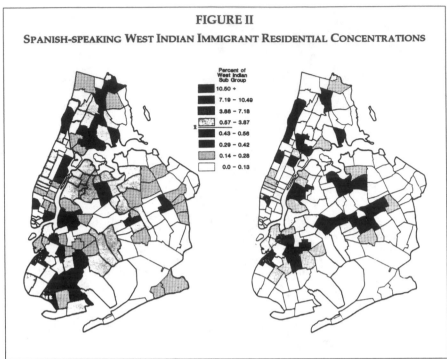

FIGURE II

SPANISH-SPEAKING WEST INDIAN IMMIGRANT RESIDENTIAL CONCENTRATIONS

Percent of
West Indian
Sub Group

- 10.50 +
- 7.19 – 10.49
- 3.88 – 7.18
- 0.57 – 3.87
- 0.43 – 0.56
- 0.29 – 0.42
- 0.14 – 0.28
- 0.0 – 0.13

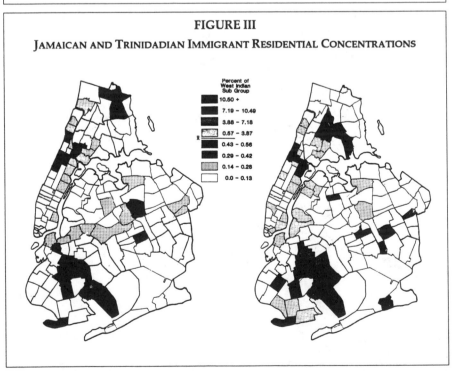

FIGURE III

JAMAICAN AND TRINIDADIAN IMMIGRANT RESIDENTIAL CONCENTRATIONS

Percent of
West Indian
Sub Group

- 10.50 +
- 7.19 – 10.49
- 3.88 – 7.18
- 0.57 – 3.87
- 0.43 – 0.56
- 0.29 – 0.42
- 0.14 – 0.28
- 0.0 – 0.13

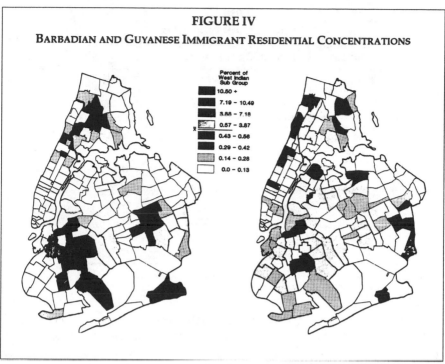

FIGURE IV

BARBADIAN AND GUYANESE IMMIGRANT RESIDENTIAL CONCENTRATIONS

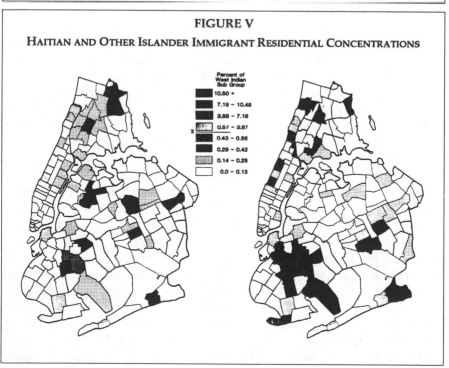

FIGURE V

HAITIAN AND OTHER ISLANDER IMMIGRANT RESIDENTIAL CONCENTRATIONS

TABLE 2
SEGREGATION INDICES[a] OF
IMMIGRANT, NATIONAL SUB-GROUPS WITH DIFFERENT
CARIBBEAN CULTURAL GROUPS IN NEW YORK CITY, 1980

Cultural Background (language)	Immigrant Sub-Group	Spanish-Speaking Cultural Group	English-Speaking Cultural Group	French Creole Cultural Group
Spanish	Dominican Republic	38.28	66.18	70.98
	Cuba	38.49	64.58	66.78
French	Creole (French) Haiti	68.35	31.12	0.00
English	Jamaica	68.67	24.07	35.71
	Trinidad & Tobago	65.77	19.87	26.39
	Guyana	58.11	28.48	34.10
	Barbados	77.00	30.19	31.50
	Other Islands	67.49	17.73	38.55

Note: [a] *See,* Footnote 1 for how these indices were derived.

tan, also Hispanics also reside in appreciable proportions in Belmont and Parkchester in the Bronx and in the Jackson Heights-Corona section of Queens (Figure IIa). On the other hand Cubans do not appear to have one recognizable core district. They do co-inhabit Manhattan with the Dominicans but their pattern is one of rather lower proportions in many neighborhoods in all the counties (Figure IIb). The Haitians appear to have concentrated in the Vanderveer Park neighborhood in Queens. As the English-speakers, fewer Haitians reside in Manhattan (Figure Va).

Grouping Caribbean immigrants into cultural groups according to the major language of their home country provides three reference groups against which the patterns of residential separation of national subgroups can be compared (Table 2). Clear differences emerge between the residential patterns of the English- and Spanish-speaking groups, with nationalities of each group exhibiting association with their own kind but considerable separation from the opposite cultural group (Table 2). The Haitian ("Creole (French)-speaking") group's pattern is much closer to that of the English-speaking group ($I_s=31.1$) than the Spanish speaking group ($I_s=68.4$). Also of interest are the relative degrees of residential separation of the Commonwealth Caribbean nationalities and their reference cultural group, the remainder of the English-speaking immigrants. "Other islanders" exhibit the least separation ($I_s=17.7$), and Trinidadians are also intermixed among their Commonwealth Caribbean "brothers and sisters" ($I_s=19.9$). Barbadians and Guyanese exhibit greater degrees of separation from other English-speaking West Indians ($I_s=30.1$ and $I_s=28.5$, respectively). Barbadians also exhibit the higher degree of separation from the Spanish-speaking cultural group

(I_s=77.0). Yet , in spite of these differences, with the English-speaking group there appears to be a greater degree of residential separation between the two Spanish-speaking nationalities, the Dominicans and Cubans (I_s=38.3 and I_s=38.5, respectively) (Table 2).

These patterns of residential separation and association clearly demonstrate the heterogeneity in residential experiences of Caribbean immigrants in New York City. In cases of separation of nationalities with a different reference culture group, the indices of residential separation approximate those estimated by other social scientists when examining Black American and Puerto Rican segregation with the White majority in New York City. Using census tract data to obtain segregation indices for 1960, Tauber and Tauber (1972) found that Puerto Ricans were segregated from other Whites by an I_s of 73, that Blacks were separated from White Americans by an I_s of 80, and that Blacks were separated from Puerto Ricans by an I_s of 62. In our study, all "Black" English-speaking nationalities[3] except Guyanese have separation indices from their Spanish-speaking counterparts exceeding the 62 of the Black Puerto Rican index, suggesting higher degrees of residential differentiation among Caribbean immigrant groups. In similar fashion, both Dominicans and Cubans exhibit greater separation (I_s=66.3 and I_s=64.6 respectively) from the English-speaking group (Table 2).

CONCLUSION

In terms of prior expectations our conviction that residential clustering would be pronounced is confirmed in this analysis. The two major cultural groups of Caribbean immigrants do exhibit considerable residential separation in New York City. Although the Barbadians among the English-speakers exhibit the highest degree of separation both from their related culture group and from the Spanish-speaking group, the range of indices reflecting different residential patterns of the Commonwealth Caribbean nationalities is relatively small. Also, contrary to expectations, the Haitians, rather than exhibiting a separate residential pattern, appear to have an affinity for residential proximity to English-speaking immigrants in New York City, especially in neighborhoods in Brooklyn and South Queens (Figure Va). In fact, Haitians exhibit less residential separation from English-speaking West Indians than do Dominicans and Cubans from each other. This supports the several impressions that there is more residential clustering among "Black" Caribbean immigrant groups than among "brown" Hispanic groups (Figures II, III, V, and Vb).

---

[3] The INS data do not distinguish the ethnicity of these immigrant nationals. Hence in the case of countries like Guyana and Trinidad and Tobago it is very likely that undocumented proportions of these national subgroups will be of East Indian or mixed races.

One conclusion logically emerging from this comparative analysis of the 1980 residential patterns of Caribbean immigrants is that more can be learned about patterns of differentiation, segregation, and succession in cosmopolitan New York City by desegregating Caribbean immigrants from the undifferentiated categories of Black and Hispanic minorities (*see,* Denowitz, 1980).

BIBLIOGRAPHY

Boswell, T.D.
1976   "Residential Patterns of Puerto Ricans in New York City," *Geographical Review* 66(1):92–95. Jan.

Burnley, I.H.
1975   "European Immigration and Settlement Patterns in Metropolitan Sydney, 1957–61." In *Urban Social Segregation.* C. Peach, ed. London: Longman. Pp. 325–343.

Cowgill, D.O. and M.S. Cowgill
1951   "An Index of Segregation Based on Block Statistics," *American Sociological Review* 16(6):820–830. Dec.

Denowitz, R.M.
1980   "Racial Success in New York City, 1960–70." *Social Forces* 59(2):440–453. Dec.

Dominguez, V.
1975   *From Neighbor to Stranger: The Dilemma of Caribbean Peoples in the United States.* New Haven, CT: Yale University, Antilles Research Program. Occasional Papers No. 5.

Hendricks, G.L.
1974   *The Dominican Diaspora: From The Dominican Republic to New York City—Villagers in Transition.* New York: Columbia University Teachers College Press.

Kessner, T. and B.B. Caroli
1981   *Today's Immigrants: Their Stories.* New York: Oxford University Press.

Lowenthal, D.
1976   "New York's Hispanic Immigrants," *Geographical Review* 66(1):90–92. Jan.

Stimson, R.J.
1975   "Patterns of Immigrant Settlement in Melbourne, 1947–66." In *Urban Social Segregation.* C. Peach, ed. London: Longman. Pp. 302–324.

Tauber, K.E. and A.F. Tauber
1972   *Negroes in Cities.* New York: Atheneum.

CASE STUDIES

Afro-Caribbean

BLACK IMMIGRANT WOMEN
IN
BROWN GIRL, BROWNSTONES

PAULE MARSHALL
Virginia Commonwealth University

If African Americans have suffered from a kind of invisibility (a subject which Ralph Ellison brilliantly explores in his 1952 novel *The Invisible Man*), and if the Black foreigner has been treated to a double invisibility (as Bryce-Laporte, 1972, suggests in an article on Black immigrants), then the West Indian immigrant woman might be said to suffer from a triple invisibility as a Black, a foreigner, and a woman. She simply has not been seen; nor have her experiences been dealt with in any direct and substantial way in the social science literature.

This chapter discusses an obscure group of women who came to the United States from the island of Barbados during the years following World War I. This period witnessed the first major wave of West Indian immigration, and coincided with the Great Migration northward of thousands upon thousands of Black Americans from the rural South. In looking at the circumstances which brought the West Indian woman to the United States in the early twenties we discern the traditional reasons which prompted most of her groups to emigrate. There was the poverty of those idyllic-looking "islands in the sun" with their single cash crop of sugar. "You know what it is to work hard and still never make a head-way?" one of the women characters in *Brown Girl, Brownstones* (1959:70) asks bitterly.

> That's Barbados. One crop. The black people having to work for next skin to nothing. The white people treating we like slaves and we taking it. The rum shop and the Church join together to keep we pacify and in ignorance. That's Barbados. It's a terrible thing to know that you gon be poor all yuh life no matter how hard you work. You does stop trying after a time.
>
> People does see you so and call you lazy, but it ain't laziness. It just that you does give up. You does kind of die inside . . . I tell

you I wouldn't let my mother know peace till she found the
money and send me to this man country.

Along with the poverty there were the tremendous population pressures
on these tiny islands, especially in a place like Barbados, which is one of the
most densely populated areas in the world. Because of these economic-de-
mographic conditions, Barbadians have always been on the move—whether
it was to resettle in neighboring areas such as Trinidad and Guyana or to try
their luck in places as far away as India, where it is known that some of them
went to help build the railroad shortly after the turn of the century.

For the women who left Barbados to come to the United States in the
twenties, the voyage north was financed in a number of ways. Money was
borrowed, a bit of family ground was sold, or a relative who had already
made his or her way to the "States" and found work dutifully sent home the
money for the ticket. Then there was what was called "Panama Money"
which, in many instances, paid the passage North. This was the name given
to the remittances sent home by the fathers and sons who had gone off to
work building the Panama Canal between 1904 and 1914. My mother, for
example, came to the States on money inherited from an older brother who
had died working on the Isthmus. "Panama Money"—it was always spoken
of with great reverence when I was a little girl.

And so the women came. The majority of them were young, the daughters
of estate workers, small landholders and artisans. My mother's father was a
cooper—a maker of barrels in which the sugar, the "life blood" of Barbados,
was exported. Most of these women were unmarried, although a number
already had children. In some cases, this was the reason for them being sent
to the States. An aunt of mine was banished to New York for having disgraced
the family with a child fathered by a pan boiler from British Guiana, who
came to Barbados every year during the grinding season to work in the sugar
factory. My mother arrived two years after my aunt as a tearful, overgrown
baby of eighteen who didn't even know how to braid her own hair. She
would never forget, she used to tell us, how awed and overwhelmed she felt
seeing New York rise shining and imperial from the sea that first day.

The search for work began almost immediately after their arrival. In
contrast to the more recent wave of West Indian women who came in the
sixties and found jobs—many of them in factories or as nurses aids and
sometimes even as secretaries, key punch operators, and the like—the only
work available to these earlier arrivals (as well as to their African American
counterparts from the South) was as domestics—or as the women in *Brown
Girl, Brownstones* termed the work they were forced to do: "scrubbing floors."

These jobs were often sleeping-in arrangements which saw these young
women overworked, underpaid, and given only every other Thursday off. A
short story published some years ago (Marshall, 1983) takes place at the wake
of a Barbadian woman who had worked as a sleep-in domestic since coming

to the United States. All she had to show for her long forty years of labor was a brownstone house in Brooklyn, which she never really got to live in very much, and closets filled with clothes she never had the opportunity to wear.

Then there was the "day's work" for the others. For the woman without a steady job, day's work was often a humiliating business of waiting on a street corner in some White neighborhood for the local housewives to come along and offer them a few hours work cleaning their houses.

Looking back on it now it seems to me that those Barbadian women accepted these ill-paying, low status jobs with an astonishing lack of visible resentment. For them they were simply a means to an end: the end being the down payment on a brownstone house, a college education for their children, and the much coveted middle-class status these achievements represented . . . As Bryce-Laporte (1972 : *passim*) points out, the Black immigrant was a fierce believer in and practitioner of the Protestant ethic.

Even when they married and had children, these women continued to work. I remember the trauma I would undergo on those occasions when I was left with a neighbor while my mother disappeared for the day to scrub some stranger's floor.

Along with work, the lives of the women revolved around house and children. Husbands, it seemed to me as a little girl, occupied a somewhat peripheral place in their wives constellation aside, of course, from their role as wage-earners. Following the traditional customs of life in Barbados, their outings with their husbands were mainly confined to church, weddings, funerals, and wakes and boat excursions up the Hudson in the summer and the annual dance of the "Sons and Daughters of Barbados" in the winter.

Apart from these occasions, the women looked to each other for their social life—and with the women in *Brown Girl, Brownstones,* as well as with my mother and her friends in real life, this consisted mainly of sitting around the kitchen table after their return from work each day and talking. Endlessly talking. Much of the talk had to do with home—meaning Barbados; the places, people, and events there as they remembered them. It was clearly an effort on their part to retain their cultural identity amidst the perplexing newness of America. Perhaps sensing the disregard in which they were held by the society, their triple invisibility as it were, they felt the need more strongly than other immigrant groups to hold onto the memories that defined them.

In terms of their relations with Black American women it seems to me from what I observed as a child that the West Indian woman considered herself both different and somehow superior. From the talk which circulated around our kitchen it was clear, for example, that my mother and her friends perceived themselves as being more ambitious than Black Americans, more hard working, and in terms of the racial question, more militant and unafraid in their dealings with White people. "Be Jesus Christ, in this white man world you got to take your mouth and make a gun," one of the women characters in *Brown Girl, Brownstones* declares.

In real life my mother used to say with pride that she probably would not live long if she were to go South since she would never like any "foolishness" from the crackers there: "They'd have to string me up from the nearest tree first," she would boast.

The distance these immigrant women sought to put between themselves and other Black women was often reinforced by the society itself which often praised them for being more reliable, trustworthy and hard-working. In *Brown Girl, Brownstones* a White woman speaks of her West Indian domestic in these terms:

> I've never been able to get another girl as efficient as Ettie. When she cleaned the house was spotless. And she was so honest I could leave my purse, anything, lying around and never worry. She was that kind of person. I've always told my friends there's something different, something special about Negroes from the West Indies. Some of the others are . . . well . . . just impossible! (1959:288).

With this kind of insidious divide and rule encouragement it is no wonder that even in the face of the racism they inevitably encountered, these West Indian women sought to escape identification with those who were considered the pariahs of the society. "If only we had had our own language," my mother used to lament—meaning by that something which would have clearly established that they were different, foreign and, therefore, perhaps more acceptable.

The racial pride and political consciousness which they believed they possessed to a greater degree than American Blacks was perhaps most dramatically expressed in their involvement in the Garvey Movement of the twenties. Not only did they faithfully contribute to the Universal Negro Improvement Association out of their meager salaries but they attended meetings, marched in parades, and served as members of the nurses' brigade, many of them when the movement was at its height. Talk of Garvey and Black self-help and Black pride still figured in their conversations long after the Movement had failed. They remain steadfast Garveyites to the end.

All in all it seems to me that these women who are now—the ones who are still living—the mothers and grandmothers of my generation, accomplished, in general, what they had set out to do in coming to America. By dint of hard work, sacrifice, and a fierce determination and will, they acquired the house, the university degrees for their children, the cars, the fur coats (which were usually, I remember, black Persian lamb) and, more recently, the trips "home" to Barbados each year to celebrate independence.

They accepted without question the materialistic ethic of this country while at the same time remaining, it seems to me, strangely aloof from America. Their aloofness, which was perhaps a defensive device, was expressed in the almost contemptuous way they insisted on referring to the United States as "this man's country." It would always, in other words, be foreign territory—someone else's turf. This sentiment was captured in a host of other ways as well, such as their speech, which remained as stubbornly Barbadian as when they first walked off the ships at Ellis Island.

They were, for all their insularity, fears and misguided materialism, women of impressive strength, authority, and style. Unfortunately, because they were women—and Black women at that—this country never saw fit to acknowledge their presence or their worth, or to make full use of the tremendous human resource they represented. Their experience as immigrant women has yet to be regarded as worthwhile historical and sociological data in its own right.

BIBLIOGRAPHY

Bryce-Laporte, R.S.
1972   "Black Immigrants: The Experience of Invisibility and Inequality," *Journal of Black Studies* 3(1):29–56. Sept.

Ellison, R.
1952   *The Invisible Man.* New York: Random House.

Marshall, P.
1984   *The Chosen Place, the Timeless People.* New York: Vintage Contemporaries.

———
1983   "Reena." In *Reena and Other Stories.* Pp.69–92. New York: Feminist Press.

———
1981   *Brown Girl, Brownstones.* New York: Feminist Press.

MIGRATION AND WEST INDIAN RACIAL AND ETHNIC CONSCIOUSNESS[1]

CONSTANCE R. SUTTON
New York University

SUSAN R. MAKIESKY-BARROW
New York State Psychiatric Institute

Although West Indian migration since World War II constitutes but the latest phase in the diaspora of English-speaking West Indians, this recent exodus differs in a number of ways. It surpasses previous migratory movements in scale; it is directed to the metropoles which colonized the Caribbean in the past and continue to dominate it today; and it is occurring during a period when both racial and political conflict have surfaced in the countries to which migrants go and in the West Indies. This article explores the impact of this migration on the racial consciousness and political awareness of both the migrant and those who remain behind.

This has been a relatively neglected topic in the study of the migration process. It has been noted that as migrants engage in the process of redefining themselves in relation to the host society, they often transform vague feelings of common ethnicity into a more articulated cultural and political consciousness. Little is known about the specific elements that contribute to this process or about how the content of the new consciousness and identity is constructed. Still less is known about how migrant ideas and identities affect those who remain at home. Yet, a significant aspect of the migration process is the change in identity and consciousness it produces. To examine these issues in relation to the recent West Indian diaspora, we found it necessary to view this migration as a bidirectional rather than unidirectional phenomenon. Whereas most studies focus on one or the other end of a migration continuum—the host or home country—we include both poles, seeing them united by social networks involving the exchange of resources and ideas.

Our approach here is to explore the character of West Indian migration to England and the United States since World War II, identify factors that

[1] This is a shortened version of a paper written in 1973 and published in 1975. The authors wish to thank Samuel Sutton, St. Clair Drake, Muriel Hammer and Antonio Lauria for their comments.

induced changes in the identity and political consciousness of the migrants, and describe the effect that the reimportation of these ideas had on those who remained on the islands. Our comparisons of West Indian responses to their status in England and the United States draw on the existing literature and on our informal discussions with Barbadian immigrants in New York City. In examining the impact of migration induced ideational changes on sending societies, we confine ourselves to Barbados where we both carried out field work in the same village during two different time periods—the late 1950s and the early 1970s.[2] Our research there, though directed to other problems, provided useful data on the repatriation of ideas at the village level, where this issue has not previously been studied.

The need to consider both ends of the migration continuum for the same group has become increasingly apparent as modern means of transportation and communication have drastically altered the nature of migration, especially between Caribbean countries and the United States. Some studies of Caribbean migration processes have sought to relate what happens at home and abroad by focusing on how social networks operate to maintain ties, interests, and social control across international boundaries. Return migrants who have by these means stayed hooked into their home societies while away are said to invest their acquired assets in the already defined economic and status systems, rather than challenging them or serving as carriers of social and cultural innovations (Philpott, 1970:18).

Our evidence from Barbados suggests that return migration has a more dynamic impact on the home society and that this is most evident in the realm of ideology—the ideas, perceptions, and evaluations that people have of themselves and their society. This view of return migration as change-producing is one that Barbadians themselves hold. Even in 1956, when the outflow of people to the metropoles had not reached the level of the following decade, Barbadians asserted the importance of leaving the island for acquiring a better understanding of Barbados. Exposure to ideas and ways of doing things abroad was believed to increase one's understanding of the oppressive nature of Barbadian society and the "narrow-mindedness" of its customs and beliefs. These observations, concretized in specific examples and illustrations, formed a major conversational theme during the lengthy village "rap" sessions which shaped the villagers' fund of knowledge and political awareness.

While racial identity was not an issue of major concern, George Lamming, with the liberties that a novelist takes in articulating possibilities that may be only faint stirrings, forecast what the migration experience to the United States could mean. In his early novel on Barbadian village life, *In the Castle of*

[2] Support for field research came from the RISM, Research Institute for the Study of Man (C.S.), Population Council (C.S.), the Wenner-Gren Foundation for Anthropological Research (C.S.), New York University Arts and Science Faculty Research Fund (C.S.), and the Foreign Area Fellowship Program of the Social Science Research Council (S.M.-B.).

My Skin (1953), Lamming captures the comparisons that engage Black West Indians as a result of their migration experiences, the ambivalence with which Barbadians regard the English—"clever" and "deceitful" on racial issues—and how the United States racial situation unmasks for them the true nature of their own condition.

> "Twas what I mean when I say you don't understan' life," Trumper said. "An' I didn't understan' it myself till I reach the States. If there be one thing I thank America for, she teach me who my race wus. Now I'm never goin' to lose it. Never never."
> "There are black people here too," I said. I hadn't quite understood him.
> "I know," said Trumper, "but it ain't the same. It ain't the same at all. 'Tis a different thing altogether. 'Course the blacks here are my people too, but they don't know it yet. You don't know it yourself. None o' you here on the islan' know what it means to find a race. An' the white people you have to deal with won't ever let you know. 'Tis a great thing 'bout the English, the know-how. If ever there wus a nation in creation that know how to do an' get a thing do, tis the English. My friend in the States use to call them the great administrators (1953:296).

Known as a "proud people," Barbadians in the 1950s expressed that pride in terms of their English-like traits and virtues. By the mid-sixties, however, a pride in being "Black people" began to emerge publicly. The form this identity took, the meaning it had to villagers, and conditions that gave rise to it must be seen in the context of an expanding social field extending beyond Barbados within which islanders increasingly operate.

To grasp how this internationalized social field influenced Barbadian identity and consciousness, we begin by briefly comparing Barbadian emigration prior to and after World War II. For the latter period, we sketch out changes in the nature of Barbadian society, perceptions of the role of race, and Barbadian preconceptions of England and the United States.[3] This sets the background for understanding how they responded to their experiences as immigrants in these two countries. It is the different structures of incorporation in these two metropoles that shaped their experiences, contradicted their expectations, and influenced their interpretations. We compare these two settings in terms of how they influenced Barbadians' newly acquired understandings concerning their racial identity. Finally, we return again to our point of departure to consider the impact of these new understandings on those who remained behind.

[3] Large numbers of West Indians, including Barbadians, have also emigrated to Toronto and Montreal during this period, but we do not have sufficient information to include Canada in our discussion.

BARBADIAN MIGRATION

Emigration has always been an integral feature of Barbadian society, intimately tied to its history as a densely populated island and a successful exporter of sugar. By the mid-nineteenth century, the Barbadian government passed legislation promoting emigration to relieve overcrowding, unemployment, and poverty among the island's superabundant population and in 1861 the island witnessed the first large-scale outward movement of Barbadians who went mainly to British Guiana and Trinidad. A second migratory movement began in 1904 when work on the Panama Canal was resumed and lasted until 1914 when this work ceased, after which migration was redirected to the United States. This lasted until 1924 when the United States restricted entry. Between 1921 and 1946, a steep decline and reversal in direction occurred as more migrants returned than left the island. Between 1861 and 1921, the total number of emigrants equaled the size of the island's population in 1921—150,000 (Roberts, 1955:276).

These earlier phases of Barbadian emigration increased the options of the island's Black majority and changed their attitudes. Remittances and the savings of returned migrants were applied to the purchase of land and houses, resulting in the rapid growth of freehold villages throughout the countryside. This decreased the rural population's near-total dependence on the plantations for loans and employment. It gave plantation workers enough of a margin to engage in a series of spontaneous sugar strikes that first began in the 1920s. Return migrants brought back not only savings but radical ideas that helped fuel the riots which broke out throughout the West Indies in the late 1930s, the watershed between the old and the new social order that was emerging (Reid, 1939). A repatriation of ideas occurred also as West Indian professionals educated abroad returned to assume leadership of the struggle for social and political reforms that were developing throughout the islands.

Emigration caused Barbadians to accord prestige and power to those with knowledge of the outside world. Out of the comparisons they made between "Bajun"[4] and "foreign" ways, a framework for viewing Barbados in a more critical light developed. This comparative view of island society contributed to the growth of new kinds of political consciousness and to demands for improvements. It also reinforced the notion that solutions to problems were to be sought outside the society. For the Black majority, this continued to mean that though things might be hard at home, elsewhere there existed opportunities they might seize.

During this early period, the success of Barbadian immigrants contributed to the growth of an ethnic consciousness based on proverbial island pride and gave support to their deeply held conviction that if you give a Bajun half

---

[4] *"Bajun"* is a colloquial term for Barbadian. It also refers to the folk language and culture of the Black majority.

a chance—just a start—he or she will make good! Reputed to be hard-work-ing and well-educated, Barbadians were favored by recruiting agents, and in the societies to which they went they gained ascendancy in the two occupa-tions that carried authority and were open to Black and Colored people at that time: they became known as the teachers and policemen of the West Indies.

As immigrants to other Caribbean territories, Barbadians became part of the West Indian community of the host society while retaining a Barbadian identity in their private lives. This was not possible for the Barbadian com-munity which formed in New York City, as is shown in Paule Marshall's novel, *Brown Girl, Brownstones* (1959). In the United States, the racial identity assigned to them by the wider society and the nature of Barbadian relations to Black Americans constantly intruded on the efforts of Barbadians to view themselves simply as another immigrant ethnic group.

World War II and the years immediately following brought changes within West Indian societies, in their relations to North Atlantic metropolitan centers, and in their patterns of migration. The war accelerated the flow of Barbadians to England, the United States, and Canada. The novelty of this migration lay in the large numbers involved and in the fact that the majority were of working-class and lower-middle-class status. The primary determi-nants of the direction of this postwar outflow were the economic situation and immigration policies of the North Atlantic industrial countries. In the United States, a sharp drop in agricultural recruitment programs and in 1952 the passage of restrictive legislation temporarily curtailed West Indian immi-gration. In Britain, however, an open immigration policy attracted West Indians to that country from 1952 to 1962. Beginning in 1962, Britain began to impose restrictions on the immigration of its Commonwealth citizens from the colonies. These restrictions, which became more stringent in 1965 and 1971, made clear Britain's political stance on race relations and deflected the direction of West Indian migration toward the United States, which in 1965 liberalized its immigration policies.

BARBADIAN SOCIETY AND BARBADIAN PERCEPTIONS

In Barbados during the late 1950s, the contours of a sugar-producing colonial plantation society were still deeply etched in the landscape and social struc-ture. The island's 166 square miles held a population of just under a quarter of a million, making it one of the most densely populated areas in the world. Some 150 White Creole families owned 85 percent of the cane fields stretching across most of the island, and the remaining small plots were owned by Colored and Black families. Interspersed along the edges of estates and crowded together at highway intersections were dwellings of a large wage-earning rural population.

Most of the Black majority lived in these rural settlements with easy access to the main town by bus, bicycle, or car. The community examined here was adjacent to the island's largest plantation. We have pseudonymously named it Endeavor because of its reputation as a district of aggressive, enterprising individuals. The plantation employed, either seasonally or year-round, some 45 percent of Endeavor's working population. Another 15 percent worked at other plantations, and the remainder worked "all about" as artisans, trades-people, shopkeepers, or domestics. Of the working population, 40 percent were women.[5]

In 1958 the 600 dwellings in the village housed some 2,500 persons related by ties of kinship, common residence, shared local history and sentiments. The outward-looking quality of life was reflected in the daily dispersal of the working population and in the fact that 11 percent of the villagers had lived and worked abroad. One quarter of the adult population was receiving money from relatives abroad in amounts varying from total support to cash supplement for purchasing specific items, covering school fees, or contributions to celebrations of births, marriages, and other rites of passage. The paternalistic control of plantation days was seriously eroded as trade unionism and mass politics brought the Black majority into the political process. While the new island leadership committed itself to raising living standards, and creating new opportunities and resources, for the Black majority, education and emigration were still the two main avenues for "rising a notch above." The target societies for the hopeful emigrants were England, Canada, and the United States.

A decade later, the Barbadian economy had shifted away from its near-total dependence on sugar cane cultivation, which, by the late 1960s was rivaled by the growth of tourism and light manufacturing. These developments, important in weakening the economic control of the Barbadian planter-merchant class, were marked by significant intrusions of North American capital into this former British preserve. Encouraged by incentives offered by the new Black government, North American investors and tourists alike were attracted by the island's reputation for political stability—an image Barbadian leaders were successful in cultivating and vigilant in maintaining, and the island came more fully into the American sphere of influence.

There were parallels in the political domain. In 1966 Britain granted Barbados the status of independent nation within the Commonwealth. But although the political leaders of independent Barbados significantly increased their role in the administration of the island's education, health, and welfare services, the ultimate economic control of the island receded overseas where it has continued to elude their grasp. The elaboration of the island's

---

[5] For a fuller account of Endeavor in 1956–1958, see, Sutton (1969). See, Makiesky-Barrow (1976) for the changes that had taken place by the early 1970s.

links to metropolitan centers at the national political and economic level was accompanied by the increased emigration of working-class Barbadians to the countries which dominated them. By the early 1970s Barbados was more firmly than ever ensconced in an international network of trade, politics, and migration, its destiny and maneuverability more than ever dependent on these external linkages. In this context, emigration provided, more dramatically than before, the most realistic avenue for meeting the increasingly consumption-oriented aspirations of the population. It is their preconceptions of the countries to which they hoped to emigrate that will now be examined.

The literature on preconceptions of England emphasizes the cultural affinities West Indians feel for the "mother country," followed by the disillusion and rejection the immigrants experience when they find that the English do not share this view (Brown, 1970; Deakin, 1970; Lewis, 1969, 1971; Roe, 1969; Tajfel and Dawson, 1965). To leave the matter here, however, would seem to imply that West Indians come to Britain with no knowledge of, or concern about, racism and discrimination. This grossly distorts the realities of social life in the West Indies, and perpetuates the myth of the island as a paradise of racial harmony. It has become increasingly evident that West Indians at home experience considerable conflict and discomfort about racial identity, in part because of the historic White bias of their societies. It does not seem, however, that these conflicts entail the internalized self-hate and inferiority complex that has been attributed to West Indians in many recent writings (Lowenthal, 1972; Fanon, 1967). Especially at the village level, we found little evidence that people attributed their disadvantaged position to inherent inferiority. Instead, they would assert that their difficulties lay in being denied the opportunity to achieve socially valued goods and positions of esteem.

Though villagers felt equal, if not superior, to Whites in inherent abilities, they granted social superiority to the local White elites and race and color were far from irrelevant in their social evaluations. In fact they were at the heart of Barbadian social stratification, which is built on an invidious grading of status distinctions, described interchangeably in terms of either chromatic shade or power and prestige. It is a system in which consciousness of race has been a divisive rather than unifying force. This is quite different from what immigrants experience in Britain (or the United States), where the racial identities assigned to them ignore differences in shade and status.

When it came to England, in the 1950s, villagers assumed that the racial prejudice of their own society was a perversion of "true" British attitudes and practices which they had been taught were, above all, "fair-minded." This faith in British fair-mindedness left many Barbadians unprepared for the differences between their nineteenth-century textbook versions and the twentyth-century realities of English culture. Nor, more importantly, were they prepared for the indifference or contempt which many British people feel for their colonial citizens. By 1971, these earlier conceptions had been replaced by newer perceptions based on the incidence of racial conflict in England, the rise of Enoch Powell, and the passage of restrictive immigration laws. By this time, the influx to England had been sharply reduced as a consequence of British policies.

Images and expectations that potential immigrants have of the United States are somewhat more complex and have been generated by diverse sources. The primary elements in the Barbadian view of "America" is a vision of riches and high standards of living which is variously perpetrated by American television shows, Hollywood movies, and upper middle-class tourists, as well as by earlier emigrants who have returned home to build large houses and develop new lifestyles. The consumer-based expectations are complemented by the recognition of less attractive features. Violence and danger, mugging and murder, are graphically portrayed in the media and elaborated by returned migrants. Even more important is the knowledge of American racism. Barbadians are aware that the White majority has brutally treated its own Black minority. There is a tendency, however, to rest part of the blame on Black Americans themselves, accused of not acting in more "self-respecting" ways and not showing more "initiative" in the face of opportunities. Evidence of the successes of earlier migrants lends credence to their view that West Indians can "get through" despite American racism.

The images of economic opportunity, violence, and a troublesome Black minority are to a large extent images which White America projects of itself. These have been modified and counteracted in recent years by cultural imports from Black America: music, dress, hair styles, verbal expressions, and the ideology of Black Power. The result in Barbados has been both an increased consciousness of American racism, and a new admiration for Black American militancy, especially among younger Barbadians who have developed a heightened interest in coming to the scene of the action.

While these preconceptions affect how Barbadians interpret and react to their encounters with the English and Americans, it is the structuring of race relations in the two societies that determines the nature of these encounters.

BRITISH AND U.S.
STRUCTURES OF INCORPORATION

Despite their similarities, England and the United States differ in their social composition and the political structuring of social differences. England has been a relatively homogeneous society ethnically and culturally, its salient divisions being those of class. Culture has been given political recognition, but within an institutionalized framework of basic consensus. Political participation is on an individual basis and the political legitimacy of ethnic group interest is denied (Deakin, 1970; Katznelson, 1973).

By 1958, racial disturbances had caused the issue of race to emerge with all of its potentiality as a key political issue. The immigration restrictions of the 1960s further crystallized the different status of the immigrants from the colonies. Summarizing the responses of English society to colonial immigration, Gordon Lewis writes:

> There has taken place a massive escalation of White racist attitudes in the society. The decade of the 1950s, which can be seen as a period of immigrant arrival, was characterized by the myth that the English and the immigrants could peacefully coexist with each other in a sort of host-guest relationship. That myth was effectively destroyed with the 1958 race riots in Nottingham and Notting Hill. Those riots were followed by the decade of the 1960s, which can be seen as a period of immigrant settlement and was in turn characterized by the myth that racialism was a product only of the right-wing lunatic fringe of British politics. That myth was effectively destroyed by the process by which, after 1962, both major political parties took over, in one way or another, racialist policies, ending with the emergence in the figure of Enoch Powell, of a white populist demagogue located at the heart and not simply on the margins of the Conservative party.
>
> The history of how the party machines surrendered to the crypto-racialist majority of their electorates is the history of the legislation dealing with immigration and race-relations put through, first, by the Conservatives and, secondly, after 1964, by the Labor Party cabinets (1971:12–13).

However, the British political elites (and the new West Indian leadership) had a stake in depoliticizing the race issue. What developed in England were buffering institutions between the immigrants from the colonies and the larger society (Katznelson, 1973). West Indian culture brokers sprang up to reassure the British that the "dark strangers" from the West Indies, working at jobs the British working class no longer cared to fill (Peach, 1968), were an intelligent, responsible, and stable people—qualities that by implication could be equated with docility and political quiescence. Paternalism was to be perpetuated as the major form for dealing with West Indians, thus domestically reproducing a quasi-colonial relationship.

Unlike England, the United States has experienced large-scale immigration throughout its history. Despite the predominance of WASP ingredients in images of "the American way of life," ethnic diversity is a recognized fact of existence—particularly in the large urban centers. More significant for West Indians, however, is the overriding institutionalized racial division between Black and White, and the presence of a large native Black population in the cities to which they migrate.

Ethnic differences in the United States have been given informal political recognition in practices such as "balancing tickets" but have never received explicit formal legitimation in law while racial differences have been formally recognized. Non-White groups throughout American history have been "differentially incorporated" into the polity. Slavery and Jim Crow set Black Americans apart as a group with special political status, as did reservation policies for Native-Americans and the World War II internment of Japanese Americans. No parallels of formal differential incorporation can be found in the history of White ethnic groups. While Britain until recently kept its non-White colonies overseas and the issue of race at arm's length, the United States internalized its "colonies" from the beginning and created a society pervaded by racial division.

EXPERIENCES IN
ENGLAND AND THE UNITED STATES

England

Barbadians moving into the relatively homogeneous White society of Britain have rather different experiences than their compatriots going to the racially-divided United States, though in both cases they meet poor housing, job discrimination, and inferior schooling for their children, as well as personal hostility from sections of the White population. Written accounts and statements of numerous West Indians in Britain document their quick realization that however acculturated they may be, their color and colonial status set them apart from the English and evoke different treatment from landlords and employers (*see*, for example, Tajfel and Dawson, 1965). It is not necessary to idealize the racial pattern of West Indian societies to appreciate the impact of this on the newcomers. As Gordon Lewis writes:

> As recently as the 1950s it was a cardinal article of faith among the newcomers that they were coming "home" to the "mother country" and particularly so for the West Indian, so much more culturally English than his Asian counterparts. The literature of disillusionment . . . is of recent growth, and to read it is to be made poignantly aware of the general figure of the West Indian, immeasurably saddened by the unexpected humiliations of his daily experience . . . There can be little doubt that, as that reservoir of goodwill slowly evaporates, he becomes increasingly radicalized in his attitude to the total problem . . . More and more, to put it succinctly, the immigrant sees himself less as a West Indian or a Sikh in English society, and more as a Black man in a White society (1969:428).

At the same time that Britain provides a setting for the growth of West Indian racial consciousness, it also promotes interaction between West Indians from different islands in a context of shared position and experiences. Though these interactions are often far from harmonious, recent reports indicate that improved relations develop over time. A Nevisian is recounted as saying in the late 1960s:

> When I first came here in 1958, the feeling was terrible. At parties, in particular, there was always fear of trouble. You never knew when arguments and fights would spark off . . . It's quieted down now, and there's far more mixing. Even mixed marriages between Jamaicans and Barbadians, those most at loggerheads. Ten years ago, that would have been impossible. Every one kept to his own kind (Brown, 1970:105).

Midgett (1971) notes that new understandings arising out of this interaction, particularly among the English-born children of immigrants, are defined in terms of Blackness, not West Indianness. In either case, they serve to break down some of the insular prejudices that have marked failures to achieve unity at home.

Just as the White racism that has emerged within British society has taken over some forms of expression from the American experience, so too do West Indians find in the struggles of Black Americans the forms in which to express their response to the racism they encounter in Britain. Thus the new racial consciousness that arises out of daily realities in Britain owes much of its rhetoric and symbols to the Black Power movement in the United States. Black Power in England has been a preeminently West Indian phenomenon in which Black American forms have been transplanted and reworked in a new environment. Providing a ready-made vehicle for expressions of Black consciousness, such American borrowing also emphasizes common features of the African diaspora on both sides of the Atlantic.

West Indians in Britain are not the only exogenous element disrupting traditional homogeneity. The postwar period has involved substantial migrations from other former British colonies as well. The largest numbers have come from India and Pakistan, but West Africans are also well represented. Studies of British racial attitudes indicate an awareness of differences between the several immigrant groups (Deakin, 1971), though for many purposes they are lumped together by the British public and race relations scholars alike under the umbrella term "colored people." Clearly, England provides a unique setting for contacts between diverse members of the Afro-Asian Commonwealth. This tends to introduce a Third-World orientation into the political ideologies West Indians develop in England, an emphasis somewhat different from that which they adopt in the United States.

United States

West Indians immigrating to New York travel a rather different route to racial consciousness than that taken in England. They bring with them a notion not of their likeness to Americans, Black or White, but of their distinctness— as Barbadians, Jamaicans, Grenadians, etc. Theirs is ethnic consciousness similar to that of earlier European immigrants. They arrive with some foreknowledge of White attitudes of racial superiority and with experiences with problems of racial inequality. However, life in New York City soon teaches them that the same characteristics of "race" which make them such a visible immigrant minority in England, make them invisible as immigrants in the already racially divided system of the United States (Bryce-Laporte, 1972). Both the problems and the achievements of West Indians are viewed by the dominant White majority, and come to be viewed by West Indians themselves in the context of Black America.

The West Indian response to this situation is ambivalent. It involves consciously emphasizing distinctness from Black Americans in some contexts and moving to establish close ties and an identification with them in others. Both cases involve a heightened consciousness of West Indians as a Black minority enclosed within a sometimes menacing, sometimes friendly, world of more powerful Whites. Recently this new consciousness has been articulated in ideologies which stress the worldwide common fate of Black people —often generalized to Third-World colonized people. The concept of "common fate," not unknown in the West Indies, takes on a new salience in the United States where West Indians learn its implications in their daily lives as they compare their own experience with those of other Black people and with Whites.

West Indian racial consciousness in America also responds to the experience of interacting with West Indians from other islands and with people from Haiti and the Hispanic Caribbean. Employment, housing, and school provide settings for this contact, and though island rivalries and jealousies may be aired, there is also a recognition of similarities of background and shared experiences as non-White immigrants, the salience of a particular identity being situationally defined.

In bringing together working-class Barbadians, Trinidadians, Jamaicans, Guyanese, etc., in situations of extended exposure, the process in New York parallels that in England. Though a recent study of Barbadian marriage patterns in New York indicates that this group remains highly endogamous and carries on its social life primarily within group bounds (Maynard, 1972), our informal observations suggest that encounters with other West Indians in the neighborhood, classroom, and work place provide a context for building cross-island relationships. On one construction site in the Bronx, Barbadian and Jamaican workers observe, provoke, and antagonize each other, but *vis-à-vis* White workers on the job and in the bar on the corner after work, they form a united West Indian front. New York offers opportunities to build common understandings among West Indians not available in the Caribbean.

A similar process operates, though one step removed, in bringing together West Indians with other Caribbean peoples. Puerto Ricans, Dominicans, and Haitians are visible parts of New York's social landscape, and though they are "foreigners" *vis-à-vis* West Indians, similarities of lifestyle and of position in the dominant society create shared understandings which are beginning to be articulated in the growing interest in the Caribbean as a region and in community forms of political action and socializing. Just as England provides a unique context for merging west Indian concerns with broader notions of Black Commonwealth and Third-World issues, New York City nourishes a Caribbean consciousness that has not been actively promoted in the Caribbean. This Caribbean consciousness is both a form of separation and a basis for relating to Black Americans with whom West Indians interact and are identified by the wider society.

West Indians are also encountering White Americans in unprecedented settings. West Indians in England discuss their initial feelings of surprise at seeing White people perform manual work. Barbadians in New York City have similar reactions. One might expect that comparable occupational status in these settings would lead to a coalition of interests emphasizing class, not race. In fact, the reverse occurs. In their contacts with White workers, West Indians often encounter direct expressions of racist attitudes and learn that their White co-workers enjoy privileges and opportunities denied to them. Thus while the opportunity to see White men and women working at menial jobs serve to demystify the racial division of labor and class privilege known back home, the experience also makes clear the independent racial basis of oppression of Blacks in America.

Both our own observations and data from the literature indicate that West Indian experiences in England and the United States result in converging developments of racial consciousness. In England, West Indians arrive with no developed sense of ethnic distinctness and only a submerged racial consciousness. They acquire a consciousness of being different—of being "Black people in a White world." In the United States, to which they go with a distinct ethnic feeling and apprehension over their racial identity, they lose their sense of ethnic difference as the full meaning of being Black in a White society is driven home. Their arrival at similar forms of racial consciousness via different routes is significant. It suggests that England and the United States share a common way of structuring their relationships to Black and colonized peoples despite their different historical ties to the colonized world.

FEEDBACK EFFECTS

One of the most interesting elements of the West Indian experience in the metropoles is its effect on the island societies. The new forms of racial and political consciousness acquired in England and the United States are relayed back to the islands through direct and indirect channels. We are able to report on some of these effects noted among the villagers of Endeavor in the 1950s and the early 1970s. This information can be taken as more or less typical of the hundreds of rural villages throughout Barbados which are similar in structure and in culture. We explore here how the experiences and ideas of West Indians abroad were perceived by villagers and operated, along with other factors, to bring about changes in their own racial consciousness.

Politics is a prominent theme in village rumshop debates, casual roadside discussions, and in general conversations at work, at home, and at social affairs. During the 1956–1958 period, though village political talk was primarily concerned with local issues, the interest shown in events outside the island was remarkable in its range. The Rosenberg case and the British treatment of Cheddi Jagan of British Guiana was still being debated. Knowledge of methods of cutting cane in Cuba was put forth, and views on the "soviet system" acquired by a cane worker who had been in Cuba during the period of radical activity on the sugar estates there in the 1930s, were discussed and compared to ideas in the Bible or with practices alleged to be followed in England.

Villagers followed with interest local newspaper and rediffusion (wired radio) reports on the progress of school integration in the United States and the White reaction in Little Rock, Arkansas. The latter incident gave the Barbados government the impetus to seek the resignation of a British *aide-de-camp*, who was accused of racial prejudice when he placed his daughter in an island secondary school known to cater to the children of the White plantocracy. His resignation over the issue was referred to as the local "Little Rock" incident, but with the moral that Barbados did not tolerate anything resembling the United States pattern of race relations. The population was very pointedly reminded how different their position was from that of Black Americans.

However, the issue of color and race on the island was not so easily buried. The following year, 1958, was marked by racial disturbances in the town of Nottingham and in Notting Hill, London, areas where the West Indian immigrant presence was being felt. The English put the riots down to the doings of irresponsible fringe elements in the society—the Teddy Boys or small native fascist groups—and denied that there was racial feeling in England or that the two incidents had a racial basis. There were also reassurances from members of the British government that the incidents would not influence Britain's open immigration policy—reassurances which hindsight has shown to be as untrue as the proclaimed absence of racial feeling in England.

These British interpretations of events were conveyed to Barbados where they did not go down so easily. Instead, the riots galvanized a sentiment of West Indian racial unity as ministers from all the unit territories flew to England to look over the situation. Local newspapers featured lengthy accounts of what life was like for West Indian immigrants in England and insular differences were momentarily forgotten as indignation ran high over the treatment they were being accorded. Latent hostility toward British colonial rule surfaced as islanders compared the hospitality shown British officials and expatriates to the rejection West Indians were experiencing in England. One local commentator wrote that Britain could never repay her debt to the West Indies which had provided her with the wealth to dominate the rest of Europe.

The riots evoked sentiments of anger that Black people were attacked, but also relish at the opportunity this afforded to embarrass White people on the island and expose British hypocrisy. A few villagers voiced the feeling that "we live with race hatred all our lives, but now our boys in England are holding out and giving them limeys a tough time." This combative view of the situation was not widely shared, however, and one woman told a group standing about chatting:

> I feel real bad and hurted over this in truth! These things, can they be fair? What are we Black people to do? We only ask for a chance to make a living and help ourselves and our families when they want to push us under the ground. It look they want to kill all the nigger people out of the world. But that can't happen because the White people can't do without we . . . even when they try to keep we down.

In Barbados the resentment provoked by the riots was channeled by the Black governing elite into programs aimed at preparing emigrants for what to expect in England. Efforts were made to emphasize the differences between the English incidents and the acts of race hatred that typified the situation in the United States. Barbadians were also informed that of all the West Indian groups in England, they were the best liked, were doing well economically, and were most successful at accommodating to the new scene.

Thus while race was an issue that lurked around the corner of all other issues—the question of the color-class hierarchy, of economic hegemony and international alignment, of emigration, and of a distinct national identity reflective of the history of their own societies—the governing elite followed the past policies of caution and avoidance of conflict, continuing to hold up British ways as a model to emulate.

By the late 1960s, Endeavor had experienced more than a decade of large-scale emigration to England and the United States, which intensified the outward-looking orientation of islanders, as the attention of villagers was directed to events in the metropolitan urban centers. The increase in the number of friends and relatives abroad gave information from these areas immediacy and personal relevance. Moreover, villagers viewed what happened in the metropoles with an eye to its implications for their own potential future abroad. News of criminal violence in the United States, for example, evoked hypothetical accounts of their own strategies for dealing with such things, while pregnant women debated whether the benefits of United States citizenship conferred by birth there outweighed the possibility that their as yet unborn sons might someday be drafted to fight in a U.S. war.

The mass media and the returned migrants served different roles with respect to information about the metropoles. While media coverage kept the community up to date with the daily happenings in those countries, interpretations of these events were provided by villagers who had themselves been there. The traditional Barbadians respect for knowledge gained "outside" was augmented by a growing recognition of the parallels in Barbados to at least some of what was occurring in America and England. This was particularly true for issues of race and Black power. The awakening racial consciousness of Black Americans drew early responses in the West Indies.

Although the university campuses of the West Indies have been the source of some of the more articulate expressions of the new racial and political consciousness, its impact on life at the village level deserves more attention than it has received. What occurred during the late 1960s in rural Barbados was a fairly autonomous reaction to the joint impact of local conditions and international racial disturbances and owed more to the return of villagers from urban centers in the United States than to the tenuous links of villagers to middle-class and student radicals.

Our first inkling of this change came in 1968 when, returning to Endeavor after a ten-year absence, we found a new mood of racial concern which entered into the always lively political conversations. "Tell me, is God a Black man or a White man?" a 35-year-old mechanic challenged his rum-shop audience. Parents expressed concern with the younger generation for flaunting openly their rejection of established norms of respect and deference behavior. Among the young people, information about Black America and Africa was actively solicited, Afro hair styles and *dashikis* were beginning to make an appearance, and Black American soul music took precedence over calypso at country *brams* and house parties. Small beginnings, but striking departures from the 1958 village scene.

The most dramatic indication of the new mood in the community was the formation by a group of young men of an organization dedicated to achieving economic autonomy for villagers. Although members of this group were not unanimous in their conceptualizations of Black power, the concept included a commitment to placing economic control of the island in the hands of the Black majority and opposition to the island's present Black leadership for their self-interested approach to politics and collaboration with their White oppressors. They showed interest in the struggles of Black people elsewhere—particularly in the United States—and sought to bring the concept of Black unity closer to home by asserting solidarity with West Indians in other islands. "We got to adjust ourselves to all of us are brothers," one young man said, "and not treat the St. Lucians like the White man treat the Black man." Above all, there was unanimous concern with the right of Black people to personal dignity and respect. Condemning their elders for their desire to "please the White man," they defied village norms of social deference, asserting their right to evaluate and validate themselves on their own terms.

This development occurred among semiskilled artisans who did not trust or accept the leadership or motives of middle-class Black Power advocates on the island. They sought their models for leadership and their formulations in Black America.[6] They quoted Malcolm X, not West Indian Walter Rodney; and in 1971, the trial of Angela Davis "a beautiful Black woman made into a political prisoner," generated active discussion. The local leaders were, predictably, villagers returning from the United States, but the issues to which they applied their new insights were predominantly those of the local community: the plantations and sugar factories and their personnel, the village "greats," and even their own parents were the focus of attack—though national leaders came in for their share of abuse. Moreover, they sought contact with groups similar to theirs which had formed in other villages on the island.

By 1971, then, the new knowledge had affected both behavioral styles and assessments of their own local situation. The demand in the village for books by Eldridge Cleaver, Malcolm X, and George Jackson, as well as writings on Africa, Cuba, and China was symptomatic of the attempt to place their local experience in a broader context. The result was a broadened consciousness of colonialism and the standards it imposes. "Ten years ago," one young militant said, "ninety percent of the Bajans thought that the White man was superior. Today, I would say that seventy percent think he just another man—or another crook—or 'tief,' we call it. And with some help by the outsiders, I think we'll make it." The outsiders referred to here were Black Americans, cited as models not only of ideology but personal lifestyle as well.[7]

[6] We do not deal with the feedback of the Black Power movement that developed in England because its impact was not as apparent, in part because there were fewer migrants who had returned from England and because the movement in the United States set the pace on the island. English race riots, immigration restrictions, and reported incidents of racial discrimination fed back into racial and political consciousness at home by changing the public image of England in the eyes of Black Barbadians and considerably reducing their identification with English culture.

[7] We do not mean to imply that the influence was one-way. West Indian symbols and forms of

Community reaction to the rhetoric of Black Power was not uniform. Cautious acknowledgments of the fact of racial oppression were followed quickly by disparagement of the disrespect and violence thought to characterize the movement. A 42-year-old plantation worker found Lord Kitchner's rather moderate calypso "Black Power" too "wicked" for his children to hear, but privately confessed that it was enjoyable "for people with understanding." Though activists were admonished to concern themselves less with Black Power and more with hard work to increase their buying power (labeled "green power") there was, at the same time, a grudging approval of the audacity of the youth, tempered by fear of its consequences.

Island political leaders also responded with ambivalence to the U.S. Black Power movement. Their support for its assertions of racial pride was tempered by the fact that demands for racial pride and independence were being turned against them. Local Black Power advocates accused their new island elite leadership of reneging on promises they had made and of equating their own political ascendance with a true independence for Barbados.

The Black leaders who brought the island to independence did so with minimal disruption of the old social structure. They discouraged any stress on racial pride as a basis for national identity. Not surprisingly, then, they have reacted to the Black Power movement by proclaiming its irrelevance to West Indian realities and asserting that "Black Power" already exists in the guise of their own leadership. They have sought to allay the influence of foreign appeals to racial consciousness by forbidding or controlling their entry into island society. Book bans in Jamaica, Barbados' alarm at Stokely Carmichael's visit, and the subsequent passage of a Public Order Act forbidding public meetings without police permission, are examples of the government s' responses, as is the denial of entrance visas to West Indian radicals from other islands. All were ploys to contain the migration of ideas by restraining their carriers.

But reactions at home required justification for such actions, and the rationale was phrased in nationalist terms: Black Power was portrayed as an example of United States cultural imperialism and placed on a par with CIA intervention and multinational corporations. This attempt by the political elite to obscure the very different relationship of Barbadians to Black and White America was a response to the real threat that a sense of unity between Caribbean and United States Blacks posed to their leadership and policies. Rather than supporting American dominance in the Caribbean, the alliance of Barbadian and American Blacks was predicated on opposition both to that dominance and to their political leaders acquiescence to it. In addition, Black American influence provided a model of behavior and leadership that was explicitly proletarian. This contrasted with the anglified styles of local leaders

---

expression such as *reggae* music, bangles, and *"Rasta"* hairdos have diffused to the United States and have been incorporated by Black Americans. But though the diffusion was two-way, the political symbols and analysis during this period were largely the articulations of Black Americans.

who tended to perpetuate the traditional social distance between leaders and followers.

The introduction of Black Power ideology and writings into the village community directly involved only a few of the returned migrants. Even those villagers, however, who were least involved in political action or ideology abroad returned from the United States as conveyors of political messages. Despite their avowed reluctance to emphasize the hard times and difficulties they faced abroad, what they did impart of their experiences reinforced in unintended ways the use of Black people as a reference group. When they talked about "America," they referred to subways and tall buildings, to expressways and snow—features of the landscape. But when they talked about "Americans," the reference was primarily to Black Americans, though Jamaicans and Puerto Ricans, Italians and Jews also figured prominently in their conversations. The traits and characteristics of these new "significant others" were dissected, analyzed, and merged into the available stock of information about the world outside.

In Barbados, the village-level expressions of racial consciousness were at their zenith in 1969.[8] Barbados did not experience the more dramatic expressions of Black consciousness that occurred in Trinidad, Jamaica, and some of the smaller islands. However, the brief period of activity left its mark. Elements of the new consciousness persist and have modified local behaviors. Much that was articulated has become submerged. Yet it remains available for elaboration and further development by those who seek to fashion new concepts of West Indian, Afro-American, Caribbean, and Third-World countries.

SUMMARY

Historically West Indian societies have been migration-oriented, a pattern especially pronounced in the case of Barbados. In this chapter we have explored how recent migration, in interaction with other factors, has produced a heightened sense of racial identity and political awareness among Barbadians.

During the nineteenth and early twentyth centuries, when Barbadian emigrants went primarily to other West Indian colonies with similar racial and social structures, they retained a pride in their national origin but tended to merge with the host population. In this period Barbadian immigrants used an ethnic identity to distinguish themselves as individuals but tended to merge with other West Indians rather than form distinctive ethnic enclaves in their host societies. Immigration to Panama and the United States, where

---

[8] The unrest of this period gave the Barbados government the leverage to compel local and foreign companies to take on non-White Barbadians at levels of management and decision-making formerly closed to them. Though entry into these positions benefited only a few, many more Black Barbadians began to feel that there was some room at the top for them.

West Indians had a racial minority status imposed upon them, constituted exceptions to this situation.

After World War II the main flow of migration was directed to the industrial centers of England, the United States, and Canada. West Indian experiences in these countries led to an emphasis on racial rather than ethnic identity, and this growth of racial consciousness had parallels on the islands. It is our contention that these developments were not independent but linked by the migration process.[9] Migration provided an important channel for the bidirectional flow of ideas such that political events at home (*e.g.*, independence) had an impact on the migrant communities abroad, while migrant experiences were relayed in the opposite direction. The combined movement generated a framework of knowledge and understanding that has led Barbadians to react in similar ways to related but different situations at home and abroad.

In Barbados we were able to observe the shift in the nature and content of the racial and political consciousness of villagers during the late 1950s to the early 1970s. This shift was toward a greater emphasis on race as a dominant idiom by which Barbadians were coming to see themselves in opposition to those with power, whether in their own society or outside. In the late 1950s, race was a latent factor in a political consciousness which focused more prominently on the need for class unity to extract concessions from the planter-merchant class that still dominated the economy. The challenge to the negatively ascribed characteristics associated with the status of being Black only began to make itself felt after the mid-1960s.

The new racial awareness stirring Barbadians abroad and at home differed from other earlier expressions of either national or ethnic identity. It was not simply an expression of national or ethnic pride but rather of cultural opposition—an explicitly countercultural assertion against the dominant values both at home and in the metropoles.

Migration alone did not create this shift in group identity and political consciousness. The situation of Barbadians at home predisposed them to have certain expectations concerning their place in the societies of England and the United States. The different structures of incorporation in these two countries led Barbadians and other West Indians to find that their status as colonized races overrode other aspects of their background and became the salient dimension of their social encounters. Political events of the 1960s resulted in West Indians in England and the United States traveling different routes to reach a convergence in racial consciousness. Finally, changes in Barbadian society during the 1960s made segments of the population partic-

---

[9] A dramatic example of this was the West Indian students' protests in 1969 at Sir George Williams University in Montreal and the Black Power revolt that took place in Trinidad a year later when some of the Montreal students returned to the island. West Indian sociologist Dennis Forsythe makes the connection between the two events explicit in his analysis of the Sir George Williams episode, viewing them as part of a single liberation struggle (Forsythe, 1971). Accounts of the Trinidad Black Power revolt can be found in Best (1970) and Oxaal (1971).

ularly receptive to the political formulations and assertions of racial pride that emerged in West Indian communities in the metropoles.[10]

There are seeming paradoxes in the juxtaposition of increased political autonomy at home (end of official colonialism) and increased West Indian migration to the countries responsible for their subjugation, past and present; in West Indians achieving an economic well-being in the metropoles unattainable at home, while simultaneously rediscovering a political and social subordination from which they have only recently emerged. It is perhaps ironic that it is as immigrants living in the metropoles that West Indians come to recognize their common problems bequeathed by colonial history and that it is here they begin to forge a West Indian/Caribbean consciousness and a basis for a unity of action. Both the paradoxes and irony are resolved once it is recognized that the bidirectional nature of recent West Indian migration has created a transnational sociocultural and political system.

BIBLIOGRAPHY

Best, L.
1970 "The February Revolution." In *The Aftermath of Sovereignty: West Indian Perspectives*. D. Lowenthal and L. Comitas, eds. Garden City, New York: Anchor Books. Pp.306–330.

Brown, J.
1970 *The Un-melting Pot—An English Town and Its Immigrants*. London: Macmillan.

Bryce-Laporte, R.S.
1972 "Black Immigrants: The Experience of Invisibility and Inequality," *Journal of Black Studies*, 3(1):29–56. Sept.

Deakin, N.
1971 "A Survey of Race Relations in Britain," *Ethnies*, 1:75–90.

———
1970 "Ethnic Minorities in the Social Sciences," *New Atlantic*, 2(1):134–159.

Fanon, F.
1971 *Let the Niggers Burn! The Sir George Williams Affair and Its Caribbean Aftermath*. Montreal: Black Rose Books.

———
1967 *Black skin, white masks*. D. Forsythe, ed. New York: Grove Press.

Katznelson, I.
1973 *Black Men, White Cities: Race, Politics and Migration in the United States, 1900–1930, and Britain, 1948–1968*. London: Oxford University Press.

Lamming G.
1953 *In the Castle of My Skin*. London: Michael Joseph.

---

[10] In the multilayered process of identity-formation, we have concentrated on the aquisition of wider identities overlaying previous ones and having implications for new forms of political consciousness and group alignments. It goes without saying that individuals carry multiple identities and that the one which is foremost at a given time will be situationally defined, influenced by the kinds of identities that the unifying and dividing forces of inequality activate.

Lewis, G.K.
1971 "An Introductory Note to the Study of Race Relations in Great Britain," *Caribbean Studies*, 11(1):5–29. April.

1969 "Protest Among the Immigrants? The Dilemma of Minority Culture," *Political Quarterly*, 40(4):426–435. Oct.

Lowenthal, D.
1972 *West Indian Societies*. London: Oxford University Press.

Makiesky-Barrow, S.R.
1976 "Class, Culture and Politics in a Barbadian Community," Ph.D. dissertation, Brandeis University.

Marshall, P.
1959 *Brown Girl, Brownstones*. New York: Random House.

Maynard, E.S.
1972 "Endogamy among Barbadian Immigrants to New York City." Ph.D. dissertation, New York University.

Midgett, D.K.
1971 "Twice Removed: West Indian or Black British?" Paper given at the American Society for Ethnohistory, Athens, Georgia.

Oxaal, I.
1971 *Race and Revolutionary Consciousness*. Cambridge, Massachusetts: Schenkman.

Peach, C.
1968 *West Indian Migration to Britain: A Social Geography*. London: Oxford University Press.

Philpott, S.B.
1970 "The Implications of Migration for Sending Societies: Some Theoretical Considerations." In *Migration and Anthropology: Proceedings of the 1970 American Ethnological Society Annual Meeting*. Seattle: University of Washington Press.

Reid, I. de A.
1939 *The Negro Immigrant: His Background, Characteristics and Social Adjustment, 1899–1937*. New York: Colombia University Press. Republished by Arno in 1969.

Roberts, G.W.
1955 "Emigration from the Island of Barbados," *Social and Economic Studies*, 4(3):245–288. Sept.

Rose, E.J.B., ed.
1969 *Colour and Citizenship: A Report on British Race Relations*. London: Oxford University Press.

Sutton, C.R.
1969 "The Scene of the Action: A Wildcat Strike in Barbados." Ph. D. dissertation, Colombia University.

Tajfel, H. and J.L. Dawson, eds.
1965 *Disappointed Guests: Essays by African, Asian and West Indian Students*. London: Oxford University Press.

WEST INDIANS IN NEW YORK CITY AND LONDON:
A Comparative Analysis

NANCY FONER[1]

State University of New York, Purchase

Since the beginning of this century, thousands of West Indians[2] have come to live in New York City. More recently, since the 1950s, large numbers of West Indians have settled in London. Whether they moved to the United States or Britain, most West Indians have usually earned more money and maintained a better living standard than they did at home. They have not, however, succeeded to the same degree in both countries in reaching the upper rungs of the occupational ladder. How and why West Indians have fared differently in these two countries is the subject of this chapter.

In New York, West Indians are known for their accomplishments in business and the professions. They have traditionally been considered more successful than Black Americans. Writers on West Indians in New York have pointed out that a high percentage of Black professionals are West Indian (see, for example, Coombs, 1970; Epstein, 1973; Forsythe, 1976; Lowenthal, 1972; Sowell, 1978) and that many people who have achieved national fame— Stokely Carmichael, Shirley Chisholm, Harry Belafonte, and Sidney Poitier, for example—are of West Indian background.

In a 1930s study, Reid (1969:121) estimated that as many as one third of the Black professional population in New York City, particularly doctors, dentists, and lawyers, were foreign born. Several decades later a *New York Times* report (1970), focusing on the professional accomplishments of West Indians in New York City, noted that Manhattan's first Black borough president, the highest ranking Black men in the city police department, and the only Black federal judges in the city were all West Indian. A recent analysis of 1970 census data shows that West Indians in the New York City metropolitan area

[1] I wish to thank Thomas Sowell and The Urban Institute for making available page proofs of relevant parts of *Essays and Data on American Ethnic Groups.* I am also grateful to Anne Foner, Judith Friedlander, and Constance Sutton for helpful suggestions.

[2] In this paper, the term "West Indian" refers only to those with origins in the English-speaking Caribbean, including Guyana.

achieve higher occupational status and higher incomes than American Blacks.[3]

Two types of explanations generally have been offered to account for the success of West Indians relative to Black Americans. One stresses West Indians' distinctive cultural heritage, arguing that they bring their ethos of hard work, saving, and investment with them when they emigrate (Glazer and Moynihan, 1970:35; cf. Forsythe, 1976). Unlike Black Americans, West Indians have come from societies where Blacks are a majority and where black skin is less of a barrier to upward mobility. They have not been subject to such a large "blast of inferiority complex pressure" or to the debilitating effects of segregation (Raphael, 1964). Their cultural tradition, based in part on the slave experience and demographic realities, promoted initiative and self-confidence rather than the "regimented dependence" fostered among Black Americans (Sowell, 1978:41–49; cf. Glazer and Moynihan, 1970:35). Other observers note that West Indian migrants bring with them an emphasis on education, and that they are "pushed to do well in America by traditions that accord status to academic success" (Lowenthal, 1972:226).

A second set of explanations focuses on West Indians' status as immigrants. It is argued that because they are strangers and marginal people, West Indians have greater chances for mobility into "interstitial statuses" (Bryce-Laporte, 1972:49). Unlike Black Americans (but like many White European immigrants), they are more often willing to scrimp and save in low-status jobs to advance themselves. By West Indian standards, United States wages are good. As immigrants from poor countries, most are also "accustomed to unemployment without welfare, hard work or underemployment, and thus relative deprivation from many of the things Black and White Americans consider basic necessities" (Bryce-Laporte, 1972:44; see also, Foner and Napoli, 1978).

While these arguments seem reasonable, when the situation of West Indians in Britain is considered, the adequacy of these explanations is put to question. Although they share a common cultural heritage and immigrant status with West Indians in the United States, in Britain, West Indians are not renowned for their business and professional accomplishments. Indeed, social commentators often emphasize their low occupational status and the barriers they face in trying to improve their position. It is not merely images of West Indians' occupational attainment that differ in the two countries. Evidence indicates that West Indians in the United States are occupationally more successful than West Indians in Britain.

My interpretation of the available data suggests that three factors may help to explain why West Indians in the United States and Britain differ in occupational status: 1) the history of West Indian migration to Britain and

---

[3] For example, 8.6% of American Blacks and 15.4% of West Indians in the New York metropolitan area were classified as professional, technical and kindred workers. The median family income for the former was $6,881; for West Indians, $8,830 (Sowell, 1978:43).

the United States; 2) the occupational background of the migrants in the West Indies; and 3) the racial contexts of the receiving societies or, in Sutton and Makiesky-Barrow's phrase (this volume), "the English and American structures of incorporation." The concluding section of this chapter considers how a comparison of West Indians' occupational achievements in the United States and Britain may broaden our understanding of why West Indians are more successful than Black Americans in New York.

Throughout the chapter, I refer to West Indians in the United States and Britain, rather than in New York and London specifically, since census data, which provide the main information on West Indians' occupations, are not available for West Indians by city. I believe, however, that the occupational trends indicated in the national data also hold for West Indians in New York and London. About 60 percent of West Indians in the United States live in the New York metropolitan area and about 55 percent in Britain live in the Greater London region (the remainder in the United States live chiefly in other northeastern cities and in Britain in the industrial centers of the midlands). Moreover, the general argument put forward to explain the differences between West Indians' occupational position in the two countries also applies to their situation in New York and London.

OCCUPATIONAL ATTAINMENT

In the United States, the 1970 census (Sowell, 1978) shows that approximately 45 percent of the West Indians in the labor force worked at nonmanual jobs, whereas, in Britain, according to the 1971 census (Lomas and Monck, 1977), this was true of only about 25 percent.[4] When it comes to the learned professions, there is also a discrepancy: 1.9 percent in the United States work force and .7 percent in the British work force.[5] In general, then, the occupa-

---

[4] Census data on West Indians in the United States and Britain are derived, respectively, from Sowell's (1978) and Lomas and Monck's (1977) analyses; Sowell's tables are based on data compiled from the 1970 census (Public Use Sample); Lomas and Monck's study is based on the special 1971 census country of birth tables. There may be problems with using these census data, and there is no way to make them strictly comparable. First, most undocumented immigrants in the United States are not included in the census, but we do not know their numbers or their occupations. Second, there are omissions in the British data in that because of inadequate information, Lomas and Monck (1977) could not classify sizeable proportions of West Indians according to occupational skill level. Third, certain occupations which are considered white collar in the American census—though probably accounting for only a small proportion of West Indians—would be considered in the manual categories in the British census. One point does seem similar in both censuses: economically-active workers in British census terminology appear to be the equivalent of those in the labor force in American census terminology.

[5] In Sowell's (1978) study, West Indians are defined as Black residents of the United States who were born in the West Indies or whose parent(s) come from there. The occupational tables he presents do not distinguish first and second generation West Indians. In the Lomas and Monck (1977) study, occupational data are presented separately for 1) those born in the West Indies, with one or both parents born there and 2) those born in Britain with both parents born in the West Indies. I have combined the data for both categories to make the analysis comparable to Sowell's. I also use the term West Indian to refer to both categories in the Lomas and Monck study.

tional distribution among West Indians in this country is skewed more toward the higher ranking occupations than it is in Britain.

West Indians also seem more successful in business in the United States although the evidence is mainly qualitative material which, as a rule, compares West Indians to Black Americans. A 1901 study indicates that West Indians were disproportionately represented in New York's Black businesses. Of the 309 Black businesses surveyed in Manhattan, 19.7 percent of the proprietors were born in the West Indies, a figure about 10 percent higher than the West Indian proportion of the total Black population (Haynes, 1968:101–102). West Indians were noted in the 1920s and 1930s for their thrift and business acumen, and enough West Indians prospered in New York to "engender an American Negro stereotype of them as 'Black Jews'" (Lowenthal, 1972:227). When a West Indian "got ten cents above a beggar," a common local saying in Harlem ran, "he opened up a business" (Osofsky, 1968:133). Ivan Light (1972:33) observes that West Indians in Harlem in the early decades of the century were more aggressive than American-born Blacks in their choice of enterprises, running grocery stores, tailor shops, jewelry stores, and fruit vending and real estate operations, businesses that put them in direct competition with White businesses in the ghetto.

Recent investigations indicate that West Indians in New York City continue to be actively involved in business enterprises. Ueda (1980:1026) claims that they own over one-half the Black businesses in the City, being especially prominent in publishing, taxi companies, real estate, advertising, banking, insurance, and retail clothing.

In Britain, by contrast, West Indians do not own many businesses. The foreword to the "Who's Who" among West Indians in Britain (*West Indian Digest*, 1973:7; *cf.* Hiro, 1971) laments that "West Indians are reluctant to go into businesses small or large." Although the 1971 census shows that 2.3 percent of the economically active West Indians in Britain were self-employed, the results of the 1974 survey conducted by Political and Economic Planning (Smith, 1977:92–93) suggest that only a small proportion of the self-employed own businesses. Among working West Indians surveyed by PEP, 6 percent of the men and 1 percent of the women were self-employed. Only 2 percent of the self-employed were shopkeepers; nearly one-half were in the construction industry, most likely individual workers operating on a freelance basis.

REASONS FOR OCCUPATIONAL DIFFERENCES

How can we account for the fact that West Indians in the United States have higher status jobs than their counterparts in Britain? Neither immigrant status nor cultural heritage can explain the difference since these two features pertain to West Indians in both countries. Indeed, the occupational differences between West Indians in Britain and the United States raise questions about Ivan Light's (1972) explanation of West Indians' business achievements in the United States. Light attributes the entrepreneurial success of New York West Indians to the traditional institution of rotating credit associations. Known as "partners," *susus*, and "boxes," these rotating credit associations, according to Light, provided West Indians with an important source of capital for business ventures. Lacking these traditional credit associations, Black Americans were more dependent on banks and lending institutions for credit, which they were frequently denied. True, rotating credit associations have also been reported among West Indians in Britain (Davison, 1966; Patterson, 1965; Philpott, 1973) and, as Light (1972:35) notes, West Indians there may well have amassed funds for purchasing homes through such associations. Yet, despite the presence of rotating credit associations in both countries, West Indians in Britain seem to have invested their savings in small-scale businesses less than have their counterparts in New York.

It is necessary, then, to look elsewhere for explanations. While the lack of data about the background of the occupationally successful in both countries means that I can only venture certain hunches, three factors appear to be important. One factor is the more recent nature of mass West Indian migration to Britain compared to the United States. Specifically, a higher percentage of West Indians in the United States have lived there longer than is the case in Britain, and hence a higher percentage of economically-active West Indians in the United States are second generation.

West Indians are not newcomers to American shores. About 2 percent (or one million) of the aliens who entered the United States between 1830 and 1970 were West Indian (Bryce-Laporte, 1972:33). A substantial part of this immigration occurred early in this century so that by the 1920s approximately one fourth of the Black population of Harlem was West Indian (Sowell, 1978:47). The 1924 Immigration Act limited West Indian immigration, however, and even more severe cutbacks were effected by the 1952 McCarran-Walter Act. Nevertheless, mass emigration to the United States was again possible after the passage of the 1965 immigration legislation, and the number of West Indian immigrants more than tripled from fiscal year 1966 to 1967 (Dominguez, 1975:11). Between 1967 and 1971 about 127,000 West Indians legally emigrated to the United States (Palmer, 1974:573). It is impossible to say how many West Indians are United States residents today because many are not legally registered. Nor are published figures available on the presumably rather sizeable number of second generation West Indians. It is rumored, for instance, that if one includes the second and third generations, some 250,000 Barbadians live in New York City (Sutton and Makiesky-Barrow, this volume). A 1972 study estimated that some 220,000 Jamaicans lived in the New York metropolitan area with another 95,000 in the rest of the country (Lambie, cited in Dominguez, 1975: 100); over one quarter of the total number of Jamaicans arrived from 1967 to 1972 as legal immigrants (Dominguez, 1975:34).

West Indians arrived en masse in Britain only after 1951. Before that year, West Indian arrivals in Britain apparently never exceeded 1,000 a year (Rose, 1969:66). The closing off of the United States as a destination for emigration in 1952, combined with postwar labor shortages and an open immigration policy in Britain, ushered in a period of mass migration to "the mother country." The West Indian population grew from an estimated 15,300 in 1951 to 171,800 only a decade later. Open immigration ended with the Commonwealth Immigration Act of 1962. This Act and the subsequent tightening of immigration controls drastically reduced West Indian immigration. West Indians who entered after 1962 were mainly dependents (wives and children) of those already settled in Britain, and in recent years the number of incoming dependents has dropped so sharply that more West Indians have left Britain than have arrived there (*New York Times*, 1978).

West Indians in Britain are a visible immigrant minority and their numbers have been counted carefully as ammunition in political debates ("the numbers game") over immigration. Prior to 1962, West Indians had the right of free entry to Britain and, by 1971, 446,200 people of West Indian origin were living there, of whom 223,300 were born in Britain (Lomas and Monck, 1977: 12). However, only about 3,000 of those British born to West Indian parents were then over 15 years of age (Lomas and Monck, 1977:17).

Because large-scale West Indian migration to the United States spans a much longer period than the mass West Indian movement to Britain, a higher proportion of the West Indian population in the United States is second generation. This may be one key to understanding the relative occupational success of West Indians in the United States since the evidence suggests that second generation West Indians, both in Britain and the United States, are better represented in white-collar jobs than their parents (Dominguez, 1975:61; Lomas and Monck, 1977:37; Sowell, 1978:44).

A second factor is the occupational background of West Indians who have emigrated to Britain and the United States. Although limited, statistics available for the recent mass movements of West Indians to the two countries indicate that West Indian migration to the United States in the past two decades has been marked by a higher percentage of professional and other nonmanual workers than the emigration to Britain in the 1950s and early 1960s (Kuper, 1976:12–13; Palmer, 1974:571).[6] Migration to both countries has been selective. Various surveys, however, show that while a high percentage of West Indian migrants to Britain in the 1950s and early 1960s were skilled workers (*see,* Palmer, 1974:574; Wright, 1968:30–40), only about 10 percent of West Indian workers emigrating to Britain could be classified as white collar. By contrast, of the approximately 91,000 West Indian legal emigrants to the

[6] The West Indian migration to the United States earlier in the century seemed to include a higher proportion of manual workers than the recent movement, although the early figures are sketchy at best. In the peak years of the migration (1906–1925), the overwhelming majority appeared to be manual workers; professionals formed from 3% to 4% of the total workers in the foreign Black migrant stream and those employed in commerce from 6% to 11% (Reid, 1969:244).

United States between 1962 and 1971 who were listed as workers, about 15 percent were classified as professional, technical and kindred workers and about 12 percent as clerical and kindred workers (Palmer, 1974:574).[7]

The third factor likely to have affected patterns of occupational achievement is the social contexts of the two receiving societies. The lower occupational attainment of West Indians in Britain cannot be explained by arguing that they merely fit the occupational profile of the total population since West Indians in Britain are much less well represented in professional and other nonmanual positions than the total population. By contrast, West Indians in the United States more closely approximate the national occupational pattern in that similar proportions of West Indians and the total population are in professional and other nonmanual employment.

A critical difference in the social contexts of the two countries is the structure of their race relations. To be sure, West Indians in the United States as well as in Britain have faced, and continue to face, barriers to occupational advancement because of their skin color. Their relative success in the learned professions and business in the United States may, however, be explained at least in part because they settled in cities with many American Blacks. In Britain, they moved into a rather homogeneous, largely White, society. Indeed, the racial context of the receiving areas has influenced the way West Indians view their own occupational attainments. While West Indians in both countries do compare their occupational status with what it was at home, West Indian achievements in the United States also "are viewed by the dominant White majority, and come to be viewed by West Indians themselves, in the context of Black America" (Sutton and Makiesky-Barrow, this volume). Such a comparison puts West Indians in a favorable light and bolsters their ethnic pride. West Indians in New York for example, stress that they work harder, save more money, and are more ambitious than Black

---

[7] There are many problems with those occupational data, based on U.S. Immigration and Naturalization Service reports and, for Britain, on various sample surveys (many carried out in the West Indies before the migrants left for Britain). In terms of the U.S. data, the figures do not include illegal aliens whose numbers and occupational characteristics are unknown (Tomasi and Keely, 1975:68–70). In addition, occupation of West Indians in the INS reports may refer to three different types of occupations: 1) current occupation of the applicant in the West Indies; 2) job on arrival in the U.S.; or 3) job held as an undocumented alien in the United States if the person is applying for a visa from within the U.S. The labor force participation of women, moreover, is undercounted since many classified as housewives worked in the West Indies and/or enter the work force soon after admission to the U.S. For a full analysis of the problems in the INS data, see Tomasi and Keely (1975:62–64). The British data on West Indian migrants' occupations do refer to their occupations in the West Indies, but these data are not without problems. The various surveys of migrants' occupations in the West Indies only cover certain years of the mass migration to Britain, for example, and only include migrants from some islands. For a summary of these surveys, see Wright (1968:30–40). Despite the limited data, it still does seem that the recent migrant stream to the U.S. includes a higher percentage of white-collar workers than the stream to Britain. If one considers all West Indians (over 150,000) who migrated legally to the U.S. between 1962 and 1971, rather than only those categorized as workers, nearly 20% were classified in white-collar occupations. In every survey of West Indian migrants to Britain in the 1950s and early 1960s a much smaller percentage of West Indians (whether based on total workers or total migrants) were white-collar workers.

Americans (*see,* Coombs, 1970). In Britain, West Indians as well as the British tend to measure West Indians' achievements against those of the White majority. Such a comparison, by contrast, puts West Indians at a clear disadvantage.

That West Indians in the United States are submerged in the Afro-American population is evident at the neighborhood level. In New York City, for instance, West Indians live mainly in areas of Black residence in central Brooklyn, and among the middle class, especially in the north Bronx and the southeastern sections of Queens. They are rarely found living outside the usual neighborhoods of West Indian residence or of the Black population (Thomas-Hope, 1975:3).

In London, as in other English cities, West Indians and other racial minorities "are concentrated in particular local authority areas; within the local authority areas they are concentrated in a few wards . . .; and even within wards they are concentrated in particular streets" (Smith, 1977:30). In spite of the fairly dense concentration of West Indians in particular areas and on particular streets, there is not the same pattern of racial and residential segregation found in the United States. According to t he 1971 census, the highest proportion West Indians formed of any London borough's population was 6.5 percent, and of a London ward population, 21.3 percent (Lee, 1977:15, 24). The percentages change little if the other main colored groups in Britain—Indians, Pakistanis, and Bangladeshis—are included. A large number of Whites lived in most South London streets where I interviewed Jamaicans in 1973,[8] and the White presence is very evident in most other areas of dense West Indian settlement in Britain.

The presence and residential concentration of so many American Blacks in the American cities where West Indians live has, I suggest, influenced their business achievements. West Indians in New York, for instance, have had a ready-made, rather large constituency they could cultivate for their enterprises: the American, as well as the West Indian, Black community. Most Black businesses in the United States depend upon Black patronage. West Indians in Britain are less likely to invest their savings in small enterprises, I would argue, because there are far fewer West Indians in British cities than Blacks in New York and other major American cities to furnish a market, because they are a minority in most boroughs and wards and because they fear that English Whites might not patronize Black businesses.

It is difficult to compare opportunities for high-level professionals because of differences in the structure of many professions in Britain and the United States. However, being part of a large native Black population in the United States seems to have provided aspiring West Indian professionals with some advantages. Even in the days before affirmative action, when entry into White universities and professional schools was extremely difficult for Blacks, all-Black colleges, Howard University in particular, provided medical

---

[8] My research on Jamaicans in London is fully reported elsewhere (*see,* Foner, 1977, 1978).

and other professional training. Reid (1969:226) notes that between 1867 and 1932 Howard University had more than 1,000 West Indians in its student body. In Britain, by contrast, no independent system of Black higher education has been available, and university education and training for learned professions have been beyond the reach of most West Indians. Moreover, in Britain, West Indians in professions based on private practices might find it difficult to establish themselves because the small size of the Black population offers only a limited market for their services, and they have to vie with British professionals for White clientele. The absence of a sizeable native Black population in Britain also has meant that potential West Indian political leaders have a narrow base, while West Indians in America have been able to utilize the Black community and the Black vote as a foundation for achieving positions of political prominence.

IMPLICATIONS: WEST INDIANS AND BLACK AMERICANS IN NEW YORK

Comparing West Indians' occupational success in the United States and Britain highlights a number of factors which might be overlooked if West Indians in only one country were examined. Such an analysis shows that West Indians' cultural heritage and their status as immigrants do not adequately account for the nature of their occupational attainments.

While being Black in America has meant that West Indians often are invisible as immigrants (Bryce-Laporte, 1972), the presence of the native Black community has provided them with a basis for upward occupational mobility. The evidence also indicates that the West Indian population in the United States includes a higher proportion of persons who were nonmanual and professional workers at home, as well as a higher proportion of working members of the second generation.

What does the comparison between West Indians in the United States and Britain tell us about why West Indians have been more successful than Black Americans in New York? Do any of the three factors that distinguish West Indians in the United States from those in Britain help us to understand the differences between West Indians and Black Americans? First, let us consider the structure of race relations. While White Americans are often said to favor West Indians over native Blacks, by and large West Indians and Black Americans have similar educational and occupational opportunities available. Sowell's (1978:44) recent study, in fact, casts doubt on the argument that West Indians' achievements are explained by different treatment from White American employers. Sowell compiled 1970 census data for second generation West Indians in the New York City area. He found that this second generation—likely to have been educated in the United States and unlikely to have an accent that would enable a White employer to distinguish them from native Blacks—not only exceeds the socioeconomic status of other West Indians and native Blacks but also that of the United States population as a whole. Second, there is the generation factor as such. It is doubtful that the relative proportion of first, as opposed to second, generation migrants among West Indians and Black Americans explains West Indians' achievements. Black Americans' immigrant origins are deep in the past. Even though most Black Americans in New York City have their roots in the rural South, a high percentage of Black American workers are second generation urban migrants.

What remains as possibly an essential factor is occupational background which may well give West Indians certain advantages over Black Americans. I have shown that, at least in recent years, a high percentage of legal West Indian immigrants to the United States were classified as professional and white-collar workers. A large number of West Indians may have had (or their families had) relatively high occupational status back home and, therefore, not only the skills but also the confidence that comes with such position.

This is not to dismiss the role of cultural heritage and immigrant status altogether. West Indian cultural heritage operates to the extent that their coming from societies with Black majorities and with a relatively wide occupational range open to Blacks gives them a basis for greater assurance and ambition than Black Americans. Because they are immigrants and tend to view work and wages in the United States by standards in "the old country," they are willing to work hard in low-status jobs and save to advance themselves—at least in the first generation. Yet, until careful and systematic studies are undertaken of the life histories and careers of West Indians in New York, as well as in London, we will not have a full understanding of the relative impact of occupational background, cultural heritage, and immigrant status on West Indians' achievements in their new environments.

POSTSCRIPT

When this chapter was first published in 1979, I relied on census data from the early 1970s. Unfortunately, recent data on the occupational composition of the West Indian population in Britain and the United States are not available, and therefore a rigorous updated analysis is not possible. Even so, I believe that the trends documented and interpretations put forward in this chapter still hold.

West Indians in the United States are almost certainly still more successful occupationally than those in Britain—although West Indians in Britain may not be lagging so far behind. For one thing, a higher proportion of the working West Indian population in the United States is probably still second generation. The proportion of employed second generation West Indians in Britain has, of course, grown since 1971, and thus it is likely that the percentage of white-collar workers among West Indians in the labor force has also increased. Moreover, in the United States, a larger proportion of the West Indian population now belongs to the first generation due to the continued, massive influx of immigrants; about 144,000 West Indians legally entered the country between 1972 and 1977, and the movement shows no signs of abating. Nonetheless, given the long history of West Indian migration to the United States, the percentage of working members of the second generation is still sizeable—and still likely to be higher than among West Indians in Britain.

Furthermore, the West Indian migrant stream to the United States continues to include a high percentage of professional and nonmanual workers. In 1978, for example, 15 percent of the legal Jamaican immigrants to the United States listed as workers were classified as professional, technical, and kindred workers, 18 percent as clerical and kindred workers. And finally, the presence and residential concentration of Black Americans in the American cities where West Indians live continues, I would argue, to give West Indians in the United States an edge over their British counterparts in establishing businesses and professional practices (see, Foner, 1983). Although West Indians in English cities represent an increasing proportion of the population of certain boroughs, there is not the same pattern of racial or residential segregation found in the United States.

In sum, despite changes in the past ten or fifteen years, I strongly suspect that West Indians in the United States still fare better occupationally than those in Britain. I believe, the explanations I advanced in 1979 to account for this difference remain valid.

BIBLIOGRAPHY

Bryce-Laporte, R.S.
1972   "Black Immigrants: The Experience of Invisibility and Inequality," *Journal of Black Studies*, (1)3:29–56. Sept.

Coombs, O.
1970   "West Indians in New York: Moving Beyond the Limbo Pole," *New York Magazine*, 13:28–32. July.

Davison, R.B.
1966   *Black British: Immigrants to England*. London: Oxford University Press.

Dominguez, V.
1975   *From Neighbor to Stranger. The Dilemma of Caribbean Peoples in the United States*. New Haven: Yale University, Antilles Research Program, Occasional Papers No. 5.

Epstein, C.
1973   "Black and Female: The Double Whammy," *Psychology Today*, 7(3):57–61. Aug.

Foner, N.
1983   *Jamaican Migrants: A Comparative Analysis of the New York and London Experience*. New York:

Center for Latin American and Caribbean Studies, New York University Research Program in Inter-American Affairs. Occasional Paper 36.

1978 *Jamaica Farewell: Jamaican Migrants in London.* Berkeley: University of California Press; London: Routledge and Kegan Paul.

1977 "The Jamaicans: Cultural and Social Change Among Migrants in Britain." In *Between Two Cultures.* J.L Watson, ed. Oxford: Basil Blackwell. Pp. 120–150.

Foner, N. and R. Napoli
1978 "Jamaican and Black-American Migrant Farm Workers: A Comparative Analysis," *Social Problems,* 25(5):491–503. June.

Forsythe, D.
1976 "Black Immigrants and the American Ethos: Theories and Observations." In *Caribbean Immigration to the United States.* R.S. Bryce-Laporte and D.M. Mortimer, eds. Washington, D.C.: Research Institute on Immigration and Ethnic Studies, Smithsonian Institution. Pp. 55–82.

Glazer, N. and D. Moynihan
1970 *Beyond the Melting Pot.* Cambridge, Mass: The MIT Press.

Haynes, G.E.
1912 *The Negro at Work in New York City.* New York: Arno Press. 1968

Hiro, D.
1971 *Black British: White British.* London: Eyre and Spottiswoode.

Kuper, A.
1976 *Changing Jamaica.* London: Routledge and Kegan Paul.

Lee, T.
1977 *Race and Residence: The Concentration and Dispersal of Immigrants in London.* Oxford: Clarendon Press.

Light, I.
1972 *Ethnic Enterprise in America.* Berkeley: University of California Press.

Lomas, G.G.B. and E. Monck
1977 *The Coloured Population of Great Britain: Employment and Economic Activity, 1971.* London: The Runnymede Trust.

Lowenthal, D.
1972 *West Indian Societies.* London: Oxford University Press.

New York Times
1978 "Mrs. Thatcher Touches a Nerve and British Tension is Suddenly a Political Issue," *New York Times.* Feb. 22.

1970 "Neighborhoods: West Indies Flavor Bedford-Stuyvesant," *New York Times.* October 28.

Osofsky, G.
1968 *Harlem: The Making of a Ghetto.* New York: Harper and Row.

Palmer, R.W.
1974 "A Decade of West Indian Migration to the United States, 1962–1972: An Economic Analysis," *Social and Economic Studies,* 23:571–588.

Patterson, S.
1965 *Dark Strangers: A Study of West Indians in London.* Harmondsworth: Penguin.

Philpott, S.
1973 *West Indian Migration: The Montserrat Case.* London: The Athlone Press.

Raphael, L.
1964 "West Indians and Afro-Americans," *Freedomways*, 4(3):438–445. Summer.

Reid, I. de A.
1939 *The Negro Immigrant. His Background, Characteristics and Social Adjustment, 1899–1937*. New York: Columbia University Press. Arno Press, 1964.

Rose, E.J.B. *et al.*
1969 *Colour and Citizenship*. London: Oxford University Press.

Smith, D.J.
1977 *Racial Disadvantage in Britain*. Harmondsworth: Penguin.

Sowell, T.
1978 *Essays and Data on American Ethnic Groups*. Washington, D.C.: The Urban Institute.

Thomas-Hope, E.
1975 "The Adaptation of Migrants from the English-Speaking Caribbean in Select Urban Centres of Britain and North America." Paper presented at the Annual Meeting of the Society for Applied Anthropology, Amsterdam.

Tomasi, S.M. and C.B. Keely
1975 *Whom Have We Welcomed?* Staten Island, N.Y.: Center for Migration Studies.

Ueda, R.
1980 "West Indians." In *Harvard Encyclopedia of American Ethnic Groups*. S. Thernstrom, ed. Cambridge, Mass.: Harvard University Press. Pp. 1020–1027.

West Indian Digest
1973 "West Indians in Britain, Who's Who, 1973/1974". Hertfordshire : The West Indian Digest.

Wright, P.L.
1968 *The Coloured Worker in British Industry*. London: Oxford University Press.

WEST INDIAN CHILD FOSTERING:
Its Role in Migrant Exchanges[1]

ISA MARÍA SOTO
New York University

Throughout their long history of migratory movements to regional and international economic centers, the West Indian peoples have been successful in maintaining and transforming a sociocultural tradition that is not territorially based. This success is predicated on the circulation between the two ends of the migration continuum—the home and host societies—not only of material resources but also of individuals and ideas. While previous studies have focused on the circulation of material resources and of ideas (Philpott, 1968, 1973; Sutton and Makiesky Barrow, this volume), this chapter concentrates on the circulation of humans and their importance in sustaining cultural continuity. This circulation will be examined from the perspective of the role that children play in an international migration situation. It is my thesis that child fostering—the care of migrants' children by kin or friends in the home society—can be considered an integral and vital part of this circular movement that works to maintain an historical and cultural continuity between the migrants and the communities that send them forth. Data to sustain this thesis are derived from ethnographic studies of West Indian societies, West Indian immigrant groups, and from fictional literature on West Indian migrants and interview material with West Indians.

The Afro-Creole population of the English-speaking West Indies will be dealt with as a unit in that these islands share a common West African heritage and a history of slavery and colonialism (Herskovits, 1958; Mintz and Price, 1976). Studies of West Indian family life among the numerically predominant nonelite populations indicate that similar cultural patterns underlie their forms of marriage and kin relations, household organizations and the fluidity of residence pattern, (Marks, 1976; Otterbein, 1966; Sanford,

[1] I want to thank Dr. Constance Sutton for the opportunity to publish this paper and for her extensive assistance in the process of formulating the ideas presented as well as editing various drafts of the paper. I also wish to thank Ms. Margaret Souza without whose advice, illuminating comments, and emotional support this paper would not have been written.

1971; Slater, 1977; M.G. Smith, 1962; R.T. Smith, 1956; Sutton and Makiesky-Barrow, 1977). This similarity also applies to child fostering, a cultural practice that plays a key role in the social reproduction of the kin groups that comprise the membership of local West Indian communities.

Fostering or fosterage is the widespread practice whereby children are taken care of by kin or nonkin at various times in their childhood years. This temporary transferral of parental rights does not entail the disruption of a child's original kin affiliations (Midgett, 1969:1; Sanford, 1971:60). Fostering is also the term used by others (Goody, 1976; Sutton and Hammer, 1985) who have studied this cultural practice in West African societies. Therefore, I use the term fostering rather than adoption because legal adoption and all that it implies is rarely the case in the West Indies.[2]

Recent studies that have investigated and analyzed the adaptive strategies of West Indian immigrant households at home and abroad (Kerns, 1983; Laguerre, 1984; Philpott, 1968, 1973) have made little reference to childcare activities or, more important, to whether or not children contribute to the success of these adaptive strategies. Either children are assumed to be a drawback to the full pursuit of economic success or, where children are the focus of analysis, two main problems are emphasized: the adjustment difficulties confronted by children as they are integrated into the host society's formal educational system and the role of children in the process of severing migrants' ties to the cultural traditions of the home society. It is from this latter viewpoint that intergenerational conflict is explained, attributing to the younger first generation and to second generation migrants the role of cultural brokers or agents of immigrant cultural assimilation into the host society (cf. Laguerre, 1984).

A different view of this younger generation is presented here in which children are regarded not only as agents of cultural change but as critical actors in maintaining cultural links between home and host societies. From this perspective, the cleavage between generations becomes muted. For even as immigrants' children change from being identified as essential workers in the daily battle for the economic survival of the international household to embodiments of upward socioeconomic mobility (cf. Pessar, 1982), the links forged in their early years with kin in the home community do not readily disappear. As adults circulate between home and host societies, channeling their resources from one to the other, children provide the link in the exchange systems between the mobile adult and the more stationary ones left at home. For all the individuals involved, this exchange is an investment. For

[2] The word fostering carries negative connotations for the West Indians who have experienced discrimination based on what is believed to be their deviant forms of family organization. From a Western ethnocentric point of view, fostering is associated with the economic and emotional abandonment of children on the part of adults. Immigrants and islanders both prefer to use the terms "minding" or "caring for" children.

the participating adults, fostering opens up a wide spectrum of active social ties across which goods flow and commitments are sustained.[3]

Thus, fostering increases the general density of possible relationships that are part of the structure of West Indian cultural systems. To either leave or send one's child to a surrogate parent communicates the desire of the absent parent to maintain links with the home community, links which represent a desire to return in the future and become an active participant within the community. For the persons who do the fostering, the activity puts them in touch with happenings in the host society and in a position of prestige vis-à-vis the biological parent(s) and children. From the children's perspective, the residential shift between home and host countries (which occurs when children are deemed capable of taking advantage of the opportunities offered by the host society), ensure that they become acquainted with their kindred and the community with whom they are expected to acquire life-long responsibilities. For the adult, the children they foster will become the symbols of their successful parenting through their potential for success in the economic arena. In sum, fostering is an activity which results in the redistribution of wealth, resources and services across international boundaries.

FOSTERING AND MOTHERING

Fostering practices have been recognized for present-day West African societies (Etienne, 1979; Goody, 1982; Sutton and Hammer, 1985) and for other populations that comprise the African Diaspora in the New World (Clarke, 1966; Covert and Cook, n.d.; Durant-Gonzalez, 1976; Stack, 1974). In West Africa, fostering reinforces claims to assistance from kin. The fostering process also serves to acknowledge the importance of kin and friends as a support system and a source of individual power in a society where success and wealth are predicated upon personal access to a dense web of social networks. In the United States, "child sharing" among Afro-American households is part of a larger system of "swapping" networks that distribute goods and services within a localized community, becoming a crucial element in their survival strategies (Stack, 1974).

[3] In seeing child fostering as an exchange activity, I am closely following the thesis put forth by Annette Weiner (1980) in her reinterpretation of Trobriand and other Oceanic societies. Weiner is concerned with looking at the role that exchange of valuable objects among the Trobriand Islanders plays in the regeneration of social life through time. These objects—yams, banana leaf bundles, etc.—are physical and ideological representations of the great amount of human energy invested in this regeneration. Objects, by virtue of their specificity, and the labor needed to reproduce them, are the embodiment of the power of past relationships and can communicate through their exchange the state of present, and expectations for future relationships between the participants in the exchange. In the West Indies, it would appear that the object-person relationship outlined by Weiner is reversed. It is my thesis that the exchange of human beings, i.e., children, serves to activate the exchange of material goods. It is the meaning embedded in the former that makes the latter possible.

The rationale for fostering practices as they are enacted at the local level is related to how mother roles are defined in the West Indies and the nature of the mother-daughter tie (Durant-Gonzalez, 1982; M.G. Smith, 1962; R.T. Smith, 1956; Sanford, 1971). These female roles and relationships have both structural and symbolic aspects (Kerns, 1983). Fostering as an activity primarily within the domain of female responsibility (*see*, Durant-Gonzalez, 1982) also exhibits these symbolic and structural dimensions.[4] First, the activity of caring for others' children is part and parcel of the role of women as forgers of social life (*cf.* Etienne, 1979; Kerns, 1983), as the focus of kin and community activities (Kerns, 1983:13 fn). Children are regarded by West Indians as women's wealth, and socially it is the distribution of this wealth that links different generations of women. Second, fostered children play an important role in creating and maintaining socially significant material and symbolic exchanges in a situation where cooperation between adults is based on consanguineal kin ties and friendship rather than on the conjugal bond. It is this local pattern that is transferred into the international arena through the migration process. In this latter arena, fostering is a crucial though little studied component of the migrant experience.

In the early literature, the specific nature of the relationship among women and their lineal kin was identified as "matrifocality" (R.T. Smith , 1956). This referred to what European observers perceived as an unusual amount of authority exercised by women in domestic relations. However, it should be noted that West Indian matrifocality, which has suffered numerous redefinitions in the literature, is not synonymous with the recognized demographic incidence of female-headed households. Rather it is an organized cultural pattern that ties women and their children together across generations—lineally and laterally—imbuing these relationships with a source of power and responsibility for women. This pattern stems from a cultural logic that identifies women as the focus of authority in the domestic realm as well as in social relations at the community level (Kerns, 1983).

Informed by this logic, West Indian women engage in a conscious activation of roles which are at once voluntary and obligatory. In addition to their own roles as mothers, women are expected to be responsible for other juniors in their community (Kerns, 1983:5). Thus the definition of what it means to be a West Indian woman cannot be extricated from her role as childbearer and childrearer (Durant-Gonzalez, 1982:14). With motherhood, a woman will achieve full adult status in her community. Yet this role does not require that the mother be the primary caretaker or the exclusive female person with rights over the child. Often the children are born into the household where

---

[4] Until recently, most of the literature on West Indian family life looked at child fostering in two problem-oriented ways. Studies of fertility looked at how "childcaring" by kin helped to diffuse the pressure of biological reproduction and alleviated individual responsibility for the children produced. Studies of West Indian mating and residence practices saw "childcaring" as a response to "absentee fatherhood," serial unions and male economic marginality (Blake, 1961; Clarke, 1966; Goosen, 1972; Marks, 1976; Otterbein, 1966; Sanford, 1971).

they will eventually be fostered. Women begin their reproductive activities early in their life cycles and may go through a series of unions before their childbearing years are over (Blake, 1961; Sutton and Makiesky-Barrow, 1977). It follows that the first and/or second child born to a woman is likely to be born in her parents or foster parents' home from a union with a man she may subsequently leave. This does not preclude the presence of male "surrogate" parents, for the organization of household and family allows for and many times requires that the adult males associated with it support its members, both emotionally and economically. As a woman, a man must ultimately prove to be a responsible parent to earn the respect of the community, although he may diffuse his parental responsibility over more than one household (M.G. Smith, 1962:234; Sutton and Makiesky-Barrow, 1977:309).

Concomitant with the value placed on motherhood is the high value of children as markers of social prestige, and the strong ties that develop between mothers and children—especially girl children.[5] There is also the expectation that the children one has "cared for" as parent or fosterer will in exchange "help care for" one as they reach adulthood. Thus, as children grow older they become an increasing source of autonomy for women, lessening their dependence on the resources that male partners may or may not make available to them. These patterns and values are not limited to the lower socioeconomic classes but cut across class differences (Durant-Gonzalez, 1982).

Through children, women are able to establish lasting emotional and economic ties with one another. One particularly interesting version of this phenomenon was illustrated by a female immigrant from the West Indies whose four children, one of whom stayed back home with the grandmother, were fathered by the same man who "sent for" her in the early 1970s.[6] Because of what she called his deep reluctance to become a responsible family man, they separated after the three youngest children were born in New York City.

[5] The importance of ties between female consanguineal kin as related to mothering functions extends to the sibling relationship as well. The eldest daughter is an important authority figure *vis-à-vis* her younger siblings and their offspring (Otterbein, 1966). This closeness and authority develop not only because of "blood" ties but also because of common residence in a household, usually the mother or grandmother's. It is also often the case that the older sister cares for the younger siblings and eventually their children. These close relationships have the potential for acquiring control over other women's labor and reproductive resources. As one woman stated: "My brother's wife owes me respect because she got something from me and I got nothing from her" (Otterbein, 1966:122).

[6] The comments from immigrants recorded in this essay are part of in-depth interviews with Eastern Caribbean immigrants as well as their families and friends left back home. The interviews were conducted for an ongoing project on Eastern Caribbean immigrants in New York City under the direction of Dr. Linda Basch for the United Nations Institute for Training and Research. The quotes come from immigrant mothers and foster parents (both male and female) in the home island of St. Vincent. Out of 44 available interviews in New York City, 22 presently or at some point in their migration experience, left or sent their children back to the island. This group of immigrants consisted equally of married and unmarried persons. Out of the 52 interviewees in the home island, at least 27 had cared for an emigrant kin's child(ren) for some period of time. I want to express my debt to Dr. Basch for making this unpublished data available to me.

Meanwhile, the woman developed a cooperative relationship with her former partner's legal spouse who had also migrated. The first woman took care of the second's child for some time. Although they were not friends, the two women were able to set aside their conflicting interests and pool their meager resources to help each other. Thus they managed to call each other once a week to share information about the children, school, store bargains, and finally to console each other when their mutually-shared partner misbehaved in some way. The cultural logic that makes the children the *raison d'être* for mutually supportive exchange was succinctly stated by this West Indian woman who explained her need to help another woman "because our children link us."

If one is to see women as the dominant actors in an exchange system which renews and transforms kin and community relations, men's participation can be seen as conditioned by their economic and affective ties to particular women and their children in this network (*cf.* Etienne, 1979). Male foster parents are rare in the West Indies. Where they do occur, they signal affinal rather than consanguineal ties between the foster father and child. In other words, while women foster their consanguineal kin, men often foster their spouses' kin (Kerns, 1983:117–18). However, an adult woman's presence in the household seems to be a prerequisite in the majority of fostering cases (Philpott, 1973:136). A man can keep children with whom he has established a close relationship if the woman in the household is incapable of doing so, as is illustrated by a widower interviewed in St. Vincent who continued, after his wife died, to take care of emigrant children's offspring.

In this cycle of social continuity, women and children are the main actors. Men selectively participate at various junctures in the cycle. Sanford (1971:99) describes West Indian women as "building their empires as mothers by appropriating their daughters' children." To build an empire you need wealth, and children as "women's business" (Clarke, 1966:180) are also women's wealth. At the apex of this empire are the women who have reached the later years of their life cycles (Kerns, 1983). Most of the older generation of women have already proven their ability to successfully carry out the expected mothering roles, having effectively extended these roles by caring for their kin's children, especially those of their daughters (R.T. Smith, 1956:148). In doing so, they also exercise the right to demand the services of the younger generation: "who owes must pay" (Kerns, 1983:189). As one 80-year-old woman interviewed in St. Vincent explained:

> I taken care of the children to the best of my ability. Now I content
> to sit back and let them take care of me. That is they duty, I think.

Interdependent ties between lineal kin create an exchange system through time. Socioeconomic interests, different aspirations and experiences may work to divide generations, but there is an acknowledged "shared substance" between them that is perpetuated through exchange. These personal bonds are represented within a larger cosmology that emphasizes the gratitude of the living for the work of the elderly, respect for the ancestors, and the recognition that the past shapes the present and future (Kerns, 1983; Marshall, 1983). The links between generations, expressed in Afro-American literature as the importance of "roots," is a renewable source of female power within the kin group. The ancestors' roles in creating women's power was described by one Afro-American novelist who has written one of the few existing novels of the West Indian immigrant experience in the United States. She proclaims of her grandmother, whom she visited for one eventful year in Barbados during her childhood:

> She's an ancestor figure, symbolic for me of the long line of Black women and men—African and New World—who made my being possible, and whose spirit I believe continues to animate my life and work (Marshall, 1983:95).

FOSTERING AND MIGRATION

Expectations of gratitude in the form of financial help (Kerns, 1983:189) and dependence on remittances—part of the acknowledged exchange relationship between older and younger generations—do not totally account for the older women's willingness to care for their kin's children. The successful upbringing of two generations of children endows these women not only with some sort of financial security but also with the maturity, seniority and prestige accorded to mothers of successful children. Both foster children and their biological parents embody the potential for achieving this form of success. But within these dependent economies, migration has become an institutionalized means to realize this potential, a response to limited employment opportunities in the home islands, and rite of passage to adulthood (Lowenthal, 1972; Philpott, 1968). It is the younger generation, and eventually their children, who will embark upon this migratory exodus, lending an international character to the localized pattern of "caring for" and socializing future generations.

For the past fifteen years, immigration to the United States, particularly to New York City, has been characterized by a large influx of Caribbean peoples. Following international trends, the majority of these immigrants are women in the twenty- to thirty-age range (Tobier, 1982; United States Department of Justice, Immigration and Naturalization Service (INS), 1971–1981). In addition, Caribbean immigrants have arrived in great numbers under family reunification preferences under the category of spouses and unmarried children of resident aliens (see, United States Department of Justice, 1971–1981).

The above trends coincide with the pattern of child fostering as it is worked out under conditions of international migration. The numbers in the immigration statistics are representative of women who not only are in their prime working ages (Tobier, 1982), but also in their prime reproductive years. These West Indian women carry with them the important responsibility of at least partially providing for kin left back home. The underrepresentation of children younger than ten years old arriving with adults (vis-à-vis those arriving under family reunification preferences) is an indication that at least initially very young children are left in the care of kin back in the home society. However, physical distance does not prevent a mother's involvement with the care of her children. After all, providing a better chance for them in life is one of the major reasons for the physical distance. As one Vincentian immigrant woman commented about her children left in the home society: "I am raising them. I am giving them more nutritious things to eat."

There are also other economic circumstances that make fostering an attractive choice for these female immigrants. According to recent analyses, these women enter the labor force through jobs traditionally reserved for non-White females—as domestics, operatives, and service workers (Mortimer and Bryce-Laporte, 1981). They work long and often irregular hours which leaves them little time for personal and family interaction. In addition, the restrictions of the immigration quotas force many women to circumvent legal entry into the host country. Thus, women immigrants often cited migrant status and job related insecurities, the expense of childcare and the lack of immediate adequate housing as reasons for leaving their children at home. Obviously, in the earlier part of the migration experience all these economically-oriented problems are of major concern. But the answer to these problems is a cultural one based on long-standing traditions.

The children left back at home, often with expectations of migrating at a later time, form an important part of the daily life of the community in the home island. They are economic and emotional assets, performing many tasks for their older relatives (Durant-Gonzalez, 1976; Philpott, 1973; M.G. Smith, 1962). One elderly Vincentian woman explained about her 19-year-old grandson:

> I care for him since he was a child and it worked out all right. I have no problem and he my all. I can send him anywhere and he go without fuss.

The statement is revealing of one possible outcome of the fostering process. An older woman may ask to "keep" a child when the mother or caretaker migrates, especially if the child was born in the household and they have developed a close relationship (M.G. Smith, 1962). However, this attachment is not without its problems. First, the older generation of Vincentians interviewed in the island can be heard to complain that today "children are raising themselves" as a result of changing social circumstances detrimental to the survival of traditional values. Second, sometimes the child gets attached to the family minding her/him and as one Vincentian foster parent explained, "when it get time for him to leave he don't want to."

The first problem is a generational one in societies undergoing rapid changes—economically, socially, and culturally. The second is more difficult to confront, but it seems that while foster parents are aware of the emotional wear and tear of this shift, they also know that there is a time for the child to stay and a time to go. The separation is viewed as a natural consequence of maturation. This process could be made more disruptive if the biological parent(s) do not attend to their duty in maintaining financial and emotional links with their society of origin. One foster mother commented: " If they not careful to keep in touch, the children won't recognize them." This statement suggests that links may be broken by immigrants. When this happens, community disapproval falls on the parent.

From the perspective of the parents in the host society, the time elapsed before sending for their children is related to their wanting the children to be able to take full advantage of both home and host society resources. This desire translates into the children spending their early childhood in the Caribbean, where it is generally agreed that the environment is safer and healthier because there are "more people to care for them." It is also where the children can learn to live by West Indian values, described as "learning to live a community life," "to respect elders," and to "cooperate with others" (see, Justus, 1976; Laguerre, 1984). Once in the host society, the child is expected to take full advantage of the educational and economic opportunities available there. The particular age when the child is deemed ready to begin this process seems to be after the children finish at least part of their primary education. Recent data on West Indian immigrants in New York City bear out this statement (United States Department of Justice, 1971–1981). Infants seem to be rarely introduced into the host situation.

Immigration statistics show that the majority of West Indian children arriving in the United States are in the ten- to nineteen-age range. Also of note is the fact that at a time when New York City's public and private school enrollment has been steadily declining, Black student enrollment in secondary schools, public and private, has increased. This increase can be attributed in part to the presence of children of West Indian immigrants (Tobier, 1982:179, 191, 192). The education and future employment of these children ensure that their parents can potentially realize their expectation of return to the homeland where, older people are "well respected."

Just as the mother-child tie is not severed when mothers leave their children to be fostered in the home island, so the migration of these fostered children does not mean that they will sever ties with those back home. Parents have been known to utilize their links with the home community by sending their children to the Caribbean in times of crisis such as illness, disciplinary problems, and family separation. This also applied to children born in the United States who are expected to learn West Indian values and to participate in kin networks back home when they visit, whether it be a short- or long-term stay (Marshall, 1983).

On the other hand, parents in the host society may make use of localized kin networks there to arrange for childcare. Information on fostering in a situation where both biological and foster parents are in the host society was only, until recently, available for West Africans and West Indians in London (Goody, 1982). More recent studies of Caribbean immigrants in New York City have recorded enough evidence to indicate that parents utilize kin networks, established both at home and in the United States, for help in childcaring activities. One work in progress shows that American-born children of Haitian immigrants participate in extensive social networks, often spending as much time in their kin's home as in their biological parents' home throughout their childhood and on to adulthood, thus developing lasting ties with peer and adults within the immigrant community (Gutwirth, 1985). The fact that this immigrant community includes individuals and families from other West Indian islands may signal the widening of the support network in the host context. Whether or not this is actually the case with English-speaking Caribbean immigrants at this time cannot be ascertained until more information is available.

The strong ties to their home societies developed by those children fostered in island communities does not preclude the possibility that they may, after migration, reject those ties. This is also true for children born or brought up from infancy in the United States. Parents worry that children will "get into bad company" and forget those values that define this international immigrant community. Because of this, they try to travel back to the Caribbean with their children in an attempt to keep these links active. Upward mobility and time could also serve to weaken the cycle of continuity. By the same token, the inherent cyclical nature of Caribbean migration, the relative ease of travel between countries, and the constant influx of new immigrants who renew the cultural dynamism of the already settled immigrant community continue to feed this system of interaction between the two ends of the migration continuum.

An important implication of this process is that English-speaking West Indian immigrants bring to the host society a cultural tradition that protects them from becoming fully incorporated and assimilated into the host society. We have to give due recognition to this cultural process along with the conditions in both the home and host societies that perpetuate the patterns of creative adaptation for which Africans in the diaspora are noted. The adaptive picture that emerges from this migrant experience is a three-person circulation involving parent, fosterer, and child, with its accompanying dense web of relationships. These relationships cross international boundaries in a pattern of constantly recirculating peoples and resources, with the older generations allowing the younger ones to seek new sources of wealth and networks that will eventually be invested in replenishing the system. The relationship of recycling between the youngest and oldest generation is again best described by Paule Marshall as she reminisces about her grand-mother:

> It was as if both us knew, at a level beyond words, that I had come into the world not only to love her and to continue her line but to take her very life in order that I might live (1983:95).

THE CASE OF THE HISPANIC CARIBBEAN

It is of interest to examine whether a comparable cultural pattern of child fostering operates within the context of the circulatory migration cha-racteristic of the Hispanic Caribbean, where there are noted differences in family and gender relationships as compared to the rest of the West Indian regions of the Caribbean.

The practice of child fostering as described above has been reported for the French, Dutch, and Spanish-speaking Caribbean (Hendricks, 1974; Laguerre, 1984; Marks, 1976; Safa, 1974; Slater, 1977). But whereas a similar ideology of cultural continuity through mothering and fostering informs the practice in English-, French-, and Dutch-speaking island societies, it is not clear how aspects of and meanings attributed to fostering practices fit into the distinctly patriarchal orientation of the Hispanic Caribbean family sys-tem. Significantly, no research on this area has focused specifically on child placement among kin and the literature on the subject is relatively scant. What information is available is embedded in the ethnographic accounts of the adaptive strategies of localized and international migrant Hispanic households—particularly those of Puerto Rico and the Dominican Republic.[7] These accounts have emphasized the same saliency of extended family forms that was observed for West Indian societies (*cf.* Garrison and Weiss, this volume; Hendricks, 1974; Padilla, 1958; Pessar, 1982; Safa, 1974). Within this kinship network, consanguineal ties are sometimes considered just as bind-ing as conjugal ties; maternal female lineal kin create long-lasting cooperative ties and the intense mother-child relationship reinforces the dominant role of motherhood within the family.

Ties between consanguineal kin help to sustain childcaring activities and create a general environment within which children become part of this network of cooperating adults. In much the same way as other Caribbean societies, a sense of adult responsibility for the junior generation pervades the community at home and in the United States. Older sisters, aunts,

---

[7] Because of the political and economic circumstances of Cuban immigrants in the United States, the role of the extended family and the fostering of children merits a closer examination and different interpretation than is provided here. This, however, is beyond the scope of this paper.

grandmothers, and godmothers care for children, and older children assume some of the responsibility for junior siblings (Padilla, 1958; Safa, 1974).

Yet, Hispanic women do not gain social power and status equivalent to that of West Indian women through their mothering role. This is not to demean individual female action against what have been called the three *bandidos* of Hispanic culture: the Hispanic male, the Catholic church, and the Spanish heritage (Zentella, 1984:3). But over and above the actions of individual women is a dominant ideology that links motherhood to wifehood, making a woman's relationship to her husband a central part of her self-definition within the family. As Padilla (1958:129) points out, even when a woman can justify her migration to care for her children's children, she can also refuse to do so, citing the ideology that a wife's duty to her husband predominates over other family loyalties. A conjugally-focused family or an extended family that centers around an older conjugal couple remains the cultural models for family organization. And, while single-headed female households appeared in significant numbers in both rural-urban migrant populations in Puerto Rico during the "bootstrap" development period of the island in the 1950s, and in the international Hispanic immigrant population in New York City during the last decade and a half (*see,* Rohter, 1985), the nuclear family still predominates numerically and ideologically above other possible choices of household compositions (Gurak and Kritz, 1982; Safa, 1974:37–41). This is unlike the pattern in West Indian societies where a conjugally based family form is but one out of a possible range of legitimate and acceptable choices (Slater, 1977). In a Hispanic household, a man, when present, is expected to be the focus of authority. More often than not, he realizes this role (Padilla, 1958:134).

The raising of *hijos (as) de crianza* ("children by rearing") and *compadrazgo* (ritual co-parenthood) are two activities in Hispanic cultures where children figure prominently, and they exhibit some similarity to West Indian child fostering. Yet, the term hijo de crianza, meaning a child reared in the household (as opposed to a child born to a parent), has no linguistic equivalent in West Indian societies. In the English-speaking West Indies, children cared for by an adult as well as children born to that adult are collectively called "my pickneys," "my children," or when referring to the co-parent relationship, "our child." While it is reported that the status of children within the Puerto Rican fostering family is equal to that of biological offspring of said family (Padilla, 1958:131), the accompanying set of cooperative exchanges that occur seem to involve a narrower range of participating kin than in comparable West Indian cases.

Placement of Hispanic children with adults of the kin group conforms to dual residence patterns related to the circulatory pattern of Hispanic migration (Padilla, 1958:129). Children may be left in the home society in the care of relatives, they may be sent to the home society after spending some time in New York City, or they may be sent to keep company with relatives in other boroughs of the City. Where long-term delegation of parental duties occurs, it can be considered as an action that weakens kin ties rather than strengthening them as well as a response to crisis situations (Safa, 1974).

A resort to child fostering under the rubric of hijos(as) de crianza is part of changing socioeconomic circumstances that have impelled Hispanic Caribbeans to emigrate and that have increased the incidence of female-headed households in the home and host communities (Rohter, 1985). In a study conducted after the 1980 United States Census (Gurak and Kritz, 1982), a sample showed that as many as 37 percent of Dominican and 43 percent of Puerto Rican immigrant households were female-headed. Of the Dominicans, only 10.7 percent of these households had children present. Aside from the relatively young age of these immigrants, it is safe to assume that some of them left their children behind in care of kin, as studies suggest (see, Garrison and Weiss, this volume). However, even while making use of extended family ties, and sending remittances to those left behind, there is not the same accompanying cultural logic that the care for a child is a main link in the creation and maintenance of exchange relationships between immigrants and nonimmigrants.[8]

Autobiographical accounts of Hispanic children in New York City emphasize the crisis aspect of leaving or sending children back to the home society (Cooper, 1972). Behavior and language problems, economic marginality, as well as the breaking up of the conjugal couple are often cited as reasons for the children's return to the home society. More often than not, the grandmother or a sister accepts the responsibility of childcare and a breakdown of communication between mother and child can ensue. In a nonmigration situation an earlier study of rural Puerto Rican communities points out that child fostering occurs mainly in a situation in which children are seen either as economic burdens or as not vital to household survival (Wolf, 1972 :257).

Compadrazgo relationships also necessitate the participation of children. This relationship entails the establishment of ritual co-parenthood ties that emphasize strong bonds of emotional and financial support among the participants (Hendricks, 1974:31). While originally these ties functioned within the confines of Catholic life cycle and religious rituals; such as baptism and marriage, the pattern of ceremonial kinship has been extended to include support in other areas of the life experience, including experiences related to the migration process. The relationship provides personalized social connections that can cut across class boundaries and can be used to advance the

---

[8] As in earlier studies of West Indian family forms, the emphasis on the crisis aspect of Hispanic fostering may be a result of research bias. In an early study of Puerto Rican immigrants, Padilla (1958) observed that those immigrants raised in the island were more likely to maintain strong ties of cooperation and obligations with kin and friends left back home than their mainland-raised counterparts. Though this was not the focus of her study, I suggest that this observation could be stretched to include children fostered in the island. A closer look into the activities of individuals involved in the fostering process might show that they do indeed provide the necessary links for the cultural continuity of the international migrant community, as I have tried to outline for the West Indian case.

personal aims of the participants involved (Hendricks, 1974; Min and Wolf, 1950). While godparents are expected to sponsor the godchild during life cycle rituals, have input in disciplinary actions and help with the godchild's educational expenses, the most important dyad in this relationship is that of the adults (Padilla, 1958:121). The child serves ritually to consolidate already existing ties. A loving relationship often develops between godparent and godchild, and the former is under obligation to see to the care of the child should an extreme crisis such as death occur to the parents. But in its most frequent form compadrazgo does not imply the same dimensions of parental care that are involved in West Indian child fostering. When a godchild becomes an hijo de crianza, it is usually a sister or other maternal relative who acts a co-parent, the godparent tie serving to further strengthen already existing kinship ties (ibid., 1958). On an intergenerational level, the concern on the part of the godparent is reciprocated with respect and obedience on the part of the godchild. But again, there is no evidence that the child is expected to contribute eventually to the support of the godparent in later years.

Compadrazgo also operates within the immigrant community in the United States. In this case, compadres and personas de confianza serve as culture brokers for the recently arrived (Hendricks, 1974; Padilla, 1958), and as links between the home and host societies. Yet this seems to be a supplementary rather than an integral part of the process of maintaining kin ties, and childcare roles do not figure prominently.

The differences noted suggest that the meanings attached to the concept of motherhood for the Caribbean Hispanic woman do not carry with them the potential for the extension of her power within the household into the community at large that they do for the West Indian woman. This does not mean that the Hispanic immigrants in the United States are not actively engaged in maintaining links between home and host societies that ensure their cultural continuity as a community. Women and children may, in fact, play a greater role in this process than has been noted. But whether they do or not, historically the cultural ideology of the Hispanic Caribbean societies has not invested them with the same import for the continuity and social reproduction of their cultural communities that women and children carry in the West Indian tradition. Nor does the Hispanic tradition, as expressed in fictional, testimonial, and ethnographic forms, contain an interweaving of notions of motherhood with personal power and relative autonomy.

While in this chapter I have tried to show how child fostering in West Indian societies operates to maintain links between dispersed members of the international migrant community, I have also suggested ways in which the pattern is both similar and different among Hispanic Caribbean populations. Forms of childcare in this latter area may exhibit striking similarities to West Indian forms, but the meanings attributed to fostering of Hispanic children have to be looked at in a different light, taking into careful consideration the relative position and status of women and children in these cultures. What remains true for both is that their patterns of child fostering as they operate in the international migration system contribute to maintaining a historical and cultural continuity between the two ends of this social system. Further research is needed to examine what role the care of children in immigrant Hispanic Caribbean communities plays in sustaining the distinctive cultural traditions with which they are concerned.

BIBLIOGRAPHY

Blake, J.
1961 Family Structure in Jamaica. New York: Free Press.

Clarke, E.
1966 My Mother who Fathered Me. London: George Allen and Unwin.

Cooper, P.
1972 Growing Up Puerto Rican. New York: Signet.

Covert, M.B. and B. Cook
n.d. "Patterns of Child Fosterage in a Caribbean Village." Unpublished manuscript.

Durant-Gonzalez, V.
1982 "The Realm of Female Familial Responsibility." In Women and the Family. J. Massiah, ed. Cave Hill, Barbados: Institute of Social and Economic Research, University of the West Indies. Pp.1–27.

1976 "Role and Status of Rural Jamaican Women: Higglering and Mothering." Ph. D. dissertation, University of California, Berkeley.

Etienne, M.
1979 "The Case for Social Maternity: Adoption of Children by Urban Baule Women," Dialectical Anthropology, 4(3):237–242. Oct.

Goody, E.
1982 Parenthood and Social Reproduction: Fostering and Occupational Roles in West Africa. Cambridge University Press.

Goosen, J.
1972 "Child Sharing and Fostering in the French West Indies." Expansion on paper presented at the 1971 Meetings of the American Anthropological Association.

Gurak, D.T. and M.M. Kritz
1982 "Dominican and Colombian Women in New York City," Migration Today, 10(3–4):14–21.

Gutwirth, L.W.
1985 "Ti Moune': Domestic and Kinship Networks of Some American-born Children of Haitian Immigrants." Unpublished manuscript.

Hendricks, G.
1974 The Dominican Diasporo. New York Teachers College Press, Columbia University.

Herskovits, M.
1958 The Myth of the Negro Past. Boston: Beacon Press.

Justus, J.B.
1976 "West Indians in Los Angeles: Community and Identity." In Caribbean Immigration to the

United States. R.S. Bryce-Laporte and D.M. Mortimer, eds. Washington, D.C.: Smithsonian Institution, Research Institute on Immigration and Ethnic Studies, Occasional Papers No. 1. Pp. 130–148.

Kerns, V.
1983   Women and the Ancestors: Black Carib Kinship and Ritual. Urbana: University of Illinois Press.

Laguerre, M.S.
1984   American Odyssey: Haitians in New York City. Ithaca: Cornell University Press.

Lowenthal, D.L.
1972   West Indian Societies. London: Oxford University Press.

Marks, A.F.
1976   Male and Female in a Caribbean Household. The Hague: Martinus Nyhoff.

Marshall, P.
1983   Reena and Other Stories. New York: The Feminist Press.

Midgett, D.
1969   "Transaction in Parenthood: A West Indian Case." Paper presented at the Meetings of the American Anthropological Association.

Mintz, S.W. and R. Price
1976   An Anthropological Approach to the Afro-Caribbean Past: A Caribbean Perspective. Philadelphia: ISHI Publications.

Mintz, S.W. and E.R. Wolf
1950   "An Analysis of Ritual Co-Parenthood (Compadrazgo)," Southwestern Journal of Anthropology, 6(4):341–368. Winter.

Mortimer, D.M. and R.S. Bryce-Laporte, (eds.)
1981   Female Immigrants into the United States: Caribbean, Latin American, and African Experiences. Washington, D.C.: Smithsonian Institution, Research Institute on Immigration and Ethnic Studies, Occasional Papers No. 2.

Otterbein, K.F.
1966   The Andros Islanders: A Study of Family Organization in the Bahamas. Lawrence: University of Kansas Press.

Padilla, E.
1958   Up from Puerto Rico. New York: Columbia University Press.

Pessar, P.R.
1982   Kinship Relations of Production in the Migration Process: The Case of Dominican Emigration to the United States. New York: Center for Latin American and Caribbean Studies, New York University Research Program in Inter-American Affairs. Occasional Paper No. 32.

Philpott, S.B.
1973   West Indian Migration: The Monserrat Case. New York: Humanities Press, Inc.

——————
1968   "Remittance Obligations: Social Networks and Choice among Monserratian Migrants in Britain." Man 3(3):465–476. Sept.

Rohter, L.
1985   "Hispanics in State in Worst Poverty: Two Studies Find No Residents in New York Poorer." New York Times, August 16.

Safa, H.I.
1974   The Urban Poor in Puerto Rico: A Study in Development and Inequality. New York: Rinehart and Winston, Inc.

Sanford, M.
1971   "Disruption of the Mother and Child Relationship in Conjunction with Matrifocality: A

Study of Childkeeping among the Carib and Creole of British Honduras." Ph. D. dissertation, Catholic University of America.

Slater, M.
1977 *The Family in the Caribbean: Legitimacy in Martinique.* New York: St. Martin's Press.

Smith, M.G.
1962 *Kinship and Community in Carriacou.* New Haven: Yale University Press.

Smith, R.T.
1956 *The Negro Family in British Guiana: Family Structure and Social Status in the Villages.* New York: Grove Press.

Stack, C.
1974 *All Our Kin: Strategies for Survival in a Black Community.* New York: Harper and Row.

Sutton, C.R. and M. Hammer
1985 "The Social World of the Yoruba Child." Unpublished manuscript.

Sutton, C.R. and S.R. Makiesky-Barrow
1977 "Social Inequality and Sexual Status in Barbados." In *Sexual Stratification: A Cross-Cultural View.* A. Schlegel, ed. New York: Columbia University Press. Pp. 292–325.

Tobier, E.
1982 "Foreign Immigration." In *Setting Municipal Priorities.* C. Brecher and R.D. Horton, eds. New York: New York University Press. Pp. 154–201 .

United States Department of Justice
1971– *Immigration and Naturalization Service Reports.* Washington, D.C.: INS.
1981

Weiner, A.
1980 "Reproduction: A Replacement for Reciprocity," *American Ethnologist,* 7(1):71–85.

Wolf, K.
1972 "Growing Up and Its Price in Three Puerto Rican Subcultures." In *Portrait of a Society.* E. Fernández Méndez, ed. Barcelona: M. Paria. Pp. 233–277.

Zentella, A.C.
1985 "Rethinking Our Lives: The Contribution of Feminist Scholarship to Hispanic Women." Unpublished manuscript.

GARIFUNA SETTLEMENT IN NEW YORK:
A New Frontier

NANCIE L. GONZÁLEZ
University of Maryland

Among the many other Latin and West Indian migrant groups living in New York City is a little-known group called Garifuna (Black Caribs). The Garifuna form small community clusters in the Bronx, Spanish Harlem, and Brooklyn, with scattered families in New Jersey, White Plains and elsewhere. Although generally indistinguishable from other Afro-Americans, they are unusual in that they speak a South American Indian language and share about one quarter of their genetic make-up with native Americans (Crawford, 1977). Despite the fact that Garifuna men have visited United States ports for three generations as sailors on Caribbean freighters, their residence in this country has only become common within the past decade.

Like the inhabitants of almost all small Caribbean islands, Garifuna men have been forced for more than 100 years to travel to find wage-paying jobs. Although in earlier times this labor was only intermittent, gradually it became the primary mode of existence for the majority of the male population during earlier adulthood. It is the argument of this chapter that migration is now essential to the maintenance of the Garifuna sociocultural system, and that the United States industrial economy provides a new labor market of enormous potential for these people. Population pressures at home, as well as throughout the Caribbean generally, have forced them to look for new frontiers, and New York City is seen as such by the Garifuna today. Their migration to this country has, in fact, allowed them to retain their distinctive ways of life at home for longer than might otherwise have been the case.

The Garifuna are basically a West Indian, Caribbean people living today on the fringes of Latin America. Their settlements are located on the Central American coastline from Dangriga (formerly Stann Creek), Belize to Bluefields, Nicaragua. The largest numbers live in Belize and Honduras, although Livingston, Guatemala, is also a major town, containing approximately 2,500 Garifuna. Their total number was estimated by Davidson in 1974 to be between 70,000 and 80,000, but I would put that at 200,000 today, with as many as 30,000 in the New York City area. I believe that Davidson's estimate was too low, and there is good evidence that their rate of increase has been and remains high.

The Garifuna, a hybrid group whose forebears came from Africa and Amazonia, have no heritage of slavery, although it is increasingly clear that their ancestors included many former and escaped slaves (González, 1984). The earliest Africans in their ancestry managed to escape or were ship-wrecked off the coast of Dominica and/or St. Vincent in the Lesser Antilles, probably during the seventeenth century. They quickly adopted most of the culture of the Carib Indians, themselves fairly recent immigrants from the tropical forests of South America. In time they intermarried with the Carib Indians and by 1797, when they were forcibly removed from St. Vincent by the British, politically and economically they were one people (González, 1984b; Taylor, 1951).

The insular lifestyle of the Garifuna was based on fishing and horticulture, although trade with various European concerns familiarized them with Western goods, languages and cultures at an early date. Their prowess on the seas in their native dugouts was both known and respected. Upon arrival in the Bay Islands off the coast of Honduras, where the British exiled them in 1797, they quickly took to the sea and made their way to the Central American coastline, planting crops and forming settlements up and down its length. Their distinctive culture, marked by a language unknown to any but themselves, facilitated their adaptation to this new environment. Not only were their native crops, especially cassava, easily grown in these parts, but their fishing technology was transferable as well. Furthermore, their penchant for travel, their interest in and familiarity with foreign cultures, and their fearless independence all contributed to what has now become their traditional way of life in Central America.

This lifestyle has served them well, for they have had an almost incredible reproductive success over the past 180 years. This seems to have been largely because of the African component which included the sickle cell genetic adaptation to malaria. This allowed them to prosper in an area where neither Europeans nor American Indians succeeded. It appears, however, that their unique sociocultural patterns, including their migratory patterns, have also been instrumental in furthering their welfare and in increasing their numbers.[1]

In earlier publications (González, 1959, 1969). I have suggested that the family and household patterns had adjusted to a way of life that included various types of migration participated in only by men during earlier times. Women who were left alone for long periods of time formed domestic bonds with other women, primarily their mothers and sisters, or with consanguine-

---

[1] Since this was first written, I have conducted considerable archival research in England, Guatemala, and the United States. It now seems clear to me that the different elements which go to make up this presently unique lifestyle were in large part borrowed from their neighbors after they arrived in Central America and blended with the remnants of the Antillean culture they had been forced to abandon (González, 1984b).

ally related males, especially brothers and sons. This tended to reinforce the solidarity among sibling sets and, in turn, weakened the marital tie. Since men hesitated to return empty handed to their wives, they often stayed away, hoping for better luck in their search for employment in a labor market which discriminated against them. Under such conditions, it is not surprising that women readily took new partners when the opportunity arose—especially if the new man had a steady income. Between partners, they depended on their brothers, uncles, or sons for those services they could not handle on their own.[2] This system allowed the group as a whole to maintain itself, both in terms of economics and in terms of ethnicity. Children were procreated, raised, disciplined, and taught to survive as had their parents. Thus, the system became "traditional," and most young men expected to spend at least part of their adult years away from their home village. Women, likewise, learned to live in a world in which men made better brothers and lovers than husbands, and were appreciated as such.

In 1956–57, I conducted a complete household survey of all Garifuna in Livingston. At that time a total of 231 out of 1,762 persons were listed as being temporarily "absent" from town. One hundred forty-two of these were males and 89 were females. Of the men, 114 were working or seeking work mostly in Belize (then British Honduras), the nearby port of Barrios (Guatemala), or elsewhere in Central America. Only two were reported to be in the United States. Many additional men commuted daily or weekly from Puerto Barrios and were not included as being "absent" in this survey.

Of the "absent" women, only twelve were working for wages, most of these as servants in Guatemala City. The others were visiting relatives and /or engaging in petty trade between Belize and Guatemala, the profits from the latter usually being minimal and barely enough to cover the cost of their trips.

About 30 absentees were children or youths boarding with relatives or living as servants with non-Garifuna families to go to school, either in the city of Puerto Barrios or in Belize (more commonly known as British Honduras, or "the colony"). Livingston schools went only through 6th grade, and Belizean schools have long had a reputation in the area for discipline and good educational results. The most important reason, however, for sending children to Belize was to give them the opportunity to learn English, which was considered an asset for coping with the outside world. All Guatemalan Garifuna under 30 at that time spoke Spanish fluently, although women tended to be less bilingual than men—not a surprising finding considering their relative isolation. In addition, many men spoke Kekchi, English, or French. Two or three whom I knew spoke all four of these in addition to their

---

[2] In a previous article (González, 1969) I described men and women's traditional roles. Briefly, however, men built and repaired homes, cleared virgin land for gardens, manufactured baskets, fishnets, wooden utensils and canoes, and fished. Women were responsible for all other household chores and the care of children. They also planted, cultivated, and harvested the crops.

native tongue. Linguistic versatility has been traditionally valued in Garifuna culture and is clearly advantageous in the migratory process.

In 1962, I returned briefly to Livingston to study reproductive behavior, health, and disease, but collected no new data on migration. In a survey of 126 households conducted in 1975, approximately 25 percent of the Garifuna households in Livingston at that time, 166 family members, were listed as "absent" and, of these, 66 were women. Furthermore, 58 of the total number were in the United States, and the greatest numbers of these resided in New York. This represented several new trends (Table 1) including an increase in the scale of migration, a major change in destinations, and a change in the sex ratio of the migrants.

TABLE 1

SEX AND WHEREABOUTS OF ABSENT MEMBERS IN
126 GARIFUNA HOUSEHOLDS, LIVINGSTON, GUATEMALA, 1975

	Guatemala City	Elsewhere in Guatemala	Belize	New York City	Total
Females	6	17	11	32	66
Males	13	46	15	26	100
Total	19	63	26	58	166

The following summer's fieldwork among the Garifuna in Dangriga (Stann Creek) and Punta Gorda, Belize, again revealed a heavy outmigration to the United States, including large numbers to Los Angeles and Chicago, as well as New York. In Belize and Livingston, a large proportion of the migrants were women—clearly a departure from earlier Garifuna migratory patterns.

In 1977 I initiated a study on the recent Garifuna migration.[3] Materials already in hand from 1975 and 1976 consisted of comprehensive data on 300 households in three towns or villages, and in early 1978, Ian González collected additional data on migration from the same Garifuna towns and villages I had first visited in 1956. In late May, 1978, a survey was conducted in New York of the migrant members of all those families surveyed in Central America, eliciting information concerning length of absence, number and frequency of return visits, remittances, expectations concerning future emigration, and the like. In this process many more migrants were found than had originally been reported. Within a short time I had talked with more than 100 Garifuna, many of them individuals whose presence I had not expected. Not only were there members of families who had disclaimed having rela-

[3] I am grateful to the Ford Foundation for a grant which has made possible the present research. I am now only in the midst of the data-gathering stage, so the comments made here are preliminary and the conclusions tentative until a more complete analysis can be accomplished.

tives in New York, but there were many individuals who had arrived be-tween the survey in Central America and the beginning of the New York phase of the study.

The Garifuna in New York number perhaps as many as 30,000, including those born in the United States. They come from all three nations (Belize, Guatemala, and Honduras) and, although they maintain ties and identify with the larger ethnic group, it is clear that they tend to cluster by nation, as well. Yet, ethnicity apparently overrides nationality, since they claim to feel less close to non-Garifuna from the same country than they do to Garifuna from other than their homeland. In spite of the continued use of their primary native tongue (Garifuna, or Island Carib), New York residence introduces new kinds of linguistic complexity. Natives of the English-speaking country of Belize and those educated there have little difficulty adapting to any part of New York or the United States in which they find themselves. On the other hand, Guatemalan and Honduran Garifuna do best when living near other Latin immigrants. Many women, especially, are only barely conversant in English, and many of the children cannot handle Garifuna well, since Span-ish is the primary language of their peers. Thus, Spanish has increasingly become the preferred tongue, although English is picked up quickly in the schools and the next generation of adults will have no difficulty with it.

The Spanish-speaking neighborhoods also offer familiar foodstuffs which ease the culture shock of living in a foreign land. These include items such as cassava, coconuts, plantains, avocados, pineapples, pigs' feet and tail, and even the flat unleavened bread made of bitter cassava they call *areba*. Span-ish-language magazines, newspapers, radio, and television programs are ubiquitous. Belizean Garifuna, since most do not speak Spanish, often feel uncomfortable in these neighborhoods unless accompanied by their fellows. Brooklyn is the home of many of the English-speaking Garifuna, where they associate with West Indians and with Black Americans.

Most of the people in the survey were employed: women as well as men; young and old. Both sexes worked in various capacities in the garment industry. Many of them were in bead and other jewelry import and manu-facturing houses. Some of the women worked as domestics, although this is neither common nor preferred. Men were found in a variety of other occu-pations, especially restaurant and other food-related industries. Some were paid quite well, although most probably barely exceeded the poverty line. Nevertheless, most of the immigrants saved money to send home for the support of relatives and to increase their wealth within the village. Thus, many built houses to which they would retire at some future date. Money was also banked, but rarely, if ever, invested in stocks or real estate. In New York most lived in rented apartments that they shared with not only their immediate family, but sometimes with more distant relatives and friends. Very few, if any, appeared to be "on welfare," by which was generally meant Aid to Families with Dependent Children. There were, however, several instances in which assistance was received from federal and state governments for help with retarded or crippled children.

One of the most interesting deviations from the social patterning found in Central America is the fact that there are more nuclear family cores in the New York households. Furthermore, many of the couples were bound by legal marriage. Several informants commented that they were "forced" to marry by the Immigration Service. Although the people attribute a "moral sense" to the law on this matter, the ruling is intended to control and facilitate immigration by more readily permitting close relatives of legal residents to join them. Spouses, children, and parents of residents are given priority in assignment of visas, a fact which reflects the United States legislative definition of "family," and which does encourage marriage between men and women who otherwise might not contemplate such a move (*see*, Garrison and Weiss, this volume).

The fluidity of the Central American domestic establishment is diminished, although not entirely lost in New York. It could be postulated that the greater living expense in the latter area, plus the urge to save money to send home, tends to make people discourage visiting kinfolk from staying on too long. New York apartments do not seem so "expandable" as houses and yards in the tropics.

Although it is as yet early to draw conclusions, there is evidence to suggest that Garifuna migration to New York is a logical extension of their normal patterns of sociocultural organization. In the past, for reasons that probably can best be explained on ecological grounds, they continually moved out from their villages to found new settlements up and down the Caribbean coastline (Davidson, 1974). By the middle of the nineteenth century and probably much earlier, wage labor by males had become an indispensable supplementary activity to the gardening and fishing engaged in by their ancestors. There is even evidence that some trading had been important to them during their residence on St. Vincent. Gradually, as the process of modernization continued during the early twentieth century, wage labor became the basis of their economy, with horticulture and fishing remaining important ways of maintaining those who remained at home. The latter, of course, were primarily women, children, older persons, and men who were "in between" jobs elsewhere.

Although I have no quantitative data to support my view, it is my suggestion that by 1956, migration was already a necessity. In 1975, when I returned to Livingston for a major restudy, I found that few people any longer engaged in fishing and farming. Not only did the young people disdain the work, they really had little knowledge of how to go about these important activities. For the most part, only a few of the most elderly still planted in the forest. At the same time, my own observations in the areas where Garifuna had been accustomed to making their slash and burn plots indicated that Kekchi Indians had largely occupied the available lands. Data copied from records in Livingston confirm that Indian in-migration has been heavy over the past decade.[4]

Thus, it would appear that the migration to New York has become an essential part of the Garifuna culture without which they could not now survive. Migration confers a number of different benefits. First, it is largely those who are reproductively active who leave, which lowers the birth rate at home. Infant and child mortality are undoubtedly lower in New York than in Central America, which results in an even greater reproductive success than this group has previously known. In addition, the money earned in New York, when redistributed and spent according to Garifuna cultural patterns, allows a better life for both migrants and those left at home. Not only do remittance checks help buy food and necessities in the villages, but large amounts of goods purchased in the United States find their way to Central America. Finally, many of those working in New York manage to save for their future retirements.

It now seems clear that the Garifuna population as a whole is increasing dramatically as a result of the present migratory process. In this sense, New York and other United States cities can be viewed as frontiers that offer both the "living room" and the necessary economic resources. Health and nutrition are improved among both the migrants and those who benefit from their remittances. Furthermore, reproduction seems in no way diminished, and may even be enhanced by the desire to bear children in the United States (see, González, 1984c).

Because of the long history of temporary and recurrent migration (González, 1961) among these people, the process may be less disruptive to the home communities than might otherwise be the case. I also suggest that it might be more fruitful to consider the individual, rather than the household, as the basic unit of the society, thus allowing maximum flexibility for the formation of differing dyadic and multistranded alignments (González, 1984a). There has always been a large number of persons absent from their home villages at any given point in time. The primary difference now is that women, as well as men, have become part of that floating pool (González, 1976c). It can also be argued that female migration is a natural outgrowth of the fact that there are many jobs for women in New York City, and that the Garifuna culture has allowed great freedom for women to travel, although until recently, few did so for the purposes of finding wage labor.

---

[4] Observations in 1984 suggest a new interest in fishing and cultivation among some young Garifuna males who have apparently become disillusioned with "civilization and its discontents." This may be related to an awakening of ethnic pride, which in turn can be seen as evidence of acculturation. The presence in Livingston over the past decade or more of young American and European men and women (locally called "hippies"), who have themselves been searching for a simpler, less technologically-complicated way of life, clearly has had an impact on some of the Garifuna youth. Research now underway should throw more light on what this contact has meant and will mean for the Garifuna of the future.

In terms of the New York experience, my impression is that Garifuna retain their ethnic identity regardless of their association with the West Indian (English) and Caribbean (Spanish) peoples who also colonize that city. At the same time, however, they continue to adopt new behavior patterns and artifacts from those with whom they come in contact, incorporating these into "Garifuna" culture, both in New York and in their home villages. Each time they return to the latter, they introduce new elements, including clothing and bodily adornments, hairstyles, musical forms, instruments, and performance styles, household furnishings, and linguistic innovations, including American slang.

It will be interesting and important to compare the impact migration has had upon the Garifuna, both in New York and at home, with that of migrants from elsewhere. The mosaic of immigrant cultures seems to find encouragement in United States urban settings, but at the same time, continual reinterpretation and modification is inevitable. The *Harvard Encyclopedia of American Ethnic Groups* (Thernstrom, 1980) lists and describes an unbelievably large number of different cultural components now identifiable within U.S. borders. Some have been here for a long time and have only recently begun to take a new interest in their cultural heritage. Others, like the Garifuna, are relative newcomers who are still not completely integrated into their new surroundings, either as individuals or as a group. Much remains to be done before we will understand the nature of immigration and acculturation. It is hoped that volumes such as this will inspire new thinking on these issues.

BIBLIOGRAPHY

Crawford, M.H.
1977 "Genetic Microdifferentiation and Admixture in Garifuna Populations." Paper presented at the Annual Meeting of the American Anthropology Association, Houston.

Davidson, W.
1974 "The Carib (Garifuna) of Central America: A Map of Their Realm and a Bibliography of Research," *National Studies*, 2(6):43–51.

González, N.L.
1986 "Giving Birth in America: The Immigrant's Dilemma." In *International Immigration: The Female Experience*. Rita J. Simon and Carolina B. Brettell, eds. Totowa, N.J.: Rowman and Allenheld. Pp. 241–253.

———
1984a "Rethinking the Consanguineal Household and Matrifocality," *Ethnology*, 23(1):1–12. Jan.

———
1984b "New Evidence on the Origin of the Black Carib," *New West Indian Guide*, 58(1):143-172.

———
1976a "Multiple Migratory Experiences of Dominican Women," *Anthropological Quarterly*, 49(1):36–44. Jan.

1976b "Types of Migratory Patterns to a Small Dominican City and to New York." In *Migration and Urbanization: Models and Adaptive Strategies*. B.M. du Toit and H.I. Safa, eds. The Hague: Mouton Publishers. Pp. 209–23.

1976c "Changes in Black Carib Sex Role Patterning." Paper presented at the Annual Meeting of the American Anthropological Association, Washington, D.C.

1970 "Peasants' Progress: Dominicans in New York," *Caribbean Studies*, 10(3):154–171. Oct.

1969 *Black Carib Household Structure: A Study of Migration and Modernization.* Seattle: University of Washington Press.

1961 "Family Organization in Five Types of Migratory Wage Labor," *American Anthropologist*, 63(6):1264–80. Dec.

1959 The Nonunilineal Descent Group in the Caribbean and Central America," *American Anthropologist*, 61(4):578–83.

Hendricks, G.L.
1974 *The Dominican Diaspora: From the Dominican Republic to New York City—Villagers in Transition.* New York: Columbia University Teachers' College Press.

Taylor, D.M.
1951 *The Black Carib of British Honduras.* New York: Viking Fund Publication No. 17.

Thernstrom, S., ed.
1980 *Harvard Encyclopedia of American Ethnic Groups.* Cambridge, Mass.: Harvard University Press.

THE POLITICS OF CARIBBEANIZATION:
Vicentians and Grenadians in New York[1]

LINDA G. BASCH

United Nations Institute for Training and Research

This chapter focuses on the political activities of two groups of West Indian[2] immigrants in New York, Vincentians and Grenadians, from the small eastern Caribbean agricultural islands of St. Vincent[3] and Grenada, each with a population of approximately 100,000. Of particular concern are the ways certain political and economic features of New York interact with the cultural traditions and experiences that these immigrants bring with them to shape their political responses in New York.

At first glance it would appear that Vincentians and Grenadians, and most West Indians for that matter, are inactive politically in the contemporary urban environment, particularly in contrast to their earlier activism in Black

---

[1] This chapter is based on data deriving from a larger comparative project on "Caribbean International and Regional Migration: Implications for Development," which focused on the adaptive strategies developed by Vincentian and Grenadian immigrants in New York and Trinidad and the nature of their ties with their home societies. This project was funded in various parts by the International Development Research Center of Ottawa, Canada, the United States Agency for International Development and the United Nations Fund for Population Activities. Material support was also provided by the United Nations Institute for Training and Research and the Institute of International Relations at the University of the West Indies in Trinidad and Tobago. The larger comparative project was undertaken in collaboration with Dr. Rosina Wiltshire-Brodber of the Institute of International Relations, St. Augustine, Trinidad, and with Joyce Toney of St. Vincent and Winston Wiltshire of Trinidad, whose myriad inputs to the ideas expressed in this paper are gratefully acknowledged. I also thank Colin Robinson, Isa Soto, and Margaret Souza, research assistants in New York, for their insights and observations. Finally, I express my appreciation to Constance Sutton for her many comments and suggestions, and to the many Vincentian and Grenadian immigrants interviewed in New York who generously provided their reflections on their own experiences.

[2] The term West Indian is used in this chapter to describe those people, characteristics, or societies deriving from the former British Caribbean territories. The term Caribbean refers to all islands lying in the Caribbean Sea between North and South America as well as to particular countries along the northern rim of South America: namely, Guyana, Surinam, and French Guyana.

[3] St. Vincent also includes the Grenadines, a series of small islands under the suzerainty of St. Vincent.

American political causes spanning the 1930s to the mid-1960s. A close analysis of the data, however, reveals that the issue is not so much an absence of West Indians' political activity as a shift in the form of their political involvements resulting from a complex of changes underway since the mid-1960s in both New York and their home countries. A prominent feature of the current West Indian political behavior is an increasing emphasis on Caribbean ethnic identity.

Recent official counts identify some 2,700 Vincentians and 5,000 Grenadians living in New York City (U.S. Department of Commerce, 1980), although inclusion of the undocumented would probably extend the combined number to over 15,000.[4] Their absolute numbers are small relative to immigrants from the larger, more economically developed west Indian countries of Jamaica,[5] Trinidad, and Barbados—for example, together they constitute only .05 percent of the West Indian totality of more than a quarter million—which makes them less secure than the others in the alienating world of New York. Nonetheless, they are a continuing component of the contemporary West Indian migration to New York and call on adaptive characteristics similar to those of the larger groups. As other West Indian immigrants in New York whose numbers markedly increased after the liberalized 1965 Immigration Act went into effect, Vincentians and Grenadians represent a relatively new presence.

Some analysts have viewed the seeming lack of current West Indian and wider Caribbean involvement in New York City's political system as a result of these groups' continuing strong bonds to their home societies, which makes political participation in New York relatively meaningless (see, Georges, 1984:33; Hendricks, 1974; Papademetriou, 1983). In this chapter, I argue that West Indians do participate in New York political life, but in ways that are shaped by the racially divisive dominant institutions of U.S. society as much as by the ties they maintain to their home countries.

In point of fact, as has often been noted, West Indians have made a substantial impact on the political landscape of New York over the past several decades. Manhattan's first Black borough president was a West Indian, as have been many of the City's Black judges, civil servants, and high-ranking Black police officers. However, through being merged with and identified as Black Americans, these West Indians were rendered politi-

---

[4] The counting of immigrants is imprecise, and numbers vary. Statistics accumulated by the Population Reference Bureau (PRB) in Washington, D.C. suggest that a larger number of Vincentians and Grenadians are settled in New York. According to the PRB, between 1960 and 1980, 10,391 Grenadians entered the United States legally (Bouvier, 1984b:7), and 6,041 Vincentians were admitted between 1960 and 1979 (Bouvier, 1984a:6). Since New York is the center toward which Vincentians and Grenadians gravitate, it is likely that more are settled in New York than the U.S. Census indicates.

[5] Contrast the combined figures for Vincentians and Grenadians with numbers of Jamaican immigrants: according to INS figures, some 180,884 Jamaicans entered the United States between 1967 and 1979.

cally invisible as representatives of a distinct immigrant ethnic group.[6] As Kessner and Caroli (1981:186) point out, in a country in which one race predominates, the distinctive subtleties of its minority segments, although carefully registered within the group itself, are not distinguished by the majority.

It is against this background that West Indian political life in New York has emerged as a complex and fluid phenomenon. Its contemporary form can be best understood by examining the interaction of three changing sets of relationships: 1) the linkages West Indians maintain with their home societies; 2) their relations to the wider West Indian community in New York, an aggregation that encompasses both "small" and "large" islanders; and 3) their relationship to Black Americans, the group to which they are most closely linked by outsiders.

This chapter argues that West Indians are in the process of changing the shape and form of their political behavior. Central to this redefinition is a heightened sense of their own ethnic identity, manifest in what may be termed a Caribbeanization of their social, cultural and political lives. This increasing sense of "West Indianness" is reinforced by the close linkages immigrants maintain with political life in their home societies, most of which have become politically independent relatively recently. Thus, the emerging emphasis on West Indian ethnicity is related to West Indians becoming more directly involved in both the political life of their home countries and the U.S.—with the involvements at the two ends representing not opposing poles, as has been suggested in the literature, but rather a single field of action comprised of a diverse but yet unitary set of interests for the immigrants. Support for these statements comes from research undertaken between 1982 and 1984 that in part addressed how the adaptation of Vincentians and Grenadians to New York City was affected by the links these two groups of immigrants maintain with their home societies.

Relatively speaking, Vincentians and Grenadians, as other West Indians in New York, are able to "make good" materially (see, Foner, 1983; Georges, 1984; Marshall, 1981). They have to work hard, however, and their success is frequently contingent upon the participation of at least two household members in the labor force. Roughly one half of the 131 employed individuals in our sample earn annual incomes somewhere between $11,000 and $30,000; of these, almost two-thirds earn between $11,000 and $20,000 and slightly more than one-third draw between $21,000 and $30,000. Another 15 percent earn between $30,000 and $50,000, while less than one-third bring home incomes smaller than $10,000 in a given year. Many of the 78 households studied have multiple income earners: three-quarters report more than one employed member, and at least one-third have between three and four workers. In terms of occupational success, more than one-half our sample fill

---

[6] See, Bryce-Laporte (1972) for a more extended discussion of the ramifications of West Indian invisibility.

white-collar, managerial and professional positions. While the majority in our sample experience downward or lateral mobility on their first jobs in New York, as do other West Indian and Caribbean immigrants, data on individual occupational and financial histories indicate that many enjoy significant upward mobility thereafter.

Most of the Vincentian and Grenadian immigrants studied fill service-type occupational roles, conforming to the pattern of immigrants providing labor for the specialized service sectors in the city (Sassen-Koob, 1981:31). They are involved in health care, banking, computers, insurance, accounting security, and the hotel industry. Some of the women—especially those who are undocumented—do paid domestic work. In addition, as other West Indians, they increasingly perform service functions for their own communities as entrepreneurs operating travel agencies, shipping companies, record and beauty shops, restaurants, and in professional capacities as lawyers, doctors, dentists, and accountants (Basch, 1985).

Many of the more recent Vincentian and Grenadian immigrants enter New York with social and economic resources that facilitate their success. Most received financial help with their migration; several had relatives in New York who supplied direct assistance upon arrival; and many possessed skill levels—82 percent had some secondary school education—that aided their absorption into the New York economy. For the majority, the basic skills and education they brought were just a starting point. Most entered training and education programs in New York, earning high school diplomas and university degrees. Over 60 percent of the sample acquired post-secondary school education, with 27 percent achieving university and post-graduate degrees.[7]

POLITICAL TIES TO HOME

A striking feature of Grenadian and Vincentian political behavior in New York is the ties these immigrants maintain with home. Among our sample, one-third actively support a political party at home and one-half report having frequent discussions about home politics with other Vincentians and Grenadians in New York—a practice easily observable at any social or organizational gathering. Some 14 percent of the sample send money to home-based political parties.

These political ties are reinforced by the close connections immigrants retain with relatives and friends in the Caribbean through telephone calls, letters, and visits, the latter made possible by the many excursion flights sponsored by Vincentian and Grenadian voluntary associations at both Christmas and Carnival. It is noteworthy that 70 percent of our sample with legal residence in New York have visited home at least once within the past five years.

[7] These figures are significant, considering that less than 20 percent possessed GCE "O" levels (roughly the equivalent of a U.S. high school diploma) at the time of migration.

The close connection with home-based politics is actively nurtured by politicians from St. Vincent and Grenada. Last year, ten government ministers from St. Vincent visited New York and met with immigrants in large auditoriums in Brooklyn, at the consulate, and privately. During the government of Maurice Bishop in Grenada, between twelve and fifteen government representatives visited Brooklyn in a given year. In fact, Maurice Bishop is known to have said that one of Grenada's largest constituencies is in Brooklyn. These meetings, which had been taking place before independence in both countries, have increased as immigrant communities have grown in size, home governments have become more firmly rooted, and their officials have had more reason to visit Washington and the United Nations.

The visits serve to tie political leaders and migrants together in an ongoing symbiotic relationship. Immigrants are made aware of development plans and problems at home and are urged to participate actively in the economic and political life of their home island. They respond by contributing to philanthropic projects at home: they send requested equipment and supplies to churches, hospitals, and schools, and donate considerable sums through their voluntary organizations in New York to disaster relief projects, the building of secondary schools, establishing scholarships, etc. Immigrants are also an important resource for their islands' industrial development through their investments in government bonds and local enterprises such as milk factories, sugar factories, textile firms, cable TV, and an airport.

Island politicians perceive immigrants as playing an important role in home electoral processes and carry their campaigns into the halls of Brooklyn, where their political authority is also validated. In the 1984 Grenada elections, for example, four candidates visited Brooklyn more than once during the campaign, and shortly after the election the prime minister and two cabinet ministers were again in Brooklyn to explain their projected plans and policies. Although immigrants in New York cannot vote in elections at home because of a one year's residence requirement, they can have an impact on these events through advising uncommitted relatives who to vote for and by making contributions to political campaigns. Participants at the recent political meetings in New York contributed between $500 to $600 with one fund-raising function yielding $1,500. During the recent elections in both St. Vincent and Grenada, some immigrants went home to campaign for favored candidates.

Given the level of material affluence immigrants achieve in New York, why do they continue to invest their energies in politics at home rather than devoting themselves to political activities in New York City where they could protect and even further their economic interests? One reason for their continued involvement in island politics is that it is a political arena where they can be more influential. In fact, they can often wield more power than islanders who, if they espoused the views put forth by immigrants, would likely be regarded as local agitators rather than successful native sons and daughters. This is because both immigrants and islanders believe that experiences abroad provide a special vantage point from which to reevaluate politics and reformulate political standards. Underpinning this perspective is the managerial and political experience many immigrants gain in their jobs and in their leadership positions in migrant organizations, as well as their exposure to new ideas and behaviors. Thus many of these immigrants also feel that they have something special to contribute to political and economic processes at home.

The urge to return home to improve one's society and bring a new political orientation has been a recurrent theme in the Caribbean diaspora, and there are many examples of migrants who have imported change-inducing ideologies to their home societies and replenished the leadership base. Riding on the crest of discontent generated in the 1930s and 1940s, Joshua, the labor leader and later prime minister of St. Vincent, brought back populist ideas from the oil fields in Trinidad to St. Vincent. So, too, did Gairy, the labor leader and first prime minister of Grenada, bring back ideas from Aruba and the United States. Similarly, Blaize, the current prime minister of Grenada, gained managerial experience in Aruba. Migrants living abroad streamed home in the dozens to give shape to Maurice Bishop's Peoples' Revolutionary Government in Grenada, and both Vincentians and Grenadians living in the United States were candidates in the 1984 elections in their respective countries.

The strong political ties forged with home and sustained through reciprocal exchanges between home politicians and immigrant leaders also have symbolic meaning for immigrants. Not only do these ties legitimate the existence of these immigrant communities as valid and important constituencies of the home society, but the soliciting of their views in dialogues with home-based political leaders imbue immigrants with a sense of importance and distinctiveness. In the racially conscious context of U.S. society where West Indians often feel demeaned both as Blacks and as immigrants, involvement in island politics provides immigrants with an alternate arena of prestige.

WEST INDIAN RELATIONS IN NEW YORK[8]

Despite the home focus, Vincentians and Grenadians, as other West Indians, are beginning to participate in the New York urban environment both as home owners and citizens, although they have not yet made their presence felt in the form of an organized pan-West Indian political group. While some

[8] Vincentians and Grenadians, as most West Indians, identify in terms of their specific islands and the larger West Indian region, which is a recognized shared context for most immigrants. The identity activated at a particular moment is in many instances situation-specific. In this and the following sections I adopt the approach of generalizing to speak of West Indians rather than Vincentians and Grenadians where both the situation and the immigrants themselves emphasize this wider identity.

believe that the continual activation of insular interests hampers the formation of such a grouping, there are other constraining factors as well that have
to do largely with the history of the islands. The Caribbean version of
colonialism involved each island in maintaining vertical ties to metropolitan
countries and competitive ones within the region. These metropolitan links
created an ideology in which the values and behavior of the metropoles were
regarded by islanders as superior and more worthy of respect and emulation
than those of local Caribbean societies. Thus, there has been little incentive
to form cross-island, horizontal ties within the West Indian region where
island life is similar but relationships between the islands are competitive.

This has remained true even though workers did migrate to other Caribbean areas, notably Trinidad, Barbados, Guyana, Panama, and Cosa Rica,
where they established social ties and even family relations. These bonds,
however, remained informal. Moreover, the subordinate status of immigrants from the more impoverished small islands created a distancing and
suspicion between themselves and the West Indians native to the larger
islands. These features are also discernible in the migrant situation that West
Indians face in New York. In most instances, Vincentian and Grenadian
immigrants prefer to socialize among themselves and belong to island-spe-
cific voluntary associations. A Grenadian immigrant activist sums up the
situation with the comment:

> You see how divided we are! We are a mirror image of our
> brethren at home. We are a divided and tormented people.[9]

Immigrants who have been in New York some time and who have distinguished themselves either occupationally or through organizations do attend parties and social events given by persons from other islands, particularly if they work together or are neighbors. As one Vincentian commented,
"West Indians first meet each other in New York, London, Toronto, Panama,
Trinidad, and Jamaica." Moreover, despite their insular histories and ideologies, West Indian immigrants in New York share both a common structural
position and a set of experiences. They generally fill the same economic
niches, live in the same neighborhoods, shop in the same stores, and send
their children to the same schools. They also share a body of cultural understandings arising from the common aspects of their histories.

In addition to the informal social mixing which has begun to take place,
West Indians have succeeded in carrying out joint activities in the explicitly
cultural realm. All West Indians can enjoy a good Sparrow or pan performance and an "ecumenical cultural celebration" at St. Patrick's Cathedral
honoring the West Indian religiocultural experience. These events, like the
West Indian Carnival in Brooklyn, nurture a developing West Indian con-

---

[9] All quotations are taken from interviews of the Caribbean International and Regional Migration project unless otherwise noted.

sciousness (*see*, Kasinitz and Freidenberg-Herbstein, this volume), and can serve as a precursor to larger organizational forms. They have not yet been translated into unified political demands on the system.

There are other attempts to merge the interests of the separate island communities. One such effort is the newly created Caribbean Research Center at Medgar Evers College in Brooklyn which caters primarily to West Indian students. It aims to develop research on the West Indian immigrant experience and "problems and issues facing the Caribbean-American community" (*Carib News*, 1985:7). On the board of directors are prominent academicians and community leaders from a wide spectrum of Caribbean islands.

The other effort is the Caribbean Action Lobby (CAL), a pan-West Indian political organization formed four years ago and dedicated to the "economic, social, and cultural development of the Caribbean and its people both at home and in the U.S." (Caribbean Action Lobby: New York Regional Chapter, n.d.). Its goals are both organizational and legislative. It aims to articulate Caribbean aspirations—whether they are in the United States or the Caribbean—to the centers of American political power. This organization has conducted citizenship information drives as a first step to the "political empowerment of the Caribbean immigrant group." It also has created an institute to further Caribbean interests with the U.S. government and to foster trade from the Caribbean to the United States.

CAL is led by Mervyn Dymally, a Trinidad-born U.S. Congressman from California and by professionals from the wider Caribbean community in New York City. While the leaders have generated a number of policy statements and proposals, at the moment their community support is small. One immigrant observed that this association's seminars and dances attract under 100 people, while the events held by the more "traditional" island-based benevolent societies attract up to 1,000.

One problem confronting the leaders of CAL is identifying and meeting the concerns of the constituency they seek to represent. At times the leadership has adopted positions that diverge from those of most immigrants. For example, the head of the organization, perhaps in consideration of the political sensitivities of his largely Mexican American constituency, did not support the Simpson-Mazzoli Bill, which most West Indians saw as providing amnesty to undocumented West Indians in Brooklyn. Similarly, the leadership was vocal in its opposition to the American invasion of Grenada, about which the majority of immigrants was ambivalent. At a rally, CAL sponsored for the Afro-American presidential candidate Jesse Jackson where the importance of voter registration was emphasized, the issue was somewhat lost on West Indians, most of whom are not citizens and cannot vote in U.S. elections.

Perhaps more to the point is the fact that many Vincentians and Grenadians perceive CAL leaders as acting in their own self-interest; they say that they do not trust this organization. This is a familiar theme in

Caribbean political behavior. It is a perception of leaders nurtured by a colonial system that co-opted the local leadership away from its mass base. To West Indians, leaders are often seen as representing the interests of the colonial powerholder and not the masses (*see also*, Basch, 1978; Carmody, 1978; Jayawardena, 1963; Makiesky-Barrow, 1976; Sutton, 1969; Wilson, 1973). These views, which have become part of their political folklore, result in a leadership situation underscored by suspicion. As one Grenadian community leader put it: "Among West Indians, a king has no honor in his own country."

Despite the class and insular-based divisions, the political situation in the Vincentian and Grenadian—and other West Indian—immigrant communities is fluid. Although insular identifications continue to dominate a sense of belonging to a larger West Indian community, a proliferation of cross-island groups in the cultural realm and on the elite level is beginning to provide a basis for a pan-West Indian unity and joint political thrusts.

WEST INDIAN/AFRO-AMERICAN RELATIONS

Vincentians and Grenadians, as part of the wider West Indian population entering New York, found their gatekeepers to the wider system to be a similar racial group already in place. Because of their shared racial characteristics and African cultural heritage, West Indians were assigned by the dominant groups—i.e., Whites—to the same sociopolitical space as Black Americans. This meant that West Indian relations to the wider society were largely mediated by Black American institutions, a situation destined to produce ambivalent feelings between the two groups.

Despite the cultural affinity born of common African traditions and similar plantation-slave experiences, there are differences in the two groups' orientations and experiences. For example, Glantz (1978) in his study of several hundred Brooklyn College students in the early 1970s found notable differences between West Indians and Black Americans concerning their expectations and values. West Indians, more than almost any other group, expressed a high value for hard work, education, and nonviolence, as well as trust in the local authority structure.

These differences are largely grounded in the groups' different historical experiences. As Cruse (1985:425) points out:

> . . . because of the contrasts in the cultural and political developments in black America and the black West Indies, there is a clash of cultural backgrounds.

The comment of a Vincentian immigrant expresses a similar viewpoint:

We get along better with people. We're not as sensitive to Black/White relations. From our upbringing, we have a pride instilled in us that Black Americans do not have.

But the major point for Cruse is the structural situation confronting the Black American group and the West Indian response to—and from Cruse's perspective, misunderstanding of—this situation.

> . . . the West Indian psychology is a thing apart—distinguishing itself through myriad ways, but principally by not accepting the American Negro social status as it has been fashioned by the American way of life *(ibid.).*

Thus, although the large number of Black Americans already in New York provided the new immigrants with a "turf" from which to operate as well as a reference group against which they could view themselves as successful (see, Foner, 1983; Sutton and Makiesky-Barrow, this volume), the demeaned status of Afro-American cultural traditions *vis-à-vis* White America has been troublesome to West Indians. As one West Indian professional asserted, "We saw their second-class status and didn't want any of it" (Kessner and Caroli, 1981:188).

One result is that West Indians have oscillated between identification and separation in their social and political relations with Black Americans. Witness the following statement in a West Indian-American newspaper and the positive emphasis on characteristics stereotypically associated with the West Indies:

> This national organization [of West Indian-Americans] naturally favors integration into the black American community and would strive to accomplish this assimilation while strongly and fiercely insisting on retaining the best in the West Indian character: a passion for education and self-pride ("Antillean Caribbean Echo" in Glantz, 1978:189).

A similar point was made by a Vincentian immigrant who observed that Vincentians tend to cluster in ethnic enclaves not only as a protective device, but "to preserve a way of life they believe is better."

There are other sources of tension between the two groups as well. Assigned to the same economic, social, and political niches by White Americans, West Indians and Black Americans feel in competition for the scarce resources allocated them. As a Grenadian commented:

> We from the islands are "aliens." People [*i.e.*, Afro-Americans] feel threatened by us—they've got to. It's like where I was in Tortola. "They" feel we've moved in to take over.

A Vincentian made a similar point: "Blacks think we're getting the breaks they worked hard for." And another Vincentian, similarly concerned with competitive relations between the two groups, made the following observation:

> Black Americans call us "Black Jews" because we stick together. They are jealous because we work well and have respect for authority. They think we take away their jobs . . . They want us to go back home.

On the other hand, the exclusion West Indians experience from the dominant institutions of U.S. society by virtue of being Black strengthens the already existing cultural bond between West Indians and Black Americans. One Vincentian immigrant described how she was refused an apartment she had wanted to rent because the owners "were not renting to Black people." This made her "realize what it meant to be Black in the United States." Her response, however, was to work so that "this could never happen [to her] again." She and her husband now own their home in Brooklyn.

The ambivalence between the two groups is particularly notable in the political realm, where relations have been in continuous flux. The West Indian migration to New York in the first half of the 20th century dovetailed with the heavy influx of Black Americans from the U.S. South. Because of greater educational opportunities available in the Caribbean, West Indian immigrants were prepared to assert their leadership and influence in the political domain.

Early accounts describe the "corner soap-box or ladder street meeting" in Harlem, a pungent West Indian type of oral journalism that emerged in the 1930s in response to the informational needs of the mostly illiterate southern Blacks and West Indians who had come to New York City (H. Robinson in Henry, 1977:457). After the 1930s, when Blacks were finally allowed to join neighborhood political clubs, it was the more educated West Indians who moved into leadership roles.

By the 1950s and 1960s, Hulan Jack, J. Raymond Jones, Constance Baker Mottley—all of West Indian extraction—controlled the political machine in Harlem, and Shirley Chisholm, Bertram Baker, George Fleary, and Sam Welcome—of similar origin—wielded political power in the clubs of Brooklyn (Moore, 1984:13). Stokely Carmichael, Roy Innis, and Malcolm X were other figures of West Indian origin active on the political scene. This was a period when the pervading force of both Black American and West Indian life in the United States was race. What is significant is that these West Indian leaders represented and articulated Black political interests to the wider American polity. Their power and identity derived from their emphasis on their "Blackness," not their West Indianness. Although the pre-1960s West Indian political activists may have led Caribbeanized social and cultural lives, in their public political lives they acted as Black Americans. According to one West Indian immigrant, Shirley Chisholm in all her years in Congress never sponsored legislation that was especially favorable to the West Indies, nor would Herman Farrell[10] have claimed he was West Indian 20 years ago.

Since the mid-1960s the Black American/West Indian political equation has undergone significant change. The most visible outer manifestation has been the loss of power by politicians of "Caribbean extraction" and their retirement from "center stage" (Moore, 1984:13). For West Indians there has been a shift, arising out of the civil rights and Black Power movements and the changing demographic presence of West Indians in New York from issues of race to an emphasis on ethnicity.

More educational opportunities and the loosening of rigid racial restrictions have increased the number of "middle class" Black Americans who now make strong and successful bids for political positions in both Harlem and Brooklyn, dislodging West Indian politicians backed by the political clubs. One commentator depicts the situation as follows:

> Today, [in contrast to the pre-1960s era] . . . there are no elected officials of Caribbean extraction in the State Senate or Congress. There is one Caribbean councilperson of a total of 12 in the borough; one Assemblyman of a total of 19 in the borough, one District leader of a total of 38 in the borough (Moore, 1984:13).

At the same time, the West Indian presence in New York City has dramatically increased. Of the 800,000 immigrants arriving in the decade of the 1970s, between 200,000 and 250,000 were from the French-and English-speaking Caribbean (U.S. Department of Commerce, 1980:4). In our sample, 60 percent of the Grenadians and 80 percent of the Vincentians arrived after 1965. This new wave of West Indian immigrants, similarly located on the pale of the political system as were the earlier West Indian migrants, is showing signs of wanting to become politically more active, as did its predecessors. This time the terms of political involvement are different. The size and complexity of the West Indian community, coupled with the apparent softening of U.S. racial barriers and attitudes, has resulted in West Indians emphasizing that they are an ethnic group as well as a race, and that they

[10] A Black American of West Indian parentage who was a candidate in the 1985 mayoral election in New York City.

form a political constituency with its subset of concerns that can best be articulated by political leaders of their own background. Also key in this process of ethnic elaboration are urban institutions which emphasize ethnicity, such as the Mayors Commission on Ethnic Affairs and the awarding of funds and various political goods through community boards, which are residentially—and in the context of New York, therefore ethnically—based.

In expressing the separateness of their political interests from Black Americans, West Indians assert that Black American politicians are insensitive to the special needs of West Indians and take them for granted.[11] Emerging immigrant political activists are emphasizing their West Indianness in addition to their blackness—even if they are second generation. As one immigrant put it: "It is now fashionable for anyone with a drop of West Indian blood to say so." And Vincentians and Grenadians, despite their small numbers relative to other West Indian groups in New York, are well represented in these activist ranks.

A contemporary dilemma for West Indian political activists concerns the basis of collaboration with Black American politicians. Some envision becoming a distinct minority group, articulating West Indian political concerns to the larger system through the mediation of Black political groups. This has worked most recently for Dominicans in New York through the older established Puerto Rican groups (Georges, 1984). There are problems with this approach on a few counts. First there is the issue of West Indian political participation. The majority of Vincentians and Grenadians—and West Indians in general—are not citizens, and citizenship drives promoted by local West Indian institutions—voluntary organizations, a local radio station, and even a bakery—have not yielded large responses. Yet there are indications of a movement in this direction. Of the Vincentians and Grenadians in our sample, 27 percent are citizens and as many more indicate an intention to become citizens as soon as they are able.

A second crucial issue concerns mobilizing a sufficient following behind leaders. Here, too, there are signs of growing participation on a wider basis. Many West Indian activists, several of whom were Vincentians and Grenadians, supported political candidates in the recent Democratic party primary for mayor. There were support groups for Koch, Bellamy, and Farrell, the Black American candidate of West Indian background. While the response of the West Indian community to the three candidates emphasizes an absence of unity, it does demonstrate an increased West Indian involvement in urban politics. Significantly, promises were extracted from the candidates for distinctly West Indian focused services. For example, Koch promised a Caribbean resource center to provide community support services, a commit-

---

[11] The same concerns that cloud relations with Black Americans are an issue *vis-à-vis* the White politicians in Brooklyn from heavily West Indian districts. As a Vincentian said: "They don't understand the Caribbean community. They look at us on Labor Day as revelers and jumpers. We have a different side culturally."

tee to address problems of West Indian children in the schools, and continued support for the Labor Day Carnival in Brooklyn.

Noteworthy within this changing framework of political relations is the increasing involvement of West Indians at the local level. Vincentians and Grenadians, as other West Indians, are seeking election to community planning boards and school boards, elections that require only permanent residence and not citizenship for candidates and voters. Others are working in the political offices of elected representatives and participating on the boards of daycare centers and private schools, some of them organized by West Indians. One means of building their political bases is through participating in home-based voluntary organizations, such as ex-teachers and ex-police associations. While most of these activities are presently limited to the community level, they generate networks that presumably could be mobilized in larger, urban situations requiring wider West Indian involvement.

ETHNICITY, CARIBBEANIZATION, AND THE STRUCTURE OF THE HOST SOCIETY

Vincentian and Grenadian immigrants in New York have been highly successful materially. More than one-half our sample own their homes on tree-lined streets in neighborhoods of Brooklyn they have contributed to rehabilitating. Several also own property in their home countries, and the majority visit home at least every five years. Their material success has been matched by their educational and occupational achievements.

While keenly aware of their economic opportunities and proud of their gains in the United States, West Indians nonetheless recognize their location on the fringe of a racially conscious and divided sociopolitical system. These racial divisions set a basic structure and tone for immigrant life in New York. The Vincentians and Grenadians in our sample claim they do not really know Whites. They are segregated from them residentially, in their social activities and community life, and for many this separateness extends into the work place, where those who work with Whites are generally involved in asymmetrical supervisor-worker relationships.

Underscoring these divisions is a perception West Indians hold of their disadvantage and exclusion vis-à-vis Whites. A quarter of the immigrants in our sample reported personal experiences of racial discrimination. These generally occurred over housing, at work, or in day-to-day street life. Moreover, fully half expressed feelings that they are negatively perceived by Whites.

On the one hand, this racial awareness leads West Indians to remain within the orbit of Black American politics. Yet, their increasing numbers, matched by their longer experience in New York,[12] and their material gains,

[12] The role played by the length of stay in New York in the immigrants' overall satisfaction with

allow West Indians to focus on their own ethnicity within the wider context of race. An ideology of ethnicity—or Caribbeanization—serves several functions for Vincentian and Grenadian immigrants. On a symbolic level, by offering its own forms of prestige, esteem and power, it buffers them against the contradictions and alienation that underpin the immigrant experience. These ethnic identifications are being constantly activated and reinforced by home-based politicians and officials who are of the view that "whether or not immigrants return home, they should have a say in the development of their country."

On an instrumental level, ethnicity provides a set of symbols around which Vincentian and Grenadian immigrants have organized a rich social and cultural life within the Caribbeanized milieu of Brooklyn. It gives small-island immigrants a meaningful anchor in a situation where they feel vulnerable and distanced not only from White Americans, but also from West Indians born in the larger, developed islands. Moreover, the associational life they create around the symbols of ethnicity gives them important organizing experience.

It is this focus on ethnicity, linked to activities that emphasize connections with their island societies, that is thought by some to prevent West Indians from becoming more oriented toward involvement in U.S. politics. Our findings among Vincentian and Grenadian immigrants, however, suggest that this is not the case. Instead, our immigrant activists spanned a range of political involvements including those in their home society, in the wider West Indian New York community, and in the political structures of New York City. The political activities of two Grenadian activists, PC and AL, exemplify this increasing tendency.

PC, a professional within the West Indian community in Brooklyn who came to the United States in 1946 after finishing secondary school and working a few years, has been active in several voluntary organizations in the Grenadian immigrant community, all focused on supporting institutions in Grenada. One organization has raised $65,000 over the years to establish and maintain a secondary school in Carriacou. At the same time, PC has been a central figure in organizing a pan-Caribbean "cultural celebration" now held annually at St. Patrick's Cathedral in Manhattan. He is also part of a West Indian health committee focused on developing medical facilities in the West Indies, has been honored by the Black American New York Urban Coalition, and was a borough chairperson for Percy Sutton's political campaign.

Within New York's political establishment, PC was the Caribbean representative to the mayors advisory committee for ethnic matters and recently spearheaded the "Caribbeans for Koch" support committee. Within the same

their new surroundings is reflected in the following finding in our study: one half of those in New York less than 10 years expressed satisfaction with their situation compared with three-quarters who were in New York between 10 and 20 years.

time period, he was chairperson of the New York support committee to elect the current prime minister of Grenada and was most recently appointed to a key international position by his home government.

As part of these committees, PC has worked with fellow Grenadians, immigrants from the wider West Indian immigrant community, and Black Americans, developing and reinforcing networks he activated in other contexts. His various activities buttress one another, allowing him to transfer his political capital from one context to another. Thus, Mayor Koch looks to PC because of his power and position within the New York West Indian community, which he gained through his political involvement with his home country as well as with the New York Grenadian community. By the same token, Mayor Koch's attention to PC, just as PC's international position for the Grenada government, attracts support for him from the New York Grenadian and West Indian populations.

AL, although a more recent immigrant, also engages in a wide range of activities. Arriving in New York in 1976, he worked as a security guard for five years, then started a West Indian newspaper in Brooklyn, and now provides technical assistance to West Indian entrepreneurs. He is also initiating a Caribbean American Chamber of Commerce. In terms of community activities, AL started the Grenada ex-policemen's association at the same time he initiated a block association to "clean up" his West Indian street in Brooklyn .

AL was recently elected vice-president of the community planning board in his largely West Indian neighborhood. He was an active member of the Caribbeans for Koch support committee and has also served as public relations officer of the New York support committee to elect the current prime minister of Grenada. In addition, AL is a member of the pan-West Indian New York branch of the Caribbean Action Lobby (CAL). There are similar examples from the Vincentian community. A recent ambassador to the U.N. from St. Vincent was previously a member of the community board in his neighborhood in Brooklyn at the same time he was chairman of the umbrella St. Vincent volcano relief committee.

The activities of PC and AL serve to link their own immigrant group to other West Indians and to the polity of the city. They demonstrate that pan-West Indian networking can coexist with an insular-based identity and provide a basis for forging race/class-based coalitions with Black Americans. It is important to note that unlike the prior alliances between West Indians and Black Americans, which were based on problems related to a common racial identification, a Caribbeanized ethnicity is now emerging as the primary galvanizing force for West Indian political efforts.

Also significant is the attention to political issues in New York City that is occurring among "grassroots" Vincentians and Grenadians as their experience in New York deepens with time. For example, the voluntary associations to which Vincentians and Grenadians belong on the basis of their common bond to their own island societies have begun to focus on issues in New York or on issues which span both the host and home society. They address such matters as New York real estate investments, citizenship, the schools, daycare centers, local crime, cleaning up neighborhoods, and local entrepreneurship. Moreover, they encourage members to participate on community boards and school boards, even while they co-sponsor meetings with politicians from their home islands and organize excursion flights home for Carnival and Christmas. It is clear from these examples that from the perspective of these immigrants, political activities in the home society and in New York City, rather than constituting opposing poles, comprise a single field of action.

CONCLUSIONS

Through an analysis of the political behavior of Vincentians and Grenadians in New York in three spheres of interaction—the home society, the West Indian immigrant community in New York, and in relation to Black Americans—the immigrants' discrete activities in each domain were seen to provide differing possibilities and constraints for their political behavior in New York. On the one hand, the political linkages they maintain with their home societies create an alternate arena of political action and acknowledged prestige that can in turn serve as a mobilizing force for organizational activities in New York. On the other hand, their ties to their specific island societies constrain the forging of wider pan-West Indian organizational structures.

Within the arena of wider immigrant relations, it is significant that West Indians live together in the same neighborhoods, shop in the same stores, work in the same offices, and send their children to the same schools, thereby sharing experiences that create a sense of West Indianness vis-à-vis other groups. This is being acted upon in the creation of a Caribbean Research Center within a West Indian-dominated college in Brooklyn, the pan-Caribbean political organization, CAL, and various jointly sponsored West Indian cultural events, of which Carnival is the most dramatic.

Opposing these unifying activities, again, is the separateness of the West Indian islands, maintained by facts of geography and history, and the relationship of inequality between large and small islands. These historical residues are constantly activated in New York by the ties immigrants maintain with home and by island-based West Indian politicians and officials who are eager to have immigrants maintain their financial and political links with their home societies.

Finally, this chapter demonstrates the complex role played by ethnicity in a pluralistic host society such as the United States, with its particular configuration of race and ethnic relations and the fluid role played by this ethnicity.[13] Of critical importance is the fact that a racial hierarchy was already in place in New York, a central feature of which was the presence of a group with historical and cultural experiences similar to those of the West Indians. This has strongly influenced the expression of West Indian ethnicity and set the basis for the reworking of political relations between Black Americans and West Indians described in the chapter.

Currently, West Indians recognize their political interests as distinct, in some respects, from those of Black Americans. As part of this process, they emphasize West Indian ethnicity in contrast to the earlier unifying theme of racial oppression. Nonetheless, Black Americans remain an important reference group and mediating force for West Indians when it comes to their dealings with the wider society, particularly in applying pressure on host institutions for goods, positions, and other rewards.

The problematic focuses on the discourse of West Indian and Afro-American cooperation. West Indians, for their part, are interested in maintaining their social and cultural autonomy while allying themselves politically with Black Americans. This depends on the ability of West Indian leaders to mobilize adequate mass support, which is a difficult task.[14] However this discourse is worked out, the research with Grenadian and Vincentian immigrants clearly demonstrates that ethnicity has emerged as an important ingredient in the mobilization of group action at this moment, not only in political activities focused on home islands but also within the political arena of New York in support committees to elect a New York City mayor, in pan-West Indian cultural associations and events, and in political caucuses with Black Americans. Within this expanded political field, West Indian ethnicity is a multifaceted and complicated phenomenon which can both unite and divide peoples.[15]

---

[13] To fully understand West Indian behavior in New York it would be important to study and analyze the same immigrant populations comparatively in such diverse host contexts as London, Toronto, and Caribbean migration centers, each with its specific structures of immigrant incorporation. Preliminary results from the larger comparative study of which this research is a part, indicate that in the particular conditions of Trinidad, small island ethnicity does not assume the salience it does in New York and is not a basis for political action. A beginning basis for comparative analysis with West Indians in England also exists: see, Jayawardena (1973) on Guyanese Indians in England; Midgett (1975) on St. Lucians in London; Foner (1983) on Jamaicans in London and New York; and Sutton and Makiesky-Barrow in this volume on Barbadians in London. See also, Marshall (1985) for preliminary findings on Eastern Caribbean migrants in Toronto.

[14] The following retort by a Black American politician to claims of West Indian political aspirants describes the sentiments of some Black American politicians regarding the political involvement of West Indians: " I organized to reach where I am and if you want power, you had better be organized" (Carib News, 1984:3).

[15] In varying ways, ethnicity has been a primary mode of relating to the wider political environment for almost all immigrant groups to New York since the beginning of the twentieth century (see, Katznelson, 1981).

BIBLIOGRAPHY

Basch, L.
1985   *Caribbean International Migration: Implications for Development.* New York: United Nations Institute for Training and Research.

——————
1982   *Population Movements within the English-speaking Caribbean: An Overview.* New York: United Nations Institute for Training and Research.

——————
1978   "Workin' for the Yankee Dollar: The Impact of a Transnational Petroleum Company on Caribbean Class and Ethnic Relations." Ph. D. Dissertation. New York University.

Bouvier, L.F.
1984a   *St. Vincent and the Grenadines: Yesterday, Today and Tomorrow.* Washington, D.C.: Population Reference Bureau Occasional Series: the Caribbean. March.

——————
1984b   *Grenada: Yesterday, Today and Tomorrow.* Washington, D.C.: Population Reference Bureau Occasional Series: the Caribbean. April.

Bryce-Laporte, R.
1972   "Black Immigrants: The Experience of Invisibility and Inequality." *Journal of Black Studies,* 3(1):29–56. Sept.

Caribbean Action Lobby, New York Regional Chapter
n.d.   The Caribbean Action Lobby.

Carib News
1985   "Caribbean Education." June 25.

——————
1984   "Political Summits." Aug. 15.

Carmody, C.
1978   "First among Equals: Antiguan Patterns of Local-Level Leadership," Ph.D. dissertation, New York University.

Cruse, H.
1984   *The Crisis of the Negro Intellectual: A Historical Analysis of the Failure of Black Leadership.* New York: Quill.

Foner, N.
1983   *Jamaican Migrants: A Comparative Analysis of the New York and London Experience.* New York: Center for Latin American and Caribbean Studies, New York University Research Program in Inter-American Affairs. Occasional Paper 36.

Georges, E.
1984   *New Immigrants and the Political Process: Dominicans in New York:* Center for Latin American and Caribbean Studies, New York University Research Program in Inter-American Affairs. Occasional Paper 45.

Glantz, O.
1978   "Native Sons and Immigrants: Some Beliefs and Values of American-Born and West Indian Blacks at Brooklyn College." *Ethnicity,* 5(2):189–202. June.

Hendricks, G.
1974   *The Dominican Diaspora: From the Dominican Republic to New York City—Villagers in Transition.* New York: Columbia University, Teachers College Press.

Henry, K.S.
1977   "The Black Political Tradition in New York: A Conjunction of Political Cultures." *Journal of Black Studies,* 7(4):455–484. June.

Jayawardena, C.
1973   "Migrants, Networks and Identities." *New Community*, 11(4):353–357.

―――
1963   *Conflict and Solidarity in a Guianese Plantation.* London: The Athlone Press.

Katznelson, I.
1981   *City Trenches: Urban Politics and the Patterning of Class in the United States.* New York: Panthelon Books.

Kessner, T. and B. Caroli
1981   *Today's Immigrants: Their Stories.* New York: Oxford University Press.

Makiesky-Barrow, S.R.
1976   "Class, Culture and Politics in a Barbadian Community," Ph.D. dissertation, Brandeis University.

Marshall, D.
1985   *Eastern Caribbean Immigrants in Canada.* Cave Hill, Barbados: Institute of Social and Economic Research, University of the West Indies.

Marshall, P.
1981   *Brown Girl, Brownstones.* Old Westbury, New York: The Feminist Press.

Midgett, D.K.
1975   "West Indian Ethnicity in Great Britain." In *Migration and Development: Implications for Ethnic Identity and Political Conflict.* H.F. Safa and B.M. du Toit, eds. The Hague: Mouton. Pp. 57–81.

Moore, C.
1984   "The Caribbean Community and the Quest for Political Power." *Carib News.* Aug. 28.

Papademetriou, D.G.
1983   *New Immigrants to Brooklyn and Queens: Policy Implication with Regard to Housing.* Staten Island, New York: Center for Migration Studies.

Sassen-Koob, S.
1981   *Exporting Capital and Importing Labor: The Role of the Caribbean Immigrant to New York City.* New York: Center for Latin American and Caribbean Studies, New York University Research Program in Inter-American Affairs. Occasional Paper 28.

Sutton, C.
1969   "The Scene of the Action: A Wildcat Strike in Barbados." Ph.D. dissertation, Columbia University.

U.S. Department of Commerce
1980   *Ancestry of the Population by State.* Washington, D.C.: Bureau of the Census.

Wilson, P.
1973   *Crab Antics: The Social Anthropology of English-Speaking Negro Societies of the Caribbean.* New Haven: Yale University Press.

Wiltshire-Brodber, R. and W. Wiltshire
1985   *Caribbean Regional Migration.* Trinidad and Tobago: Institute of International Relations, University of the West Indies.

ALL IN THE SAME BOAT?
Unity and Diversity in Haitian Organizing in New York

Nina Glick Schiller, Josh DeWind, Marie Lucie Brutus,
Carolle Charles, Georges Fouron, Antoine Thomas

As immigrants settle in the United States, they create voluntary associations, clubs, agencies, and numerous other organizations. Social scientists
have studied these organizations with the assumption that immigrants from
the same national or cultural background share an identity that enables them
to unite as a community and promote their common interests. Indeed scholars such as Glazer and Moynihan (1970:1xxxiii) view such ethnic organizing
as one of the most important means by which urban immigrants have taken
advantage of the economic and political opportunities in the United States.

On the other hand, immigrants have often failed to unite. Historians have
recorded how members of the same immigrant "community," with opposing
identities and antagonistic interests, have contended fiercely with one another (Olsen, 1979:185, 278). A major cause of disunity has been the persistence of distinctions among immigrants based on class (Gorelick 1982:32), and
on differing political (Vassady, 1982:42–43), religious (Sowell, 1981:24), and
regional identities (Schermerhorn, 1949:247). These differences, brought by
the immigrants from their home countries, have retained significance in the
United States.

Immigrants' organizing efforts have frequently been directed toward influencing political struggles in their country of origin. Immigrant leaders
have been known to rally their constituents together on the basis of a
national identity to pursue political goals in their country of origin (Georges,
1984:21; Handlin, 1951:194, 260). The organization of the Irish American
community to support first the creation of the Irish Free State and then the
unification of Ireland is just one example of numerous attempts to unify
immigrants for nationalistic purposes.

Social scientists often treat "ethnic" and "national" identities as interchangeable (Schoenberg, 1984:417). Although the two identities are sometimes addressed simultaneously by the immigrant leaders themselves in
appeals for community unity, they imply different orientations and courses

of action. Ethnic organizing is aimed at achieving recognition, status, and resources for an immigrant community as an interest group within the American political system. Nationalistic organizing is directed toward influencing the political system in the country of origin rather than attempting to establish a niche in American society. Recent research into the origins of the "new immigration" (Bryce-LaPorte, 1980) has established a theoretical framework that helps to explain trends toward organizational unity and diversity among immigrant populations in the United States. Starting from a global perspective, social scientists have begun to see international migration as a product of the integration of advanced industrial and relatively underdeveloped nations into a single world capitalist system (Portes and Walton, 1981; Sassen-Koob, 1981). Upon this international stage immigrants became actors with multiple roles to play in both their home and host countries (Sutton and Makiesky-Barrow, this volume; Basch, this volume). As a result, immigrant organizations adopt various, and at times contradictory, goals and identities related to their interests in their home and host countries.

The necessity of examining immigrant organizing in an international context to understand trends toward unity or diversity is illustrated in the following analysis of Haitian organizing in New York City. In this case study we examine how conditions both in the United States and Haiti influence the development of Haitian organizations in New York City. The conditions produce the seemingly contradictory unification of the "Haitian community" based on nationalist or ethnic identities while blocking that unity by maintaining diverse interests, organizational goals, and identities.[1]

The migration of Haitians to the United States has been part of a more general large-scale migration from the Caribbean. Each of the migrant streams from individual islands and the subsequent organizing activities of the migrants in the United States has been shaped by migrants' prior experience with foreign domination. The migrants come from countries that were once European colonies and are now neocolonial dependencies of the United States. Yet Haiti also stands apart from other islands. Haitians won an early political independence from France at the beginning of the nineteenth century to become the first "Black republic" in the world. Yet, since 1957 Haitians have been subjected to the most oppressive dictatorship and poverty in the hemisphere.

[1] The data on which this paper is based was collected during field work in New York City in 1969–71 and 1985–86. Research in 1985–86 included an extensive interview with the leaders of 90 Haitian organizations, and participant observation in numerous events, meetings, church services, and demonstrations. This research was supported by the National Institute of Child Health and Human Development. We would like to thank Constance Sutton and David Schiller, for their helpful editorial assistance; Nancy Bonvillain, Eva Friedlander, Hannah Lessinger, Betty Levin, Fran Rothstein, and Ida Susser for their assistance with an earlier version of this article. Our thanks also to Karen Abbott for her skillful word processing and endless patience. Some of the material in this article was presented at the 87th meeting of the American Anthropological Association in Washington, D.C., December, 1985.

In the United States, Haitians also share with other Caribbean immigrants the experience of being received as members of a minority population defined largely in terms of race. Categorized as "Black," Haitians and other Afro-Caribbean immigrants are relegated to the low social status of a minority group in American society regardless of their social standing in their home countries (Laguerre, 1984:143, Fouron, 1983.)

HAITIAN MIGRATION TO THE UNITED STATES

Ever since Haiti became an independent nation small numbers of its citizens have emigrated (Laguerre, 1984:160–169), but after François Duvalier took power in 1957, the flow of migrants reached major proportions. Suffering under the political dictatorship and dismal economic conditions imposed by the Duvalier regime, some 900,000 Haitians, or 15 percent of the nation's population felt compelled to leave Haiti between 1957 and 1984. The majority of the migrants, perhaps 600,000, settled in the United States (Allman and Richman, 1985:5). Roughly 400,000 are now concentrated in New York City alone.

Among the first migrants to leave Haiti after François Duvalier took power were opposition political leaders and their closest supporters who quickly became targets of Duvalier's notorious henchmen, the *ton ton macoutes*. These migrants were generally members of two upper-class groups who had fought each other for access to the spoils of government since Haiti won its independence from France in 1804. One group was comprised mainly of rural land owners, speculators, and merchants who controlled internal commerce. Predominantly, but not exclusively, Black, this group has frequently advanced its political interests on the basis of an idealogy of "negritude." The second and more elite group was more closely tied to international trade. Predominantly mulatto, this group used its lighter skin color as a marker of superior status.

Historically, both upper-class groups distinguished themselves from other Haitians by maintaining French colonial prejudices, expressed most notably in their preference for French, rather than Creole.[2] They sent their children to Europe for higher education and extolled French culture. They professed Catholicism and, at least publicly, showed disdain for the African-derived *vodoun* practiced by the lower classes.[3]

These upper class migrants to the United States were soon joined by members of Haiti's middle and lower classes. After Duvalier consolidated his dictatorial control over the government in 1965 and declared his election as

[2] Creole is linked grammatically to the languages of Africa. Its vocabulary incorporates words from several languages, most noticeably French (Pressoir, 1947).

[3] The nature of the Haitian class system, and the extent of cultural differences between the classes has been a topic of controversy. Discussion of the topic can be found in Leyburn (1966), Pierre Charles (1967), Moral (1978), and Lundahl (1979).

"President-for-Life," Haiti's shopkeepers, teachers, low-level government bureaucrats, and skilled workers began to leave Haiti in large numbers. These people shared with the upper class a high evaluation of French language and culture, although less familiar with it.

After Jean-Claude Duvalier donned his father's mantle of "President-for-Life" in 1971, economic conditions in rural areas continued to deteriorate despite the new leader's proclamation of an "economic revolution"—and political oppression continued, although in a somewhat less bloody style than before. By the end of the 1970s thousands of peasants and unskilled urban workers had begun to flee Haiti. To a certain extent these later emigrants were culturally different from their predecessors. Many lacked the gloss of French language and culture: they spoke primarily Creole and were most comfortable with the African-based culture which Haitian peasants maintained in the countryside.

Over the three decades that Haitians have settled in significant numbers in the New York metropolitan area, their organizing activities have gone through four somewhat distinct phases reflecting trends toward both unity and disunity.[4] Through these phases, the notion of a "Haitian community" defined either as ethnic or national has progressively been developed, modified, and finally used as the basis for political activity. Meanwhile many organizations with Haitian memberships have asserted and maintained separate identities and goals, sometimes in reaction to appeals for unity. In the following pages we outline and illustrate how organizing by Haitians in New York evolved through each phase in response to changing conditions in both Haiti and the United States.

PHASE I: 1957–1964.

A POPULATION DIVIDED BY CLASS AND POLITICAL RIVALRIES

Today there is an ideology of community among Haitian immigrants, and some leaders organize the immigrant population by making appeals for unity. The notion of "community," however, was not part of the original organizing efforts of Haitians when they settled in New York. These early organizations fostered and maintained class and political divisions which originated in Haiti. The members were oriented toward returning to Haiti where they hoped to displace the Duvalier regime and restore their own upper-class political and social positions. Not open to all Haitians, these

---

[4] Similar trends in the development of Haitian organizations, modified by variations in the racial and ethnic composition of the local populations and the political history of each city, seem to have occurred in both Miami and Boston.

organizations did not claim to represent or speak in the name of a Haitian community.

Clustered around former presidential candidates who had lost to François Duvalier was a group of political exiles who were more interested in building the reputation of their candidate than in pulling together a broad anti-Duvalierist opposition. A radio station that gave voice to nonpartisan opposition had little effect in creating any sense of common identity among Haitian immigrants in New York because its programs were transmitted only to Haiti. Haitian historian Lyonel Paquin describes these political groups, whose disunity reflected the divisive effects of class and color in Haitian politics:

> [Haitian] politicians [in New York] were more concerned with their own images than burying their differences . . . Our leaders, instead of fighting Duvalier, were building a list of their enemies in exile to prevent them from returning to Haiti when the new regime assumed power. While people were dying in Haiti, the so-called political leaders were busy organizing phantom governments in New York . . . They all strived to build a Machiavellian reputation. They were convinced that the more difficult they behaved with each other, and the more devious their behavior, the more they would be judged by their peers and posterity as having been shrewd and cunning leaders (Paquin, 1983:198–201).

There were also several exclusive social clubs that perpetuated the upper-class status of the members. Club Elite was such an association.[5] Its main activities were dances and formal balls. Membership was so exclusive that not everyone invited to the balls was considered acceptable for club membership.

The social distinctions and political rivalries from Haiti were not the only obstacles to organizing as a community. The racial prejudices newcomers encountered in New York City further discouraged such organizing. With its categorical distinction between Blacks and Whites, the U.S. racial system left little social space for the organizing of distinctive Black ethnic groups. Race, not culture, became the overriding mark of identity in relation to the wider society.

Haitian immigrants responded to racial discrimination in two different ways. Together with other Caribbean populations, some Haitians joined Black American organizations where they participated as Blacks in the civil rights movement. In an attempt to obtain more prestige and social acceptance than was accorded native Blacks, a large number of Haitians of all classes

[5] All names of Haitian organizations and individuals in this chapter have been changed so as to respect the promises of confidentiality made to respondents.

identified themselves in public as French in language and culture. They spoke of "staying Haitian to avoid being Black twice." While they welcomed the label "Frenchie," they made no attempt to create organizations based on this identity.

PHASE II: 1965–1972.

CONCEPTS OF COMMUNITY ARE FORMULATED BUT NOT WIDELY ACCEPTED

In the second phase of organizing, emergent leaders formulated a concept of a Haitian community, issued calls for this community to unite, and attempted to speak to and for the entire Haitian immigrant population. A struggle developed over the purpose and direction of efforts to build a common consciousness and a shared identity. Some leaders spoke of a Haitian community competing with other ethnic groups for resources, position, and power within American society. Others struggled to build a new political consciousness that would unite a Haitian community in a struggle to liberate Haiti. These first efforts to unite Haitians for either ethnic or nationalist goals elicited few positive responses from the majority of the immigrant population. The leaders were unable to convince even members of their own organizations to set aside class and political rivalries for some greater good.

Both ethnic and national organizing were influenced by political developments in both U.S. society and abroad. In response to the U.S. civil rights movement and the growing protests of Blacks against a political system from which they were excluded, the federal government developed the "War On Poverty." This program created a system of patronage that bypassed the entrenched political party machines and offered inducements for Black people to participate in the new government bureaucracy. In response to social eruptions in urban ghettos and the growth of a powerful Black liberation movement, the participitory programs were extended to ethnic groups under an emerging ideology of "ethnic pluralism." Competition developed between racial and ethnic groups for programs and funding. Not only did these programs create social space for variations of Black ethnicity, but such variations were encouraged.

During the same period, Haitian migration increased noticeably, spurred by a wave of terror unleashed by the Duvalier regime. Revisions of the U.S. immigration laws in 1965 and labor recruitment by U.S. employers facilitated the entrance of Haitians into the United States. Impressed by the growing size of the Haitian immigrant population and influenced by the burgeoning ideology of ethnic pluralism, American politicians, church officials, and educators began to encourage ethnic organizing among the Haitians. Because Haitians were linguistically and culturally different from other Black populations in the United States and had a long history of national pride, they were seen as perfect candidates for the status of a new ethnic group.

Representatives of the New York City government, the Democratic Party, the Catholic Church, and schools of social work recruited individuals from professional backgrounds in Haiti to become ethnic leaders. The American officials presented the United States as a land of competing ethnic groups whose leaders and populations achieved upward social mobility by organizing along ethnic lines. With American support, the Haitian leaders began in 1965 to develop several community centers, social programs, and church congregations which were identified specifically as Haitian and as representative of an emergent New York City Haitian ethnic community (Glick Schiller, 1972, 1975).

The Haitian American Political Organization (HAPO) was one of the organizations that developed in the context of this ideology of ethnic pluralism. Like a number of the very early immigrants, HAPO's founder, Joseph Maxime, had first experienced American politics while working as a Black with other politicians of West Indian origin who identified themselves as Black Americans. However, Maxime was encouraged to organize as a Haitian by the Nationalities Division of the Democratic National Committee who wrote him that on "the highest level" the party thought it was good for the United States that Haitians organize as a separate ethnic group.

Unlike the Haitian exile organizations and the elite social clubs which were oriented toward Haiti, HAPO referred to Haiti only for symbols of common heritage and pride. The organization avoided reference to social, economic, and political conditions in Haiti which they feared would be divisive. HAPO was created to improve conditions for Haitians as an ethnic group within the United States, not to improve conditions in Haiti itself.

Stating that they were committed to "uniting the community," HAPO leaders were among those who had begun to speak of the Haitian population as sharing a single identity and waiting only to be organized. However, during HAPO's attempts to organize fundraising activities and to support what they called "community projects," the members split into upper-class and middle-class factions, which supported only their own projects regardless of merit. Even though the organization preached an ideology of community, its members were unable to act in terms of a community of interest.

Not everyone who began to speak in terms of the Haitian community accepted the framework of ethnic organizing. In this period, nationalist organizing also addressed itself to the "Haitian community." Inspired by liberation struggles around the world and by the Black liberation movement in the United States, a handful of Haitians formed organizations whose goal was to carry out a revolution in Haiti. Drawing on the experiences of the communist movement in Haiti and of radicalized Haitians who participated in the student movements of 1968–1969 in Haiti, France, and the United

States, these leftist organizations began their political work by promoting cultural activities. They sought to develop a cultural nationalism based on a sense of the Haitian people's African roots and expressed in the Creole language. One group established a radio program for the Haitian community; another formed Troupe Liberation, a theatrical group that appealed to the "community" to participate in a new type of nationalist cultural experience.

Performing at the Brooklyn Academy of Music, Troupe Liberation presented skits ridiculing what they saw as Haitian "bourgeois pretensions" and "French mannerisms," and sang songs bespeaking the need to liberate Haiti. The Troupe was initially greeted with mixed reactions. While some applauded, many in the audience were uncomfortable with the attack on their lifestyle. Moreover, the Duvalier regime cast a long shadow over events in New York, and many in the audience were frightened at being present at an event which publicly attacked the Haitian government. They feared reprisal against kin and friends in Haiti.

PHASE III: 1972–1982.

THE CULTURAL BASIS OF THE COMMUNITY IS REDEFINED: A NATIONALIST COMMUNITY EMERGES

The third period of organizing began with a decline of Haitian ethnic organizations and a struggle to define a new cultural basis for a Haitian community. The Haitian ethnic associations began to founder or disappear in the seventies, as federally-funded community corporations, a mainstay of ethnic politics, were dismantled. Moreover, in the wake of a recession there were less resources available for the politics of pluralism, and in the course of the decade the emphasis on ethnicity in the larger society diminished. By 1980, Haitians who aspired to power or influence in the American political system had to make new political contacts and negotiate new political relationships.

In New York City, a new bureaucracy composed of area policy boards and youth boards was established to provide a much reduced level of social service. Black Americans began to be incorporated directly into those structures, and Haitians who were attempting to build a separate Haitian ethnic community had to come to terms with Black American leaders who claimed to speak for all Blacks. In addition, several leaders of Haitian ethnic organizations returned to Haiti, believing the promises of reform being issued by a new Haitian president, Jean-Claude Duvalier.

Meanwhile the debate about culture appeared to be destroying any semblance of community. The debate focused on the use of Creole (*see*, Buchanan in this volume). Underneath the dispute over language and culture were questions of class. Would Haitian culture be defined as predominantly French or African in its roots? Would the culture of the bourgeoisie or the peasantry be promoted?[6]

At the center of the controversy were the "Blessed Priests," a group of Haitian priests who were strongly influenced by liberation theology. They preached pride in Haitian peasant culture and a nationalist opposition to the Duvalier regime and to the foreign domination of Haiti. In New York City, the priests began to say Catholic masses in Creole and sought to unify the Haitian population through the use of Creole as the true Haitian national language (Buchanan, this volume).

Initially, the efforts of the "Blessed Priests" to create revolutionary nationalist sentiment among Haitian immigrants met with tremendous opposition. Many people of all classes refused to attend Creole masses and resisted the use of Creole as a symbol of their common heritage. Although many of the Haitian immigrants rejected Creole as inappropriate for public occasions, by participating in the debate they were implicitly accepting the underlying notion that Haitians can share interests and a common identity. Thus, the controversy laid the foundation for greater unity in the future.

Into the midst of this controversy came thousands of new Haitian immigrants, many of them from peasant or urban working-class backgrounds and unfamiliar with French culture. At the same time, some members of the Haitian upper classes together with other well-educated Haitians returned to Haiti. These changes in the migrant stream would affect all efforts to build a Haitian community throughout the 1970s.

In 1971, François Duvalier died and was replaced as President-for-Life by his nineteen year-old son, Jean-Claude. The new president promised to carry out a political liberalization and to promote economic development. Although Jean-Claude wielded political power less brutally than his father, his efforts at increasing political freedom were superficial and short-lived and repression remained pervasive. Throughout the 1970s, an influx of international capital created a small industrial sector. This development provided some low-wage employment opportunities for Haitian workers. A large number of technicians and professionals returned to Haiti from the United States to take up administrative and managerial positions.

For the vast majority of the Haitian population, Jean-Claude's presidency meant a continuation of intolerable political and economic conditions. Many believed that their only hope lay in coming to the United States. Those who

---

[6] The same reaction was also observed in Haiti around attempts to make Creole the "national language." Motions were passed in the Haitian Congress to make Creole the language of instruction in the first five primary grades in the Haitian schools, but they were very unpopular and French was kept as the "official language."

couldn't manage to obtain a visa, whether official, forged, or borrowed, came by small boat. The first boat arrived in 1972 and was followed by an increasing number every year throughout the decade. By mid-1981 the Immigration and Naturalization Service has apprehended approximately 45,000 Haitians landing on Florida's coast (Buchanan, 1981:49).

In the early 1970s, the U.S. economy was falling into a recession. Foreign workers were portrayed as competitors for American jobs and sentiment against them increased. Various directors of the Immigration and Naturalization Service (INS) focused national attention on undocumented immigration, calling it a "silent invasion" and a "national dilemma" and blaming undocumented immigrants for the rapid growth of unemployment and the decline of social services (Chapman, 1976; Bustamante, 1980). In this climate U.S. immigration officials targeted Haitian "boat people" for rapid apprehension and deportation back to Haiti with little observance of due process of law (Stepick, 1982:178–95).

In the spring of 1980, 125,000 Cubans arrived by boat in southern Florida. This "Mariel" exodus and the rapid processing and acceptance of the Cubans' applications for asylum inspired a surge in Haitian boat migration. Nearly 25,000 Haitians landed in Florida during 1980 compared to roughly 5,000 the year before (Buchanan, 1981:49). The American government detained the Haitian "boat people" and subjected them to unsanitary conditions in crowded detention camps.

From the early arrivals of these boat people, newspaper headlines portrayed Haitian immigrants as ragged, impoverished, and illiterate. This image contributed to a growing public sentiment that the United States should not continue to accept the "tempest-tossed" from the "teeming shores." The media image of Haitians as weak, pitiful, and ignorant sent shock waves through the Haitian population of New York. Many shunned any identity which would equate them with the boat people. Human rights organizations that made efforts to win better treatment for the boat people were puzzled by the fact that many Haitian organizations wanted nothing to do with the boat people.

However, certain Haitian groups took an early and enduring interest in the boat people. The activist "Blessed Priests," the Haitian political left, and Haitian exile organizations came forward to represent the community. Together with American organizations such as the National Council of Churches, the Emergency Civil Liberties Committee, and the Congressional Black Caucus, they worked to have the boat people accepted as political refugees rather than as economic migrants seeking jobs and economic opportunity. Status as "political" as opposed to "economic" refugees would provide a positive image for the boat people around which a Haitian community could be organized. Organizations which tried to obtain refugee status for the boat people argued that all Haitians who were forced to flee the repressive Duvalier government belonged to a community and should be granted political asylum. Taking this line of argument, Haitian community organizations found themselves organizing a political attack on the Duvalier government. Those who had organized, participated in, or supported actions in behalf of the boat people came to feel that united and vocal political action could bring results. In June 1980, the federal government recognized those who had come by boat prior to October 1980 as "Haitian entrants" and gave them the right to work in the United States and to receive certain medical, educational, and financial benefits. The Spellman decision in June 1982 "paroled" many people who had been imprisoned in detention centers.

A new, politicized Haitian identity began to emerge. In 1981, an estimated 10,000 Haitian immigrants and many Americans came to Washington D.C. to demand the release of Haitians from immigration detention centers. In 1982, a crowd of approximately 5,000 people, predominantly Haitians, marched down Eastern Parkway in Brooklyn to make the same demand. This organizing was supported, encouraged, and assisted by U.S. church organizations and private voluntary organizations involved in securing freedom for the boat people.

The demonstrations were organized in the name of the Haitian community, a notion which seemed to come to life for the large number of people who marched down the street together. For these demonstrators the stigma of the boat people had turned into a source of pride.

Through these demonstrations and the subsequent organizing many Haitian organizations emerged which used Creole as the language of their meetings and public gatherings. These organizations accepted a new conceptualization of Haitian culture, one built on the efforts of the activist priests to define the popular, not the elite, culture as the basis for the Haitian community. Organizations that wished to be identified as representative of "the Haitian community" for both the Haitian population and the larger society stopped claiming that Haitians were a people with a French-based culture.

PHASE IV: 1982–1986.

THE FLOWERING OF ORGANIZATIONAL DIVERSITY AND A FURTHER DEVELOPMENT OF COMMUNITY

At first, attempts to establish a broader Haitian identity and greater unity of action were threatened in two ways. First, all Haitians were inaccurately but very publicly linked with the dreaded disease AIDS (Acquired Immune Deficiency Syndrome). In response, many Haitians had not only distanced themselves from efforts to organize a Haitian community, but had ceased even to identify themselves as Haitian. Second, before the overthrow of Jean-Claude Duvalier in early 1986, many Haitian immigrants feared the consequences of an open anti-Duvalier stand implied in the new, politicized definition of the Haitian community. Both of these developments contributed to a flowering of organizations which did not identify themselves as Haitian and worked against the unifying sentiment of a Haitian community that had developed.

In 1982, the Federal Centers for Disease Control and the New York City Department of Health placed Haitians on the list of populations at risk for the contraction of AIDS. Haitians were the only members of a nationality group so identified. The stigma they had first incurred when identified by the media as boat people was now greatly increased. Haitian school children found themselves shunned by both teachers and students; Haitians lost jobs, friends, and apartments. By 1985 when the federal and city governments decided to remove Haitians from the category of a group at risk of contracting AIDS, Haitians had already become firmly linked in the public mind as carriers of AIDS. This experience of being ostracized and shunned because they were from Haiti served to reinstate the long-standing tendency of many individuals and organizations not to identify themselves as part of a Haitian community.

Sectors of the Haitian immigrant population also pulled away from identification with the Haitian community because the term "community" had become a term identified with anti-Duvalierist politics. These people feared such a political stance would prevent them from maintaining their ties with their family and friends in Haiti. Moreover, they saw any politics as the domain of competition between personally ambitious leaders and wanted no part of it.

Thus, an increasing number of immigrants organized around a number of alternative identities. Currently, over 250 organizations exist among Haitian immigrants. Of the 91 organizations we interviewed in 1985, the majority were organized around regional, religious, occupational, fraternal, or Caribbean identities. Many were religious groups including new storefront Protestant churches and an organization of Haitian Taoists.

Leaders of Association Antille, one of the numerous regional associations which developed during this phase, were clear about their relation to the rest of the Haitian immigrants: they wanted nothing to do with them. "The opinion of the organization," stated one leader, "is not to build ties with anyone from other countries or even from other parts of Haiti." The sole interest of such groups has been to raise money for projects back in their hometowns. The leaders and members used the organization to obtain or maintain prestige and influence back home as well as among their networks in New York. Politics have endangered the base they are building back home.

Yet at the same time, the funding and support provided by the government, foundations, and private voluntary agencies for the settlement and adjustment of the Haitian "entrants" gave a new impetus to ethnic organizing. A new Haitian citizens' association and a Haitian student organization were developed with the explicit goal of obtaining power and position for Haitians as a group within the American political system. These associations were among a handful of Haitian groups working to forge political connections in New York City and to make their way in an ethnic political situation which had increased in complexity.

A dinner for high school graduates given by the Association of College Graduates revealed some of the complexity of these connections. The guest of honor was State Assemblyman David Harris, a Black American. He spoke to the Haitians as fellow Black people, part of a community who share a fate of racial discrimination. In contrast, the Haitian leaders who welcomed the graduates did so on behalf of the Haitian community, and avoided submerging that identity in a broader racial category.

While Assemblyman Harris did not publicly recognize the Haitians as a separate ethnic constituency, other Black American politicians readily did so. Black American leaders differed as to whether they recognized ethnic divisions within the Black population as a whole. These leaders were in competition with a new grouping of Black politicians who identified themselves as Caribbean (Basch, this volume; Kasinitz, *n.d.*). Caribbean leaders included Haiti in their definition of Caribbeans and encouraged the participation of Haitian leaders in their organizing efforts.

In contrast, White politicians, such as Edward Koch who was the Mayor of New York City, played classic ethnic politics, publicly lauding "the unique cultural heritage of the Haitian people" and welcoming the Haitians into the ranks of New York's multitude of ethnic groups. Since 1980 every October 17[7] has been declared "Haitian Solidarity Day" by the Mayor of the City of New York and several of the borough presidents. In 1985, Mayor Koch held a breakfast in Gracie Mansion with a "Haitian Task Force" and proclaimed New York's first "Haitian Culture and Awareness Week." Ethnic organizing, even with its new complexities, seemed firmly established.

Yet within a few months the orientation of organizing efforts changed dramatically and portended the beginning of a new era of nationalist organizing. The pull of events in Haiti again had a profound effect on the leaders and organizations bent on establishing a Haitian community in New York.

In November 1985, the ton ton macoutes attacked a demonstration and killed three high school students in the town of Gonaive in central Haiti. Towns and cities throughout Haiti erupted in openly antigovernment demonstrations which protested the killings in Gonaive. By January the people began attacking the macoutes, government officials, and the central government was no longer in control of the hinterland. In Haiti, calls of the people for "*Liberté*" were supported not only by the Catholic clergy but by an ever

---

[7] October 17 is the anniversary of the assassination of Jean Jacques Dessalines, the founder of the Hatian Republic, who proclaimed the Independence of Haiti in 1804.

widening circle of forces including the usually conservative Protestant denominations, the Association of Haitian Doctors, and the Association of
Haitian Industrialists. Finally, Jean-Claude Duvalier fled, replaced by a six-
member junta, five of whom had played important roles within the Duvalier
government.

Day by day Haitians who watched from abroad became more involved in
the political drama unfolding in Haiti. In the two months preceding
Duvalier's flight and in the weeks which followed, tens of thousands of
Haitian immigrants came together in picket lines, marches, church services,
and meetings in support of the uprisings in Haiti. In the words of a statement
signed by seven regional Haitian associations in New York, these Haitian
immigrants expressed their "solidarity and [upheld] without reservation the
Haitian people in their heroic struggle for justice, well-being and democracy." The fact that this statement came from previously apolitical regional
associations was significant. The upsurge of struggle in Haiti had brought a
wider circle of organizations into a nationalistic political struggle, uniting
them under the rubric of a Haitian community.

Leaders who just a few months before had been using their ties to American politicians to win recognition of the Haitians as one of New York's ethnic
groups were now politicking to end American support for Duvalier. When
Duvalier fell, several of these leaders immediately declared they planned to
return to Haiti. Determinedly nonpolitical Protestant leaders showed up at
events supporting the struggle in Haiti, or helped lead a Protestant service
of thanksgiving after Duvalier's departure.

A proud identification with the Haitian community, which community
organizers had been working to instill for twenty years, was established. On
February 8, 1986, an estimated 25,000 Haitians marched and danced through
the streets of Brooklyn. Many carried red and blue Haitian flags, or wore red
and blue clothing. When speakers said that the Haitian people had finally
"stood up" and once again showed the world that Haitians can struggle for
freedom and justice the crowd roared approval. This new pride in being
Haitian was based on identifying the Haitian community in New York as a
part of the Haitian nation. People chanted, "Ayiti pou Ayisyens! Ameriken, pa
met men sou Ayiti," (Haiti for Haitians. Americans, keep your hands off Haiti).
They followed this with "Makut, bam peyi mwen" (Macoutes, give me my
country), and the country they meant was Haiti.

Calls for unity were frequent during the months after Duvalier's fall.
However, while many organizations came forward to speak to and for the
community, any unity between organizations was destined to be extremely
tenuous and short-lived. Looking to play a leading role in Haiti, leaders in
New York tended to build up their own special constituencies rather than
unite in a common cause. When it became clear that all New York leaders had
been excluded from the post-Duvalier government, an ad hoc coalition called
for a "massive demonstration." The coalition, obtained endorsements from a

broad range of organizations, but also exacerbated underlying differences and tensions. Thus, at the very moment when increasing numbers of the Haitian immigrant population came to identify with a Haitian community, personal ambitions, class divisions, and differences in political programs continued to divide that community.

CONCLUSION

Several themes have emerged from this historical overview. First, we have shown that Haitians, like other immigrant populations, have organized around many identities other than as members of a single community. These diverse identities reflect forces at work in both Haiti and in the United States and are maintained, in part, because Haitian immigrants are actors in the social systems of both countries. Looking back toward Haiti, the first leaders to form organizations among Haitian immigrants were those who wanted to preserve social and political differences within the population both in New York and in Haiti. Since that time, Haitian immigrants have developed various types of identities often trying not to publicly identify as Haitian.

Second, throughout the four phases of organizing, Haitians have had to confront the question of race. But while race remains a constant factor, our study shows that the identities adopted by a Black immigrant population can vary over time. In the first phase of settlement, Haitian and other Caribbean immigrants found that they were able to organize politically only as Blacks. In contrast, during the second phase, the politics of ethnic pluralism encouraged some Haitian leaders to define themselves with a separate Haitian identity so as to be different from and even compete with Black Americans and other Black groups. Although the perception that the attacks on the Haitian boat people had an underlying element of U.S. government racism rallied numerous Black people to oppose the attacks, Haitian leaders organized their defense activities primarily around the identity of a distinct Haitian community defined in political opposition to Duvalier. During the last phase of organizing some Haitian leaders again turned toward ethnic organization. They built both political alliances as Black people and competed with Black and Caribbean leaders as representatives of a separate Haitian community.

Finally, we have traced the way in which the concept of a Haitian community developed in the context of political and economic developments in both the United States and Haiti. The notion of a Haitian community began as an ideology or model of the way immigrant life is lived in America. The concept of a Haitian ethnic community was taught by representatives of American institutions to members of the Haitian immigrant population. Though this notion was "made in America," it was reshaped by Haitian leaders and their organizations in relation to events and social forces in the United States, Haiti, and around the world. In developing a model of community, Haitian immigrants, like others before them, utilized both ethnic and nationalistic concepts of identity.

When Haitian immigrants organized as an ethnic group they saw themselves as an interest group within American society competing with similar groups for power, influence and prestige in the United States. When Haitian immigrants organized as "the Haitian community" for nationalistic goals, they sought to change the regime in Haiti and return triumphant to Haiti. In both cases the concept of a "Haitian community" played a key role in structuring the actions, speech and identity of participants.

As leaders and organizations with ethnic and nationalist aspirations appealed to their members and built their constituencies in the name of the "Haitian community," some members of "the immigrant population" responded. The ideology of community came to shape group action. In the course of the attacks on the boat people, the ideology of community allowed organizations with different goals to coalesce and brought increasing numbers of Haitian immigrants into political action. The ideology of community was transformed from a set of abstractions into the practice of people acting together.

However, underneath the unity of action the contradictions between the interests and political aspirations of various classes and sectors of the population have continued. At times of political crisis, such as the uprising in Haiti against the Duvalier regime, such contradictions lead to greater divisions in the leadership of the community. Meanwhile, a greatly enlarged number of organizations and individuals identify themselves with the Haitian community.

At the moment, increasing numbers of organizations are being politicized and pulled into identification with the Haitian nation and the actions and fate of the Haitian people. At some later date, this new level of unity may be used as a base for further efforts to participate in the American political system. As in the case of previous ethnically organized immigrants, political action within the United States may be used to influence events back home as well as to obtain resources and position in the United States settled in the United States.

BIBLIOGRAPHY

Allman, J. and K. Richman
1985   "Migration, Decision Making and Policy, the Case of Haitian International Migration, 1971–1984." Paper presented at the Population Association of America Meetings, Boston.

Bryce-Laporte, R.S., ed.
1980   *Sourcebook on the New Immigration: Implications for the United States and the International Community.* New Brunswick, New Jersey: Transaction Books.

Buchanan, S.
1981   "Haitian Emigration: The Perspective from South Florida and Haiti," Port-au-Prince: U.S.
       Agency for International Development. Mimeographed.

Bustamante, J.
1980   "Immigrants from Mexico: The Silent Invasion Issue." In *Sourcebook on the New Immigration:
       Implications for the United States and the International Community.* R.S. Bryce-Laporte, ed.
       New Brunswick, New Jersey: Transaction Books. Pp. 140–144.

Chapman, L.F.
1976   "Illegal Aliens: Time to Call a Halt." *Readers' Digest,* 109:88–92. Oct.

Fouron, G.
1983   "The Black Immigrant Dilemma in the U.S.: The Haitian Experience." *Journal of Caribbean
       Studies,* 3(3):242–265. Winter.

Georges, E.
1984   *New Immigrants and the Political Process: Dominicans in New York.* New York Center for Latin
       American and Caribbean Studies, New York University Research Program in Inter-Amer-
       ican Affairs. Occasional Paper No. 45.

Glazer, N. and D.P. Moynihan
1963   *Beyond the Melting Pot: the Negroes, Puerto Ricans, Jews, Italians and Irish of New York City.*
       Second Edition. Cambridge, MA: The M.I.T. Press.

Glick Schiller, N.
1977   "Ethnic Groups Are Made, Not Born." In *Ethnic Encounters: Identities and Contexts.* G. Hicks
       and P. Leis, eds. North Scituate, MA: Duxbury Press. Pp. 23–35.

_____
1975   "The Formation of a Haitian Ethnic Group," Ph.D. dissertation, Columbia University.

Gorelick, S.
1982   *City College and the Jewish Poor.* New York: Schocken Books.

Kasinitz, P.
n.d.   "West Indian Diaspora: Race and Ethnicity in Minority Politics." Unpublished manuscript.
       New York University Department of Sociology.

Handlin, O.
1951   *The Uprooted: The Epic Story of the Great Migrations that Made the American People.* New York:
       Grosset & Dunlap.

Laguerre, M.S.
1984   *American Odyssey: Haitians in New York City.* Ithaca: Cornell University Press.

Leyburn, J.G.
1966   *The Haitian People.* Revised edition. New Haven: Yale University Press.

Lundhal, M.
1979   *Peasants and Poverty: A Study of Haiti.* London: Croom Helm.

Moral, P.
1978   *Le paysan haïtien: etude sue la vie rurale en Haïti.* Port-au-Prince: Fardin.

Olsen, J.
1979   *The Ethnic Dimension in American History.* New York: St. Martin's Press.

Paquin, L.
1983   *The Haitians: Class and Color Politics.* Brooklyn, NY: Multi-Type.

Pierre-Charles, G.
1961   *L'economie haïtienne et sa voie de development.* Paris: Maisonneuve & Larose.

Portes, A. and J. Walton
1981   *Labor, Class, and the International System.* New York: Academic Press.

Pressoir, C.F.
1947 *Debat sur le creole et le folklore.* Port-au-Prince: Imprimerie de L'Etat.

Sassen-Koob, S.
1981 "Towards a Conceptualization of Immigrant Labor." *Social Problems* 29(1):65–85. Oct.

Schermerhorn, R.A.
1949 *These Our People.* Boston: D.C. Heath.

Schoenberg, U.
1985 "Participation in Ethnic Associations: The Case of Immigrants in West Germany." *International Migration Review* 19(3):416-437. Fall.

Sowell, T.
1981 *Ethnic America: A History.* New York: Basic Books.

Stepick, A.
1982 "Haitian Boat People: A Study in the Conflicting Forces Shaping U.S. Immigration Policy." *Law and Contemporary Problems* 45(2):163–196. Spring.

Vassady, Jr., B.
1982 "The 'Homeland Cause' as a Stimulant to Ethnic Unity: The Hungarian American Response to Karolyi's 1914 American Tour." *Journal of American Ethnic History*, 2(1):39–64. Fall.

POSTSCRIPT

HAITIAN TRANSNATIONAL PRACTICE AND NATIONAL DISCOURSE

Nina Glick Schiller
January 1992

The major findings and conclusions of the article "All in the Same Boat?" remain relevant seven years later. In the article we argued that social scientists must look at both home and host societies in order to understand the context within which immigrants organize and develop collective identities. We traced the changing conditions in the United States and Haiti that had shaped Haitian organizing in New York City.

Beginning in 1957 when there was little organization and no collective Haitian identity, the article outlined four stages in the emergence of a public Haitian presence in New York. By 1986, Haitian immigrants were participating in organized activities oriented to both life in the United States and life in Haiti. While earlier these immigrants had hesitated to identify with other Haitians and had organized around multiple identities, there was evidence by 1986 that Haitian immigrants were identifying themselves as members of a Haitian community. The article noted a tendency, then newborn, to link together the two societies by identifying the Haitian community in New York as part of the Haitian nation. However, the article did not comment on this development nor report on the widespread practice among Haitian immigrants to build and maintain their links to Haiti, even as they developed social networks and activities that linked them to the daily life of their neighborhoods and work places in New York.

Therefore, to a certain extent, our analysis "missed the boat"; we were unable to explore the implications of the growing density of multiple layers of home ties and the passionate identification with Haiti of Haitian immigrants who were firmly embedded in U.S. society. We paid insufficient attention to this aspect of Haitian migration despite the fact that Haitian members of our research team, Marie Lucie Brutus, Carolle Charles, George Fouron, and Antoine Thomas were themselves well established in the United States and yet Haiti was an ongoing part of their daily lives and activities.

It was only when Linda Basch, Cristina Szanton Blanc and I began to compare the experiences of migrants from the Eastern Caribbean, from the Philippines and from Haiti and similar patterns emerged that the full implications of these trends became clear. The three of us developed an analytical framework that could account for the praxis and discourse of the three immigrant populations. (Basch, Glick Schiller and Szanton Blanc, in press; Glick Schiller, Basch and Szanton Blanc, 1992).

We have defined transnationalism as the processes by which immigrants build social fields that link together their country of origin and their country of settlement. Immigrants who build such social fields are designated "trans migrants." Transmigrants develop and maintain multiple relations—familial, economic, social, organizational, religious, and political—that span borders. Transmigrants take actions, make decisions, and feel concerns, and develop identities within social networks that connect them to two or more societies simultaneously (Glick Schiller, Basch and Szanton Blanc, 1992).

We hypothesized that contemporary immigrants are increasingly transnational because of the following factors "1)labor sending countries in a dependent relationship with capital core countries 2) the construction of transnational social fields 3) the insecurities generated by present shaky conditions of world capitalism, and 4) the racially exclusive dominant national construction of citizenship in core capitalist countries that presume whiteness" (Basch, Glick Schiller and Szanton Blanc, 1991). Having begun to perceive the phenomenon of Haitian transnationalism, Haitian members of the research team and I turned to an exploration of various aspects of Haitian transnationalism (Glick Schiller and Fouron, 1990; Charles, 1990, 1992; Fouron, 1992). In this same period a number of other scholars began to conceptualize transnationalism as a major trend in contemporary international migration (Sutton, 1987; Kearney, 1990; Rouse, 1992).

Social scientists in the United States have long pictured immigrants as "the uprooted," who cut their ties with their country of origin and were obliged to adapt to their new country (Handlin, 1951). In contrast, populations who refused to settle and continued to agitate for changes in their homeland were seen not as immigrants but as exiles or political refugees. Immigrants themselves, in part influenced by assimilationist pressures of both social science and public policy, have debated their relationship to the United States in terms of these same antimonies. Haitian immigrants interested in overthrowing Duvalier urged people to keep alive their identification with Haiti. They urged people to see themselves as only temporary residents of the United States. These forces, were spearheaded by the "Haitian Fathers"—radical activist priests exiled by Duvalier—who popularized the word "diaspora" to convey the sense of a displaced Haitian people whose mission was to return to the homeland. Others argued it was hopeless to expect political change in Haiti in their lifetimes, and the task at hand was to engage in the urgent problems face by the Haitian populations in New York by entering actively into the U.S. political process. The question was posed as either/or.

However, despite this conceptual dualism, many persons, including "leaders," members of organizations, and the unaffiliated were engaged both in maintaining ties to Haiti and in settling in the United States. Various forms of organizations such as regional associations and Protestant churches, people with occupations which included musicians (Glick Schiller and Fouron, 1990), technocrats, and *mambo* and *houngon* (voodoo priestesses and priests) (Richman, 1990), and persons engaged in business activities were increasingly operating in both societies simultaneously. Family members went back and forth for reasons of health, to celebrate weddings or funerals, or to visit. Remittances went back to Haiti, and news of family and friends arrived on cassettes or via telephones. Much of this establishment and maintenance of home ties had begun quietly in the 1970s although it became much more prominent in the years following the overthrow of Jean-Claude Duvalier.

By 1992 many Haitian immigrants in New York have become transnational in their activities and their identities, playing a role in both societies. Many seem to be attempting to firmly plant their feet in the United States and to maintain their familial, social, and economic ties to Haiti. They are determined to build the best possible situation for themselves in their new land of settlement, while not giving up the land of their birth. Moreover they try, sometime successfully and sometimes not, to bring their children up to continue to identify with both societies.

However, an awareness of this transnationalism and a conscious commitment to it, has emerged only slowly. The term diaspora became much more widely known and its meaning began to change. While in 1985 most Haitian leaders we interviewed were not familiar with the term, by 1991 it had entered into Haitian Creole in both the United States and Haiti. In the United States, diaspora meant those who were settled a long time in the United States but continued to have a commitment to and active involvement in developments in Haiti. (In Haiti it could mean Haitians abroad or have more of a pejorative gloss such as "upstarts.") In popularizing this term Haitian leaders made reference to Zionists who in the Haitian conception were Jews in the United States who were part of the polity and society in the United States but felt that they had a "homeland" in Israel.

When Pascal Truillot became interim President in 1990, the active engagement of the diaspora in the political affairs of Haiti became apparent in several ways. Truillot came to power as the result of a coalition of political forces in Haiti in which the Haitian Fathers played a seminal role. These priests had returned to Haiti in 1987 but had extensive transnational networks which linked the United States and Haiti. Truillot appointed, as representatives of the Haitian government in Washington and New York, two long-time members of the diaspora, one of whom was the director of a Haitian community center organized since the 1960s to represent Haitians as an ethnic group in New York.

However, it was Father Jean Betrand Aristide who gave to the Haitian population, both in Haiti and abroad, a new way to conceptualize their transnational experiences. On the day of his inauguration in February 1991, Aristide addressed representatives of the diaspora with whom he was meeting in the Presidential Palace as the *"Le Dixieme Departement"* (The Tenth Department), (Richman, 1992). The territory of Haiti is divided into nine geographic divisions called *"Departements."* By conceptualizing Haitians abroad as part of the territory of Haiti, Aristide became one of an increasing number of Third-World leaders who define their dispersed populations as part of a "deterritorialized nation" (Basch, Glick Schiller and Szanton Blanc, 1991; Basch, Glick Schiller and Szanton Blanc, in press). Concepts of the deterritorialized nation recognize the necessity for a large proportion of the population of Third-World countries to live outside of their countries of origin. However, these populations are constructed as remaining part of the nation—economically, socially, and politically—no matter where they may settle and no matter what other citizenships they may acquire.

The concept of *"le dixieme"* struck a resonant note among a number of middle-class Haitian immigrants and aspiring political leaders in the United States and they proceeded to hold a series of meetings to organize the manner in which they would assist Haiti and to choose official representatives of the Tenth Department. The concept was less popular among those, both inside and outside Haiti, who opposed Aristide. This opposition included the majority of the Haitian Parliament who refused to allow the Tenth Department to have any official status.

Aristide's overthrow in September 1991 occasioned rallies and marches in the United States and Canada culminating with an estimated 50,000 people who demonstrated for Aristide in October in New York City. This massive demonstration which included a strong representation of both men and women, young and old, newly arrived and long-term residents, undocumented and naturalized citizens, workers and middle class was organized by

Le Dixieme. Among the speakers who addressed the demonstration was Mayor Dinkins, the African-American Mayor of the City of New York.

Whatever the immediate political situation in Haiti, the demonstration made clear the tremendous transformation of the Haitian immigrant population in the course of the past three decades. The days when Haitian immigrants kept apart from each other, seeking no common activities in the United States and no public identification as Haitian or with the Haitian state, were gone. The presence of Mayor Dinkins signaled that the Haitian immigrant population was part of the political process in the United States and seen by major political actors as significant players in U.S. ethnic and racial politics. At the very same time, Haitian immigrants were publicly and actively participating in the political processes of Haiti by responding to the call of the leaders of le dixieme and coming out in large numbers to demand the restoration of Aristide. Aristide's rhetoric built among these immigrants a conscious identification with the Haitian nation-state. This was a consciousness that had been developing ever since Haitians took to the streets in New York in the joyous days that followed the overthrow of Jean-Claude Duvalier.

In one sense Haitian transnationalism had come of age. The concept of Le Dixieme allowed Haitian immigrants to express their continuing ties to Haiti without eschewing their ties within the United States. However, as a construction which focuses Haitian transmigrant energies on the Haitian nation-state, there is much in the Haitian transnational experience that the identity as members of Le Dixieme does not encompass. Through their social relationships and their actions, Haitian transmigrants experience the intersection and interpenetration of their countries of origin and settlement. They may be conceptualized and even come to see themselves as a population sharing the experience of living their lives stretched between the United States and Haiti. However, this is a population that remains diverse in class backgrounds, history of settlement and current class position. No single identity has been, or possibly can be, formulated that could fully give voice to the complexity of their lives lived across national borders in a world divided into nation-states.

BIBLIOGRAPHY

Basch, L., N. Glick Schiller and C. Szanton Blanc
In   The Transnationalization of Migration: New Perspectives on Ethnicity, Race, and Nation.
Press New York: Gordon and Breach.

1991 "Transnationalism and the Construction of the Deterritorialized Nation: An Outline for a Theory of Post-National Practice." Paper presented at the 90th Annual Meeting of the American Anthropological Association, Chicago.

Brown, K.
1991   *Mama Lola*. Berkeley: University of California Press.

Charles, C.
1990   "A Transnational Dialectic of Race, Class and Ethnicity: Patterns of Identity and Forms of Consciousness Among Haitian Migrants in New York City." Ph.D. dissertation. SUNY, Binghampton.

———
1992   "Transnationalism in the Construct of Haitian Migrants' Racial Categories of Identity in New York City." In *Towards a Transnational Perspective on Migration: Race, Class, Ethnicity and Nationalism Reconsidered*. N. Glick Schiller, L. Basch and C. Szanton Blanc, eds. New York: New York Academy of Sciences.

Fouron, G.
1992   *Dependency and Labor Migration: Haiti in the Fold of Global Capitalism*. Durham, N.C.: Duke University Press.

Glick Schiller, N., L. Basch and C. Szanton Blanc
1992   "Transnationalism: A New Analytic Framework for Understanding Migration." In *Towards a Transnational Perspective on Migration: Race, Class, Ethnicity and Nationalism Reconsidered*. N. Glick Schiller, L. Basch and C. Szanton Blanc, eds. New York: New York Academy of Sciences.

Glick Schiller, N. and G. Fouron
1990   "'Everywhere we go we are in danger.' Ti Manno and the Emergence of a Haitian Transnational Identity." *American Ethnologist*, 17(2):329–347.

Handlin, O.
1951   *The Uprooted: The Epic Story of the Great Migrations that Made the American People*. New York: Grosset and Dunlap.

Kearney, M.
1990   "Borders and Boundaries of State and Self at the End of Empire." Unpublished manuscript.

Rouse, R.
1992   "Making Sense of Settlement: Class Transformation, Cultural Struggle, and Transnationalism among Mexican Migrants in the United States," In *Towards a Transnational Perspective on Migration: Race, Class, Ethnicity and Nationalism Reconsidered*. N. Glick Schiller, L. Basch and C. Szanton Blanc, eds. New York: New York Academy of Sciences.

Richman, K.
1990   "Ritual, Remittances, and Development: Rethinking Conscious Consumption in a Transnational Community." Paper presented at the 89th Annual Meeting of the American Anthropological Association, New Orleans.

———
1992   "'A Lavalas at Home/A Lavalas for Home': Inflections of Transnationalism in the Discourse of Haitian President Aristide." In *Towards a Transnational Perspective on Migration: Race, Class, Ethnicity and Nationalism Reconsidered*. N. Glick Schiller, L. Basch and C. Szanton Blanc, eds. New York: New York Academy of Sciences.

Sutton, C.
1987   "The Caribbeanization of New York City and the Emergence of a Transnational Sociocultural System." In *Caribbean Life in New York City: Sociocultural Dimensions*. C. Sutton and E. Chaney, eds. Staten Island, New York: Center for Migration Studies. Pp. 25–29.

LANGUAGE AND IDENTITY:
Haitians in New York City

SUSAN BUCHANAN STAFFORD*
Community Relations Service, U.S. Department of Justice

All immigrants to the United States have experienced conflicts of social identity when confronted by the necessity of remaking their lives in a new society. For Afro-Caribbean immigrants, in this case, Haitians, the issue is complicated by the fact that they arrived with a deep ambivalence over their racial and cultural heritages, the legacy of a colonial, slave-based past. These conflicts are exacerbated by the position of Afro-Caribbean immigrants within the United States race and socioeconomic systems and by the social identities ascribed to them by the dominant White society. In responding to this situation, Afro-Caribbean immigrants choose to emphasize different elements from their traditions of linguistic and cultural dualism according to their strategic value in different social contexts.

The use of two sets of cultural values and two forms of language and speech patterns by Afro-Caribbean populations is a widely noted and distinctive aspect of their traditions (see, Abrahams, 1970a, 1970b; Makiesky, 1973, 1976; Reisman, 1970; Sutton, 1974; Wilson, 1973). Rooted in the interplay of African and European derived forms, "biculturalism" and language dualisms in the New World context are linked to issues of power, class, and status, and sociocultural identity. The contradictory evaluations of language and culture that these dualisms permit often make selective use of forms a matter of contention. Thus, cultural and linguistic dualisms in Afro-Caribbean societies can, on occasion themselves, become the direct focus of social and personal conflict.

This chapter focuses on identity and status conflicts experienced by Haitian immigrants in New York City and expressed in their debates over language usage.[1] In Haiti, both Haitian Creole and French are spoken, and

*The analysis put forth in this article is my own and does not represent the views of the U.S. Department of Justice.

[1] Material for this chapter was drawn from the author's doctoral dissertation and based upon field work conducted among Haitian immigrants in New York City between Oct. 1974 and Jan. 1977. The research was partially funded through the generosity of David Kriser by a Charles Kriser Foundation fellowship. I should like to thank Constance R. Sutton, Nancy Bonvillain, Mary Ann Castle, Penney Hills, and Donald C. Buchanan, and several Haitian friends who must remain anonymous for their comments and editorial assistance.

language is an important aspect of personal and social identity. As I intend to show by analyzing the struggle over the primary language to be used in the Catholic Mass at a Brooklyn church,[2] the issue of language not only continues to express identity and status conflicts among Haitian immigrants, but it is also a vehicle for debating the leadership within the Haitian milieu and the representation of the Haitian community to the wider society.

LANGUAGE IN HAITI

As in many other Caribbean nations, the clash of Africa and Europe in the Americas left Haiti with two languages.[3] Haitian Creole is universally spoken, but only a minority of 2–5 percent of the population also speak French fluently. Although Haitian Creole derives much of its vocabulary from French, the two languages are mutually unintelligible. Their linguistic relationship has been described as one of diglossia; that is, the coexistence of two languages (or varieties of language) within the same speech community, one of which is accorded high prestige, the other, low prestige (Ferguson, 1959; Pride, 1971). The majority of Haitians are monolingual Creole speakers, but French, as the official language, is endowed with high prestige. Historically, the French language and culture of Haiti's former colonizers have been used by the dominant minority to validate its claims to power and high status, and to block the majority of Haitians from full participation in the national life. The language situation thus not only mirrors, but reinforces the social, economic, and cultural differences which separate the educated elite and growing middle class from the illiterate and impoverished peasantry and urban proletariat. In addition, the positive and negative evaluations of Haitian Creole and French, their African and European associations, and the contexts deemed appropriate for their use also reveal the complex and contradictory feelings Haitians have about their racial and cultural identities (see, Efron, 1954; Hall, 1953; Leyburn, [1941] 1966; Stewart, 1963; Valdman, 1975). Herskovits ([1937] 1971) characterized these attitudes as "socialized ambivalence" (see also, Bourguignon, 1970).

In general, Haitians of all social classes have tended overtly to "accept" the ranking of Whiteness and colonially-derived cultural behavior and language

[2] English was not perceived as an alternative in this controversy, hence, I have not discussed its meaning and associations for Haitian immigrants. Most Haitians regard English as a language necessary for survival and as the language of the younger generation. For many Haitians who do not speak French, English is replacing French as their language of status and prestige and is a means of culturally validating their achievements in United States society. English and its cultural associations are naturally becoming an important part of the social identity of Haitian children born or educated in the United States. It is possible that more Haitians now speak English rather than French as their second language. In Haiti, English has become a third language for a small but increasing number of Haitians, especially those involved in business and tourism. The growing importance of English in Haiti reflects the United States presence there and Haiti's status as an American satellite colony.

[3] See, Hymes (1971) for a general discussion of issues in Creole linguistics. A vast body of literature on Haitian Creole exists and some of the major works are cited in the bibliography.

as superior to Blackness and the African-based cultural and linguistic forms. Consequently, French, a language with international stature, is considered to be the appropriate language to use in all Haitian national settings and to project Haiti's national identity to the world. Fluency in French is associated with power, authority, formal knowledge and high social status; it is essential for social mobility. A symbol of the refined and cultivated aspects of Haitian life, the French language is admired and respected, as are those who speak it well.

Despite the growth of Haitian nationalism during the twentieth century and increased recognition of the necessity of using the majority language as the major medium of communication, Haitian Creole is still relegated to a secondary status.[4] Knowledge of only Haitian Creole indicates lower-class origin, ignorance and illiteracy. Notwithstanding a growing literary tradition and a wealth of linguistic evidence to the contrary, Haitian Creole is stigmatized as *patois* and disparagingly referred to as broken or corrupt French. These prejudices against treating Haitian Creole as a formal language are partially responsible for the fact that few Haitians are, or wish to be, literate in their mother tongue.[5] Support of Haitian Creole as the official language of Haiti is negatively associated with radicalism, opposition to the government, and subversion.

The above evaluations of language mask another set of reverse values and associations. Equally strong feelings exist that French is the language of pretense, duplicity, deceit, and falseness: conversely the "lowness" of Haitian Creole is identified with positive traits such as truth, integrity, sincerity, and genuineness. According to this schema, French represents the inherent divisiveness of the Haitian color-class hierarchy and Haitian Creole signals equality: the national and racial unity of the Haitian people. Haitian Creole connotes authentic Haitian identity, drawn from the African heritage, while French is associated with an imposed, artificial identity linked to the European heritage and colonialism. Haitian Creole is currently a symbol of resistance to the growing economic and cultural domination of Haiti by Western, industrialized nations, especially the United States and France.

[4] The surge of nationalism during the United States occupation of Haiti (1915–1934), which provoked military resistance on the part of the peasants and a search for Haiti's African roots by intellectuals, coincided with the Haitian Senate vote to recognize French as the official language of Haiti in the Constitution—114 years after independence. This inclusion was meant as a gesture of defiance to the North Americans and as protection against the imposition of English as the official language of Haiti. Even François Duvalier (1957–1971) maintained French as Haiti's official language, although during his Presidency Haitian Creole was recognized in the Constitution (Article 35) and its use "permitted and even recommended to safeguard the material and moral interests of citizens who do not sufficiently know the French language," in certain undefined cases and circumstances.

[5] The issue of literacy in Haiti, where approximately 90% of the population is illiterate, is a complex problem. Literacy in Creole is generally regarded as a transitional step to literacy in French rather than as an end in itself. The prejudices against the use or Haitian Creole in the education system, and the lack of one universally accepted orthography and of educational materials in Creole further complicate the issue. *See,* Berry (1975) and Dejean (1975, 1976).

The contexts deemed appropriate in Haiti for the use of French and Haitian Creole reveal the evaluations and associations assigned to them.[6] As the language of government and business, as well as of polite society, French is considered appropriate mainly in formal contexts whether public or private. As the language of emotion and intimacy, Haitian Creole is regarded as suitable in private and public mainly for unofficial business, daily routine, small talk, and gossip.

In practice, however, Haitian Creole is now spoken in all but the most formal settings and is widely used in radio and television especially for advertising. Its use in formal institutions, such as schools and churches, is still limited mainly to the lower classes, but progressive church personnel and educators are working to broaden its acceptance among the upper classes. Governmental and public resistance to recognition of Haitian Creole as the official national language persists. It is bolstered by the French government which has retained economic and cultural hegemony despite Haiti's early independence (1804) from France.[7]

HAITIAN MIGRANTS IN NEW YORK CITY

For Haitians, migration to the United States is a matter of economic survival and escape from political harassment. Approximately 300,000 Haitians live and work in the New York City metropolitan area.[8] Most of them have arrived within the last ten years, some legally and many as undocumented migrants. They come from all sectors of Haitian society—the elite, the middle class, the urban proletariat, and the peasantry. Their presence in the United States reflects the expansion of Western capitalism on the island, the demands of the United States labor market, the grinding poverty of Haiti, and the years of political terrorism and corruption under the Duvalier regimes.

[6] Rules for the functional distribution of French and Creole have not been precisely defined, although Stewart (1962) delineates two domains in terms of two intersecting variables: public versus private and formal versus informal. Studies by Reisman (1970), Abrahams (1970a; 1970b) and Makiesky (1973) on the subtleties and complexities of interrelationships between language use and cultural values in Antigua, St. Vincent, Tobago, and Barbados suggest what appears to be a more general pattern that also applies to Haiti.

[7] Since Haiti's 1860 Concordat with the Vatican, the Haitian Catholic Church and educational system have largely been controlled and staffed by natives of France or other French-speaking foreigners. These institutions have been the primary conduits of French culture and language in Haiti and perpetuators of the myth of superiority over traditions derived from Haiti's African heritage. Bebel-Gisler (1976) and Bebel-Gisler and Hurbon (1975) provide illuminating discussions on the interrelationship of language and colonialism in Guadeloupe and Haiti.

[8] This estimate is based upon the informed judgments of several Haitian sources and upon Immigration and Naturalization Service statistics. The large number of undocumented migrants in this population makes a precise enumeration impossible.

Occupational and Residential Distribution

The vast majority of these immigrants, including some highly educated members of the upper classes, work at menial unskilled jobs in factories, service industries, domestic service, and the like. Only a small percentage, primarily of earlier immigrants, hold professional, technical, or managerial positions, or own small businesses. Most Haitians reside in neighborhoods populated by Black Americans, Hispanics and other Caribbean immigrants: the ghetto and working-class areas of Brooklyn, Manhattan and the Bronx, and the working or lower middle-class parts of Queens. Only a minority can afford to live in middle-class neighborhoods in these boroughs or in Westchester County and Long Island. In general, the upward mobility of Haitians is hampered by their inadequate knowledge of English, their status as undocumented migrants, their lack of skills relevant to an urban, industrialized society, and heavy financial commitments to families in Haiti.

Social and Legal Status

Although individual Haitians have experienced some upward mobility, group progress is blocked by the racial composition of the population. By United States criteria, a small percentage of Haitians are classified as Caucasian. Most are phenotypically Black, and thus are relegated to the lowest status category in United States society. Their reputation as a French-speaking and a culturally French people, however, also allows them to perceive themselves and to be perceived by the wider society as an ethnic population (Sutton, 1973:145). Like other Caribbean immigrants, they "suffer double invisibility (in Ellison's terms) as immigrants and Black immigrants or double visibility as Blacks in the eyes of Whites and as foreigners in the eyes of native-born Blacks" (Bryce-Laporte, 1972:54 fn). In addition, Haitians bear the stigma of being suspected "illegal aliens" and of coming from the poorest country in the Western Hemisphere. As a population in economic and political exile, confronted by enormous problems in the United States, it is little wonder that they experience conflicts over the nature of the identity they wish to project.

CASE STUDY: THE LANGUAGE DISPUTE IN A BROOKLYN CHURCH

During two years of fieldwork among Haitian immigrants in New York City, I witnessed a complex dispute over the language of a Catholic Mass and control of a parish group at a Brooklyn church. This conflict provided a key to my understanding of one of the principal preoccupations of Haitians: the issue of identity.

The Parishioners

In this particular Haitian/Hispanic/Black American parish, Haitian parishioners came from nearly all class backgrounds. Many were undocumented migrants and worked in unskilled jobs. Two particularly influential men from the Haitian middle class held white-collar jobs, one as a bookkeeper, the other as a social worker. Some parishioners came to the United States between eleven and twenty years ago, but most arrived within the last nine years. Reflecting their social backgrounds, only a few, including the bookkeeper and the social worker, spoke French fluently or understood it well. Haitian Creole was the primary language used by most parishioners. Few of them had a good command of English.

The French Mass and the Introduction of Creole Mass

Between 1969 and 1974, a North American parish priest of Irish descent, assuming that French was the Haitian vernacular, recruited a succession of non-Haitian and Haitian priests to conduct a weekly Mass in French for the Haitian parishioners. Haitians from outside the parish were also welcome to attend. In 1971, a formal Haitian parish organization began in which the bookkeeper and the social worker played active roles as officers. The organization and the Mass in French endured until mid-1974 when a Haitian priest residing at the rectory left. Following his departure, three exiled priests (two Haitians and one French national) from outside the parish offered their assistance to the United States parish priest. They recruited another Haitian priest to live in the rectory while he pursued his university studies.

All four priests were ardent proponents of Haitian Creole as the official language of Haiti and as the only valid national language for Haitians. They were critics of the Duvalier regime and of neocolonialism in Haiti. They also devoted a great deal of time and energy to raising funds for Haitian refugees and helping other Haitians, notably the undocumented, solve the numerous practical problems they face here. With the exception of the resident Haitian priest who could not be too public about his political opinions as he eventually had to return to Haiti, these priests participated in and organized meetings, conferences, and demonstrations about the above issues. The activism of these priests was indicative of their adherence to liberation theology, a progressive ideology current among Latin American/Caribbean clergy which expresses the pastoral ministry of clergy through the active social and political involvement of the Church.

This parish, then, planned to introduce a Mass in which Creole would be the only language used. This Mass would contrast greatly with the previous Mass said primarily in French with Creole playing a minor role in the priest's sermon. The priests began soliciting support for this idea among the parishioners. Meanwhile, a European priest continued to say the weekly Mass in French.

Opponents of the Creole Mass

The idea of an exclusively Creole Mass created a furor among some of the Haitian parishioners who insisted that the Mass continue to be conducted in French. The opponents (some of whom spoke French and some only Creole) were led by the bookkeeper and the social worker, who not only favored French, but who resented the presence of the priests, especially the resident priest, whom they viewed as competitors for positions of leadership among the parishioners. A victory for Haitian Creole would signal the loss of some of their influence, which arose partly from the implications of their knowledge of French.

The opponents argued that Creole is a patois suitable for Voodoo ritual, but indecent and inappropriate in the formal, sacred setting of the Catholic Church. They claimed that the priests would be depriving the parishioners of the more "edifying" and "civilized" aspects of Haitian culture by eliminating French from the Mass. The opponents feared that such emphasis upon only one of Haiti's heritages—the African—would increase the isolation of Haitian immigrants from the dominant White culture. In the opinion of the opponents to the Haitian priests, Creole would not be a "suitable" language for New York City as it would make Haitians *noua de foua* (Black and hence, inferior, twiceover). The opponents bitterly denounced the priests as "troublemakers and dictators who expected the same obedience to their authority as they enjoyed in Haiti." They strenuously objected to the priests' involvement in "nonreligious" affairs such as the demonstrations and rallies, and to their outspoken criticism of the Duvalier regime. Politics, they held, did not belong in the Church.

Proponents of the Creole Mass

The priests and their supporters (again some French and some monolingual Creole-speakers) argued that the use in church of French which few Haitians understand or speak contradicts the idea that the message of Christ is for everyone. Use of French thus infringed upon most Haitians' rights of access to this message. They stressed that Creole is the mother tongue of all Haitians while French is an alienating, imposed language which "whitewashes" Haitians by denying their race, culture, and authentic Haitian identity. Emphasizing French as a continued source of division among Haitians in the United States, they urged parishioners to abandon it and to unite to solve their common problems as an exploited, foreign, Black minority within North

American society. They accused the bookkeeper and the social worker of wanting to manipulate the parishioners for selfish ends; it was common knowledge that the two men had visions of creating a citywide federation of Haitian community groups with themselves as leaders.

Resolution of the Language Question and the Consequences

At a meeting to decide the language issue, the merits of the two languages were hotly debated in both French and Creole. The majority of parishioners voted in favor of an all-Creole Mass which began shortly thereafter, complete with mimeographed songsheets (later a book) and biblical selections printed in Creole.

Outraged by the decision, some pro-French parishioners angrily severed their ties with the church and recruited a Haitian priest to say the Mass in French at a church nearby. Others stayed in the parish, demonstrating their contempt for Creole and the priests by attending Masses in English and Spanish, languages they did not understand well. The bookkeeper and the social worker also remained, but regularly attended the Creole Mass. They hoped to reassert their authority among parishioners and eventually to reestablish a Mass in French. Ostensibly, however, they committed themselves to working with the resident Haitian priest to develop a new parish organization which would broaden the appeal of the Creole Mass, educate parishioners in Creole, and plan social and cultural activities, particularly for the parish youth.

The harmony was short-lived. The bookkeeper and the social worker continually opposed the priest and constantly disrupted meetings by reviving the language issue. Even after officers were finally elected, they pushed for the election of "better, more serious" officers, i.e., themselves. Failing in these ends, they tried to organize a parallel community group, using the church as a meeting place and as a base for recruiting members. In this endeavor, they also failed.

The bookkeeper and the social worker also played upon the negative political connotations of Creole and Haitians' fear of anti-Duvalier political involvement by spreading rumors that the New York City police would arrest anyone attending the Mass (a double threat for parishioners in the U.S. without proper documents). Attendance at the Mass dropped off for a short while until it became clear that no arrests would be made.

These efforts undermined the attempts of the resident priest and his supporters to sustain a viable parish organization. After this priest completed his university studies and returned to his pastoral work in Haiti in mid-1975, and several of his staunchest followers moved to other neighborhoods, the organizational attempts ended. One of the other pro-Creole priests returned each Sunday to say the Mass, but without a resident Haitian priest and with the loss of parishioners to other neighborhoods, interest in and attendance at the Mass dwindled. The bookkeeper and the social worker began seeking support for their cause among Haitians attending one of the Brooklyn churches where the Mass in French is still held.

The merger of the parish with an adjacent one shifted the Creole Mass to the church where the pro-French dissenters had moved the Mass in French. Although this French Mass had been discontinued by the time of the parish merger, its opponents again refused to attend the Creole Mass and actively discouraged other Haitians from doing so. The Creole Mass again failed to take root because of the opposition, the lack of a resident Haitian priest, and the continuing decrease in the resident Haitian population. Only a handful of Haitians, mainly loyal supporters from the first parish, now hear the Mass in Creole at this church.

ANALYSIS

Why did the language issue create such consternation and anger among the Haitian parishioners in the Brooklyn parish? This question may be examined in relation to: 1) the issue of status within the Haitian milieu and the wider society; 2) definitions and uses of self and group identity; and 3) the problem of leadership within the church and representation of Haitians in United States society.

Language, Status, and Identity within the Haitian Milieu

Many Haitians in the United States continue to operate within the same social categories they have transferred from Haiti. The traditional class system, as they define it, based upon education (knowledge of French), wealth, color,[9] and family name still provides the ideological and behavioral frame of reference for them; United States society does not. Thus, they attempt to re-create Haiti on foreign soil. Attempts to maintain the traditional Haitian class system in New York City, however, have become threatened first by the new possibilities for social mobility of Haitians from lower-class backgrounds through increased access to the cultural and material symbols of elite status, and second by changing standards for the evaluation of status and prestige. Thus, French language and culture are invested with new importance in New York as markers of status differences, especially by

[9] Following Dominguez (1975:31–32), "it is to be understood here that 'color' refers to position on a continuum of racial mixture between European and African, and not merely to one's color of skin. Determination of position on such a continuum depends on the evaluation of hair form and facial features, as well as of color of skin."

upper-class Haitians who have suffered downward economic and social mobility. Knowledge of French becomes one way they continue to maintain social distance by excluding from their social circles and organizations Haitians of lower social standing who do not speak French well.

By insisting upon the use of Creole at the Mass, the Haitian priests challenged their parishioners' identification with the traditional class system and underscored the futility and destructiveness of perpetuating these divisions among Haitians in New York City. The priests asserted the right to all Haitians, particularly monolingual Creole-speakers, to reject the elitist version of Haitian culture and identity based upon a European model, and to develop a Haitian identity based upon cultural symbols drawn from their African heritage—an identity the Haitian clergy regarded as authentic.

Not all the pro-Creole parishioners agreed with the priests' political opinions or wished to take political action themselves. They were, however, amenable to the idea of Creole as a dominant symbol of their enhanced self and group identity as Haitians and as a symbol of the unity and equality among Haitian immigrants within the parish or, more generally, in New York City. Their acceptance of Creole in this situation, however, did not eradicate the deeply ingrained ambiguities they felt about the two languages; many still valued French highly and used it as a symbol of identity in other social situations.

Similarly, the parishioners who refused to abandon their cherished French self and group images did not altogether reject Creole. The bookkeeper and the social worker, for example, maintained a show of solidarity with the other parishioners by using Creole at meetings and at the Mass when making announcements. Ironically, to impress others with the sincerity of their objections to Creole and to be understood, they had to express themselves in Creole. Even those Haitians who prefer French equate denial of knowledge of Creole with a repudiation of Haitian nationality and identity. The ability to speak Creole is believed to be practically a genetic trait: it is part and parcel of being Haitian. The pro-French parishioners, however, did not want Creole to be selected from the tradition of linguistic and cultural dualisms as the dominant symbol of self and group identities.

Language, Status and Identity within the American Milieu

The high value placed upon retaining the French language and culture as symbols of identity by both French and monolingual Creole-speakers is also a response to the institutionalized racism of United States society. Like many other foreign-born Blacks, Haitians have learned that presentation of the "proper credentials," *i.e.*, cultural, behavioral, and linguistic features perceived as superior to those of Black Americans, often bring tangible and intangible benefits from White Americans, although these same features may also evoke resentment and hostility in Black Americans and Caribbean peoples (see, Bryce-Laporte, 1972; Dominguez, 1975; Green, 1975; Sutton, 1973). Thus, for Haitians, the French language, culture and identity constitute the "proper" means for eliciting favorable responses from White Americans (see, Fontaine, 1976:117–118), while having the double benefit of distinguishing them from native Black Americans. This strategy plays upon the American and Haitian stereotypes of French-speakers as educated, cultivated people, and also implies that Haitians have a superior cultural status to White Americans whose language and culture Haitians generally hold in low esteem.

Speaking Haitian Creole also distinguishes Haitians from Black Americans, but the pro-French parishioners associated Creole, a marker of low social status in Haiti, with the low status of native Black Americans. Creole and its associations, they feared, would also stigmatize them as the illiterate citizens of a poverty-stricken nation. On the other hand, while they rejected or denied Creole in this particular circumstance, in other situations, they would openly criticize Haitians who tried to "pass" as Whites or who claimed to be from any other country.

The pro-Creole group essentially rejected the French identity and the idea of whiteness as superior to blackness; their insistence upon Creole and its associated positive values made Haitians unambiguously Black and brought the objective reality of their identity as Haitians and their position as a minority within a minority to the forefront. This does not imply, however, that pro-Creole Haitians totally accepted identification with the native U.S. Black minority. That is, for pro-Creole Haitians, racial identity was not promoted to the exclusion of ethnic identity since Creole remained a symbol of their cultural distinctiveness as Haitians. This ideology, however, has the potential for linking Haitians with Black Americans and other Caribbean immigrants to resolve their common problems as low-status, oppressed minority groups in a predominantly White society. Currently, this effort is limited by the reciprocal negative attitudes held by Haitians, Black Americans, and Caribbean groups.

Most Americans do not recognize the distinctions Haitians draw among themselves and perceive Haitians as both an ethnic and racial population. The parish priest (of Irish descent), for example, was completely bewildered by the linguistic controversy, especially as he was constantly assured that all Haitians speak Creole. Although he did not overlook their racial characteristics, he perceived them as an undifferentiated ethnic population whose particular needs could be met by the church (see, Glick, 1972 for a discussion of the institutionalized pressures contributing to ethnic group formation among Haitians in New York City). Haitian organizations have successfully used both their racial and ethnic identities to solicit support from groups ranging from labor unions to the Congressional Black Caucus, and also from other Caribbean immigrant organizations. Sometimes they stress their problems as a Black people, sometimes as an "invisible" immigrant ethnic population, and sometimes as an exploited Third-World people, depending upon the situation.

Language and Leadership

The language debate was not only a conflict over the issues of status and identity, but also over the question of leadership and the representation of the Haitian community to outsiders. The lack of a common interpretation of Haitian identity became the vehicle for competition among the most influential leaders in the Church: the resident Haitian priest, the bookkeeper and the social worker. The influence they wielded derived not only from their knowledge of French (and its associations), but also from their knowledge of English and their experience with United States institutions. The pro-Creole parishioners used the language issue to reject the bookkeeper and the social workers as their leaders and mediators with the institutions of the wider society. They did not want the parish organization used as a launching pad for the careers of either man as a spokesman for this community.

By voting for Creole, the pro-Creole parishioners sought to equalize the opportunities for gaining status and prestige within the church and the parish organization. Thus, no one would need to feel unqualified or embarrassed to participate actively because of lack of fluency in French. The pro-Creole parishioners were mainly concerned with these problems and thus lacked the firm commitment to the deeper religious and political concerns that spurred the priests. Moreover, the traditional ambiguity of meanings assigned to French and Creole allowed the bookkeeper and the social worker to undermine support among the pro-Creole group when it came to the issue of embracing and internalizing the ideology behind Creole as the dominant symbol of self and group identities.

CONCLUSION

The common experience of exile and of being Black and foreign in a predominantly White society has not united Haitians. Restratification and relegation to the lowest status category of United States society have exacerbated the transferred conflicts over social identity. The attempt to re-create the traditional class system has become a source of contention and conflict. The Haitian leadership in New York City remains fragmented, with various groups seeking to establish differing status and identity claims, thus inhibiting them from uniting on issues which concern the future of Haitians. The conflicts and divisions inherited from the colonial slave past continue to plague Haitians in their new conditions of exile. The linguistic and cultural dualisms of Haitian society are now invested with new ambivalent meanings as Haitians attempt to develop into a united community within New York City.

BIBLIOGRAPHY

Abrahams, R
1970a "A Performance-Centered Approach to Gossip," *Man,* 5(2):290–301. June.

_____
1970b "Patterns of Performance in the British West Indies." In *Afro-American Anthropology.* N.E. Whitten Jr. and J.F. Szwed, eds. New York: The Free Press. Pp. 163–179.

Bebel-Gisler, D.
1976 *La Langue Creole, Force Jugulée.* Paris: Editions L'Harmattan.

Bebel-Gisler, D. and L. Hurbon
1975 *Cultures et Pouvoir dans la Caräibe.* Paris: Editions L'Harmattan.

Berry, P.
1975 "Literacy and the Question of Creole." In *The Haitian Potential: Research and Resources of Haiti.* V. Rubin and R.P. Schaedel, eds. New York and London: Columbia University Teachers College Press. Pp. 83–113.

Bourguignon, E.
1969 "Haiti et L'Ambivalence Socialisée: Une Reconsideration," *Société des Americanistes,* 58:173–205.

Bryce-Laporte, R., Jr.
1972 "Black Immigrants: The Experience of Invisibility and Inequality," *Journal of Black Studies,* 3(1):29–56. Sept.

Buchanan, S.H.
1980 "Scattered Seeds: Haitian Migrants in New York City." Ph. D. dissertation, New York University.

Dejean, Y.
1976 *Orthographie Créole et Passage au Français.* Brooklyn. New York: n.p.

_____
1975 *Dilemme en Haiti: Français en Peril ou Peril Français?* Port-au-Prince: Editions Connaissance d'Haiti.

Dominguez, V.R.
1975 *From Neighbor to Stranger: The Dilemma of Caribbean Peoples in the United States.* New Haven: Yale University, Antilles Research Program. Occasional Papers No. 5.

Efron, E.
1954 "French and Creole Patois in Haiti," *Caribbean Quarterly,* 3(4):199–213. Aug.

Faine, J.
1936 *Philologie Créole.* Port-au-Prince: Imprimerie d'Etat.

Ferguson, C.A.
1959 "Diglossia," *Word,* 15(2):325–340. Aug.

Fontaine, P.M.
1976 "Haitian Immigrants in Boston: A Commentary." In *Caribbean Immigration to the United States.* R.S. Bryce-Laporte and D.M. Mortimer, eds. Washington, D.C.: Smithsonian Insti-

tution, Research Institute on Immigration and Ethnic Studies. Occasional Papers No. 1. Pp. 111–129.

Glick, N.
1972 "The Formation of a Haitian Ethnic Group." Ph. D. dissertation, Columbia University.

Green, V.
1975 "Racial versus Ethnic Factors in Afro-American and Afro-Caribbean Migrations." In *Political Conflict*. H.I. Safa and B.M. du Toit, eds. The Hague: Mouton Publishers. Pp. 83–96.

Hall, R.
1953 *Haitian Creole*. Washington, D.C.: American Anthropological Association. Memoir 74.

Herskovits, M.
1937 *Life in a Haitian Valley*. Garden City, New York: Doubleday and Company, Inc. 1971.

Hymes, D., ed.
1971 *Pidginization and Creolization of Languages*. Cambridge: Cambridge University Press.

Leyburn, J.
1941 *The Haitian People*. New Haven: Yale University Press. 1966.

Makiesky, S.
1976 "Class, Culture and Politics in a Barbadian Community." Ph.D. dissertation, Brandeis University.

_____
1973 "The Politics of Language Use in a West Indian Society." Paper presented at the 72nd Meeting of the American Anthropological Association. New Orleans.

Pride, J.B.
1971 *The Social Meaning of Language*. London: Oxford University Press.

Reisman, K.
1970 "Cultural and Linguistic Ambiguities in a West Indian Village." In *Afro American Anthropology*. N.E. Whitten, Jr. and J.F. Szwed, eds. New York: The Free Press. Pp. 129–144.

Stewart, R.A., Jr.
1963 *The Functional Distribution of Creole and French in Haiti*. Washington, D.C.: Georgetown University, Monographs in Language and Linguistics.

Sutton, C.R.
1974 "Cultural Duality in the Caribbean: A Review." *Caribbean Studies*, 14(2):96–101. July.

_____
1973 "Caribbean Migrants and Group Identity: Suggestions for Comparative Analysis." In *Migration: Report of the Research Conference on Migration and Ethnic Minority Status and Social Adaptation*. Rome: United Nations Social Defense Research Institute. Publication No. 5. Pp. 133–148.

U.S. Department of Justice, Immigration and Naturalization Service
Various *Annual Reports*. Washington, D.C.: Government Printing Office.
Years

Hispanic Caribbean

PUERTO RICAN LANGUAGE AND CULTURE IN NEW YORK CITY[1]

JUAN FLORES
Queens College, City University of New York

JOHN ATTINASI
Indiana University/Northwest

PEDRO PEDRAZA, JR.
Hunter College, City University of New York

ARE PUERTO RICANS BECOMING AMERICANIZED?

Most observers agree that the distinctive signs and qualities of Puerto Rican culture, including the Spanish language, are giving way to the seemingly inexorable sweep of Yankee pluralism. Here, however, the consensus ends. Directly after observing and recording the signs of cultural assimilation come the vexing tasks of analyzing and evaluating them. Is the process desirable or undesirable? Should it be facilitated or denounced? How far along is it and are there limits to its full realization? Is it inevitable or reversible? Is the main obstacle to total Americanization to be found in national or "ethnic" resistance or in the very structural relationship between the United States and Puerto Rico? More fundamental, perhaps, is the question of what it means for Puerto Ricans to be "Americanized." Which of the essential features of Puerto Rican cultural life are being integrated? Which are being obliterated by pervasive colonial influences? Which aspects of North American culture are seen as the most potent forces promoting assimilation among Puerto Ricans, especially those living in the United States? Which other U.S. historical experiences of conquest, domination, or absorption through migration are pertinent for Puerto Ricans? Is the issue of Puerto Rican cultural identity best posed as that of an immigrant group, or of an ethnic or racial minority? Are Hispanics set off by language of origin, or are

---

[1] This chapter is a shortened version of "La Carreta Made a U-Turn: Puerto Rican Language and Culture in New York City," (Flores, *et al.*, 1981).

they Third-World victims of internal colonialism, or participants in the culture of poverty?

There is some validity in each of these approaches, and interpretations thus far have generally been based on one or a combination of such models. To what extent, however, do these models measure the nature and degree of Puerto Rican acculturation? Finally, if Puerto Ricans do not consider the process either desirable or inevitable what alternatives remain? We suggest that the persistent affirmation of a discrete Puerto Rican national culture, and particularly its multidimensional traditions of anticolonial resistance, is consonant with an ever deeper immersion in the cultural life of the United States.

Such a situation of dual cultural reference is rarely, if ever, addressed by commentators on the Americanization of Puerto Ricans in the United States, despite agreement that assimilation is far from complete and in fact highly problematic. For example, although Puerto Ricans are gaining command of English, they are by no means abandoning their native Spanish. The debate invariably falters in the face of this reality, with North American sociologists and anthropologists continuing to consider Puerto Ricans in the United States as problematic "newcomers" in the long line of ethnic immigrants, including Blacks from the South, who occupy the lowest rung on the ladder of social mobility.

Puerto Rican observers, on the other hand, emphasize the distinctiveness of Puerto Rican migrants who, unlike their European predecessors, come from a nearby colonial nation and keep their national ties active. Assimilation theory provides the theoretical context here also, and commentators both inside and outside the Puerto Rican community have come full circle in predicting the eventual incorporation of "Puerto Rican Americans" into the pluralist mainstream. The most basic problem, then, is the method common to both approaches, since it accommodates two divergent currents of interpretation. Both are glaringly inadequate—that of American social scientists, because it omits or minimizes the colonial dimension of the relationship between the United States and all Puerto Ricans, and that of Puerto Rican writers, because it lacks a consideration of class relations and the cultural struggle in the United States.

This complex theoretical debate and the corollary ethnographic assertions rarely refer to one obvious source of evidence: the firsthand cultural production of Puerto Ricans in the United States and their linguistic practices. The case against cultural imperialism and the data base of urban anthropology have all but ignored the explicit testimony of the community as expressed in its daily verbal interactions, not to mention its painting, drama, music, poetry, and dance. Pathologies are extensively documented, the "requiem" is pronounced, proofs and disclaimers are raised on such telling issues as group intermarriage, the relative successes of bilingual education, and patterns of upward mobility—while the practical communicative and creative experiences of Puerto Ricans in the United States go largely unanalyzed. Matters of cultural representation, for the most part, are left to the artistic circles themselves. In the galleries, workshops, and ensembles, and among the painters, poets, and musicians, "Puerto Rican culture" is the substance and product of everyday work not merely an intellectual issue or category, but a directly and creatively re-expressed reality. Similarly, policy-makers and scholars speculate extensively on the Puerto Rican language predicament and its implications for public policy, without ever taking as a point of departure the virtuosity of speech resources in the context of home, work place, and social interchange.

In this essay we will attempt to tap these active currents by turning to specific instances of Puerto Rican expression in the United States.[2] The conclusions drawn from a long-term study of linguistic practice and attitudes on a single block in El Barrio[3] note the particular complexity of sociolinguistic change in the Puerto Rican case. These conclusions challenge many guiding assumptions of previous discussions of bilingualism, and have important consequences for the finding of educational policy for Hispanics, especially since these findings rest on an understanding of the historical and political position of Puerto Ricans in U.S. society.

THE SOCIOLINGUISTIC EVIDENCE

For language minorities in the United States, the acquisition of standard English is presumed to signal both a willingness to assimilate and an effort to take the most crucial first step to gain the knowledge and skills that enable social advance. Learn the language, it is said, and the doors of the "larger" society will swing open. There is, of course, a kernel of accuracy to such reasoning and it impels millions of Puerto Ricans, Chicanos, and other Latinos to struggle daily for educational opportunity, employment, and access to social services.

However persuasive it may appear, though, the language-as-lever rationale is riddled with contradictions. As it informs public opinion and policy, it is little more than a rationalization used to conceal the element of coercion that runs through the entire history of language contact under colonial conditions. The very term bilingualism has itself been used as a convenient cover for the imposition of English in Puerto Rico throughout much of the twentieth century. What is touted as the most desirable circumstance—trad-

[2] The original version of this article included a lengthy discussion of contemporary bilingual Puerto Rican poetry.

[3] For a description of El Barrio, the oldest Puerto Rican settlement in New York City, see, page 211.

ing Puerto Rican Spanish for communicative skills in English—turns out to be not so much a life-enlarging choice as an outright obligation.

Vague definitions and tenuous premises, such as the ingrained assumption that "correct language" somehow implies good behavior and intelligence, are further rationales for the adoption of the standard variety of English (Bernstein, 1965).[4] The insidious system of stratification identifies undesirable speech as the speech of undesirables. The consequences of this circular rationale are felt by the poor and working class of all nationalities, but the magnified disadvantage for language minorities is obvious. Rather than assessing intellectual abilities—whether based on oral or written language— standards of measurement mainly detect deviations from a prestige dialect and the learned routines of social interaction. Clearly, the bias inherent in such hierarchical rankings complement and reinforce the elaborate tracking system at work throughout the educational process and in the society as a whole.

The most telling case against emphasizing language choice and use is the growing evidence that points to social status as the key to educational success, and not vice versa (Coleman, 1966; De Lone, 1979). Formal schooling and language acquisition, although held up as a ready panacea to economic and political disadvantage, have made only minor inroads into the stubborn system of class and national stratification. To a large extent, in fact, they have served to obfuscate the need for deeper social change. Making it through school and gaining command of English afford little real prospect of alleviating the vast inequities and discrimination that keep the majority of Puerto Ricans on the bottom rung of the social ladder.

The main arena of struggle has concerned the establishment of bilingual programs in the public schools. The effectiveness of these efforts has been at best uneven, the most visible impediment being reluctant and piecemeal institutional commitment. Many bilingual programs have also been hampered by the unclear, diffuse, and often conflicting goals of the legislators and educators involved. Here, too, numerous issues are fraught with confusion: the choice between English proficiency and Spanish maintenance, or their potential compatibility; the meaning and content of "bicultural" curricula; and the range of language practice among the student population.

The last issue is most pertinent to this essay; the widespread ignorance and disregard for actual linguistic experience results in gravitation toward the accepted norms of Spanish or English language "standards." Only recently— and half-heartedly—has attention been paid to dialect usage as a legitimate mode of social communication compatible with broader educational objec-

---

[4] Standard language is widely assumed to be evidence of clear thought and more elaborated ideas. Bernstein (1965) asserts this linkage; he argues (1972) that social control is exercised through hegemony of such ideas (a virtual withdrawal from the controversies spawned by his work). Althusser's (1971:132–33) insights on the ideological aspects of language standardization and social behavior are pertinent here.

tives, rather than as a mark of deviance and retardation to be rooted out in favor of sanctioned language norms.

It is here, in the description and assessment of how Puerto Ricans actually communicate, that a reformulation and redirection of language and educational policy must begin. The results of an intensive look at language use in a Puerto Rican community follow. To study bilingualism concretely, we sought to understand the norms of speaking in daily interaction by observing residents in a single block in New York City over an extended period of time. We also conducted linguistic studies and an attitudinal survey to complete the description of language use and to take account of community members' own perceptions of the language problem (Centro de Estudios Puertorriqueños, 1978a, 1978b, 1979a, 1979b, 1980a, 1980b, 1980c; Attinasi, 1978, 1979).[5]

We chose El Barrio, or East Harlem, as our site of study because it is a large, old, stable Puerto Rican community, with three generations of U.S.-based Puerto Ricans as well as recent and circulating migrants. Except for the absolute size and ethnic density of the community,[6] the demographics of East Harlem are similar to those for the total Puerto Rican population in New York: the majority were born in the United States or have lived here for more than ten years; slightly over half were born in Puerto Rico; 50 percent are under 25 years of age. It is a poor neighborhood where one third of the residents live below the poverty level. No single sample, of course, is fully reliable for purposes of generalization. The richness of the present data base, however, and our diversified sociolinguistic approach, ensure that the cultural and political implications to be drawn contain valid suggestions for new lines of thinking and analysis.

A person's placement within the social organization of this working-class community is determined as much by the facts of migration—frequency,

---

[5] The linguistic evidence reported in this section derives from an interdisciplinary study of the Language Policy Task Force (LPTF), which included co-authors Pedraza and Attinasi, and Shana Poplack and Alicia Pousada. The work was sponsored by the Ford Foundation, the National Institute of Education, and the Center for Puerto Rican Studies, City University of New York. Pedraza was responsible for most of the field work and the ethnographic description of speech (*See*, Centro de Estudios Puertorriqueños, in press).

The main sociolinguistic conclusions in the present article are treated at greater length by the LPTF in Centro de Estudios Puertorriqueños (1980a), and are contextualized in Attinasi (1978), which has been reprinted as the LPTF's Working Paper No.1. Specific studies concerning the types of code-switching and their relation to bilingual ability may be found in Poplack (in press) (also Centro de Estudios Puertorriqueños, 1978a); Poplack (Centro de Estudios Puertorriqueños, 1979a); and David, Sankoff and Poplack (Centro de Estudios Puertorriqueños, 1980b).

Regarding linguistic structure, the analysis of the verbal system appears in Pousada and Poplack (Centro de Estudios Puertorriqueños, 1979b), and pluralmarking is examined in detail by Poplack (1980) (also Centro de Estudios Puertorriqueños, 1978b) and Poplack (Centro de Estudios Puertorriqueños, 1980c). The attitudinal report appears in greater detail in Attinasi (1979).

[6] The block we studied is 90% Puerto Rican, greater in ethnic density than most Puerto Rican communities, dense even in comparison with the rest of El Barrio. Actually, only 20% of Puerto Ricans in the United States live in neighborhoods where they are the majority, with an average density at 25% (U.S. Department of Commerce, 1970; U.S. Department of Labor, 1975; Waggoner, 1978a and 1978b).

recency, and other particulars—as by age and sex.[7] Language use, skills, and outlook connect to these factors in rather complex and surprising ways. Language preference was not decisive among the various motives for community association, and the range of linguistic abilities, although wide, did not obstruct communication.

In contrast to the traditional immigrant pattern of transition from the foreign language to English over three generations, with grandparents and grandchildren being virtually monolingual in one or the other language, nearly all Puerto Ricans are bilingual to some degree, with second-language skills acquired, for the most part, outside any formal language instruction. There seems to be a life cycle of language use in the community. The younger children learn Spanish and English simultaneously, hearing both languages from those who use them separately and from those who combine them in various ways. The older children and adolescents speak and are spoken to increasingly in English, which accords with their experience as students and as members of peer groups that include non-Hispanics. In young adulthood, as the school experience ends and employment responsibilities begin, the use of Spanish increases, both in mixed usage and in monolingual speech to older persons. At this age, then, the Spanish skills acquired in childhood but largely unused in adolescence become notably reactivated. Mature adults speak both languages. Older persons are, for the present at least, Spanish monolingual or nearly so.

The new roles associated with adulthood involve more serious relationships with family members of all ages. The familial networks, like the general community, are affected by circulating migration, making bilingualism necessary. Migration patterns not only place certain persons of all ages in the Spanish-speaking environment of Puerto Rico, but also require that those who remain in New York communicate with persons who circulate between the two places, with recent arrivals, and with persons who came as adults and who continue to speak Spanish. Although there are social institutions that tend to reinforce one or the other language, the Spanish-maintaining counterforces become prominent as Puerto Ricans pass from adolescence to adulthood.

How, then, are we to characterize the dynamic bilingualism of Puerto Ricans? Our research indicates that an historical framework is required. For just as four centuries of Spanish colonialism have been responsible for the

---

[7] In all, we discovered nine major networks of social interaction at this research site, with subgroupings in each. These were all informal associations of men, or women with or without children, or mixed adults, or adolescents, who shared leisure-time activities. Some were heterogeneous, centered upon a locale or institution; others were defined more by similar characteristics of age, sex, or family. If a network consisted mainly of members of similar age and sex, the subgroupings were divided according to migration experience; if a network was defined by similar migration history, subgroupings were delineated by age and sex. All the networks interconnected in the neighborhood through friendship and familial ties. We did not follow the extensions of these networks outside the community, and we focused our observations principally on public and semipublic settings.

Caribbean variety of Spanish that Puerto Ricans speak, so, too, is U.S. colonialism crucial to the language dynamic current in the last part of this century. The colonial status of Puerto Rico underlies such social conditions as complex and circular migration patterns, economic stratification, American citizenship, and monolingual language policies. Given the dialectical nature of these social factors, the same processes that instigate change also have stabilizing influences within the community, counteractive to the more obvious effects of assimilation. Bilingualism that makes use of nonstandard and class-based vernacular speech is qualitatively different from separated bilingualism comprised of literate standards. Interpretation of the sociolinguistic situation of Puerto Ricans in the United States must therefore be placed within the context of working-class culture and language practice.

Before treating combined usage, it must be recognized that both poles in Puerto Ricans' bilingual range are colonial dialects. Puerto Rican Spanish, with its admixture of indigenous, African, and peasant qualities, is stigmatized to this day as a corruption of the "pure" Spanish mother tongue and its supposedly more faithful Latin American variants. The class basis of this judgment is obvious. The acquired language—the urban varieties of American English most immediately accessible to Puerto Ricans—may also be a downgraded dialect, distinct from, but sharing much with, Black English. The studies and struggles surrounding the recognition of that variety are most pertinent. Having learned English well enough to communicate actively with their working-class peers, Puerto Ricans—even those who speak little Spanish—enter school with the prospect of having to relearn the language to use it "properly." The transfer, within a generation, from Spanish to English is merely the first step toward social success and acceptance. Class placement then forces still another language adjustment if Puerto Ricans are to "succeed"—the transfer from the colloquial English of the neighborhood and work place to the more formal language of educational and professional life.

Most Puerto Ricans in the United States, however, are not located at either end of the Spanish-English spectrum, but range throughout it. The resulting phenomenon is the interpenetrating usage of both languages—derogatorily called "Spanglish"—in a wide range of circumstances, especially for in-group communication. We found that balanced bilinguals engaged in more intimate, intricate kinds of switching, while those with fluency in one language avoided syntactic risks by switching between sentences or switching only independent particles and exclamations. Rather than compensating for monolingual deficiency, code-switching often signals an expansion of communicative and expressive potential.

There are subjective factors that reveal pressures felt and exerted in the sociolinguistic situation and that condition the use of language in everyday interaction. In our language attitude survey, we found a conscious and widespread connection to bilingualism, so much so that bilinguals are perceived to be most prevalent in the Puerto Rican community.[8] Most of those interviewed found no conflict between speaking English and being Puerto Rican, or speaking Spanish and being actively involved in American culture. They readily admit that many speakers mix both language in discourse, and view this positively. Both languages are valuable. English is recognized as an asset, and Spanish remains important both as a marker and a component of the culture (see, Vidal, 1980). On the other hand, none of those interviewed advocate complacency toward the preservation and development of Spanish language skills, tasks that are viewed as a responsibility of the group itself and as a legitimate right in a democratic society.

This was true even for young people who admitted to not knowing much Spanish. The feeling was that Spanish should be audible and visible wherever Puerto Rican culture exists, an attitude that connects to both observed language use and the postulated life cycle of language competence. This is concretely manifested in the norms of etiquette in which Spanish-speakers are almost always accommodated.

Puerto Ricans also want to learn English; for most, a person who is more fluent in English than in Spanish is neither a paradox nor an anomaly, much less a case of deliberate or unwitting cultural betrayal. These findings reveal that both linguistic and cultural identity are changing in response to economic and social transformations, and that interpenetrating bilingualism is the idiom in which these cultural changes are expressed.

There was nearly unanimous support for the principle of bilingual education, although unfortunately this consensus also tended to be uncritical and somewhat confused. Education that both elaborates standard skills and recognizes the communicative value of community speechways, and education that begrudgingly concedes a program to remedy the lack of English, are fundamentally different. This is evident not only from the very conceptualization of the problem, but also at the concrete level of interaction with the bilingual or potentially bilingual child. A community that is composed of people in movement between Latin America and the United States and that communicates bilingually will surely want bilingualism. It misses the point to pose the problem of language choice—Spanish or English—as a simple connection between language and cultural identity.

Thus a realistic understanding of the language-culture nexus calls into question both conventional linguistic approaches to Puerto Rican experience and the assimilationist or cultural nationalist orientations in which they are grounded. Rigorous linguistic description is of course indispensable in exposing the profound complexity of the language contact situation in its own right. In addition, a comprehensive conception of language as a system of interaction may help overcome the frozen dichotomy that ties English and

---

[8] A language attitude survey was conducted through personal tape-recorded interviews, using a questionnaire of over 174 items. The sample included 91 persons chosen as representative by Pedraza in the course of the ethnographic observation.

Spanish to monolithic cultural blocks, while the analysis of verbal communication serves to illuminate some of the most distinctive qualities of contemporary artistic production and innovation. Explaining these sociolinguistic conditions and even elaborating the rules that govern their practical workings calls for placing linguistic considerations in a wide-ranging context of cultural and political theory.

Two dimensions of Puerto Rican language and culture in the United States—national resistance and the vantage point of the have-nots—provide valuable coordinates for assessing the theoretical debate over assimilation. In general, the discussion has laid excessive stress on one or the other, depending on whether the commentator is Puerto Rican or North American. Island-based writers such as Eduardo Seda-Bonilla (1972), Manuel Maldonado-Denis (1976), and Luis Nieves-Falcón (1975), tend to view assimilation as a fatal assault on the national culture of a colonially-oppressed people. Many North American social scientists such as Oscar Handlin (1951, 1959), Joseph Fitzpatrick (1971), and Oscar Lewis (1965) interpret assimilation as the problematic insertion of still another ethnic subculture into the variegated current of the North American immigrant experience.

Such a "sociodemographic" approach, which aligns squarely with Milton Gordon's paradigm (1963) fails to recognize or take account of the colonial nature of this interaction, and for the most part implicitly, if not forthrightly, denies that Puerto Rico has so much as a national culture. Even the "radical" critiques of this mainstream research model, as for example in *Divided Society: The Ethnic Experience in America* (Greer, 1974), attach the issue of ethnic assimilation too mechanically to factors of economic and social mobility to assist reliably in assessing the specific cultural direction of Puerto Ricans as a colonial "minority." Increased economic advantage with inevitable cultural integration—often in the supposedly egalitarian, pluralist sense—is still the abiding assumption.

Puerto Rican commentators usually steer clear of these illusions; they see assimilation as the forceful loss of the national culture in its glaringly unequal contest with imposed foreign values. There is, of course, a formidable tradition of assimilationism and cultural accommodation among colonial thinkers, couched most typically in cosmopolitan occidentalist terms. The writings of Eugenio Fernández Méndez (*see*, 1970) clearly exemplify this tradition, though many of the apologists for Commonwealth status, with all their appeals to the cultural patrimony, share the same universalizing orientation. The Puerto Rican intellectuals who have been most vocal about the assimilation process in the United States all depart from anti-imperialist, cultural nationalist premises. Among them, Seda-Bonilla and Nieves-Falcón lean more heavily on North American sociology, while Maldonado-Denis, José Luís González (Díaz Quinones, 1976), and Juan Ángel Silén (1974) attempt to ground their interpretations in a Marxist framework. They are in agreement, though, in their stress on racial and linguistic differences, which stem from the social oppression of a colonized nationality, as the essential defining element in the cultural experience of Puerto Ricans in the United States.

This political emphasis is appropriate, particularly as a means to controvert the immigrant analogy and ethnic pluralism that pervade North American analysis. Social scientists in the United States tend to reduce the national and colonial dimension, but the Puerto Rican writers also fall into reductionism, although of a different kind. They pose the clash of national cultures as an absolute polarity, with each culture understood in static, undifferentiated, and outdated terms. Thus, any disappearance of Puerto Rican traits and the taking on of present U.S. cultural lifeways signifies the surrender of the Hispanic tradition to that of Anglo-Saxon—in a word, assimilation. The complex class dynamic at work in both Puerto Rican and North American history, and at the basis of the migration itself, falls from view in this assessment.

Yet, both the overarching Hispanic and Anglo-Saxon traditions have been subject to constant challenge from cultural forces within their own societies, forces that are subordinate and oppositional and that may therefore converge in ways that cannot be written off as mere "assimilation." Upward mobility is not involved here, nor does such convergence necessarily indicate the abandonment of authentic national "roots." One thinks of the indigenous and Afro-Caribbean traditions in Puerto Rican culture and how they inter-weave with Black and other Caribbean cultures in the United States. Even the elements of coercion and inequality, so central in culture contact within an imperialist framework, play no role in this kind of interaction. Rather, shared and parallel social experiences primarily influence the cultures and language practice of working people.

At the level of popular culture, as distinct from the dominant national heritage of each society, the question of assimilation must be viewed from an angle quite different from that of the opposing flanks in the theoretical debate. Popular culture not only places in question the privileged status of the elite tradition, which presumes to define the indispensable features of entire cultures, but is also in constant tension with the very tenets of "nation-ality" itself, to the extent that these tenets are confining and at odds with other sources of social identity. In this respect, a strong countercurrent to the assimilation process that affects Puerto Ricans in the United States entails an "internationalization" of inherited cultural experience. Rather than being subsumed and repressed, Puerto Rican culture contributes, on its own terms and as an extension of its own traditions, to a new amalgam of human expression. It is a fusion, significantly, at the popular level of shared work-ing-class reality, and one expressive of recognized marginalization and ex-clusion. The existing racial, national, and class divisions in U.S. society allow for, indeed necessitate, this alternative course of cultural change.

BIBLIOGRAPHY

Althusser, L.
1971 "Ideology and Ideological State Apparatuses." In *Lenin and Philosophy*. New York: Monthly Review Press.

Bernstein, B.
1972 *Class Codes and Social Control*. New York: Wiley.

1965 "A Sociolinguistic Approach to Social Learning." In *Penguin Survey of the Social Sciences*. J. Gould, ed. Hammondsworth, England: Penguin. Pp. 144–68.

Centro de Estudios Puertorriqueños
In Ethnographic Observation of Language Usage in East Harlem. New York: Hunter College, Press Centro de Estudios Puertorriqueños.

1980a *Social Dimensions of Language Use in East Harlem*. New York: Hunter College, Centro de Estudios Puertorriqueños. Language Policy Task Force Working Paper No. 7.

1980b *A Formal Grammar for Code-Switching*. New York: Hunter College, Centro de Estudios Puertorriqueños Working Paper No. 8.

1980c *Variable Concord in Sentential Plural Marking*. New York: Hunter College, Centro de Estudios Puertorriqueños Working Paper No. 6.

1979a *Sometimes I'll Start a Sentence in English y Termino en Español: Toward a Typology of Code-Switching*. New York: Hunter College, Centro de Estudios Puertorriqueños. Language Policy Task Force Working Paper No. 4.

1979b *No Case for Convergence: The Puerto Rican Spanish Verb System in a Language Contact Situation*. New York: Hunter College, Centro de Estudios Puertorriqueños Working Paper No. 5.

1978a *Syntactic and Social Constraints on Code-Switching*. New York: Hunter College, Centro de Estudios Puertorriqueños Working Paper No. 2.

1978b *Deletion and Disambiguation in Puerto Rican Spanish: A Study of Verbal—/#n/ -*. New York: Hunter College, Centro de Estudios Puertorriqueños Working Paper No. 3.

Attinasi, J.
1979 "Language Attitudes in a New York Puerto Rican Community." In *Ethnoperspectives in Bilingual Education Research: Bilingual Education and Public Policy in the United States*. R. Padilla, ed. Ypsilanti: Eastern Michigan University. Pp. 408–461.

1978 "Language Policy and the Puerto Rican Community," *The Bilingual Review*, 5(1–2):1–40. Jan.–Aug.

Coleman, J.S.
1966 *Equality of Educational Opportunity*. Washington, D.C.: U.S. Department of Health, Education, and Welfare.

de Lone, R.
1979 *Small Futures: Children, Inequality and the Limits of Liberal Reform*. New York: Harcourt Brace.

Díaz Quinones, A., ed.
1976   *Conversación con José Luís González*. Rio Piedras, Puerto Rico: Ediciones Huracan.

Fernández Méndez, E.
1970   "Assimilación o enquistamiento?: los polos del problema de la emigración transcultural puertorriqueña." In *La identidad y la cultura*. San Juan: Instituto de Cultura Puertorriqueña. Pp.245–258.

Fitzpatrick, J.P.
1971   *Puerto Rican Americans: The Meaning of Migration to the Mainland*. Englewood Cliffs, N.J.: Prenctice Hall.

Flores, J., J. Attinasi, and P. Pedraza
1981   "La Carreta Made a U-Turn: Puerto Rican Language and Culture in New York City." *Daedalus*, 110(2):193–217. Spring.

Gordon, M.
1963   *Assimilation in American Life*. New York: Basic Books.

Greer, C., ed.
1974   *The Divided Society: The Ethnic Experience in America*. New York: Basic Books.

Handlin, O.
1959   *The Newcomers: Negroes and Puerto Ricans in a Changing Metropolis*. Cambridge, Mass.: Harvard University Press.

_____
1951   *The Uprooted: The Epic Story of the Great Migrations that Made the American People*. New York: Grosset and Dunlap.

Lewis, O.
1965   *La Vida: A Puerto Rican Family in the Culture of Poverty*. New York: Random House.

Maldonado-Denis, M.
1976   *Puerto Rico y Estados Unidos: Emigración y colonialismo*. Mexico: Siglo XXI.

Nieves-Falcón, L.
1975   *El emigrante puertorriqueño*. Rio Piedras: Edil.

Poplack, S.
In   "Syntactic and Social Constraints on Code-Switching." In *Latino Language and Communi-*
Press *cative Behavior*. R. Duran, ed. Norwood, N.J.: Ablex.

_____
1980   "Deletion and Disambiguation in Puerto Rican Spanish: A Study of Verbal—/#n/-," *Language*, 52(2): Summer.

Seda-Bonilla, E.
1972   *Requiem por una cultura*. Rio Piedras, Puerto Rico: Bayoan.

Silén, J.A.
1974   "Aspectos sobresalientes del problema nacional puertorriqueño y la nueva lucha de independencia," *The Rican*, 2(2–3):14–20.

U.S. Department of Commerce, Bureau of the Census
1970   *New York Tract No. 166*, U.S. Population Census. Washington, D.C.: U.S. Government Printing Office.

U.S. Department of Labor
1975   *A Socio-Economic Profile of Puerto Rican New Yorkers*. New York: U.S. Bureau of Labor Statistics.

Vidal, D.
1980   "Hispanic Newcomers in City Cling to Values of Homeland," *New York Times*, May 11.

Waggoner, D.
1978a "Geographic Distribution, Nativity, and Age Distribution of Language Minorities in the

United States, Spring 1976." Washington, D.C.: U.S. Department of Health, Education and Welfare, National Center for Educational Statistics. Bulletin No. 78 B-5.

1978b "Place of Birth and Language Characteristics of Persons of Hispanic Origins in the United States, Spring 1976." Washington, D.C.: U.S. Department of Health, Education and Welfare, National Center for Educational Statistics. Bulletin No. 78 B-6.

DOMINICAN FAMILY NETWORKS AND UNITED STATES IMMIGRATION POLICY:
A Case Study

VIVIAN GARRISON
Teachers College Columbia University
and Charles R. Drew Postgraduate Medical School

CAROL I. WEISS
New Jersey Division of Mental Health and Hospitals

With a population (6.2 million) considerably less than that of New York City and a per capita gross national product roughly one half that of Puerto Rico ($1380) (Population Reference Bureau, 1985), the Dominican Republic is a major source of immigrantion to the United States. Beginning in 1961 and coinciding with the assassination of Trujillo, dictator from 1930, Dominican migration to the United States spiraled to an estimated cumulative total of 100,000 by 1970 (Pérez Montás, 1973:1, 3). Between 1961 and 1968, the Dominican Republic sent more documented aliens to the United States than any other Western Hemisphere nation with the exception of Mexico, Cuba, and Canada (González, 1970:158). From 1960 through 1983, 1.74 million persons were recorded as arrivals from the Caribbean to the United States; of these, 300,617 were Dominicans. Among Caribbean countries, only Cuba (695,120 arrivals between 1960–1983) and Barbados (491,537 arrivals) had more immigrants to the United States than the Dominican Republic (Pastor, 1985:8).

Urban migration places the migrant in an unfamiliar physical and social world, a world where options for survival are limited. Decisions to migrate and responses to the difficulties of urban life are frequently made with both the needs and resources of kin in mind. The kin group may extend from the city back to the community of origin and adaptation may involve what Graves and Graves (1974:128–132) have termed "group-oriented strategies," including "chain migration," in which new migrants are successively brought to the city on the initiative of kin who are already there. For economic as well as legal reasons, the early phases of migration may favor adult wage earners rather than children or other dependent kin.

United States immigration policy has always favored "reunification of the family," but the definition of the "family" for purposes of immigration regulations does not reflect the cooperating kin group that is frequently the unit of these adaptive strategies. This policy and definition has implications for the economy, the politics, and the population, as well as the future of the family, in both the receiving and sending societies. This chapter examines the case of one characteristic Dominican family for the light it may shed on: 1) how extended families adapt to United States immigration policy; and 2) the long-run implications these adaptations may have for the traditional Dominican family.

THE CASE OF THE DOMÍNGUEZ FAMILY[1]

The year 1962 marked the beginning of the migration of the Domínguez family, as well as the beginning of increased Dominican migration to the United States. At that time, the family consisted of a father (Papá) 54 years old, a mother (Mamá) 45 years old, six females ranging in age from nine to 24, and two males, ages eleven and ninenteen (see, Figure I). With the exception of the three oldest sisters, Emilia, Rosa, and María, who were married and living outside the family home, the family shared one household in the capital, to which the parents had moved from the Cibao (an agricultural region) at the time of their marriage.

Papá, an enterprising man with great pride in "taking good care of the family," had made sufficient money in a passenger van business in his village to be able to purchase the four-bedroom house in which they resided. Papá and the eldest son (Raúl) were both in the military service and the household was supported entirely by the wages of these two members. The income was meager, but the Domínguez family never considered itself poor.

When the story begins, the family had one connection in the United States. A sister of Papá had been something of an adventuress and, after traveling throughout the Caribbean and South America, had married an American and taken up residence in Florida twenty years before.

Four events during the years 1962 and 1965 disrupted the stability of this family, overloaded the carrying capacity of the household, and gave impetus to the chain migration that has since dominated the history of the family. First, María's husband was killed in an accident on the job. María, who as yet had no children, first returned to live in the family household, but soon the husband of her American cousin (daughter of papa's sister) died, leaving the mother and a two-year-old child in need of assistance. María immigrated to the United States legally to do domestic work in that household.

---

[1] All names used in this paper are pseudonyms.

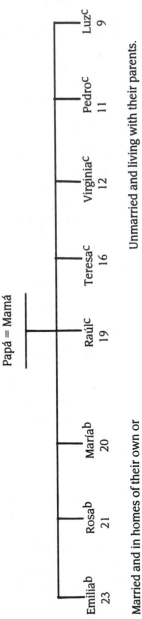

FIGURE I

THE DOMíNGUEZ[a] FAMILY IN SANTO DOMINGO, 1962

Papá = Mamá

| Emilia[b] | Rosa[b] | María[b] | Raúl[c] | Teresa[c] | Virginia[c] | Pedro[c] | Luz[c] |
| 23 | 21 | 20 | 19 | 16 | 12 | 11 | 9 |

Married and in homes of their own or of their husband's families.

Unmarried and living with their parents.

Note: [a] All names are pseudonyms and identifying features have been altered to obscure identity without distorting the facts of the case.

[b] Married and in homes of their own or of their husbands' families.

[c] Unmarried and living with their parents.

Two years later, Emilia, the oldest daughter, was shot by her husband in a family tragedy. Emilia left one eight-year-old daughter and a four-year-old son, who were taken into the family household to be raised by the grandparents. Upon the death of her sister, María returned to the Dominican Republic. Soon, however, Rosa's husband died of natural causes. Rosa and her two children, a two-year-old and an infant, moved back into the family household. María returned to the United States to make room in the house for Rosa, but also with the intention of arranging for Rosa's immigration to the United States as well.

Finally, during the 1965 Revolution,[2] the husband of the fourth daughter, Teresa, who had married by then, was shot by police during a demonstration, although he was only a bystander. Teresa had a two-year-old child and a two-month-old baby, and all three moved back into the family household. The baby, with whom Teresa was unable to cope in her grief, became the unofficial ward of the grandparents.

The four-bedroom household in 1965 thus consisted of five adults and nine children under eighteen and was organized as shown in Figure II.

Rosa sewed at home and Teresa occasionally helped out, but the work, like other jobs open to women in the Dominican Republic, paid little, and there were few employment opportunities for women outside domestic service (Lanz, 1969; Tancer, 1973; Ramirez, 1974:17).

In the United States, María met a man, whom we will call Jorge, and they planned to marry. However, Jorge was a permanent resident and María asked him to do her the "favor"' of first marrying her sister so that she could come to the United States. Jorge went to the Dominican Republic and married Rosa. Rosa then came to the United States as the wife of Jorge, necessarily leaving her two children in the care of their grandparents until such time as she became a permanent resident and could "ask" for her children.

At the same time that Jorge was doing this for María, he asked María to do him the "favor" of marrying his brother so that he could enter the United States. This "marriage for favor" (matrimonio de favor), as it is called by our informants, was also carried out.

During the period of the marriages for favor, Rosa lived with María, with whom Jorge also lived as consensual husband. Jorge's brother lived elsewhere. All four worked in the same factory. María and Jorge's brother reported María's address while Rosa and Jorge reported the address of the patrilateral cousin with whom María previously had lived.

Consider the complexities of management of the presentation of self in this situation where there are four noncongruent impressions to be given to different persons at different times: 1) the meaningful consensual bond between María and Jorge; 2) the legal marriages for favor about which a fiction must be maintained; 3) the reported legal residences; 4) the actual

---

[2] Marked by U.S. military intervention on behalf of a conservative faction.

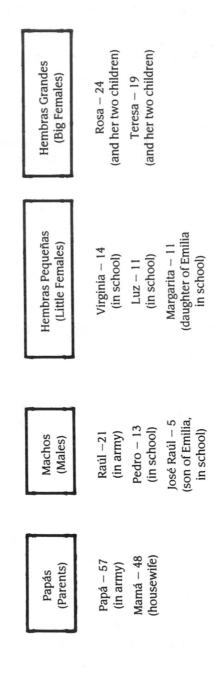

FIGURE II

THE DOMINGUEZ FAMILY HOUSEHOLD IN SANTO DOMINGO, 1965 (FOUR BEDROOMS)

Papás (Parents)	Machos (Males)	Hembras Pequeñas (Little Females)	Hembras Grandes (Big Females)
Papá – 57 (in army)	Raúl – 21 (in army)	Virginia – 14 (in school)	Rosa – 24 (and her two children)
Mamá – 48 (housewife)	Pedro – 13 (in school)	Luz – 11 (in school)	Teresa – 19 (and her two children)
	José Raúl – 5 (son of Emilia, in school)	Margarita – 11 (daughter of Emilia in school)	

Note: [1] The first child in each generation bears the name of his father, grandfather or great grandfather. Raúl is the name used here, but other names have been added to reduce the confusion.

residences, which include one household in which two sisters live with one man who is consensually married to one, but legally married to the other.

In 1967, Papá had a heart attack. He had to retire from the Army with a pension of approximately $70 per month. Despite contributions from María and Rosa in the United States, the family had a very hard time maintaining itself. Raúl, the oldest son, then 24, also in the military and earning approximately $90 a month, applied for a tourist visa to go to the United States to visit his paternal aunt and ask help for his father. He went to Florida, received help, and delivered the money back to his father in the Dominican Republic. Meanwhile, a letter had arrived from Rosa suggesting that he take advantage of his tourist visa to make a visit to New York to see how life was there. With three days left on his visa, he arrived in New York, overstayed his visa, and became an "illegal alien."

Approximately eight months later, Raúl married "for love," in the church and by law, a Dominican woman who was a permanent resident of the United States. While this should have made it possible for him to legitimize his status, it did not. He believed that her family suspected that he had married her only *por interés* (*i.e.*, to obtain permanent residence status). He, therefore, refused to permit her to "ask" for him in order to avert these suspicions. After their first child was born, his wife applied for him without his knowledge. When the papers arrived he tore them up. Five years, two children, and three applications later, he accepted his visa to the United States as husband of his permanent resident wife.

During this same bad period in the history of the Domínguez family, Virginia, the next-to-youngest sister, also came to the United States on a tourist visa with the intention of working to help the family in the Dominican Republic. She spent two years in the same factory as the others after which she returned to the Dominican Republic, "because," according to the family, "she was so young and not responsible".

By this time Rosa had received her permanent resident visa. She then asked for her parents and her children. Her children arrived about a year later, after three years separation from their mother. Rosa then divorced Jorge and married a Puerto Rican with whom she had fallen in love since her marriage de favor to Jorge. This couple now has two more children who are American-born citizens.

In 1971 , Papá and Mamá arrived with resident visas. Papá was and still is head of the family, despite his illness and retirement ("We have this rule," Rosa explains, "that our Papá always knows what it is we are going to do"). Papá obtained employment quickly as a maintenance man, and allocated his pension in the Dominican Republic to the maintenance of his family there. Left behind in the Dominican Republic were: the widow, Teresa, and her two children; Pedro, their youngest son, then 22 and employed; Virginia, who had proven "too irresponsible" to live in New York; and Margarita (17) and José Raúl (11), their grandchildren-wards (children of the deceased eldest daughter), all living in the family household. Also there was Luz, their youngest daughter, then ninenteen, married with one child and another to be born, living with the family of her husband.

As guardian of his family, Papá was determined to bring other members of the family to the United States. The first was the youngest child of Teresa. As Teresa had been so distraught at the time of her husband's death, she had neglected to register the birth of her baby. The grandparents, therefore, claimed him as their natural child at the time of their own immigration and subsequently asked for and secured his resident visa. He arrived after approximately one year to live with his grandparents as their natural son, while his mother remained in the Dominican Republic. About the same time, a man who had been a resident in the United States for seven years visited the Dominican Republic, met, fell in love with, and married Teresa. He returned to the United States and made a petition for her to join him. This marriage was, however, seen as suspect by immigration authorities and an investigation was instigated. Four years passed without result, the romance waned and this couple is now planning to divorce. Teresa remains in the Dominican Republic.

Pedro had a good job and intended to stay in the Dominican Republic, but his childhood sweetheart had immigrated with her parents to New York. Unhappy with their separation, Pedro took a vacation and came to New York on a tourist visa "to settle matters" with her. Papá obtained a job for Pedro prior to his arrival. Although they felt "he was young for a man to get married," the family influenced him in every way they could to see that he married and remained. He stayed, married, became a permanent resident and now has one child and expects a second.

The eldest orphaned granddaughter, Margarita, was the next to come to New York in 1974. She was then 20, married, and pregnant. She came for a visit with no intention to stay and returned to the Dominican Republic after her visit. However, while in New York, she "was taken by surprise by the birth of her child." This chance birth of an American-born citizen gave Papá the opportunity to implement another strategy. Virginia had given birth in the Dominican Republic at approximately the same time as Margarita to a child of the same sex. Virginia's infant was said to be "choleric, with diarrhea, vomiting and anemia." Papá believed this child could get well in the United States with better medical care. He went to the Dominican Republic, borrowed the papers of Margarita's baby, and brought Virginia's infant to this country on those papers. The latter, now three years old, continues to reside in the United States with his grandparents, but with papers that show him as their great-grandchild. The household of Papá and Mamá in the United States now consists of the two grandparents and two grandchildren, one claimed as a natural child and the other as a great-grandchild. Papá worked in New York for five years, was retired at 65, and now receives Social Security.

Mamá also receives assistance for the maintenance of the two dependent children.

Before Jorge was legally divorced from Rosa, María and Jorge had produced a daughter who is permanently disabled and requires special, costly medical care and rehabilitative services, including multiple operations, special schools, and expensive prosthetic equipment. From her birth there was no possibility that she could be maintained by their earnings. Moreover, the child required the kind of care that made it impossible for María to work.

Welfare, and above all Medicaid, were absolutely necessary for the survival of this child. Medicaid was available to María only as long as she and Jorge were not married. María and Jorge, therefore, after a stable consensual union which had survived the legal marriages of both partners to other persons, were nonetheless unable to legitimate their own marital bond. Jorge, then, did another "favor" and married a patrilateral cousin who came for a visit and wished to stay. This legal marriage de favor lasted two years while the cousin arranged her residence.

The last of the Domínguez immediate family to come to the United States was Luz, the youngest daughter of Mamá and Papá. She says, "I came the worst." Santiago, Luz's legal husband and father of her two daughters, now eight and five, worked for an American company in the Dominican Republic. In 1974 he came to the United States on a business trip with a three-month tourist visa to seek future employment with the same company in the United States. Raúl, however, procured an immediate job for Santiago in building maintenance work to which the whole family had by then transferred from the factory. "He earned in one week what he did not earn in one month in the Dominican Republic." As the primary source of support not only for his wife and two children, but for his mother, two sisters, and two nieces as well, Santiago was tempted by these greater wages, overstayed his visa, and became an illegal alien, separated from his wife and children. He wrote Luz asking her to divorce him so he could make a *matrimonio de negocio* (marriage for business), become a legal resident, divorce, remarry her, and eventually apply for her. Luz was naturally reluctant to comply with his request, but in the end she "trusted him," procured a divorce for $148, and began the long wait for a time when she and her children could rejoin her husband. Santiago lived in the home of Mamá and Papá and sometimes with Rosa while he was legally married por negocio to a friend of the family who gave him a slightly reduced rate for this service ($700 instead of the usual $1,000). Santiago was forced to leave his job at one point because of a threatened investigation by the INS. In spite of assistance from the family who gave him lodging and food and helped with remittances to his dependents in the Dominican Republic, the eight people there for whom he was responsible were in dire straits.

A year after the geographical separation of Santiago and Luz, Papá impatient with the long processes involved in the matrimonio de negocio, had saved the $1,200 necessary to "buy" a passport. These "purchased passports," as they are called, are actually rented passports with a tourist visa, which are used for a single one-way trip and then returned to the "seller" for use by another customer.

Luz came to the United States with a "purchased passport," leaving her two daughters in the care of their paternal grandmother and aunts to await a time when Santiago had his residence permit, had divorced his "wife of business," and could remarry Luz and apply for her legally. Currently, Luz refuses to have her daughters brought "like me on false passports with false names." She remarked, "One comes here out of necessity, in order to give a better life to one's children, in order to feed them, educate them, to get medical care, not to have to be asking loans and forever paying back loans just to go to the doctor." "Also," she contends, *la vida* (life) comes easier here, one lives more comfortably." Luz, however, misses her children, whom she has not seen for three years, and they miss her. For Santiago it would now cause a great hardship to return to the Dominican Republic. One of his sisters dependent upon him is enrolled in the university; the other has two children in school. A large part of his earnings ($ 165 a month regularly, plus whatever extras are required) goes for their maintenance. Luz works as a domestic and also sends a large part of her income to Santiago's family for the maintenance of her daughters.

The Domínquez family living in the United States now includes most of those who were residing in the family household in 1965 (Figure II) and their offspring. Exceptions are: Teresa, separated from her U.S.-resident husband for almost five years and reconciled to staying in the Dominican Republic; Teresa's daughter, Virginia, who was "too irresponsible" in New York; Margarita, who, Papá says, "is too weak *(debil)* to suffer life in New York," and her child; and, finally, Luz's children, who all are anxious to reunite with Luz and Santiago as soon as possible.

When the family constellation in the Dominican Republic was reduced to the three unmarried or separated women with two children and the two children of Luz (living with their father's family), Papá rented a small house for Teresa, Margarita, and Virginia for $40 and rented out the larger family house for $75. The net gain from the rental and Papá's military pension provide $105 per month which is allocated to the maintenance of this small household. Papá, María, Rosa, and Luz also periodically send Teresa and Margarita extra monies to support the children in school, to buy shoes and to meet other extraordinary expenses.

The attitude of the family toward life in New York compared to life in the Dominican Republic is that New York "is the best place to get ahead, or to improve your life, but the Dominican Republic is the best place to be if you are down and out or have problems." Unlike many Dominicans in the studies of González (1970:170) and Hendricks (1974:86–87), only two have any illusions of ever returning to live in the Dominican Republic. One is Jorge, who expects to inherit a farm upon the death of his father, but who cannot return now without leaving his wife and handicapped daughter behind because the medical care and special training the daughter receives is not available in the Dominican Republic at any price. The other is Luz, whose nostalgia for the Dominican Republic is related more to her longing for her children than to an actual desire to return there to live. She sometimes explains her desire to study English in the United States (which she has begun) as a means to improve her job prospects in the Dominican Republic.

The Domínguezes recount their trials and tribulations in the immigration process without rancor, without self-pity, and without guilt. They are grateful for the opportunities that immigration has given them, although these may appear meager to the average working-class American. Whenever the relatives in New York gather for a joint meal, Raúl is expected to look around the table and say in Spanish, "Anyone who is hungry here, raise your hand." When no hands are raised, what follows, in English, is frequently quoted by the rest of the family as Raúl's favorite expression: "God bless America!"

THE DOMÍNGUEZ FAMILY AND THE DOMINICAN MIGRANT COMMUNITY

To what extent can the migration experiences of the Domínguez family be generalized to other Dominican migrants? Both descriptive statistics and ethnographies of the Dominicans over the past ten years in New York and in urban and rural settings on the island (González, 1970 and 1975; Hendricks, 1974; Walker, 1972) indicate that this family shares much in common with fellow Dominicans. As with close to one-half of their countrypeople, the Domínguez family came from an urban area and worked in nonfarming occupations (Peréz Montás, 1973:4). With the exceptions of Mamá and Papá, all have three to six years of schooling, which is average in the Dominican Republic (González, 1975:216). Mamá had borne eight children, a typical completed family size for women in her age group in the 1969–71 census (Ramírez, 1974:31). Her daughters who live in the United States have had consistently fewer children than their counterparts in the Dominican Republic, as has been true for other Dominican migrants (CONAPOFA, 1976:80).

Recurrent themes in the Dominican accounts are cooperation and sharing within a family consisting of three generations of siblings and first cousins. Interdependence within this unit is part of the childrearing process, and adults beyond the conjugal pair as well as older siblings participate in socialization. The oldest man, or woman, is likely to assume authority over family decisions and welfare. Brothers and sisters, however, of the same generation, married or not, are also involved in promoting the social and financial growth of the family. Both shame and success are a collective responsibility. These patterns of reciprocal family obligations persist among kin dispersed between New York and the Dominican Republic. Kin in New

York are expected to contribute money and goods for the support of those left behind, and "there are whole villages for which remittances from the United States are one of the primary sources of income" (González, 1970:167). Where resources are limited, however, mutual aid can rarely extend beyond the family unit as described by Garrison and Thomas (1976:228–230); Roberts (1966:74); Walker (1972:103–104).

This family form, bilateral in descent, with or without a patrilateral bias, limited by the extent of mutual economic interests, has been called a "stem kindred," which may be defined as " . . . a corporately functioning, self-perpetuating kindred, united by consolidated socioeconomic interests and obligations that come into being in the process of socioeconomic mobility" (Walker, 1972:103; see also, Whitten, 1965:140). It is one of the most frequent family forms in the Dominican Republic. It is the form taken by the Domínguez family, a family that could also be considered a "personal kindred" organized around Papá (Walker, 1972:103). Like other Dominican families, it contrasts with the ideal type of the American family.

FAMILY TYPES AND U.S. IMMIGRATION POLICY

The corporate functioning of the Dominican kin network bears scant resemblance to the conjugal partnership in the protypical North American home. The U.S. family, as an ideal type, is viewed as consisting of the conjugal pair and its offspring. The family is judged to be incomplete should either parent or minor children not live together in a common dwelling. The nuclear family is exclusively responsible for its own maintenance and for the social adjustment of the children (Schneider, 1968:33–45).

For many Americans, adulthood and independence center on moving out from one's parents' household and establishing a home of one's own. For Dominicans, separation from the parental residence does not constitute an act of "independence" nor imply separation from parental influence. While one may move to another dwelling upon marriage, a single or married adult may also remain in the same household with the older generation and other siblings. A married daughter may move into her husband's parents' household while her married brother brings his wife to join his people. Young couples may also establish separate residences in close proximity to the parents of either mate. What is significant is that, regardless of where the adult or adult couple live, a pattern of cross-generational cooperative interdependence is present.

The emphasis on consanguineal versus conjugal ties in the Dominican families is highlighted by this statement from Luz, "My husband is the father of my children and I respect him. But if it comes down to it and my husband asks me for something and Papá, Raúl, or Rosa ask me for something, I will give to Papá, Raúl, or Rosa before I will give to my husband because they have done more for me." Luz is not unusual among Dominican women in her sense of primary loyalty and obligation to parent and siblings rather than husband. Even when the conjugal bond is close, enduring and reciprocally supportive, as in the case of Luz and Santiago, this is the expectation and cultural pattern. There is a striking contrast then between what constitutes the cooperating unit among American and Dominican families. The "primary family" is a different unit of kin in the two cultures. U.S. immigration policy favors "reunification" first of families of citizens and second of permanent resident aliens. For the permanent resident alien, the family reunion policy is based on the U.S., and not the Dominican, concept of family. The relationships between the Dominican concept of family and the concept of family presented in U.S. immigration policy are diagrammed in Figure III. A hypothetical center for the family constellation is presented by a black triangle, "ego." Generations appear vertically. A box encloses those individuals permitted to enter as relatives of a permanent resident alien under the preference system in effect since 1976. Dotted lines enclose the relatives of a permanent resident alien who, under the immigration laws in effect from 1965 to 1976, could enter the United States without labor certification. During that period, permanent resident aliens could bring in their parents but not their siblings; under the preference system instituted for the Western hemisphere in 1976 (AICC, 1976; Carliner, 1977), they can only bring in spouses and their own minor and adult unmarried children. At all times the "family" recognized for immigration purposes was much smaller than the interdependent Dominican family.[3]

Another aspect of Dominican family concepts which differs from U.S. cultural assumptions reflected in immigration policy is the legitimacy of marital ties. Dominicans, like Americans, prefer civil and/or religious marriages but, unlike U.S. immigration policy, they also recognize consensual unions as valid bonds involving obligations of mutual support and childcare. In the eyes of the Dominicans, more important than the type of marital union is the cooperation of the conjugal pair, their bearing children and the biological father's acknowledgement of his children (Roberts, 1968:84; Walker, 1972:97). The U.S. immigration preference for only legally married spouses invalidates for immigration purposes the affectively binding and socially recognized commitments of the consensual pair, while it validates some temporary legal contracts between couples who have married simply to facilitate immigration. The more flexible Dominican attitude toward what constitutes a legitimate marriage makes this relationship most adaptable to the exigencies of U.S. law. At the same time the strategies of evasion in which this relationship is manipulated undermine the social conventions of the traditional Dominican marital bond.

[3] Under legislation currently before the Congress (as this book goes to press) these provisions remain unchanged.

FIGURE III

FAMILY TIES IN DOMINICAN CULTURE, WITH IMMIGRATION PROVISIONS
FOR THE PERMANENT RESIDENT ALIEN

THE DOMINICAN FAMILY

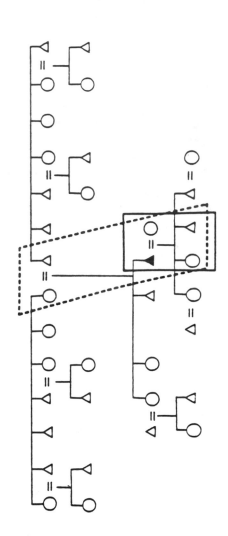

Key: All relationships shown constitute the economically interdependent "stem kindred" frequent in the Dominican Republic.

Blood relationships = Maritial ties (legal or consensual)

○ Female   △ Male   ▲ Ego

○ Kin of permanent resident aliens in preference categories for visas (within quotas) under laws in effect since 1976.

☐ ⌐ ¬ Kin of permanent resident aliens exempted from labor certification under 1965-1976 regulations.
  └ ┘

THE DOMÍNGUEZ FAMILY
AND IMMIGRATION POLICY

Figure IV shows in schematic outline the chain migration process as it occurred in the Domínguez family and as it might have occurred wholly or in part in other Dominican families immigrating during this period. Several consequences of immigration law as it was operating during this period are obvious from this single case study.

First, it is clear that U.S. immigration regulations, despite their intent to "unite" families, function to separate the viable, cooperating and closely knit families of permanent resident aliens typical of the Dominican and other Caribbean groups. Not only are parents and their adult offspring and siblings (not included in preference categories) separated, but spouses (preferred), legal as well as consensual, and parents and their minor children (preferred) are frequently separated for long periods. These separations average two-and-a-half to three years in the Domínguez family.

Second, the extra-legal and illegal mechanisms the Dominicans have developed to circumvent these regulations, function to reunite the family. All of the illegal mechanisms used by the Domínguez family were employed in the interests of reuniting kin within the "immediate family," as perceived and defined by Dominicans. Had they come after 1976, such mechanisms might also have been used to move Mamá and Papá, who would not have had preference for residence visas or labor certification exemption under current regulations.

Third, immigration regulations did not prevent the entry of an expected number of kin based on what might have been projected on the basis of the family constellation in 1965 (Figure I). Regulations merely caused delays in the movement of some and created stresses and strains for both conjugal and consanguineal relationships. Regulations also stimulated the development of a number of strategies which, while adaptive in the short run, cannot be conducive to the long-term stability and cohesiveness of the Dominican family.

The mechanisms, legal and illegal, used by the Domínguez family to reunite in the United States are (in the order of attitudinal acceptance):

1) Papers for work arranged from the Dominican Republic (*e.g.*, María, "The one who came best");

2) Being "asked for" with residence visa arranged in the Dominican Republic (Rosa's children, Papá and Mamá);

3) Matrimonio de favor (Rosa);

4) Overstaying a tourist visa (Raúl, Virginia);

5) "Borrowed papers" (Virginia's infant);

6) Matrimonio de negocio (Santiago);

FIGURE IV

THE DOMÍNGUEZ FAMILY CHAIN MIGRATION AS IT OCCURRED

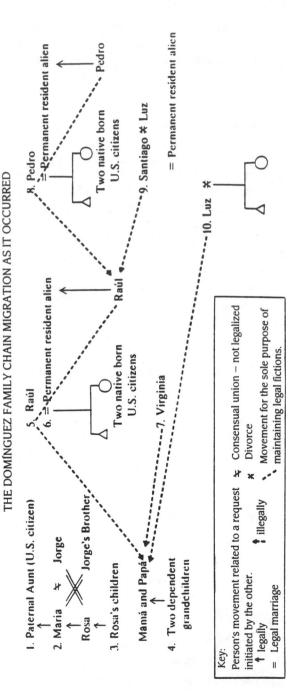

Key:

Person's movement related to a request
initiated by the other.
　↑ legally　　↑ illegally

♣ Consensual union – not legalized

✘ Divorce

╍╍╍ Movement for the sole purpose of
　　　maintaining legal fictions.

= Legal marriage

1. Legal entry for work with papers arranged in the Dominican Republic,
   and return to U.S. on prior work papers to other employment.

2. Marriage de favor to facilitate movement of siblings.

3. Legal entry of dependent children and of parents under 1965-1976 regulations.

4. One grandchild claimed as a "natural child" to permit entry in preference
   categories. The other given false identity as a U.S. born citizen ("borrowed papers").

5. Tourist visa overstayed.

6. Marriage to a permanent resident alien and subsequent legal entry with

   the fiction that marriage took place in the Dominican Republic (Delay of
   five years for "pride").

7. Tourist visa overstayed. Subsequent return to the Dominican Republic as
   "too weak" to adapt to the U.S.

8. Tourist visa overstayed, with subsequent re-entry as spouse of a permanent
   resident alien with the same fiction as 6.

9. Tourist visa overstayed with subsequent divorce of legal and affective wife to
   permit matrimonio de negocio and legal entry as spouse of a resident.

10. Entry with "purchased passport" paid by Papá in the interests of the affective
    marriage of Luz and Santiago. Two children left behind.

7) "Purchased passport" (Luz, "The one who came worst").

The following two mechanisms, also identified as used by Dominicans, were beyond the range of acceptability for the Domínguez family:

8) Crossing borders illegally without any papers at all;

9) Marrying a resident or citizen con interés (with interest, opportunism) in order to obtain resident status. (Notice Raúl refused to accept residence status through his wife because he might be accused of matrimonio por interés.) Other members of the family tell this story with pride.

There is still another mechanism which has been widely assumed and reported, but which the Domínguezes say "is very rare." This is one in which a Dominican tries to pass as a Puerto Rican because of the advantages of citizenship involved. This deceit might appear easy to North Americans who may think all Spanish-speaking people "look" or "sound alike." Among the Spanish-speakers, however, where this deceit would have to be conducted, the difficulty would be of the magnitude of, for example, a Texan trying to pass as a Bostonian, or a New England Yankee trying to pass as a Southerner. The general Puerto Rican attitude toward such illegal aliens who try to pass as Puerto Ricans is hostile, and Dominicans are deterred from using this strategy for fear they will be reported to immigration by other Spanish-speakers.

All of these mechanisms listed in this section for obtaining entry or residence in the United States, legally and illegally, have been identified in other, more quantitative, studies (González, 1970; Hendricks, 1974; and others). What is unknown is the frequency with which each strategy is employed. The fact that each is known in the Dominican community by a short phrase which elicits an account of the full process by the hearer suggests they are not uncommon.

What has not been fully recognized, however, is how the combination of these legal and illegal mechanisms actually alters the immigration process, from that intended by the policy underlying the regulations to a process that is not intended or desired by either immigrants or the receiving society.

Although the Domínguez stem kindred has adapted itself to the U.S. immigration regulations and preserved itself as a cooperating unit, this has involved severely disruptive influences upon the family over a ten-to-fifteen-year period. Ironically, the bonds which have suffered most are precisely those which U.S. immigration policy intends to protect—the relationships between spouses and between parents and children.

Disruptive influences, which can be expected to have long-term effects upon the stability and cohesiveness of the Dominican conjugal bond are: 1) the divorce of legally married pairs and the preclusion of legal marriage for persons in stable consensual unions to accommodate marriages "for favor" or "for business"; 2) the need for dissimulation of actual socially recognized conjugal bonds in favor of legal fictions; and 3) long separations of spouses which sometimes terminate in divorce, as with Teresa.

Other disruptive influences which may have long-term effects upon the social and emotional stability of children reared under these circumstances are: 1) the long separations of parents and children; and 2) the legal status of children born to parents of a consensual union when one or both partners are legally married to others and the child cannot be legally recognized by its true father.[4] Consider also the possible developmental effects on children of growing up with legal fictions about who their biological parents are.

There are other traditional Dominican family obligations—support and care for widows, aged or dependent parents, orphans, and "irresponsible" or "weak" family members—that are all undermined by U.S. immigration policy. These disruptive forces when repeated in many Dominican families over many years are likely to have long-term implications for change in Dominican society and culture.

Finally we should like to note that, regardless of the members of the Domínguez family which reside in New York or in the Dominican Republic at any one time, the stem kindred remains the interdependent economic unit. This unit, whose members live in both countries, is supported in large part by the U.S. economy. The support comes from the combined earnings of the family. Public assistance, contrary to popular opinion, plays a small part in the support or motivations of the Domínguez family, being used only for the benefit of the two minor wards of Mamá and Papá and the disabled child of María and Jorge.[5]

CONCLUSION

U.S. immigration policy, rather than fostering the unity and solidarity of families, has forced the separation of families, however defined, provoking the development of illegal mechanisms to effect "reunification." An immigration policy which recognized: 1) the importance of the sibling bond; 2) the dependency of children who are not natural children or "legitimate" children of the supporting adult(s); and 3) the possible dependency of parents on adult offspring or of adult offspring on parents, would go a long way toward

---

[4] In the United States, the biological fathers in "nonlegal" unions cannot be held legally responsible for child support, but technically the "husband for business" could. In Dominican society the biological father is held socially responsible, although legal sanctions are difficult to administer.

[5] The consequences of U.S. immigration policy for population, economic, and political issues are beyond the scope of this paper. We do wish to point out however, that a quota system which specifies a certain number of individuals, with preference for nuclear kin, is not only disruptive of family life but it also appears to be ineffective in controlling the increase in U.S. population or the economic interdependencies between the United States and the Dominican Republic. A more satisfactory immigration policy would be one mindful not only of the interdependencies of the larger Dominican family, but of those of the two countries as well.

reducing the reliance upon illegal mechanisms, the number of illegal aliens, and the stresses in the Dominican migrant community. A more realistic immigration policy must acknowledge that it is families rather than individuals who are admitted to the country within the immigration quotas, and that the concept of what comprises a "family" varies cross-culturally.

BIBLIOGRAPHY

American Immigration and Citizenship Conference
1976   "Fact Sheet—Major Immigration Provision of the Immigration and Nationality Act, as amended by P.L. 94–571." New York: AICC. Nov. 18.

Carliner, D.
1977   *The Rights of Aliens: The Basic American Civil Liberties Union Guide to Alien's Rights.* New York: Avon.

CONAPOFA—Cosejo Nacional de Poblacion y Familia
1976   *Encuestsa Nacional de Fecundidad: Informe General.* Santo Domingo: CONAPOFA. Oct.

Garrison, V. and C.S. Thomas
1976   "A Case of a Dominican Migrant." In *Alienation in Contemporary Society: A Multidisciplinary Examination.* R.S. Bryce-Laporte and C.S. Thomas, eds. New York: Praeger. Pp. 216–260.

González, N.L.
1975   "Migratory Patterns to a Small Dominican City and to New York." In *Migration and Urbanization: Models and Adaptive Strategies.* B.M. du Toit and H.I. Safa, eds. The Hague: Mouton Publishers. Pp. 209–223.

_____
1970   "Peasants' Progress: Dominicans in New York," *Caribbean Studies,* 10(3):154–171. Oct.

Graves, N.B. and T.D. Graves
1974   "Adaptive Strategies in Urban Migration." In *Annual Review of Anthropology.* B. Siegal, ed. Stanford, California: Stanford University Press. Pp. 117–152.

Hendricks, G.L.
1974   *The Dominican Diaspora. From the Dominican Republic to New York City—Villagers in Transition.* New York: Columbia University Teachers College Press.

Lanz, S.J., G.
1969   "Servicio Domestico: ¿Una Esclavitud?" *Estudios Sociales,* 2(4):197–207. Oct–Dec.

Pastor, R.A.
1985   *Migration and Development in the Caribbean: The Unexplored Connection.* Boulder, Colorado: Westview Press.

Pérez Montás, H.
1973   "Dominican Republic," *Country Profiles* 1–7. Washington, D.C.

Population Reference Bureau—PRB
1985   "World Population Data Sheet." Washington, D.C.: Population Reference Bureau.

Ramírez, N.
1974   "Situación y Tendencias Demográficas Actuales en la República Dominicana," *Estudios Sociailes,* 7(1,2):5–52. Enero-Junio.

Roberts, T.D.
1966   *Area Handbook for the Dominican Republic.* Washington, D.C.: U.S. Government Printing Office.

Schneider, D.M.
1968   *American Kinship: A Cultural Account.* Englewood Cliffs, New Jersey: Prentice-Hall.

Tancer, S.B.
1973   "La Quisqueyana: The Dominican Woman, 1940–1970." In *Female and Male in Latin America: Essays.* A. Pescatello, ed. Pittsburgh: University of Pittsburgh. Pp. 209–229.

Walker, M.T.
1972   *Politics and the Power Structure: A Rural Community in the Dominican Republic.* New York: Columbia University Teachers College Press.

Wirkin, M.J.
1975   Statement of Melanie J. Wirkin, Political Director, Zero Population Growth before the Subcommittee on Immigration, Citizenship, and International Law, Committee on Judiciary, House of Representatives, 94th Congress 1st and 2nd Session October 9. Washington, D.C.: Government Printing Office, Serial No. 34. Pp. 213–225.

Whitten, N.E., Jr.
1965   *Class, Kinship, and Power in an Ecuadorian Town: The Negroes of San Lorenzo.* Stanford, California: Stanford University Press.

THE LINKAGE BETWEEN THE HOUSEHOLD AND WORKPLACE OF DOMINICAN WOMEN IN THE U.S.

PATRICIA R. PESSAR
Georgetown University

In contrast to earlier functionalist claims about the conflicting values and roles for women of family and work (Parsons, 1955), contemporary analysts insist that the household and workplace are interdependent spheres of ideological, social, and material production. One component of the household-workplace link consists of the subsidy to employers that the non-remunerated domestic work of women provides for the daily maintenance and generational replication of workers (cf. Fox, 1980; Barrett, 1980). A more positive outcome for women of the household-workplace connection is the improvement in status and worth within the home that is often a by-product of women's waged employment (Oakley, 1981; Abadan-Unat, 1977; Pessar, 1986a, 1986b). Turning to the values and social relations women carry to the workplace from the household, we find that their skills in building social networks and organizing collective tasks within and between households may prove to be sources for creating solidarity among workers (Kessler-Harris, 1981; Tax, 1980). As one ethnographer found in her study of a walkout by ward secretaries in a large southern hospital, working-class family values can be transformed within the workplace into concrete collective actions for improvements in wages and work options (cf. Sacks, n.d.).

In this study of Dominican immigrant workers it is argued that an interdependency of spheres does not necessarily imply symmetry in the outcomes of the exchange between household and workplace. While Dominican immigrant women's participation in waged work contributes to an improvement in domestic social relations and ideology for women, these household level changes do not in turn stimulate modifications in female workers' consciousness and demands for improved conditions in the workplace.[1]

---

[1] Estimates of the total number of Dominicans residing in the United States as resident aliens

The first section of this article examines how, and in which domains, Dominican immigrant women's status in the household improves as a consequence of waged employment. The second section will explore why and how women's ideological and social rootedness in households promotes a middle-class identity and orientation to work which is not conducive to collective struggles to improve working conditions. This article concludes with a consideration of the inconsistency between the ideology and aspirations of immigrant households for a middle-class standard of living on the one hand, and the future employment opportunities for their children, on the other. It is suggested that this situation may be resolved by Dominicans bringing family ideology and loyalty to the service of collective action aimed at improving the conditions in secondary sector industries where both they and their children are likely to be working in the future.

The data upon which this chapter is based come largely from field work conducted in the United States and the Dominican Republic during the period 1980–1983. The generalizations reached about immigrants' experiences in the United States are based on structured interviews with informants, as well as casual conversations and participant observation in households, workplaces, and social gatherings over a two year period. Two principal groups form the basis for much of the data and analysis presented below: members of 55 immigrant households who provided information over a year's period on topics such as social networks, decision-making, income generation, control over budgeting, and beliefs about sex roles; and sixteen female garment workers who were queried about the above topics as well as the nature of their workplace and beliefs about their roles as workers. These informants were obtained through various means. They include previous contact with an individual or family member in the Dominican Republic and introductions by other informants and community leaders.[2]

In selecting these households and informants, some diversity was sought to explore how the immigrant experience might be differentially affected by variables such as class background, time of arrival, age, marital status, household composition, and work history. In this study, to account for women's common and contrasting experiences in the household and workplace, I have concentrated on the elements of class identification, marital status, household organization, and labor force participation.

---

and as undocumented immigrants range from 200,000 to 500,000. The majority have emigrated during the last two decades and approximately 80% currently reside in the New York Metropolitan area. According to Douglas Gurak's 1981 probability survey of Dominicans living in the borough of Queens and the northern half of Manhattan, 60.4% of the Dominican population is female. For this female population the average age of arrival was 22.2 and the median years of education is 8.0.

[2] This research was funded by the National Institute of Health, the National Science Foundation and New York University's New York Research Program in Inter-American Affairs. I would like to acknowledge the work of my research assistant, Catherine Benamou, who contributed to the design and administering of the garment worker questionnaire.

WOMEN'S IMPROVED STATUS
IN THE HOUSEHOLD

Observers of the Dominican family have distinguished two basic forms of domestic organization, the single mate and multiple mate pattern. The two are buttressed by different patterns of postmarital residence, household composition, authority and division of labor in domestic activities (*cf.* Brown, 1975; Ferrán, 1974; Instituto Dominicano de Estudios Aplicados, 1975; González, 1970, 1976; Tancer, 1973; Pessar, 1982).[3]

For the purposes of this chapter, it is the contrasting patterns o f authority found within these two forms of domestic organization that merit attention. In the single mate household, authority resides largely with the senior male; in the multiple mate unit, women tend to command authority (*cf.* Brown, 1975; Ferrán, 1974). A third model for domestic authority, which will be examined below, has emerged in many Dominican immigrant households. There has been a movement away from the hegemony of one sex over decision-making and control over domestic resources to a more egalitarian division of labor.

Inasmuch as the single mate form predominates among the middle strata of the Dominican population—the sector from which the majority of the Dominican immigrants originates—most immigrant households have experienced a movement away from patriarchal relations and values toward greater egalitarianism. These changes are most evident in three areas: belief about household authority, the allocation of household members to house work tasks, and budgetary control.

For most Dominicans the status of household head is equated with the concept of "defending the household" (*quien defiende la casa*). This "defense" is conceived of in largely materialistic terms. As women demonstrate their capacity to share this responsibility with men, so they begin to expect partnership as head of the household. Thus, in response to my questions, "Who is the household head now?" and "Who was the head previous to your emigration?" the majority of the informants interviewed (70%) echoed the words of the following woman:

> We both are the heads. If both husband and wife are earning salaries then they should equally rule in the household. In the Dominican Republic it is always the husband who gives the orders in the household (*manda lo de la casa*). But here, when the two are working, the woman feels herself the equal of the man in ruling the home (*se siente capacitada de mandar igual al hombre*).

---

[3] The multiple mate pattern should not be confused with female-headed households. Depending upon its origin (*e.g.*, widowhood versus the temporary absence of a male companion), and the way in which the domestic unit is organized to meet its social reproduction requirements, a female-headed household may be classified as single mate or multiple mate.

The problem of the double burden is one area in which immigrant women report significant modifications in men's willingness to entertain change. Women complain to their husbands that, like them, they are generating an income by laboring outside the home. However, they are being treated unjustly when they are forced to extend their work day by toiling in the home after work and on weekends. The "compromise" reached by the majority of the women I have interviewed involves the husband's minor participation in housework. The degree of participation usually varies in accordance with the domestic cycle of the household and its gender composition. The man's contribution increases when the children are young and decreases once daughters are old enough to help their mothers. The most commonly shared domestic tasks are cooking and weekly shopping.

Women tend to view their husband's help in housework as a moral victory. That is, by his minor assistance the husband recognizes the value of the woman's domestic activities and acknowledges her sacrifice for the household. Women realize, as do their husbands, that the latter do not, and perhaps should not provide an equal contribution to household maintenance. The majority of the women I have interviewed expressed the belief that a man's equal participation in all phases of housework is emasculating. As confirming "evidence," I have been told of women who insisted that their sons and daughters share equally in household chores, only to discover later that their sons have become homosexuals.

These latter beliefs emanate from a conceptual framework of the place of gender in the social universe. This cultural model ascribes men "by nature" to the "public sphere" and women to the "domestic sphere." This view was repeatedly expressed by informants in their responses to the following question: "In some households the woman goes out and works for wages and the man remains behind and assumes the childcare and housekeeping responsibilities. Do you think this is right, and do you think the man can do as good a job as a woman?" The following quote is representative:

> I know of such cases where the man assumes the housekeeping
> and childcare responsibilities. But, I don't believe a man can be as
> good as a woman; she is made for the home and the man is made
> to work.

Economic necessity has often required Dominican immigrant women, at least temporarily, to leave the domestic sphere for part of the day. This practice has in turn tempered the patriarchal dichotomy concerning men's and women's natural place in the world. The workplace has become an ideological resource drawn upon by women to redefine and renegotiate certain features of the sexual division of labor within the household. It is for this reason that I believe it appropriate to claim that for many working immigrant women, the workplace mediates between the "public sphere" and the "domestic sphere." This new orientation to the workplace challenges the more traditional ascription of men to the public workplace and women to the private household. Work heightens women's self-esteem as wives and mothers, affords them an income to actualize these roles more fully, and provides them with heightened leverage to participate as equals to men in household decision-making.

This finding adds to the growing body of literature on women, work, and the household that challenges earlier functionalist dichotomies between the family and workplace. For example, Parsons and Bales (1956) promulgated the belief that women would experience profound role conflicts if they added the status of worker to their primary status as housewife and mother. The overly facile, not to say ideologically rooted nature of such thinking, is attested to by the following. The very same women who claimed it was in the nature of the woman to do housework and for the man to labor outside of the home, also stated that the aspect of her life that most satisfied her was her role, "as a worker, because I can buy things for my daughter that I could not afford in the Dominican Republic."

Having made the point that many Dominican women utilize their access to the workplace and to wages to attain greater equality with their husbands in the home and to provide their children with more benefits, I want to stress that employment has not provided women with a new status as working women that challenges or subordinates their primary identities as wives and mothers. To the contrary, in many cases work has reinforced these statuses because it has allowed women to redefine their roles as wives and mothers in a more satisfying manner than existed prior to their employment and residence in the United States.

The other domain in which renegotiation and change has occurred is in household budgeting. As Table 1 shows, for the 55 migrant households for which I have budgetary data, the dominant mode of control prior to emigration was as follows: ten were characterized by the traditional patriarchal form; 28 operated with the household allowance pattern; and seventeen pooled household income. Of this last group, fifteen of the domestic units

TABLE 1

DOMINANT MODE OF BUDGETARY CONTROL IN THE
DOMINICAN REPUBLIC PRIOR TO EMIGRATION AND IN DOMINICAN IMMIGRANT
HOUSEHOLDS IN NEW YORK

Mode of Budgetary Control		
	Prior to Migration	Subsequent to Migration
Traditional Patriarchal Form	10	2
Household Allowance	28	15
Pooled Income	17	38
(n)	55	55

were female-headed. In sixteen of the 38 households where men controlled the household revenue, women, either as wives or daughters, contributed income on a regular or semiregular basis. Among the units characterized by the household allowance mode, the woman's income was most commonly directed toward household, rather than personal items of consumption. Women tended to specialize in "luxury" items rather than staples. Both objectively and symbolically, the direction of these women's savings to nonessential prestige items reinforced the image of the man as the breadwinner and the woman, at best, as the bestower of modern status goods, and at worst, as the purchaser of *tonterías* (frivolties).

There has been a profound change in budgetary allocation for Dominican households residing in the United States. The households in which the 55 informants are currently found are characterized by the following forms of budgetary control: two follow the traditional pattern; in fifteen households, which are characterized for the most part by the wife's nonemployment or participation in industrial homework, the women receive a household allowance. Thirty-eight households pool their income, and of these domestic units, twenty are nuclear and eighteen are female-headed (owing either to the absence of a senior male or to his irregular and limited financial contributions to the household as measured against those of the senior woman).

The predominant mode of budgetary control, income pooling within nuclear households, brings women advantages unknown in the three premigration patterns. First, responsibility for meeting the basic reproduction costs of the domestic group are distributed among members, regardless of gender, thus mitigating the invidious comparison between "essential" male contributions and "supplementary" female inputs. Second, according to informants, the greater participation by men in decision-making and in developing strategies for strengthening the household budget and managing irregularities in income flow has led them to appreciate more fully the experience and skills women bring to these tasks.

Women recognize that strides have been made in the United States with regard to women's control over the fruits of their labor. In a few cases women have had to struggle with husbands and fathers to acquire this right. Of the 55 women in this sample, eighteen were divorced or separated from a partner while in the United States. Fourteen cited the right to control their income more equitably as one of the primary factors leading to the disbanding of the union. Nonetheless, in most cases the senior male adapted relatively easily to a more egalitarian mode of budgeting. Several factors are important contributors to this change. The first will be discussed in greater detail below. It involves the ideology of emigration as a shared household experience. This collective orientation to relocation appears to lessen social distance and power inequities along gender and generational lines. Second, both Dominican women and men have expressed a desire to emulate what they believe is a more modern and less conflictual American pattern of sharing household decision-making between men and women. While these two social processes facilitate the adoption of a more egalitarian form of household budgeting, there was an additional material element operating. This became evident in those cases when women significantly reduced their level of contribution to the household budget. Whether this change occurred in the United States or upon return to the Dominican Republic, the man commonly asserted his dominance by allocating a household allowance to his wife and reducing her authority over budgetary decisions.

We have noted how women's amplified role in production has advanced their status in the domestic sphere and increased their sense of self-esteem. When the household-workplace equation is reversed to examine whether the experience of acquiring greater equity with men in the home has spurred women to struggle in the workplace to reduce the power differential between workers and owners, we find no supporting evidence. To the contrary, women's experiences in immigrant households help to create a highly individualistic, largely satisfied group of workers.

DOMINICAN WOMEN IN THE WORKPLACE

Labor force participation is high among Dominican women in the United States. According to the Hispanic Settlement in New York City Survey, 91.5 percent of Dominican women had worked for pay at some time since their emigration, with 49.7 percent currently in the labor force (employed or seeking employment). Of these women, 61 percent were engaged in manufacturing; 42 percent were employed in the garment industry, making it the single largest employer of Dominican women (Gurak and Kritz, 1982:5).

In-depth interviews were held with sixteen female apparel workers to examine whether and how household ideology and organization affect women's perceptions of and orientation to work and themselves as workers. The general characteristics of the informants are presented in Tables 2a and 2b. Among the topics addressed in the questionnaire were: current workplace organization, work history, class identification, knowledge about and attitudes toward the shop, union, and the apparel industry, household composition, and pre- and postemigration control over and participation in domestic activities.

The informants' work experiences have been conditioned by, as well as typify, the difficulties confronting the New York garment industry. For example, seven of sixteen women had been laid-off for at least a week one or more times over the past year. This job instability is a by-product of irregularities in production—a trend that has intensified as the New York apparel industry has assumed the role of a "spot market." That is, over the last two decades more stable, standardized production within the industry has moved from the Northeast to the southern United States and abroad. New York has come to specialize in the unstable components of demand. These

TABLE 2a

GENERAL CHARACTERISTICS OF INFORMANTS,
DOMINICAN GARMENT WORKERS IN THE NEW YORK METROPOLITAN AREA

Identification (Pseudonyms)	Age	Marital and Household Situation	Education
1. Zelda	42	Divorced; lives with son (23)	12 years
2. Florida	40	Divorced; lives with 4 children (19, 15, 9, 6)	11 years
3. Eva	24	Separated; lives with 2 children (3 1/2, 6 months) and divorced sister	13 years
4. Carmen	17	Divorced; lives with grandmother, aunt, and aunt's five children (11, 9, 8, 5, 3)	12 years
5. Marilu	21	Single; boarder in an apartment	0 (self-educated)
6. Rosa	62	Married; lives with husband; 2 children (26, 24) and a niece.	5 years
7. Susana	56	Widow; lives with daughter (22)	2 years
8. Marcela	48	Married; lives with husband and children (23, 18)	8 years
9. Ivalise	44	Married; lives with husband and daughter (24)	3 years
10. Gertrudes	36	Married; lives with husband and 2 children (13, 4)	6 years
11. Anita	25	Single; lives with mother	12 years
12. Juana	23	Single; lives with boyfriend	11 years
13. Marina	22	Separated; lives with 2 children (7, 3)	12 years
14. Maria	32	Married; lives with husband "comadre," and "comadre's" daughter	5 years
15. Lupita	42	Married; lives with 4 children (19, 10, 9, 22 months)	8 years
16. Esperanza	39	Divorced; lives with 6 children (21, 19, 18, 14, 11, 8) and 1 grandchild	3 years

TABLE 2b
GENERAL CHARACTERISTICS OF DOMINICAN INFORMANTS

	Years in U.S.	Last Residence in D.R.	Occupation (D.R.)	Occupation (U.S.)	Net Average Earnings Wkly	Net Average Household Earnings/Wkly
1.	15 yrs.	San Francisco (Rural)	Housewife	Sewing Machine Operator	$140.00	$140.00 (1 worker)
2.	3 yrs.	Santo Domingo (Urban)	Nurse	Sewing Machine Operator	$170.00	$170.00 (1 worker)
3.	3yrs.	Santo Domingo (Urban)	Student	Sewing Machine Operator	$125.00	$303.00 (2 workers)
4.	1 yr.	Santo Domingo (Urban)	Student	Presser in Sweatshop	$ 55.00	$365.00 (2 workers; 1 welfare recipient)
5.	8 yrs.	La Romana (Urban)	Student	Sewing Machine Operator (Laid-Off)	$100.00	$100.00 (1 worker)
6.	17 yrs.	Santiago (Urban)	Sewing Machine Operator	Sewing Machine Operator (Laid-Off)	$165.00	$745.00 (3 workers)
7.	20 yrs.	Santiago (Urban)	Sewing Machine Operator	Sewing Machine Operator	$177.00	$257.00 (1 1/2 workers)
8.	14 yrs.	San Juan de Maguana (Rural)	Housewife	Sample Maker	$203.00	$702.00 (3 workers)
9.	16 yrs.	Juancalito Abajo (Rural)	Housewife	Sewing Machine Operator	$140.00	$440.00 (2 workers)
10.	15 yrs.	Juancalito Arriba (Rural)	Housework in parental home	Sewing Machine Operator	$129.00	$330.00 (2 workers)
11.	1 yr.	Santiago (Urban)	Sewing Machine Operator	Sewing Machine Operator	$129.00	$249.00 (2 workers)
12.	1 yr.	Santiago (Urban)	Saleswoman	Floorworker (Laid-off)	$111.00	$160.00 (1 1/2 workers)

TABLE 2b (continued)

GENERAL CHARACTERISTICS OF DOMINICAN INFORMANTS

Years in U.S.	Last Residence in D.R.	Occupation (D.R.)	Occupation (U.S.)	Net Average Earnings Wkly	Net Average Household Earnings/Wkly
13. 7 yrs.	Valverde (Urban)	Nurse's Aide	Homeworker and Welfare Recipient	$100.00 (sewing/ welfare)	?
14. 1 yr.	Santo Domingo (Urban)	Sewing Machine Operator	Sewing Machine Operator	$120.00	$355.00 (2 workers)
15. 14 yrs.	Savana Verde (Rural)	Nurse's Aide	Sewing Machine Operator (Laid0off)	$150.00	$150.00 (1 worker plus irregular contributions from husband)
16. 6 yrs.	San Jose de las Matas (Rural)	Domestic	Floorworker	$130.00	$365.00 (1 worker plus irregular contributions from son; and food stamps)

components include: 1) fashion-sensitive product lines, where demand fluctuates seasonally as well as in accordance with vagaries in consumer demand; and 2) re-orders of standardized lines which cannot be managed by larger, more routinized manufacturers (cf. Abeles et al., 1983; Waldinger, 1985).

Within the apparel industry job experience is not appreciably rewarded with increases in wages or occupational mobility. While in 1950 the average hourly earnings of workers in all manufacturing and apparel in New York was $1.57 and $1.67 respectively (i.e., apparel workers' earnings were 106.4 percent of all manufacturing workers), by 1981 the comparative wage was $6.90 and $5.87 (i.e., apparel workers' earnings were 85.1 percent of all manufacturing workers [Abeles et al.]).

The average hourly wage of $4.36 (gross) earned by sixteen informants in 1982 was significantly lower than the New York figure.[4] It should be noted that most of the informants worked at piece rates rather than at a fixed hourly rate. One might expect that with experience such workers' earnings would significantly increase. A common strategy employed by owners to control such salary hikes is to augment piece rate quotas to ensure that increases in productivity do not lead to appreciably higher wages for individual workers.

---

[4] This difference is attributable, in large part, to the inclusion in the latter calculation of men's wages which tend to be significantly higher than women's.

The work histories of the women demonstrate little or no job mobility within the industry. Most of the women entered as floorworkers and rose to machine operators in one or two years' time. However, for all save the sample maker, Marcela, job mobility has stopped at this juncture. The organization of most garment shops poses a severely limiting factor for mobility. This is due both to gender stereotyping which excludes women from positions such as cutter and pleater, and to the relatively shallow division of labor in most shops, which results in very few paths for advancement.

It is within such insecure, dead-end spheres of production that social analysts have often predicted the emergence of working-class consciousness and solidarity (*cf.* Edwards, *et al.* 1975). This has not been the case for the Dominican garment workers interviewed in this study.

THE MIDDLE-CLASS IDENTITY OF THE DOMINICAN INFORMANTS

While objectively the jobs held by the Dominican garment workers would place them in the ranks of the working class, as Table 3 shows, the majority of these women identify themselves as middle class (66.5%).

Several questions were included in the questionnaire to determine whether the informants brought an individualistic or collective orientation to issues such as social advancement and employment. Two representative examples are provided below.

When asked to choose the most and least effective means for Hispanics to progress, the informants answered as follows (*see*, Table 4):

We find an overwhelming emphasis upon education, as a vehicle for individual mobility rather than support of more broad-based, popular institutions. Belief and action are congruent. All of the women with children in their late teens and twenties had at least one child attending college part time or full time. None of the women participated in political associations. Only one was a member of a social club and its orientation was recreational. The clear rejection of the legislative process reflects both the belief that as Dominicans they could expect no political assistance from the U.S. government and a more general lack of confidence in politics. One woman commented, "It isn't a good thing getting involved in politics" (*No está bien meterse en política*). Another claimed, "an individual comes to no good involving him or herself in politics" (*La persona se va abajo con la política*).

The informants' strong beliefs in "the work ethic" is reflected here in the claim by eight women that welfare is the least effective means for Hispanics to progress.

Consistent with a middle-class ideology, the women's explanations for underemployment in the garment industry reflected a situational rather than a structural approach to job supply. If the informant claimed that since

TABLE 3

CLASS IDENTIFICATION OF DOMINICAN GARMENT WORKERS
IN THE NEW YORK METROPOLITAN AREA

Identification (Pseudonyms)	Perception of Class Prior to Emigration	Perception of Class Position in U.S.	Anticipated Class Position Upon Return to D.R.
1. Zelda	Middle Class	Middle Class	Middle Class
2. Florida	Middle Class	Middle Class	Middle Class
3. Eva	Middle Class	Working Class	Middle Class
4. Carmen	Working Class	Working Class	Middle Class
5. Marilu	Poor	Poor	Poor+
6. Rosa	Middle Class	Middle Class	Middle Class
7. Susana	Middle Class	Middle Class	Middle Class
8. Marcela	Middle Class	Middle Class	Middle Class
9. Ivalise	Middle Class	Middle Class	Middle Class
10. Gertrudes	Middle Class	Middle Class	Middle Class
11. Anita	Middle Class	Middle Class	Middle Class
12. Juana	Middle Class	Middle Class	Middle Class
13. Marina	Middle Class	Poor	(N.A. Does not anticipate a return)
14. Maria	These question unanswered because informant returned to the Dominican Republic.		
15. Lupita	Middle Class	Poor	Middle Class
16. Esperanza	Poor	Poor	Poor

arriving in the United States, it has become increasingly difficult for Dominicans to find work in the garment industry, she was queried, who is the most and least responsible for this difficulty. Responses were:

1. The owners, because they close their factories here and move to other sites in the United States or abroad;

2. The U.S. government for not having placed quotas upon imported products.

3. The unions, because they inflate the salaries forcing factories to close or move their operations to another site where the salaries are lower.

TABLE 4

Preference for Mechanisms for Hispanic Progress in the U.S.

The Most Effective	
Legislative process	0
Collective action of the Hispanic community	0
Unions	0
Education	15
Other	1*
(n)	16

* "To have a good goal and faith in oneself"

The Least Effective	
Legislative process	8
Collective action of the Hispanic community	0
Unions	0
Education	0
Other	8**
(n)	16

** "Welfare"

4. The larger number of legal and undocumented immigrants who compete for a diminishing number of jobs.

As Table 5 reveals the majority of the informants perceived the problem of unemployment and underemployment in neoclassical terms of supply and demand. There were too many immigrants competing for a limited number of jobs. Several of the women cited the United States government's failure to impose quotas on imports as a factor promoting a diminishing job supply. This is a position fostered by labor unions (*cf.* Chaikin, 1976). At its root, it pits more exploited foreign workers against less exploited domestic workers. Only one informant, Esperanza, perceived the problem as one between the conflicting interests of owners and workers. Not surprisingly, she is the only woman who consistently identified herself in the Dominican Republic and United States as working class, using such terms as "we" and "they" when speaking of fellow workers and employers.

If one were to analyze fully the lack of working-class identification and the individualistic orientation to social issues characterizing most of the informants' responses to the above mentioned questions and others, it would be necessary to include several arenas in which the meanings of work and attitudes toward the workplace are forged. Among these are the work setting,

TABLE 5

BELIEFS ABOUT THE ORIGIN OF UNEMPLOYMENT AND UNDEREMPLOYMENT
IN THE GARMENT INDUSTRY

Agents deemed most responsible	
Owners	1
U.S. government	3
Unions	2
Migrants	7
N.A.	3
(n)	16
Agents deemed least responsible	
Owners	9
U.S. government	0
Unions	1
Migrants	3
N.A.	3
(n)	16

with its technology and organization of production (cf. Edwards, 1979, Zimbalist, 1971), and unions and political associations that have attempted to organize and mobilize Dominicans (cf. Benamou, 1984; NACLA, 1977; Georges, 1984). Space precludes such an in-depth analysis. Nonetheless, in focusing upon the household, we find one highly important source for the beliefs and orientations described above.

THE CONSTRUCTION OF WORK
WITHIN THE IMMIGRANT HOUSEHOLD

Immigration is foremost a household initiative. From an analytical perspective, it may be viewed as a strategy whereby household members seek to establish a fit between the material and social resources at the group's disposal (e.g., land, capital, labor), the consumption needs of its members (informed by ideologies of standard of living), and the alternatives for productive activity. For the lower middle class, the social strata to which the majority of Dominican emigrants belonged, this dynamic fit became harder to maintain as consumption needs outpaced income and opportunities for supplementing household funds (see, Table 6).

A Dominican middle class emerged in the latter part of the Trujillo regime (cf. Cassá, 1980; Bosch, 1980). It became an increasingly important sector

TABLE 6

LAST OCCUPATION HELD BY IMMIGRANTS PRIOR TO MIGRATION

Occupation	Males (%)		Females (%)	
No Occupation	53	(23.8)	198	(58.8)
Professional Workers	20	(9)	29	(8.6)
Managers, Proprietors, Officials	12	(5.4)	8	(2.4)
Clerical Workers	24	(10.8)	28	(8.3)
Sales Workers	12	(5.4)	5	(1.5)
Domestic Services	0		9	(2.7)
Other Service Workers	24	(10.8)	5	(2.7)
Farmers, Farm Laborers, Miners, etc.	14	(6.3)	0	
Skilled, Blue-Collar, or Craft Workers	17	(7.6)	3	(.9)
Semiskilled Operative	30	(13.5)	32	(9.5)
Unskilled Nonfarm Laborers	5	(2.2)	9	(2.7)
Unknown	12	(5.4)	11	(3.3)
(n)	223		337	

Source: The Hispanic Settlement in N.Y.C. Survey, 1981.

during the Balaguer presidency (1966–1978) owing to policies that encouraged massive foreign investments, national industrialization based on import substitution and the creation of a cadre of technocrats.

This program began to founder midway into the Balaguer period. At this time commodity export prices generally worsened, while food and oil costs increased, contributing to a tripling of the nation's trade deficit between 1972 and 1976 (World Bank 1978:143). The country was no longer attracting large numbers of investors. The domestic market was saturated, and plantation agriculture and mining were less profitable. By the mid-1970s the country experienced a net dollar outflow, between debt service payments and capital repatriations. And in the last years of the Balaguer regime, for every dollar of new foreign investment, $1.60 left as expatriated profits (NACLA, 1982:12).

Contradictions in Balaguer's economic model challenged the viability of middle-class households in several ways. The overall economic instability and lack of productivity threatened owners' profits in commercial enterprises; salaried workers faced possible dismissal or reduced opportunities for career mobility. Tremendous increases in the cost of living, *e.g.*, 17.0 percent in 1973 and 1974 and 21.3 percent in 1975, were experienced at the household level (Guiliano Cury, 1980:250). Between 1969 and 1978, real wages dropped from $80 a month to $54 (*op. cit.* 1982:9). While the earning power of this social class declined, there was a marked increase in the means of communication that encouraged people to objectify their status as members of the middle class[5] by consuming commodities—often beyond their financial means.[6]

International migration became a solution for this highly vulnerable group. They had the social contacts and discretionary income to facilitate this resettlement.

With this background material, we can return to the original question: "Why haven't the work experiences of most of the informants promoted a working-class identification?" I would suggest that the orientation to their status as workers has been profoundly influenced by their motive for emigrating and laboring in the United States. The goal is to buttress or attain a middle-class status for the household, as measured against Dominican standards.

Changes in the organization of immigrant households—the pooling of income and more egalitarian decision-making over budgeting—have assisted Dominicans in attaining this end while residing in the United States. That is, by tapping the collective fund of multiple wage earners, household members have been able to purchase consumer goods and services that symbolize a middle-class standard of living. Let me turn to two research findings to substantiate and elaborate upon this claim.

First, the role that income pooling assumes in stretching the low wages of individual garment workers and allowing them to acquire durable consumer goods is apparent when comparing the response of Marilu (5), Marina (13), Lupita (15), and Esperanza (16) with those of Rosa (6), Marcela (8), Ivalise (9), and Gertrudes (10). The first group of women who consider themselves "poor" reside in households with an average of 1.5 wage earners and a dependency ratio of 3:1. In contrast, among the second group, who claims to be middle class, there are 2.5 wage earners and the dependency ratio is 1:1. The differences in the consumer power between these two groups were apparent in their diet, housing furnishing, and use of leisure lime. To take two extreme examples, Esperanza's family of eight resides in a one-bedroom apartment and shares three beds, while Ivalise's garden apartment has a guest room, living room, and den.

Second, in other studies (Pessar, 1986, 1987) I have shown how women in income pooling, egalitarian households attempt to direct expenditures to durable, consumer goods which make life in the United States more comfort-

[5] For example, between 1961 and 1976 the number of Dominican radio stations increased from 36 to 105, the number of television stations from 2 to 5 and the number of daily newspapers from 5 to 7. In Santo Domingo there were 8 publicity agencies in 1966 while in 1978 the number had grown to 38 (Ureña and Ferreira 1980:156, 150).

[6] Independent development throughout the Third World has involved the opening of new markets and the creation of new needs through the importing of First World commodities (Lipset and Bendix, 1959; Ureña and Ferreira, 1980). While these have been "staples" for decades for the working class of advanced industrial societies, they are markers of modernity and mobility for the majority of the inhabitants of less developed countries. This temporal and spacial skewing of access to valued commodities benefits the employers of immigrant workers.

able materially and socially. Not surprisingly, women in these households unanimously viewed their current class position as middle class. On the other hand, women who worked and resided in households where they did not participate so fully in income allocation were more likely to classify themselves as working class. What is striking is that this occurs in several households where the salaries are equal or higher than that found in income-pooling households. The determining element appears to be the men's control over the allocation of income and their resistance to purchase consumer goods whose payment might delay the households' return to the Dominican Republic. Both research findings point to the fact that the behavior that informs many Dominican immigrants' conceptions of social class is the consumption of prestige goods.

Do these findings mean that for the majority of Dominicans in the United States there is little or no positive correlation between immigrants' experiences in households and working-class identification and struggle? The answer at present would appear to be affirmative. In the future, however, we may see a significant change if the following prognosis proves correct.

IMMIGRANT IDEOLOGY AND TRENDS IN THE U.S. AND DOMINICAN LABOR MARKETS

There is an emerging contradiction between the ideology and aspirations of immigrant households for a middle-class standard of living, on one hand, and the potential employment opportunities for their children, on the other. While a middle-class standard of living is possible for some immigrant households, for others this goal is transferred to their children and is embodied in their higher education. Referring back to the sixteen garment workers, the extreme importance ascribed to education accounts for the middle-class identification reported by Zelda (1) and Susan (7). While both have modest incomes and live frugally, they each have university-educated children with whose achievements they strongly identify. For example, Zelda explained that one was going to be an historian and the other a philosopher. She then added, "And do you know what I am going to be? I am going to be all of this, because little by little I will be picking up something from each of them and from their friends. I will be listening and learning." Both women also indicated that they looked forward to a comfortable retirement owing to the financial support of their educated children.

While many Dominicans view their children's education as a primary vehicle for the families social mobility, there are two factors militating against this goal. First, many of the parental generation intend their educated children to return to the Dominican Republic where they can apply their U.S. training. There is unfortunately little reason to believe that the Dominican economy will develop sufficiently to absorb the U.S.-educated cohort. These young people join the increasingly large number of young Dominicans whose labor force participation has been temporarily delayed through admission to technical schools and universities, whose numbers have expanded tremendously over this decade.[7] In fact, one already encounters university-educated Dominicans—residing legally and illegally in the United States, who have emigrated due to a lack of job prospects. Their employment often does not reflect nor take advantage of the human capital these individuals bring to the United States. Second, many social scientists point to an increasingly profound bifurcation in the U.S. labor market between high-skilled white-collar jobs and low-skilled secondary sector jobs (O'Connor, 1974; Sassen-Koob, 1983). As competition increases at the top of the employment hierarchy it is likely that Hispanics will suffer from both blatant discrimination and more subtle forms emanating from their lack of access to prestigious social networks. In short, the latest wave of immigrants may find that the social mobility enjoyed by earlier groups of second generation ethnics will be much more circumscribed for them in the United States. In the light of these developments we can conclude that unless structural changes occur in their country of origin or the most recent prognosis of the U.S. economy proves erroneous, the social mobility Dominicans anticipate may indeed prove illusory. An Hispanic lower working class may become a more or less permanent feature of the United States' political economy.[8]

While caution must be exercised given the very small number of workers who were interviewed, I believe that the findings and analysis presented above do suggest certain directions that might be pursued by labor and political organizations which seek to promote working-class solidarity and action among immigrant populations. Organizers often claim that women as a group are harder to win over than men. Nonetheless, women will probably prove more receptive than men to the message that their daughters and sons may not provide them with the prestige and security in old age that parents anticipate. This is the case because gender ideology continues to root women's sense of achievement and well-being to the household. If women are educated about likely ethnic and gender discrimination that will eventuate in their children's restricted mobility in a bifurcated U.S. economy, they may be more receptive to struggling now collectively to improve conditions in these secondary sector jobs.

The importance of incorporating immigrant women into the union movement is underscored when we consider the changes already occurring in the industries that recruit immigrants, ethnics, and women. We are already

---

[7] In 1965 there were only 2 Dominican universities, by 1976 the number had increased to 7 and matriculation had expanded from 6,963 to 58,907, that is, by approximately 850% (Ureña and Ferreira, 1980:153).

[8] Unlike the parental generation, the second generation will evaluate their consumer power and lifestyle against American standards. This point of reference should distinguish them from the first wave of Dominican immigrants who experienced a "middle class " standard of living that native-born Americans associate with the working class.

observing the breakdown of vertically integrated, unionized shops in the apparel and other manufacturing industries. These are being replaced by nonunionized subcontracting shops with a small labor force (Bluestone and Harrison, 1982; Christopherson, 1983). The ability of unions to organize such small, dispersed firms, an admittedly difficult task would be eased if organizers could rely upon the presence of individuals who are familiar with and positively disposed to unionization. If workers in these firms do not have available to them the higher wages, greater job security, and other social benefits unions have historically brought to laborers, it is likely that their economic vulnerability will be attributed by many to "immutable" characteristics of this work force. That is, the probable lesser mobility of these immigrant workers and their children, as compared to that of earlier European groups (cf. Borjas, n.d.) will be attributed to gender, race and national background rather than to the new political-economic constraints facing the newest wave of immigrant labor.

CONCLUSION

Drawing upon the case of Dominican, immigrant women, this article has explored the interdependence between the household and workplace. We have noted that wage employment has helped Dominican women to gain greater equity in their households. On the other hand, it has been shown that a supply of women workers who approach their jobs as satisfied individuals is a by-product of the changes in the organization of Dominican immigrant households as well as their members' attitudes toward emigration. Nonetheless, there are indications of a contradiction emerging between the immigrant household ideology and future opportunities for Dominican children. Its resolution may yet transform individual female workers into women who conceive of their identity and future as tied to the fate of the larger domestic working class.

BIBLIOGRAPHY

Abadan-Unat, N.
1977 "Implications of Migration on Emancipation or Pseudoemancipation of Turkish Women," *International Migration Review*, 11(1):31–58. Spring.

Abeles, Schwartz, Hackel and Silverblatt, Inc.
1983 *The Chinatown Garment Study*. New York International Ladies Garment Workers Union.

Barrett, M.
1980 *Women's Oppression Today*. London: Verso Editions.

Benamou, C.
1984 *"La Aguja": Labor Union Participation Among Hispanic Immigrant Women in the New York*

Garment Industry. New York Center for Latin American and Caribbean Studies, New York University Research Program in Inter-American Affairs. Occasional Paper 44.

Bluestone, B. and B. Harrison
1982   *The Deindustrialization of America.* New York: Basic Books.

Borjas, G.J.
n.d.   "The Impact of Assimilation on the Earnings of Immigrants: A Reexamination of the Evidence." Unpublished manuscript, Economics Department, University of California, Santa Barbara.

Bosch, J.
1980   Composición Social Dominicana. Santo Domingo: Editoria Alfa y Omega.

Brown, S.
1975   "Love Unites Them and Hunger Separates Them: Poor Women in the Dominican Republic." In *Toward an Anthropology of Women.* R. Reiter, ed. New York: Monthly Review Press. Pp. 322–332.

Cassá, R.
1980   *Modos de producción, clases sociales, luchas políticas.* Santo Domingo: Editora Alfa y Omega.

Chaiken, S.
1976   "The Needed Repeal of Item 807.00 of the Tariff Schedules of the United States." Report presented by the Sub-Committee on Ways and Means, U.S. House of Representatives.

Christopherson, S.
1983   *Segmentation in Sunbelt Labor Markets.* San Diego: Center for U.S.-Mexican Studies, University of California, San Diego. Research Report Series.

Edwards, R.
1979   *Contested Terrain.* New York: Basic Books.

Edwards, R, M. Reich and D. Gordon
1975   *Labor Market Segmentation.* Lexington: D.C. Heath and Co.

Ferrán, F.
1974   "La familia nuclear de la subcultura de la pobreza dominicana," *Estudios Sociales.* 7(3):137–185. Julio–Sept.

Fox, B.
1980   *Hidden in the household.* Ontario: The Women's Press.

Georges, E.
1984   *New Immigrants in the Political Process: Dominicans in New York.* New York: Center for Latin American and Caribbean Studies, New York University Research Program in Inter-American Affairs. Occasional Paper 45.

González, N.
1976   "Multiple Migratory Experiences of Dominican Women." *Anthropological Quarterly,* 49(1):36–44. Jan.

_____
1970   "Peasants' Progress: Dominicans in New York." *Caribbean Studies.* 10(3):154–171. Oct.

Guiliano Cury, H.
1980   *Reflecciones acerca de la economía dominicana.* Santo Domingo: Editora Alfa y Omega.

Gurak, D.
1981   *The Hispanic Settlement in New York City Survey.* New York: Hispanic Research Program, Fordham University.

Gurak, D. and M. Kritz
1982   "Settlement and Immigration Processes of Dominicans and Colombians in New York City." Unpublished paper presented at the Annual Meetings of the American Sociological Association, San Francisco.

Instituto Dominicano de Estudios Aplicados
1975 "La condición de la campesina dominicana y su participación en la economía." Santo
      Domingo: Secretaría de Estado de Agricultura.

Kessler-Harris, A.
1981 Women Have Always Worked. Old Westbury: Feminist Press.

Lipsett, S. and R. Bendix
1959 Social Mobility in Industrial Society. Los Angeles: University of California Press.

NACLA (North American Congress for Latin America)
1982 "Dominican Republic—The Launching of a Democracy," NACLA 16(6):1–35. Nov./Dec.

_____
1977 "Capital's Flight: The Apparel Industry Moves South," NACLA 11(3):1–25. March.

O'Connor, J.
1974 The Fiscal Crisis of the State. New York: St. Martin's Press.

Parsons, T.
1955 Family, Socialization and Interaction Process. Glencoe, Illinois: Free Press.

Pessar, P.
1986a "The Role of Gender in Dominican Settlement in the United States." In Women and Change
      in Latin America. J. Nash and H.I.T. Safa, eds. South Hadley, MA: Bergin and Garvey. Pp.
      273–294.

_____
1987 "The Constraints Upon and Release of Female Labor Power: The Case of Dominican
     Migration to the United States." In A Home Divided: Women and Income in the Third World.
     D.H. Dwyer and J. Bruce, eds. Stanford: Stanford University Press.

_____
1982 "Social Relations Within the Family in the Dominican Republic and United States: Conti-
      nuity and Change." In Hispanics in New York: Religious, Cultural and Social Experiences. New
      York: Office of Pastoral Research, Archdiocese of New York. Vol. 2, pp. 211–221 .

Sacks, K.
n.d. "Computers, Ward Secretaries and a Walkout in a Southern Hospital." Unpublished
      manuscript, Business and Professional Women's Foundation. Washington, D.C.

Sassen-Koob, S.
1983 "The New Labor Demand in Global Cities." In Capital, Class and Urban Structure. D. Smith,
      ed. New York: Sage.

Tancer, S.
1973 "La Quesqueyana: The Dominican Women, 1940–1979." In Female and Male in Latin
      America. A. Pescatello, ed. Pittsburgh: University of Pittsburgh Press. Pp. 209–229.

Tax, M.
1980 The Rising of Women: Feminist Solidarity and Class Conflict 1880–1917. New York: Monthly
      Review Press.

Ureña, E. and A. Ferreira
1980 "Modelo de dominación y sectores medios en la República Dominicana: 1966–1978." B.A.
      Thesis in Sociology, Universidad Autonoma de Santo Domingo.

Waldinger, R.
1985 "Immigration and Industrial Change in the New York Apparel Industry." In Hispanics in
      the U.S. Economy. G.J. Borjas and M. Tienda, eds. New York: Academic Press. Pp. 323–349.

World Bank
1978 Dominican Republic: In Main Economic Development Problems. Washington, D.C.: World
      Bank.

Zimbalist, A.
1979   *Case Studies on the Labor Process.* New York: Monthly Review Press.

FORMAL AND INFORMAL ASSOCIATIONS: Dominicans and Colombians in New York

SASKIA SASSEN-KOOB[1]
Columbia University

All immigrant workers, whether in Western Europe or the United States, whether North African or Latin American, whether Colombian or Dominican, share many of the same characteristics and are engaged in similar struggles. Investigating particular immigrant groups is a necessary step in the more general task of understanding the category immigrant labor. It is then possible to move from the particular back to the analytical as a means of formulating general propositions rooted in the actual historical experience of the immigrant groups .

Voluntary associations in the Dominican and Colombian communities of New York City were selected as the subject for comparison in this study for two primary reasons. Initially, these associations operate as an adaptive mechanism in situations of rapid change undergone by urban migrants coming from peasant and tribal societies (Little, 1965; Anderson and Anderson, 1962; Parkin, 1966; Doughty, 1970; Hammer, 1967). On the other hand, voluntary associations also serve to strengthen the consciousness of a group's culture of origin (Doughty, 1970; Little, 1962; Meillassoux, 1968) and reproduce aspects of the traditional institutional order in a new, urban-oriented form (*e.g.*, the model of the replicate structure in Anderson and Anderson, 1962). Both Colombians and Dominicans, as recent immigrant groups to an urban environment, are currently in a situation of change requiring adaptation. Both groups also exist as, and are perceived as, Hispanic communities.

In a comparative analysis these two immigrant communities are most interesting since they retain significant similarities and differences. These characteristics can be tentatively identified as cultural-ideological and struc-

[1] I wish to thank the Latin American students (especially Ana Falla) who requested the course from which this chapter emerged. I also wish to thank all the members of the two communities for spending time with us. Finally, I want to thank the Research Foundation of the City University of New York for funding a larger project on Third World International Migration.

tural. This chapter does not suggest that these categories be opposed as if they contained rival explanatory variables, which they do not (see, Peel, 1973). Rather, it is the contention here that these categories serve to organize the various attributes descriptive of each community. Dominicans and Colombians both share a common language, the dominance of Catholicism, and a number of cultural-ideological constructs originating under Spanish colonial rule. When placed in the context of New York City, these factors are associated with a "Latin" or "Hispanic," as opposed to an "Anglo," identity. Although generated in large part by the objective cultural content of the communities, this Hispanic identity is a product of the immigration process, and the migrant becomes an ethnic (or a member of a race). Yet, there are important differences in the socioeconomic structures of the places of origin of these immigrant groups, even though both are defined by a situation of dependence in the world economy. The Dominicans in New York typically originated in rural areas where the predominant forms of socioeconomic organization are a peasantry and rural wage labor. The Colombians are typically from the urban middle and increasingly from the lower middle class, some of them low-income and self-employed.

Given the characteristics of voluntary associations and given the similarities and differences between the Colombian and Dominican immigrant communities this chapter proposes that the incidence and types of voluntary associations in an immigrant community can be used as an indicator of the differential weight of cultural-ideological and structural factors in the articulation of the immigrant community with the receiving society.[2]

The choice of voluntary associations as such an indicator is based on certain methodological and political constraints. Because of the political implications, there are difficulties involved in obtaining information about immigrant communities. Voluntary associations, however, are usually visible, accessible, and they provide a community-legitimized source of information about particular aspects of the community.

THE TWO COMMUNITIES IN NEW YORK

Dominicans and Colombians are the two largest foreign Hispanic populations in New York City. Precise figures on their size are unavailable since they, as many other immigrant communities, contain significant numbers of undocumented migrants. For reasons discussed below, we accepted the figures provided by the Archdiocese of New York which estimate that there are at least 400,000 Dominicans and 200,000 Colombians in New York City.[3]

---

[2] Elsewhere, I have discussed some of the methodological issues involved in considering structural and cultural-ideological factors in the analysis of immigrant, ethnic or racial communities (Sassen-Koob, 1973, 1978), including a critique of the category "adaptation."

[3] There are estimated to be 170,000 Ecuadoreans, 150,000 Peruvians and growing numbers of

The recorded number of annual immigrant and nonimmigrant entries has grown steadily for both groups.

The influx of Dominicans and Colombians rose in the early 1960s because of political push factors, including Trujillo's murder and later Juan Bosch's revolution in the Dominican Republic (Gutiérrez, 1974), and the aftermath of the decade of "La Violencia" in Colombia (Fals Borda, 1967). Not surprisingly, those from this period were mostly middle-class immigrants. In the late 1960s there was a pronounced increase in the number of entries, and the flow began to include many more persons of lower-class origin. In 1967, the United States admitted 78,791 Dominicans and 32,197 Colombians with nonimmigrant status. By 1971 entries had grown to 105,191 and 59, 031 respectively; and by 1976, to 155,930 and 101,419. Both populations have had increases in the numbers admitted with immigrant status, although after 1970 the numbers of Colombians declined. In 1965 there were 9,504 Dominicans and 10,885 Colombians admitted as immigrants; by 1976 these figures had changed to 12,526 Dominicans (a 32% increase over the 1965 level) and 5,742 Colombians which represented a 47 percent decline over the 1965 level (Immigration and Naturalization Service, various years).

If we consider the nonimmigrant entries and the fact that an unspecified number simply remains after their visas expire, it is clear that the actual resident population of each nationality can easily approximate and surpass the estimates of the Archdiocese of New York.[4]

More than one-half the number of Dominicans probably live in Manhattan's Upper West Side, notably in the Washington Heights section, with smaller concentrations in the Lower East Side and in the Corona section of Queens. Our research was focused on Manhattan's upper West Side colony. Colombians tended to be clustered in Queens, although a growing number were moving out to Long Island towns (a step up the social ladder). In Queens, Colombians were concentrated in Jackson Heights, Jamaica, Elmhurst, Woodside, and Sunnyside and we focused on these areas. (For a

---

Argentineans, Chileans, and Brazilians. It must be stressed that these estimates and all those contained here are speculative.

[4] For a number of reasons, the Catholic Church probably has the best statistics on this group. First, the considerable geographic concentration of Dominicans, Colombians and other Latin nationalities allows for rather homogeneous parishes. (A number of clergy who serve in Hispanic migrant communities barely speak—and hardly need to speak English [see also, Chaney, 1976:117–118; Hendricks; 1974:117–121].) Second, most Colombians and Dominicans are Catholic, and the local church usually has either direct or indirect access to most of its parishioners. Third, the priests also act as culture brokers in these immigrant communities, along with travel and real-estate agents. The priest fulfills functions which go beyond his institutionally defined role (see, Little, 1965, on how traditional institutions such as the Church take on a new role in a situation of change). During our research we found a number of priests, including Anglo priests, with high visibility and considerable trust among the community members even when individually criticized (see, Hendricks, 1974:117). We also found the priests had rather detailed information about their parishes, the educational and occupational distribution of their members, and shifts in the nationalities dominating a parish. Finally, we found the priests to be well informed and protective of undocumented persons in their parishes.

description of the colony in Jackson Heights, *see*, Chaney, 1976.) Generally, the Dominican community of the Upper West Side is more homogeneous in terms of economic status and national origin than the Colombian community of Queens. In the latter, there are growing numbers of Eduadoreans and lesser numbers of Peruvians, Argentineans, and Chileans. This study did not include high income Colombians and Dominicans who have lost, or never had, ties with immigrant communities.

NEW YORK AND THE DOMINICAN AND COLOMBIAN EMIGRATION

New York plays very different roles in the emigration flows of Colombians and Dominicans. With insignificant exceptions, emigration for Dominicans, *ir allá* (to go there) means going to New York. A large share of the migrants are peasants and agricultural laborers who formerly would have entered the internal rural-to-urban migration flow but now simply jump that stage.[5] For Colombians, Venezuela is equivalent to New York. Using estimates of the total Colombian population in New York and Venezuela, it would seem that the former receives less than one sixth of the Colombian emigrant flow. In contrast, New York receives an estimated 90 percent of the Dominican population.

Given the obstacles of language, literacy, a foreign urban milieu, and access only through controlled ports of entry requiring some sort of visa, it is rather astounding that such a large number of rural Dominicans have made it to New York City. Unlike Mexicans crossing into the United States, and Colombians crossing into Venezuela, Dominicans have to obtain a visa, even if it is just to go to San Juan, Puerto Rico, and from there enter the continental United States as "Puerto Ricans." A number of complex historical factors have combined to make New York City a realistic option for rural Dominicans.[6] In addition to the basic relationship of dependence, certain events such as the recent flight of middle-class Dominicans to New York and the 1965 United States military occupation of the Republic, set in motion various social processes which created channels of access.

---

[5] The term peasant is problematic. The view I find most adequate is that which sees peasant societies not as a distinctive or intermediate type, but as one of the forms which noncapitalist modes of production take in response to capitalist penetration, specifically, penetration in agriculture (*e.g.,* Ennew, *et. al.,* 1977; de Janvry and Garramon, 1977). *See also,* the notion of Caribbean peasantries as reconstituted peasantries (Mintz, 1974).

[6] Even those Dominicans who come to New York after a short-term residence in a city are basically rural. *See,* Tinker on how rural-to-urban migrations in the Third World cause no qualitative change in the city, merely an expansion in their size, or on the notion of a "ruralization of urban environments" in the Third World (Tinker, 1971). This points to a possible fallacy in studies on Third World emigration that classify emigrants as urban simply because they were living in a city (often a necessary step to obtain a visa) at the time of departure.

Extended kinship promotes maintenance of linkages with Dominicans in New York and conversations about New York in the Republic. Something akin to an oral history about life in New York, its accessibility, and its rewards, has evolved, topped by an entire folklore on how to get a visa (*see*, González, 1970:163–168; Hendricks, 1974:40–70). Not surprisingly, the new occupation of United States visa-broker has emerged in many rural communities. Bringing New York even closer to the Dominican countryside is the large emigration from the Cibao region of the Republic. Almost everyone in the Cibao has a relative, *compadre*, or friend in New York. One consequence of this is that most people in the Cibao can talk at length about New York (and United States visas), and generally find the subject a compelling one. Inevitably, potential emigrants become familiar with the migration process. As the United States Consulate in Santo Domingo becomes increasingly cautious in granting visas, Dominicans become increasingly knowledgeable about getting them.

There is one final obstacle. It may cost up to $500 to obtain the required documents and get to New York City. This is a large amount in an economy where the average annual income of peasants and rural laborers is below this figure and where subsistence depends in good part on home production and barter (*see*, Westbrook, 1965). Although the Cibao region is among the wealthier in the country, it is nonetheless very poor (*see*, Hendricks, 1974:11–39; Kayal, 1978; República Dominicana, 1970).[7]

There seem to be two ways in which the sum for migration can be obtained. One is through remittances from those already in New York, as either a gift or a loan. The obligations associated with kinship and *compadrazgo* continue to weigh heavily, even though they are not perceived as burdensome because of the ultimate collective benefit. (For a detailed description of how these obligations continue to operate for Dominicans in New York, *see*, Hendricks, 1974; and Garrison and Weiss, this volume.) A second way is based on a rotating-credit association operating in rural and marginal urban milieus in the Dominican Republic.[8] Referred to as *San*, little is known about this phenomenon (for a description *see*, Norvell and Wehrly, 1969). Although common in Africa and Asia, rotating-credit associations were thought to be few in America, and confined to Barbados, Guyana, and Jamaica (Ardener, 1964). Now rotating-credit schemes are found to be widely used among peasants as alternative to modern credit institutions. The Dominican San fits Geertz's definition of an association (a limited number of participants who agree to make regular contributions to a fund which is given to each contributor in rotation, either in whole or in part). San is frequently used to finance those social rituals, *e.g.*, weddings and funerals, which require large, single outlays of money. Although we have been unable to obtain precise informa-

---

[7] Editors' note: *see also*, Grasmuck, 1982 and 1984; Pessar, 1982.

[8] The use of such an alternative credit institution in a city supports Tinker's notion. *See*, footnote 6.

tion, it seems that San is also used by Dominicans in New York City to finance various kinds of activities, a fact which may explain at least in part the rising number of small shop owners in the community. We also found indications that it is used to finance the documents, travel, and initial settlement costs involved in coming to New York.

It would appear that the rural origin of Dominicans plays a dual role in their emigration to New York. It is an obstacle in that it makes Dominicans foreign to the ways of a city, particularly a city in which English is a practical necessity. Yet, it is precisely the structure of rural society which produces a support system for emigration to a foreign and urban milieu.

In the case of Colombia, rural emigrants do not go to New York, but rather to Venezuela and, though in much smaller numbers, to Ecuador and Panama. Rural emigrants can avoid documents and application forms and simply walk to Venezuela through the *caminos verdes* (green pathways). Venezuela is also increasingly the main immigration country for urban, middle-class Colombians. The last few years have seen a marked rise in this trend. By 1976 there were 300,000 legal residents and an estimated 700,000 undocumented Colombians living in Venezuela (Consejo Nacional de Recursos Humanos, 1977:138; *see also*, Ministerio del Trabajo, 1978:18). Thus, the immigrant Colombian community of New York represents a second choice to Venezuela, and the colony accounts for only a small proportion of the total population of Colombia.[9]

The Colombian immigration to New York however, appears to be more selective. Up to 1965, migrants were overwhelmingly highly trained professional and technical personnel (Chaparro and Arias, 1970; Cruz and Castaño, 1976; Chaney, 1976:96–102). As emigration increased markedly toward the late 1960s, the constitution of the flow changed to a growing share of nonprofessional middle and lower middle-class persons. In 1972 the Colombian government sought the return of its professionals through various concessions (Ministerio del Trabajo, 1978:44–45). Yet, the results were disappointing (*see also*, Cruz and Castaño, 1976, on the possibility that emigration of professionals may be a temporary move benefiting Colombia in that returning professionals will have acquired additional training and financial resources). The highest rate of return was for Bogotá, with 13 percent of technical and professional personnel coming back. The government has recently begun another program with the same objectives (Ministerio del Trabjo, 1978:45–47; Mármora, 1978).

[9] This will become even more pronounced with the implementation of the free labor circulation system among the member countries of the *Pacto Andino*. It contains explicit stipulations aimed at regularizing the status of undocumented workers (*Comisión del Acuerdo de Cartagena*, 1977: *Capítulo* VIII). Of interest here is the case of one Colombian family in New York which found that they were not doing so well as a brother who had migrated to Venezuela several years ago and now owned his own small factory. One of the objectives of our larger project is to uncover this kind of comparative information.

These measures point to the selectivity of the emigrant flow to the United States. Although all major cities, and especially Bogotá, have a rapidly growing number of poor and *marginales*, they also have a large middle class with a relatively high level of education. Increasingly, it seems to be in the lower income segments of this middle class that the emigration flow originates.[10]

These migrants inevitably experience downward mobility in coming to the United States (Chaney, 1976). Their urban origins entail familiarity with the large, complex, impersonal, bureaucracy-dominated systems of large cities, therewith making the move to New York less of a step into foreign territory. It is our impression that in these areas there is not quite the folklore about getting United States visas and about life in New York that is so present in the Cibao region of the Dominican Republic (*but see,* Chaney, 1976:111). The equivalent of the latter can be found in some rural Colombian communities where a large number of the people have emigrated to Venezuela.

Thus, although Colombians and Dominicans have a number of cultural-ideological variables in common which, in the context of New York City, become subsumed under the category "Hispanic" or "Latin," there are important differences which this categorization omits. These differences are visible when we observe the structural variables descriptive of the localities the migrants come from and the role of New York in their respective emigration flows. Henceforth, this complex constellation of variables will be referred to by the descriptive terms "urban" and "rural." These terms are inadequate, however, in that they fail to convey the basic process underlying the differences in the places of origin of Colombians and Dominicans, *i.e.,* two different forms of incorporation into both the national class system of each country and the world economy. In other words, "Dominican peasantry" and "Colombian urban middle and lower middle class" are historical forms indicative of these different forms of incorporation. They are not diametric poles on some continuum showing different stages of modernization. Although clearly inadequate, "urban" and "rural" are a convenient shorthand (Sassen-Koob, 1978).

VOLUNTARY ASSOCIATIONS AS A MODALITY OF ARTICULATION

Thirty-six Dominican associations were located in Manhattan's Upper West Side, mostly in the Washington Heights section, and sixteen Colombian associations were found in Queens. There were several Dominican associations in Queens and a few in the Bronx, but these fall outside the focus of our study. We spoke with leaders, members, and nonmembers, examined

[10] Although a large share of the population of Bogotá is made up of migrants, many become integrated into the middle stratum. Only 9% of rural migrants in Bogotá lacked schooling and many have high levels of education (Cardona, 1973:163–177).

incorporation charters, and, to a limited degree, participated in associations' activities.

Findings

The incidence and types of associations in each community showed some differences. Accepting the estimates of population size given earlier, it would appear that the Dominican community of the Upper West Side is not markedly larger than the Colombian community of Queens. Yet, the former has more than twice as many associations. Second, there also appeared to be a predominance of civic-cultural and professional associations in the Colombian community with a rather clear tendency toward self-attribution of "elite" status or at least high status within the stratification system internal to the community.[11] The existence itself of this stratification system seemed to be another trait distinguishing the two communities. The Dominican associations were more typically recreational and in some ways reflected the greater socioeconomic homogeneity of that community. The Colombian associations on the other hand, were mostly "elite." Bitter comments were expressed from "nonelite" persons in the Colombian community about the inaccessibility to and lack of assistance from the "elite" associations. This was not apparent in the Dominican community. Antagonisms there seemed to be more rooted in political issues concerning both the home country and the relationship between the latter and the immigrant community.

Keeping in mind these general characteristics, the information obtained can be organized into the following three groups of voluntary associations.

First, while there were a large number of small recreational, mostly incorporated clubs in the Dominican community, there were very few associations of this type in the Colombian community. Although the incorporation charters of these clubs may include various community-oriented and mutual help goals, in practice they tended to be pure ly recreational. They appeared to be, in some ways, a substitute for the extended kinship and compadrazgo system of the sending country. At the same time, they facilitated the continuity of those bonds in a new, urban form. An example of this was the decision by a group of families to initiate a club after a fire destroyed the building they occupied in Corona and they were unable to find a common living situation in the Upper West Side where they had moved. One Dominican informant even noted that some of these clubs exist simply to provide members with the opportunity of dining out regularly as a group.

The closest equivalent to the Dominican groups in the Colombian community was the Colombian Soccer League, an umbrella organization grouping

---

[11] This stratification system does not include upper-class Colombians or Dominicans residing in the United States who are not and never were members of the "immigrant community." Thus, the term "elite" as used by members of this community is relative only to the latter. The objective category it describes is an upwardly mobile middle class.

a dozen sports clubs, half of which were in Queens. These clubs all share the premises of the Pan-American Soccer League, an even wider organization grouping soccer clubs from various Latin American nationalities. These groups resemble the Dominican clubs in that they cater to "nonelite" members of the communities. These clubs still, however, do not quite provide the context for patterns of interaction and bonds reminiscent of kinship and compadrazgo although they no doubt approximate this for the men involved. This is partly because they are not family clubs and lack their own meeting premises.

Second, a much larger number of cultural and civic associations were found in the Dominican than in the Colombian community while a larger number of professional associations were found in the Colombian community. Many of the associations were small; some were incorporated and others were not; some had their own meeting premises; and others simply met in the homes of members. The explicit objectives of these associations tended to be maintenance or diffusion of one or another cultural aspect of the society of origin, support to fellow countrymen, or, simply, social interaction. A large number of women were involved in these kinds of associations, often carrying most of the duties involved in their operation. Notably, in the Colombian community, it was found that some of the most active leaders were women. Nonmembers in both communities described their activities as often simply being attempts to engage in certain social rituals considered to be part of the life of an "upper class," going all the way from cocktail parties and formal celebrations to tourist trips.

There is a clear class distinction between the two communities in terms of these kinds of associations. In the words of a Dominican, many of the association members are "factory or service workers but have pretensions to being something else." In the Colombian community, these groups were definitely considered "elite" associations. Some of the associations in both communities tended to have vaguely defined political objectives, often aimed at the home country. In both communities a handful of associations were found which defined themselves as charity organizations. Their drives took place in New York but their clientele was in the home countries and, it seems, formed part of the actual or potential constituency of one or another political bloc.

Given the presence of effective leadership, these two kinds of associations can be used to mobilize a broad segment of the immigrant community in support of various struggles. This actually occurred in the Dominican community in the early 1970s when an umbrella organization called the Concilio de Organizaciones Dominicanas, grouping fifteen separate clubs, was formed to support the struggle for the rights of undocumented Dominicans. The fragility of this kind of mobilization for a broader struggle became visible when the leaders of the Concilio began to surrender their objectives because of the lack of effective and long-term support by the member clubs. This may

also be indicative of the endurance of the more traditional kinship orientation present in these clubs; *i.e.*, it is kinship obligations which will evoke the
more effective response (*see also*, Hendricks, 1974:42–44).

The closest approximation to a broad community-oriented organization in
the Colombian community was the recently formed Colombo-American
Civic committee. Unlike the Dominican Concilio, its constituents were merchants and restaurant owners. This association was seeking to revive and
organize the economic life of Sunnyside in Queens where settlement of
Colombians has resulted in the upgrading of various neighborhoods.

Although most Colombian associations fell under this second category,
their place in the community was quite different from that of the Dominican
associations of this kind. In the latter case the associations were somewhat
indistinguishable from recreational clubs and they tended to fulfill a similar
function. In contrast, participation in the Colombian associations entailed
not so much a reproduction of kinship and compadrazgo situations as it
involved the active creation of new links with the host society. For this reason
I included most of the Colombian associations under the instrumental type
discussed below.

Third, Dominicans have lagged behind Colombians in initiating organizations with fundamentally instrumental objectives. This is reflected in the
fact that Dominicans have only recently organized to obtain certain political
rights. In March 1978, they formed the Asociación Nacional de Dominicanos
Ausentes (ANDA), the most important and immediate objective of which was
to get the right to vote in Dominican elections for emigrants residing in the
United States. The Colombians had gained this right several years earlier.
Furthermore, in the words of one of the principal Dominican leaders and
organizers of ANDA, the latter is consciously shaped after the Colombian
model. This is particularly significant given the fact that the Dominicans in
New York represent an estimated 10 percent of the total Dominican population, a share notably higher than that of the Colombians in New York. ANDA
has a young leadership and appears to be very effective and people-oriented.
Its objectives include providing legal assistance for the defense of civic and
political rights of resident Dominicans.

It is our impression that the mobilization of the Colombian associations
goes a step further than that represented by ANDA's goals—which are,
moreover, goals which the Colombian community has already attained. In
October, 1978, the Asociación de Profesionales Colombianos called a meeting
attended by the director of the most important New York Spanish language
paper and a Colombian ambassador to the United Nations to protest formally
and to organize against the image propagated by the United States media
about Colombians in New York, particularly the notion that most are directly
or indirectly linked with the illicit drug traffic. Subsequent to that meeting,
similar statements continue to be made, always involving situations where
United States agencies or officials are present. Associations like the Colom-

bian professionals seek to force representatives of the host society into a direct exchange with the immigrant community, an exchange in which the latter refuses a position of ideological subordination.

Summary

We found a) a much larger number of associations in the Dominican (36) community than in the Colombian (16); b) almost all Colombian associations to be of "elite" status in terms of the stratification system internal to the community, and almost none of the Dominican to be such; c) a majority of Dominican associations to be basically recreational clubs, and a majority of Colombian to be cultural-civic and especially professional; d) that while the Dominican associations appeared to approximate recreational associations, the Colombian ones, although also recreational, had clearly instrumental objectives; and e) a more developed strategy for the use of voluntary associations as instrumental in the attainment of political objectives in the Colombian community.

DISCUSSION

Generally, a clear tendency toward expressive associations in the Dominican community and toward instrumental associations in the Colombian community may be noted. Although different in type, both kinds of associations may be seen as providing mechanisms for the transition process involved in migration.

Instrumental associations tend to involve more exchanges with an external, generally dominant group, elite, class, either within the receiving society or in the home country (e.g., ANDA). Furthermore, these kinds of associations may be seen as seeking to redefine at least certain aspects in the articulation of the immigrant community with the host society. Insofar as they introduce an element of power in the political and economic identity of the immigrant community, they can be said to help change its condition from that of a powerless to that of a "mobilized diaspora" (cf. Armstrong, 1976).

This change toward mobilization would seem to go against the role played by the more expressive associations in the articulation with the host society in that these tend to promote something akin to cultural separatism. It is in this sense that Hendricks (1974:121) views associations as being maladaptive and preventing needed resocialization. Certainly, the proliferation of associations in the Dominican community can be seen as reproducing and ensuring the continuity of the institutions of kinship and language.

Cultural separatism is a problematic term. As a category of analysis it suggests disarticulation and disengagement. Yet, historically cultural separatism has been one of the modes in which immigrant or racially distinct communities become articulated with the receiving or dominant society. I should like to argue that cultural separatism is a mode of articulation and that what appear as two opposites, the cultural separatism promoted by the expressive associations and the political mobilization promoted by the instrumental associations, are, in fact, complementary modalities of articulation. Indeed, while the first type of association can be seen as reproducing traditional institutions in a new urban form, the second type does so by seeking benefits for the community, the attainment of which are dependent on external recognition of its separateness (e.g., being a Dominican United States resident as a condition for the right to vote in the Republic; being a Colombian as a condition to demand rectification of the community's public image). In their exchanges with external, generally dominant entities, the instrumental associations found in these two communities emphasized national distinctiveness (rather than a still mythical "Hispanic unity"), a determination not to become Americanized or assimilated.

Comparing the Dominican and Colombian communities suggests two questions. First, why are there so many more voluntary associations in the Dominican community; and, second, why has the latter lagged behind the Colombian community in forming instrumental associations?

The proliferation of expressive associations within the Dominican community can be seen as a way in which a rural population adapts to a new, urban milieu by reproducing traditional institutions in a new, urban-oriented form (see, the notion of the "replicate structure" in Anderson and Anderson, 1962; Little, 1962; and Rogler, 1972:5, on how voluntary associations represent "collective efforts to compensate for the loss of communal life"). This reproduction of traditional institutions, and the affirmation of ethnicity, is not necessarily an attachment to the past but rather a response to the needs generated in a new urban context (see, Sutton, 1975:183). In this regard, it could be argued that Hendricks' finding that voluntary associations are maladaptive because they promote cultural separatism, rests on a failure to distinguish between voluntary associations as mediating agents and as directly promoting the urbanization of a rural population. It is our finding that expressive voluntary associations are mediating agents. Thus the urbanization of the rural population should not be seen as the reason for forming (and the criterion for evaluating) such associations, but rather as the context within which they reproduce traditional institutions in a new, urban form. This would also explain their greater proliferation in the Dominican community than in the Colombian. The far more pronounced disparity between place of origin and receiving society in the case of the Dominicans determines the need for a more elaborate transition process if basic social needs are to be met. It would also explain the absence of such associations among the lower strata within the Colombian community, since they are mostly urban in origin.

There is some evidence in this regard within Latin America. Doughty (1970) found a proliferation of voluntary associations among Peruvian Highlands Indians who had migrated to Lima. The fact that some of these clubs were elitist (Jongkind, 1974) does not invalidate the fact that a significant disparity between place of origin and receiving society is an important variable in the formation of these clubs (Skeldon, 1977). On the other hand, Dotson (1953) found little affiliation with such associations among low-income people in the Mexican city of Guadalajara. Furthermore, a detailed study on affiliation in Bogotá (Calderón, et. al., 1963) found affiliation to be directly related to income and almost nonexistent among low-income neighborhoods, a finding similar to the case in the United States where low-income natives have far lower affiliation rates than middle-class natives. That is, long resident urban groups of comparable income and occupations to those of Dominicans in New York do not have equally high affiliation rates (cf. Little, 1964; Parkin, 1966; Anderson, 1971). This also suggests that expressive associations do not necessarily flourish because of the weakening of the family and face to face communities but are, rather, a way of ensuring their continuity. It is also interesting to note their absence in low-income urban milieus of either Colombia or the Dominican Republic (Hendricks, 1974; Corten, 1965; Gutiérrez de Pineda, 1968; Calderón, et. al., 1963; see also, Cohen and Kapsis, 1978, on Blacks and Puerto Ricans in New York City).

One final point to be raised is why the Dominican community lagged behind the Colombian in forming instrumental associations. An important factor here, again, is the disparity between place of origin and destination. Before the community can engage in direct, instrumental exchanges with external, typically dominant agents of the host society, it has to elaborate or discover more general internally oriented group structures through which its individual members may find ways of drawing on their experience to confront new situations. The anthropological literature on voluntary associations lends support to this thesis. Furthermore, the facts of race and class probably play a significant role in this process as well. Although there is definitely racism in the Spanish Caribbean (e.g., Booth, 1976; see also, Bryce-Laporte, 1972; and Moore, 1977) it does not involve the strict categorizations present in the United States (see, Sutton, 1973; Mintz, 1974:264–265). The incorporation of Dominicans, a good share of whom are dark enough to pass as Black by United States standards, into the racial system prevalent here produces both objective and ideological burdens, including the somewhat novel experience of being identified in racial terms. As for the issue of class, there is evidence that the presence of middle-class individuals in an association will generate a push toward instrumental objectives. Rogler (1972), in his detailed study of a Puerto Rican association, found that as the core group became increasingly middle class, the association went from docile and expressive to militant and instrumental; from being community-oriented to making demands from the city's government agencies. As this transformation took place, the association lost its low-income members. For these middle-class members, participation entailed forging new links with the host society and a sense of obligation to nonrelatives (1972:219, 214). Hendricks in his analysis of middle-class Dominican associations (1974:106–109) found that their failure was due to divisive political issues rooted in the home country. That is to say, these associations were far more instrumental than the ones we located, which suggests that the class issue is quite central in determining whether an association will become instrumental. It would seem, then, that the disparity of place of origin, the incorporation into the United States racial system, and the predominance of low-income persons explain, to a large extent, why Dominicans are different from Colombians regarding the organization and use of instrumental associations.

CONCLUSION

The different incidence and types of voluntary associations in the Colombian and Dominican communities of New York City can be seen as an indicator of different modalities of articulation with the receiving society. This lends support to the hypothesis of differential adaptation within the structural uniformity of cities (*e.g.*, Little, 1967; *see also*, Parkin, 1966 and Meillassoux, 1968). The relative similarity of cultural-ideological variables in these two communities, brought out by the attribution of a common "Hispanic" as opposed to "Anglo" identity, tends to have less weight in the articulation with the receiving society than the structural differences of their places of origin and the disparity between place of origin and destination. The greater incidence of voluntary associations in the Dominican community and their less instrumental character is rooted in the nature of the gap between place of origin and receiving society, a gap much larger in the case of the Dominican than the Colombian community. The cultural separatism superficially visible in the "Latin" culture of both communities and in a deeper way in the reproduction of traditional institutions in new forms through voluntary associations, represents a distinct mode of articulation with the receiving society, not a form of disarticulation or disengagement. Finally, a shift was found in both communities from internally-oriented group activities to those involving active exchanges with the wider society, that is, a shift toward a condition of a "mobilized diaspora."

BIBLIOGRAPHY

Archdiocese of New York
1982 *Hispanics in New York: Religious, Cultural and Social Experiences* (2 vols.). New York: Office of Pastoral Research.

Anderson, R.
1971 "Voluntary Associations in History," *American Anthropologist*, 73(1):209–222. Feb.

Anderson, R. and G. Anderson
1962 "The Replicate Social Structure," *Southwestern Journal of Sociology*, 18(4):365–370. Winter.

Ardener, S.
1964 "The Comparative Study of Rotating Credit Associations," *Journal of the Royal Anthropology Institute*, 94(1,2):201–209. Jan.

Armstrong, J.A.
1976 "Mobilized and Proletarian Diasporas," *American Political Science Review*, 70(2):393–408. June.

Booth, D.
1976 "Cuba, Color and the Revolution," *Science and Society*, 40(2):129–172. Summer.

Bryce-Laporte, R.S.
1972 "Black Immigrants: The Experience of Invisibility and Inequality," *Journal of Black Studies*, 3(1):29–56. Sept.

Calderón, L., with the collaboration of J. Doreselaer and A. Calle
1963 *Problemas de Urbanización en América Latina*. Bogotá: Oficina Internacional de Investigaciones Sociales de FERES: Estudios Sociologicos Latinoamericanos No. 13.

Cardona Gutiérrez, R.
1973 *Las Migraciones Internas*. Bogotá: Editorial Andes.

Chaney, E.M.
1976 "Colombian Migration to the United States (Part 2)." In *The Dynamics of Migration: International Migracion*. Washington, D.C.: Smithsonian Institution, Interdisciplinary Communications Program. Occasional Monograph Series 5(2): 87–141.

Chaparro, O.F. and O.E. Arias
1970 *Emigración de Profesionales Técnicos Colombianos y Latinoamericanos, 1960 1970*. Bogotá: Fondo Colombiano de Investigaciones Científicas.

Cohen, S.M. and R.E. Kapis
1978 "Participation of Blacks, Puerto Ricans and Whites in Voluntary Associations: A Test of Current Theories," *Social Forces*, 56(4):1053–1071. June.

Comisión del Acuerdo de Cartagena
1977 *Instrumento Andino de Migración Laboral*. Decisión 116. Lima. Feb. 14–17. Mimeo.

Consejo Nacional de Recursos Humanos
1977 *Informe Sobre la Situación General y Perspectivas de los Recursos Humanos*. Caracas. Mimeo.

Corten, A.
1965 "Cómo vive la otra mitad de Santo Domingo: Estudio de dualismo estructural," *Caribbean Studies*, 4(4)3–19. Jan.

Cruz, C.I. and J. Castaño
1976 "Colombian Migration to the United States (Part 1)." In *The Dynamics of Migration: International Migration*. Washington, D.C.: Smithsonian Institution, Interdisciplinary Communications Program. Occasional Monograph Series 5(2):41–86.

de Janvry, A. and C. Garramon
1977 "The Dynamics of Rural Poverty in Latin America," *Journal of Peasant Studies*, 4(3):206–216. April.

Dotson, F.
1953 "A Note on Participation in Voluntary Associations in a Mexican City," *American Sociological Review*, 18(4):380–386. Aug.

Doughty, P.L.
1970   "Behind the Back of the City: 'Provincial' Life in Lima, Perú." In *Peasants in Cities*. W. Mangin, ed. Boston: Houghton Mifflin. Pp . 30–46.

Ennew, J., *et. al.*
1977   "'Peasantry' as an Economic Category," *Journal of Peasant Studies*, 4(4):295–322. July.

Fals Borda, O.
1967   La Subversión en Colombia. Bogota: Ediciones Tercer Mundo.

González, N.L.
1970   "Peasants' Progress: Dominicans in New York," *Caribbean Studies*, 10(3):154–171. Oct.

Gutiérrez, C.M.
1974   *El Experimento Dominicano*. México: Editorial Diógenes.

Gutiérrez de Pineda, V.
1968   *Familia y Cultura en Colombia*. Bogotá: Universidad Nacional de Colombia.

Hamer, J.H.
1967   "Voluntary Associations as Structures of Change Among the Sidamo of Southwestern Ethiopia," *Anthropological Quarterly*, 40(2):73–91. April.

Hendricks, G.L.
1974   *The Dominican Diaspora: From the Dominican Republic to New York City—Villagers in Transition*. New York: Columbia University Teachers College Press.

U.S. Department of Justice, Immigration and Naturalization Service
Various   Annual Reports. Washington, D.C.: Government Printing Office.
Years

Janvry, A. de and C. Garramon
1977   "The Dynamics of Rural Poverty in Latin America," *Journal of Peasant Studies*, 4(3):206–216. April.

Jongkind, F.
1974   "A Reappraisal of the Role of the Regional Associations in Lima, Perú," *Comparative Studies in Society and History*, 16(4):471–482. Sept.

Kayal, P.
1978   "The Dominicans in New York," *Migration Today*, 6(3):16–23. June; 6(4):10–15. Sept.

Little, K.
1967   "Voluntary Associations in Urban Life: A Case Study of Differential Adaption." In *Social Organization: Essays Presented to Raymond Firth*. M. Freedman, ed. London: Cass.

_____
1965   *West African Urbanization: A Study of Voluntary Associations in Social Change*. London: Cambridge University Press.

_____
1962   "The Urban Role of Tribal Associations in West Africa," *African Studies*, 21(1):1–9.

Mármora, L.
1978   *El Desarrollo de la Política de Migraciones Laborales en Colombia*. Bogotá: Ministerio de Trabajo y Seguridad Social, Servicio Nacional de Empleo. Mimeo.

Meillassoux, C.
1968   *Urbanization in an African Community: Voluntary Associations in Bamako*. Seattle and London: University of Washington Press.

Mintz, S.W.
1974   *Caribbean Transformations*. Chicago: Aldine.

Moore, B.L.
1977   "The Retention of Caste Notions Among the Indian Immigrant in British Guiana During the Nineteenth Century," *Comparative Studies in Society and History*, 19(1):96–107. Jan.

Norvell, D.G. and J.S. Wehrly
1969 "A Rotating Credit Association in the Dominican Republic," *Caribbean Studies*, 9(1):45–52. April.

Parkin, D.
1966 "Urban Voluntary Associations as Institutions of Adaptation," *Man*, 1(1):90–95. March.

Peel, J.D.Y.
1973 "Cultural Factors in the Contemporary Theory of Development," *Archives europeennes de Sociologie*, 14(2):283–303. Biannual.

Republica de Colombia, Ministerio de Trabajo y Seguridad Social
1978 *Politicas de Migraciones Laborales en Colombia*. Bogotá: Ministerio de Trabajo. Mimeo.

Republica Dominicana, Oficina Nacional de Estadistica
1970 "Cífras oficiales preliminares." Santo Domingo: Boletin, 5. July.

Rogler, L.H.
1972 *Migrant in the City: The Life of a Puerto Rican Action Group*. New York: Basic Books.

Sassen-Koob, S.
1978 "The International Circulation of Resources and Development: The Case of Migrant Labor," *Development and Change*, 9(4):509–546. Oct.

_____
1973 "Non-dominant Ethnic Populations as Parts of Total Society," *Aztlan*, 4(1):15–32. Spring.

Skeldon, R
1977 "Regional Associations: A Note on Opposed Interpretations," *Comparative Studies in Society and History*, 19(4):506–510. Oct.

Sutton, C.R.
1975 "Comments." In *Migration and Development Implications for Ethnic Identity and Political Conflict*. H.I. Safa and B.M. du Toit, eds. The Hague: Mouton. Pp. 175–188.

_____
1973 "Caribbean Migrants and Group Identity: Suggestions for Comparative Analysis." In *Migration: Report on the Research Conference on Migration, Ethnic Minority Status and Social Adaptation*. Rome: U.N. Social Defense Research Institute.

Tinker, H.
1971 *Race and the Third World City*. New York: The Ford Foundation, International Urbanization Survey. Mimeo.

Westbrook, J.T.
1965 "Socio-Economic Factors Related to Success and Failure in Agrarian Reform: The 'Caracol' Project, República Dominicana." In *The Caribbean in Transition*. University of Puerto Rico, Institute of Caribbean Studies: Second Caribbean Scholars Conference. Pp. 293–325.

A COMMENT ON DOMINICAN ETHNIC ASSOCIATIONS

EUGENIA GEORGES
University of Texas Health Science Center

Until recently, Sassen-Koob's pioneering article represented the only study of Dominican and Colombian associations in New York City. It is her thesis that there are more "affective" (largely recreational and social) organizations among Dominicans and "instrumental" (cultural-civic, goal-oriented) organizations among Colombians, and that this difference can be explained by the "structural differences of their places of origin, and the disparity between place of origin and destination."

This thesis requires amendment and clarification in the light of recent research. My comments are restricted to the Dominican case, drawing primarily on my own study of Dominican ethnic associations initiated in New York from the early 1960s to 1984 (Georges, 1984a, 1984b).[1]

My research indicates that both the origins of Dominican immigrants in their home society and the characteristics of their associations in New York are considerably more heterogeneous than Sassen-Koob suggests. She says that Dominicans in New York "typically originated in rural areas" and are "peasants and agricultural laborers who formerly would have entered the internal rural to urban migration flow." In contrast, Colombian immigrants are said to be predominantly urban and middle class in origin.

Survey research published since 1978, however, has modified our understanding of the composition of the Dominican migrant stream. Ugalde, et. al., (1979), Pérez (1981), Kritz and Gurak (1983), and Grasmuck (1983) agree that the majority of Dominican immigrants to the United States were born in urban areas, and many others have had some urban experience prior to migration. There also is widespread agreement that not only the poorest Dominicans migrate; the middle class is also well represented (Ugalde, et. al., 1979; Pessar, 1982; Grasmuck, 1983; Georges, 1983). This body of research now places the Dominican case squarely in line with what is known of the sociodemographic characteristics of international labor migration from other areas of the Caribbean (Cornelius, 1979:91 ff.).

[1] This research was funded by a grant from New York University's New York Research Program in Inter-American Affairs.

Still, it might be argued that even if most Dominicans have urban backgrounds, it is those from rural areas who predominate in the many "affective" organizations found in New York, since one of their purported functions is to replicate the close knit personal ties of the village left behind. Here, too, recent evidence does not support this claim. My analysis of data from Douglas Gurak's 1980 Hispanic Settlement Survey (Gurak, 1982; Gurak and Kritz, 1982; Kritz and Gurak, 1983, inter alia) found that Dominicans who join ethnic associations in New York do not have predominantly rural backgrounds. In fact, the rural/urban origins of association members are nearly identical to origins of the total sample population of Dominicans in New York: 60 percent "of association members were born in the four largest cities of the Dominican Republic, compared to 61 percent of the total sample population, while only 20 percent of association members were born in villages or towns with populations of less than 10,000. This is important, because Sassen-Koob bases her explanation of the differences between Dominican and Colombian associations on the putative "ruralness" of the Dominican stream and on the theoretical consequences of this ruralness.

What then are the differences between Dominican and Colombian associations? In the first place, Sassen-Koob states that there are more than twice as many Dominican as Colombian associations in New York, a finding taken as another indicator of adaptation of a rural population to an urban setting. But this finding ignores the fact that the Dominican population in New York is estimated to be about twice the size of the Colombian (Urrea, 1983), and the even more significant question of the evolution of immigrant institutions over time. Put simply, the longer an immigrant population has resided in a receiving area, the greater are the possibilities it will organize and create autochthonous institutions (Jongkind, 1974; Okamura, 1983).

Dominicans began arriving in New York in significant numbers before Colombians. Kritz and Gurak (1983:6) found that the average Dominican in their sample had resided in New York 11.3 years, and the average Colombian, 8.7 years. Although Dominican migration began to "take off" in 1961, and the first ethnic organization appeared in 1962, I found fewer than a dozen associations were formed by 1971. In contrast, Sassen-Koob identified 36 Dominican associations on the Upper West Side alone in 1978; by 1984 there were about 90 in that area, and a total of about 125 in the city as a whole. The fact that 81 percent of the Dominicans I interviewed in 1984 had joined or formed associations after five or more years of residence in the city, and 26 percent joined after ten or more years, suggests that the proliferation of immigrant associations may indicate adjustment in the receiving society rather than serve as a means to achieving that adjustment. That is, it may be necessary to invert traditional anthropological explanations of the functions of immigrant voluntary associations (Mangin, 1959; Little, 1967; Doughty, 1972). Thus, it is quite possible that the contrasts Sassen-Koob found in the nature of ethnic associations reflect differences in the length of residence of

Dominican and Colombian immigrants and that, in time, "affective" associations among Colombians will proliferate.

This hypothesis is supported by what is known of other immigrant organizations in New York. Although limited, the information suggests that the first associations were generally elite, middle-class, civic-cultural clubs. Among Puerto Ricans, for example, it was not until the 1950s that grass-roots organizations began to appear in any numbers (Estades, 1978:22). Similarly, among Dominicans, the dozen associations created in the early and mid-1960s included professionals, businessmen and consular officials—Dominicans who had more ties to other Hispanic middle-class persons in New York than to working-class Dominicans. The first Dominican grass-roots organizations did not emerge for roughly another decade.

To understand why organizations with distinct class compositions and goals develop at different times in the history of an immigrant community, it is essential to examine the changing characteristics of the migrant stream. It is also necessary to understand the political-economic context of both sending and receiving societies at the moments under scrutiny. There are several watershed events that have had profound consequences on the composition of the migrant stream, and, consequently, on the associations Dominicans created. The earliest migration was strongly influenced by the restrictions Trujillo placed on outmigration during his long regime (1930–61). Obtaining a passport was a dangerous and expensive undertaking, assumed by few who were not well connected to the dictator or his associates. With the exception of political exiles, the 10,000 Dominicans who emigrated to the United States before 1961 were a select group. Their associations—many of which are still active—were restrictive with respect to social class and political orientation, and their objectives were and continue to represent a class-based view of Dominican society and culture.

After Trujillo's death, emigration increased tenfold between 1961 and 1965, while the defeat of the liberal Constitutionalist faction in the Revolution of 1965 provided additional impetus for large-scale migration of participants in the revolt: members of left-wing and social-democratic parties, labor organizers, and dissident students from the National University of Santo Domingo, a key opposition sector during the period (Gutiérrez, 1972). Politically-motivated migration continued well into the 1970s, as the rapid industrial growth that took place between 1968 and 1974 was accompanied by increased repression and the violation of human rights. This small, but focal element of political exiles and dissidents reorganized their Dominican political parties in New York and mobilized grass-roots associations to oppose the regime of Joaquin Balaguer.

During this period, a foundation for future political mobilization was laid in the flowering of Dominican associations, social clubs and self-help organizations, culminating in the formation by 1984 of two federations of associations—the Association of Clubs and the Dominican Day Parade Committee.

With the 1978 electoral victory of the social democratic Partido Revolucionario Dominicano and the end of gross human rights violations in the Republic, the political agenda of many Dominicans in the United States began to change. A number of young, U.S.-educated activists in New York began to mobilize Dominicans for greater participation in U.S. politics, turning primarily to the parapolitical structure created by Dominican ethnic associations. Thus, the horizontal links forged among association members over the years provided a base from which Dominican activists could mobilize voters and candidates for community elections.

All this suggests that ethnic organizations are complex institutions whose functions are not easily categorized. Only by paying adequate attention to the evolution of the migrant stream in its specific historical context can the process of immigrant organization and active adjustment to the sending society be usefully illuminated and understood.

BIBLIOGRAPHY

Cornelius, W.
1979   *Mexican and Caribbean Migration to the U.S.* La Jolla: Program in U.S.-Mexican Studies, University of California, San Diego. Monograph No. 1.

Doughty, P.
1972   "Peruvian Migrant Identity in the Urban Milieu." In *The Anthropology of Urban Environments*. Edited by T. Weaver and D. White. Washington, D.C.: Society for Applied Anthropology, Monograph No. 11. Pp. 39–50.

Estades, R.
1978   *Patrones de participatión politica de los puertorriqueños en la ciudad de Nueva York.* San Jose, Puerto Rico: Editorial de la Universidad de Puerto Rico.

Georges, E.
1984a *New Immigrants and the Political Process: Dominicans in New York.* New York: Center for Latin American and Caribbean Studies, New York University Research Program in Inter-American Affairs. Occasional Paper 45.

_____
1984b "Dominican Diaspora: Putting Down Roots?" *Hispanic Monitor,* 1(2):6. May.

_____
1983   "El impacto de la emigración internacional sobre una comunida de la Sierra Occidental Dominicana." Paper presented at the Seminar on Dominican Migration to the United States, Museo del Hombre Dominicano, Santo Domingo.

Grasmuck, S.
1983   "Las consecuencias de la emigración urbana para el desarrollo nacional: el caso de Santiago." Paper presented at the Seminar on Dominican Migration to the United States, Museo del Hombre Dominicano, Santo Domingo.

Gurak D.T.
1982   "Immigration History: Cubans Dominicans and Puerto Ricans." In *Hispanics in New York: Religious Cultural and Social Experiences,* V. II. New York: Office of Pastoral Research, Archdiocese of New York.

Gurak, D.T. and M.M. Kritz
1982   "Dominican and Colombian Women in New York City: Household Structure and Employment Patterns," *Migration Today,* 10(3/4):14–21.

Guttiérez, C.
1972   *The Dominican Republic: Rebellion and Repression*. New York: Monthly Review Press.

Jongkind, F.
1974   "A Reappraisal of the Role of the Regional Associations in Lima, Perú." *Comparative Studies in Society and History*, 16(4):471–82. Sept.

Kritz, M.M. and D.T. Gurak
1983   "Kinship Networks and the Settlement Process: Dominican and Colombian Immigrants in New York City." Unpublished manuscript.

Little, K.
1967   "Voluntary Associations in Urban life: A Case Study of Differential Adaptation." In *Social Organization: Essays Presented to Raymond Firth*. Edited by M. Freedman. London: Cass. Pp. 153–165.

Mangin, W.
1965   "The Role of Regional Associations in the Adaptation of Rural Migrants to Cities in Peru." In *Contemporary Cultures and Societies of Latin America*. Edited by R. Adams and D. Heath. New York: Random House. Pp. 311–323.

Okamura, J.
1983   "Filipino Hometown Associations in Hawaii." *Ethnology*, 22(4):241–353. Oct

Pérez, G.
1981   "The Legal and Illegal Dominican in New York City." Paper presented at the Conference on Hispanic Migration to New York City : Global Trends and Neighborhood Change, The New York University Research Program in Inter-American Affairs.

Pessar, P.R.
1982   *Kinship Relations of Production in the Migration Process: The Case of Dominican Emigration to the United States*. New York: Center for Latin American and Caribbean Studies, New York University Research Program in Inter-American Affairs. Occasional Paper 32.

Ugalde, A., F.D. Bean and G. Cárdenas
1979   "International Migration from the Dominican Republic: National Survey." *International Migration Review*, 13(2):235–254.

Urrea Giraldo, F.
1982   *Life Strategies and the Labor Market: Colombians in New York City in the 1970s*. New York: Center for Latin American and Caribbean Studies, New York University Research Program in Inter-American Affairs. Occasional Paper 34.

RESPONSE TO COMMENT

SASKIA SASSEN-KOOB
Columbia University

Since it first appeared in 1979, my article on associations among Dominicans and Colombians in New York City has raised several issues among scholars. Its republication, along with Georges' comments, offers an occasion to respond.

There are two lines of criticism. One holds that new information showing Dominican immigrants to be largely urban in origin invalidates the key variable in my analysis, disparity between places of origin and destination. The other criticism is specific to Georges and based on her later research in the same Dominican immigrant community in New York City, where I found a predominance of noninstrumental associations. I shall comment on each point separately.

THE CATEGORY "URBAN"

New data, collected mostly since 1978, show that over one half of Dominican immigrants are urban born, and an even larger share has some urban experience. A key conceptual issue is how urban is defined.[1] Population size has been useful in defining the degree to which a settlement is urban in those countries where large numbers are an indicator of an array of modern social and economic arrangements. However, such "urban" characteristics do not describe large sectors of Third World cities today.

First, the growing number of dwellers in Third World cities are not being incorporated into institutions that are characteristic of the urban in the "western" experience,[2] notably the labor market, the network of public

---

[1] In using "urban" and "rural," I stated in the original article that these terms are "inadequate, but a convenient shorthand for a complex constellation of variables." Urban-rural is only one of several forms that disparity between places of origin and destination can assume. Disparity should not solely be equated with the urban-rural distinction.

[2] Similarly, we need an historical perspective on the nature of the urban in highly industrial economies. Of particular note here is the emerging "informalization" of many economic activities, especially in large cities (Sassen-Koob, 1984). Informalization can easily be seen as a consequence of the large Third World immigration. I would argue, however, that there are specific conditions at work in the current phase of highly industrialized economies that promote a reorganization of the work process wherein informalization is one important tendency. The presence of a large immigrant population from Third World countries where informal sectors are common may facilitate but cannot cause this development. There are fundamental differences in the way such cities are

services, education, and the associated rights and obligations of city life. Culturally, many city dwellers have little experience of the highly mediated character of life in a large city. Tinker's (1971) study on the ruralization of urban environments found that a significant portion of the urban population maintains strong linkages to the countryside. There is extensive informal circulation of goods and people between city and country, and rural dwellers sell some of their produce to their kin in the cities (Bhatt, 1984).

Second, given my concern with disparity between places of origin and destination, differences among cities are important, particularly the character of everyday life in the social strata from which immigrants come. It seems to me that differences in daily life between New York and Santo Domingo, and again between Santo Domingo and Bogotá are highly relevant for understanding how immigrants reconstitute their daily lives in a foreign location.

TRANSFORMATION IN THE DOMINICAN IMMIGRANT COMMUNITY

Georges found three important changes six years after I did my research. First, there was a larger number of associations. Second, there was a change in orientation among these associations toward U.S. issues. And third, she found a new, young, mostly U.S.-educated leadership. Georges' excellent study is a contribution to our understanding of the Dominican community in New York City: My problem is not with her findings, but with her evaluation of my study in the light of her findings.

Georges says that the larger number of associations among Dominicans indicates that they are more "adjusted" because the longer an immigrant community has resided in a foreign area, the greater its possibilities for organizing "autochthonous institutions." She claims I err in arguing that Dominicans are less adjusted.

First, my concern was to identify differences in modes of articulation of diverse immigrant communities, and to avoid reducing such communities to one common denominator (in this case, Hispanic culture). Further, my purpose was to decode those forms that are considered traditional, and hence assumed to be maladaptive in an advanced industrial society, to show that they, too, constitute forms of articulation.[3] I was concerned with showing that the class composition of immigrant communities is a key factor in shaping the forms of articulation, a point on which Georges and I concur.

---

incorporated in the world economic system. Expansion of an informal sector may, however, provide immigrant communities with forms of sociability and survival, and immigrants may participate in the growth of informalization.

[3] I view these associations, whether expressive or instrumental, as instances of articulation. Both types are political, although the forms assumed by the first do not correspond to conventional definitions of what is political. The terms expressive and instrumental probably are inadequate because they fail to convey the broader meaning of "political."

Second, my concern was to replace the notion of "adjustment" with the concept of articulation based on a combination of three variables: type of associations, their number, and the disparity between places of origin and destination among those who join. The much larger number of associations among Dominicans in recent years is understood by Georges as a function of length of residence, and hence as showing that the more adjusted a group, the greater the proliferation of associations.[4] I would suggest, as with "urban," the concept of "length of residence" needs to be given theoretical and historical content. It is not simply a measure of time, but of transformation in the class composition of immigrant communities, and changes in the degrees of disparity between places of origin and destination. The few instrumental associations initiated by the earlier wave of middle-class Dominicans confirm my hypothesis that the lower the degree of disparity, the higher the prevalence of instrumental objectives. However, it was not this group that predominated in Washington Heights at the time of my study.

Georges reports that most of the Dominicans she interviewed joined an organization after five or more years of residence, and that this indicates a greater adjustment. I claim that to make such an affirmation, we need to decode what length of residence and number of organizations stand for in each immigrant community.

Third, Georges herself mentions that the new leadership is a crucial factor in the changed orientation of Dominican organizations, away from the home country and toward the United States. Most of the new leaders spent their formative years in the United States, a fact suggesting a marked reduction in the disparity between place of origin and destination and the greater likelihood that a group would engage in instrumental activities, particularly direct exchange with the larger society aimed at empowering the immigrant community.

How many of these associations are now instrumental? Georges comments do not give an answer, although she suggests that most are. She says that the new leadership "turned primarily to the para-political structure created by Dominican ethnic associations in New York," a development I predicted in my earlier article. What raises questions, in terms of my analysis, would be the prevalence of a large number of instrumental associations. If this is so, I think that this development would point to a new phase in the mobilization of the Dominican immigrant community, one that begins to resemble that of citizen minority communities in periods of high political activity, notably that of Blacks, Chicanos and Puerto Ricans. At the same time, Georges' findings on the continuing importance of home country politics among

---

[4] Georges' notion that the contrasts I found between Colombian and Dominican associations reflect differences in the average length of residence of each population is not supported by the evidence to which she refers. There is an intermediate step that is not explicated: length of stay stands for transformations in the class composition of immigrant communities. Once this is made explicit, my analysis holds. A real test would require examining the length of residence in relation to an immigrant community that experienced no changes in its class composition.

Dominicans in New York is an important variable underscoring the distinctiveness of today's immigrant mobilization.

BIBLIOGRAPHY

Bhatt, E.R.
1984   "The Unintended City: The Case of India." Paper presented at the Conference on The
       Urban Explosion: Chaos or Mastery, United Nations Research and Training Institute and
       Association Mondiale de Prospective Sociale, Geneva.

Sassen-Koob, S.
1984   "The New Labor Demand in Global Cities." In *Cities in Transformation*. Edited by M.P.
       Smith. Beverly Hills, CA: Sage Annual Review in Urban Affairs. Pp. 26.

AFRO-CARIBBEAN RELIGIONS IN NEW YORK CITY:
The Case of *Santería*

STEVEN GREGORY
New School for Social Research

One aspect of Caribbean culture that has made a significant impact in New York City during the past few decades is the practice of African-derived religions. Introduced with the arrival of large numbers of Cuban and Haitian immigrants during the 1960s, the practices of Afro-Cuban *Santería* and Haitian *Vodoun* have increasingly come into prominence. The presence of these African-derived religions has been given further import by the fact that Black Americans, as well as persons of diverse West Indian and Hispanic descent—the second generation of Caribbean immigrants—have adopted Santería in recent years. Conferences, exhibitions and publications on African-derived religions sponsored by publicly- and privately-funded organizations in New York City, such as the Caribbean Cultural Center and the Museo del Barrio, point to a growing interest in African culture, particularly among the City's Caribbean and Black American populations.

Santería has received considerable attention from social scientists, health professionals, as well as from the established churches.[1] Much of this literature has focused on Santería's belief system and rituals (González-Wippler, 1973, 1982) or on its folk healing practices particularly, as these latter affect the delivery of professional physical and mental health care services (Garrison, 1977; Ruiz and Langrod, 1977; Sandoval, 1977). While some researchers have offered explanations for the practice of Santería by Cuban immigrants (Halifax and Weidman, 1973) and *espiritismo* by Puerto Ricans (Koss, 1975), these explanations focus on the psycho-therapeutic function of the religion for its practitioners who as immigrants are assumed to be experiencing undue stress.[2]

---

[1] A study on Hispanics in New York prepared by the Archdiocesan Office of Pastoral Research (1982) provides survey data on the religious beliefs and practices of Hispanics and background papers on aspects of Hispanic life in New York City.

[2] This focus on the psychotherapeutic function of African-derived religions has a long history

This chapter examines aspects of Santería's historical development, belief system, and social organization that I believe account for its vitality in the Hispanic, Black American and, to a lesser extent, West Indian communities of New York City.

My thesis is that Santería constitutes a world view, a cosmology that provides a meaningful and critical alternative to that affirmed by the dominant secular and religious institutions of American society. This cosmology is linked to a social structure that realizes its beliefs in the everyday social relations, economic activity, and religious discourse of practitioners. Practitioners of Santería are, thus, directly engaged in mediating what they perceive to be the significant forces in their lives—forces that are conceived of and treated as kinship relations between human beings and deities.

Secondly, the development of Santería in New York City will be considered in light of political, economic and social conditions in the United States that have influenced not only the reconstitution of the religion, but also the sense of cultural and ethnic identity held by practitioners. I will argue that these sociohistorical factors link Santería in New York City to its colonial origin in Cuba, as a culture of resistance to the dominant society.

Vodoun shares with Santería a similar historical development, cosmology and set of religious beliefs and practices. However, the more recent arrival of the Haitian immigrants, their less secure migrant status, plus a variety of other sociocultural factors, have limited the visibility of Vodoun and confined its practice to Haitian communities, described by Laguerre as "separate ecological niches" within New York City (1984). My own exposure to Vodoun in New York City indicates that its practitioners show greater concern for concealing its practice from the larger society than do practitioners of Santería.[3] Because of the relative lack of published scholarly material on the practice of Vodoun in New York City, the following discussion focuses on the practice of Santería, which has been the subject of my research during the past two years.[4]

The term Santería is used by Cubans and other Hispanic immigrants to refer to a variety of African religious complexes that were practiced by African

in the anthropological literature, beginning with the pathfinding studies of Nina Rodrigues in Brazil (1935). Harry Lefever (1977) has critically discussed the more widespread tendency among social scientists to portray "religions of the poor" as compensations for the conditions of lower-class life or as escapes from such conditions.

[3] I believe that Vodoun also has a stronger negative social stigma within the Haitian community than does Santería among Hispanics. Many Haitians—particularly of the middle classes—associate Vodoun with ignorance, superstition, and peasant life. On the other hand, Santería is closely associated with popular music, dance, and the visual arts in the Hispanic community. This in part accounts for its visibility and acceptance as a central component of Hispanic culture by all classes.

[4] Material for this chapter is based on field work I conducted in New York City since March 1984 and is incorporated into my doctoral dissertation (1986). This research was funded in part by the National Science Foundation and by a John R. and Elsie Everett Fellowship, provided through the New School for Social Research. I should like to thank Dr. Constance R. Sutton, James Norman, and Dr. Stanley Diamond for their comments and editorial assistance.

slaves and their descendants in Cuba and were later adopted by wider segments of the Cuban population. Practitioners of Santería, however, are more likely to use the term *Ocha* when referring to the worship of the Yoruba-derived deities called *orishas*, and *Palo* when referring to *brujería* or sorcery which is primarily of Bantu origin (Bastide, 1971; Thompson, 1983). It is Ocha, however, that is considered to constitute the religious core of Santería and define its character. As in most African religions, the spiritist component of Santería involves the propitiation of ancestors in particular, and *eguns*, or the spirits of the dead, in general.[5]

Each individual orisha such as Elegúa, Ogún, Yemayá, and Shangó, is thought to "rule over" a particular aspect of the universe. Elegúa, for example, is the divine trickster and "messenger" of the orishas and can "open the road," or change the destiny of a human being. The female orisha Yemayá encompasses the ocean, the concept of fertility, as well as the notions of vengeance and danger associated with the depths of the ocean. Ogún, the master of energy and iron, "rules over" warfare and justice and "owns" the iron tools and weapons with which human beings both create and destroy society. Shangó, the mythic king of the Yoruba city-state of Oyo, "rules over" lightning and fire which he uses to purge human society of hypocrisy, deception, and thievery.

Human beings are thought to manifest characteristics of the orisha, although with varying degrees of intensity. The relationship of a person to a particular orisha can be gleaned from his or her interests, temperament, as well as from a variety of other character traits, both positive and negative, which can be said to constitute one's individuality. The intensity of a practitioners personal identification with an orisha is further strengthened by his or her association, through divination, with a particular manifestation or "road" of that orisha; each road further articulates the attributes of an orisha and corresponds to a period in his or her mythological life. Thus in the younger roads of the warrior orisha, Ogún, he is thought to be more belligerent and unruly than in his later, more mature roads.

Religious practice in Santería is oriented toward developing and sustaining a relationship of balanced reciprocity with the orishas in general and with the specific orisha who "rules the head" of the individual practitioner.[6] Through making offerings to the orishas, sponsoring ceremonies in their honor, and living according to their will as it is revealed through divination,

[5] It is important to distinguish the African-derived spiritist component of Santería from *espiritismo*, influenced by the 19th century writings of Alan Kardec. Although some syncretism between Santería and espiritismo has taken place (Garrison, 1977), particularly among Puerto Rican religious groups, practitioners of Santería with whom I have worked strongly oppose this tendency and consider it a weakening of the Afro-Cuban tradition.

[6] Each individual is thought to have a special relationship with a particular orisha who guides and assists the practitioner during the course of his or her life. As one's involvement in the religion increases, this relationship becomes stronger and more clearly defined. Upon initiation into the priesthood, the orisha is thought to be actually "seated" in the hand of the practitioner.

practitioners ensure both the support and protection of the orishas in their daily lives. These reciprocal relations between practitioners and orishas are mediated through a network of ritualized kinship relations that binds practitioners together in religious communities known as *casas* or "houses."

In Cuba, African-derived religious practices were promoted through the establishment of *cabildos*, or fraternal associations, by slaves and free Blacks. These cabildos, formed by Africans of the same ethnic group or "nation," not only sponsored religious ceremonies and cultural activities, but also functioned as mutual aid societies, enlisting the support of their members for various cooperative endeavors, such as the financing of a members manumission (Knight, 1970).

While the organization of these "nations" and their cabildos was often encouraged by colonial authorities to promote ethnic rivalry among slaves and free Blacks, this divisive tactic sometimes back-fired: cabildos often provided the infrastructure and religious inspiration for rebellions and other acts of resistance in New World societies (Bastide, 1978; Genovese, 1979; Taussig, 1979). Moreover, although founded on the principle of common ethnicity, these cabildos eventually came to be associated with a particular African cultural heritage regardless of the ethnic composition of their members (Bastide, 1971).

Thus, from its outset, the practice of Santería linked the transmission of aspects of African culture to a social framework for resisting the dehumanizing system of colonial domination. Over time, Santería integrated practitioners from diverse African and non-African ethnic groups under a common sociocultural system, distinct from and often in opposition to the ideology and politicoeconomic interests of the dominant groups in Cuban society.

The resistance aspect of Santería in Cuba was accentuated by its suppression both during and after slavery. In response, practitioners disguised the identity of African deities and certain aspects of ritual behind a facade of Catholic icons and rites. Moreover, Santería developed esoteric traditions which served to conceal the practice of the religion from the dominant groups within Cuban society. The capacity of Santería to integrate diverse ethnic groups under a common system of religious beliefs, its resistant posture *vis-à-vis* the dominant society, and its esoteric tradition are all significant factors affecting its reconstitution in New York City.

It is difficult to ascertain when Santería first appeared in New York City. Pancho Mora, a Cuban *babalawo*, or diviner, reported that he was charged by the Asociación de San Francisco (an organization of babalawos, or priests to the orisha Orúnla) in Havana with bringing the religion to the United States in the 1940s (González-Wippler, 1983). During the 1940s and 1950s, Cubans and others wishing to be initiated as *santeros* (priests) would travel to Cuba where the necessary ritual specialists, materials, and facilities could be found. Following the Cuban Revolution and the exodus of large numbers of Cubans to the United States, Cuba became closed as a place to "make Ochas," or to conduct initiations, for those who had gone in to exile. By the early 1960s, Cuban exiles, Puerto Ricans, as well as Black Americans, who had become involved in Santería during the late 1950s, were being initiated in Puerto Rico, Miami and New York.[7]

In 1959, two Black Americans were initiated as santeros in Cuba. Both men had been active in the movement among Black Americans to define and assert an African cultural identity as an integral part of the struggle for political rights. During the mid-1960s, these men were instrumental in founding the Yoruba Temple of Harlem, along with a number of other Black Americans who had become practitioners of Santería or, as they were to refer to it, Yoruba religion. Some Temple members considered Yoruba religion to be the spiritual core of the African American nation and a necessary component of the Black Power movement. For this reason, they set out to purge Santería of its Catholic, or latinized content.

The linking of Santería, or Yoruba religion, to a nationalist ideology produced a number of consequences. On the one hand, some Cuban immigrants opposed the association of Santería with the Black Nationalist movement. Their reasons were political as much as religious. For one, the high visibility that members of the Yoruba Temple were giving to Santería (media interviews, parades, etc.) conflicted with the interests of Cuban immigrants, many of whom wanted to assimilate in to American society. It also ran counter to the esoteric tradition that the religion had maintained in Cuba. Many Black Americans, however, felt that Cuban opposition was motivated mainly by their racist attitudes.

On the other hand, Cuban opposition hardened the resolve of Temple members to develop outside of the larger Hispanic community of practitioners, despite the fact that the ritual status of Black American santeros was linked to their "spiritual descent" from Cuban santeros.[8] However, this ritual kinship link did serve to mediate the rift between Temple members and Cuban practitioners as well as between Black American and Hispanic practitioners who were just then getting involved in the religion.

While this encounter tended initially to polarize practitioners of Santería/Yoruba religion along ethnic, political and, to some degree, racial lines, it also laid the groundwork for a broader-based notion of group identity among Hispanic and Black American practitioners. During the past three decades, partly as a result of the political movements of the 1960s, many Caribbean immigrants and Black Americans have become aware of both the African roots of aspects of their cultures and their comparable socioeconomic positions within American society. Their changing cultural and political

---

[7] Most practitioners agree that Santería did not become firmly established in Puerto Rico until after the Cuban revolution.

[8] Black Americans during the 1960s were also dependent on Cuban santeros to perform specialized ritual functions such as divination, sacrifice, and the initiation of santeros to certain orishas.

consciousness, which Santería in part helped to promote, was a significant factor in the dissemination of Santería across ethnic boundaries.

Turning now to the actual practice of Santería in New York City, to its social organization, and to the meanings it holds for its practitioners, we find that the religion's social organization is based on a principle of ritual descent, while the core concept of its belief system is that of balanced reciprocity. As we shall see, these two fundamental aspects of Santería are critical to its capacity to mediate ethnic and socioeconomic differences among practitioners and to resist the ideological and structural pressures exerted by the dominant society.

Practitioners of Santería constitute religious groups organized on the basis of a principle of ritual descent. These groups, called *casas de santos* or "houses of Ocha," generally coalesce around a santero (male) or *santera* (female) who has established a reputation based upon his or her experience in the religion. Such a person establishes a house by accepting a number of "godchildren"— apprentices/proteges who refer to their "godparent" as *padrino* (male) or *madrina* (female).

The relationship between santero/santera and godchild lies at the very core of the social organization of Santería. It connotes a ritualized parent-child relationship paralleling the relationships existing between the living and their ancestors and the orishas and humankind. The role of the padrino/madrina is to direct the spiritual development of the godchild and provide a wide array of advice and assistance. In return, the godchild participates in and supports the ritual and secular activities of the padrino's or madrina's house. Godchildren provide both the labor and the money necessary to sponsor rituals and other religious activities. The status and viability of a house is therefore directly tied to the skill with which its padrino or madrina establishes and orchestrates these reciprocal bonds with godchildren.[9]

The acceptance of a godchild by a santero/santera is occasioned by the former's receipt of strings of symbolically colored and arranged beads, each of which is consecrated to a particular orisha. The ritual accompanying the receiving of beads marks the initiate's entrance into the religion and membership in the house of his or her padrino/madrina. Through this first ritual of initiation the novice is thought to be reborn out of the Ocha, or spiritual essence of the orisha received by his or her padrino/madrina upon the latter's initiation into the priesthood.

---

[9] Barber (1981:728) has noted that among the Yoruba of Okuku, Nigeria, the status of a "Big Man" was similarly dependent upon his ability to incorporate followers:

Recruitment of people was crucial in a Big Man's rise in two ways. First, they were actual factors in the production of wealth, as labor on the Big Man's farm and—in the case of wives—also as producers of the future labor of the children they bore. And second, in a fairly flexible social structure where individuals could make their own position for themselves, attendant people were the index of how much support and acknowledgement the man commanded, and thus how important he was.

In a conceptual sense, the term "house" is used to refer to all those persons, living and dead, who can be traced back for generations through the spiritual line of the padrino/madrina. Thus upon initiation, the practitioner becomes a member of a new kinship group which is a ritualized version of a genealogical model of kinship. Many houses trace their ritual lines of descent back to African slaves who lived in Cuba during the nineteenth century. During most important rituals, these ancestors of the house are invoked by name in chronological order. Most santeros can recite the names of all of the members of their house who were initiated to their Orisha, going back for generations.

A house also constitutes an active ceremonial community. The ceremonial center of this community is usually the residence of the santero/santera who presides over the house. Generally, the members of the house maintain their own residences elsewhere. These ritual godchildren may, of course, be the same age or older than their padrino/madrina. Although this kin group constitutes the membership of a house, nonmembers, such as santeros/santeras from other houses or friends and family of members often participate in its ceremonies.

A santero or santera with a large number of godchildren must have adequate resources and facilities to sponsor ceremonies and to fulfill the many responsibilities incumbent upon one who has achieved such stature. These facilities include space for the conducting of ceremonies, the storage of ritual materials, and the housing of altars. In addition, one must have kitchen facilities adequate to feed large gatherings of people and sleeping areas to accommodate practitioners visiting from out of town. A well-run house functions like a corporate family: its various tasks, such as the preparation of food, the purchase of ceremonial materials, the conducting of rituals, and the maintenance of the house are delegated to godchildren. On ceremonial occasions, large numbers of people become engaged in intense activity that often continues for a number of days.[10]

"Houses of Ocha" in New York City vary considerably with respect to their ethnic composition, religious beliefs and practices, and social organization. Some houses are composed entirely of Black Americans or Puerto Ricans, while others remain exclusively Cuban. Still others are multiethnic. Puerto Rican houses have a reputation for being more involved in European-derived spiritism than the more orthodox Afro-Cuban houses. Black American houses on the other hand eschew both spiritist and Christian influences—such as the identification of the orishas with Catholic saints—and stress the "pure" Yoruba tradition. Despite this variation and the relative autonomy enjoyed

---

[10] Practitioners of Santería use the term "work" to refer to both ritual and secular activity. "Working Ocha" describes the ritual activities (such as the making of offerings, sacrifice, etc.) involved in establishing a relationship of balanced reciprocity with the orisha. Similarly, all tasks within a house, such as cooking, cleaning and providing assistance to its members are considered to be sacred. Fernando's reputation, in part, is based upon the fact that all of his godchildren "work," regardless of their ritual status. This transformation in the nature and meaning of labor within a house of Ocha is the foundation upon which ritual kinship relations are constructed.

by individual houses of Ocha, there is considerable interaction among the members of distinct houses.[11] This interaction ensures the adherence to traditional beliefs and practices in important areas of ritual practice: the reputation of a house and of its padrino or madrina rests largely on how orthodox its beliefs and practices are perceived to be by ritual specialists from other houses.

For the past two years my research has focused on a predominantly Cuban house of Ocha in the Bronx, which I shall refer to as "Fernando's house." Fernando, who enjoyed a considerable reputation in Cuba as a santero, left there during the late 1960s, and after a brief stay in Spain, arrived in New York City in 1972 when his house was established. Fernando's house is well respected in the Santería community, is multiethnic, and is representative of the major Cuban houses in the United States. The active membership of the house consists of approximately 150 Cubans, 25 Black Americans, five persons of West Indian origin, five Puerto Ricans and two White Americans. In addition to these active members, the house includes a number of persons living in Miami, Chicago, and other areas of the United States and Puerto Rico who, for obvious reasons, do not regularly attend ceremonies.

Among Cuban and Puerto Rican members of the house, there is roughly an equal number of male and female practitioners. However, about 85 percent of its Black American members are women, as are all of its West Indian and White American members. Some houses, particularly those presided over by a madrina, show a clear predominance of female over male practitioners. This predominance of women is also evident in many Black American houses.

In Fernando's house, there is no division of labor on the basis of gender: the conducting of rituals, cooking, cleaning and other tasks are performed equally by both men and women. Traditionally in Santería, however, women cannot use a knife when making sacrifices, prepare food and perform certain ritual tasks while menstruating, or be initiated as babalawos, or *Ifá* diviners.[12]

The socioeconomic status of the members of Fernando's house varies considerably. The house includes college-educated professionals, civil servants and other members of the working classes, as well as persons of low

---

[11] There is no hierarchical organization among houses of Ocha in Santería. Members of houses tend to interact with other houses that are related through kinship relations. Consequently, it is difficult to estimate the total number of practitioners of Santería in New York City. There are no reliable estimates in the scholarly literature. The estimates of practitioners vary widely, from 250,000 to 500,000. This difficulty is compounded by the fact that many people visit santeros for health and other personal reasons and do not get more deeply involved in the religion. The New York Archdiocese's study (1982) estimated that there are 70,000 to 80,000 Hispanics in the archdiocese (which excludes the boroughs of Brooklyn and Queens, but includes Westchester County) who patronize *botánicas*—stores that sell religious paraphernalia for use in Santería. Since the survey 's respondents were informed that the study was being conducted by the Catholic Church, these figures no doubt represent exceedingly low estimates.

[12] Women are permitted to use other methods of divination, such as divination with cowrie shells (the "16 cowries"). This latter is the principal method of divination used by santeros. In Fernando's house, babalawos (priests of the Orisha Orúnla) are seldom used as diviners in rituals.

socioeconomic status. The relative proportions of these various socioeconomic groups within the house appear to be representative of the Hispanic and Black American population in general.[13] Ritual status, determined by seniority in the priesthood, cuts across these socioeconomic categories, as well as across age, sex, and ethnic boundaries.

The majority of the active members of Fernando's house are middle-aged (30–50), are santeros and have been involved in the religion for at least ten years. In addition, some older Cubans have been santeros for over 30 years. Most of the younger Hispanic practitioners were exposed to the religion through parents or other family relations who are also members of Fernando's house. Black American members of the house, generally in their 20s and 30s, were exposed to Santería through friends and acquaintances. Since santeros often bring their entire family to major ceremonies, there is strong tendency to transmit the religion across generational lines. The children of santeros in the house generally become Fernando's godchildren at a very early age; some are themselves initiated as santeros before the age of sixteen. Although children do not play major roles in ritual, they are accorded the respect due their seniority in the religion.

The members of Fernando's house take pride in its conservative adherence to the religious practices of the *Lucumi;* the term used for descendants of Yoruba slaves in Cuba. Fernando's reputation for orthodoxy, as well as his seniority in the priesthood, attract important santeros from many areas of the United States to attend ceremonies sponsored by his house. Moreover, he frequently travels to Miami and other cities where Santería is prominent to preside over initiations and other major rituals. This interaction between major houses of Ocha in the United States not only extends the scope of ritual kinship relations but also ensures that rituals are performed correctly. Santeros act as witnesses at rituals sponsored by houses other than their own.

Black Americans first became involved in Fernando's house during the early 1970s. Some of these persons had been initially exposed to the religion through their involvement with the Yoruba Temple or its members during the 1960s. Bob, the first Black American santero to be initiated in Fernando's house, told me that many of its Hispanic members were at first prejudiced against Black Americans and made it difficult for him to increase his knowledge and participation in ritual. He felt that the fact that Spanish was almost exclusively spoken in the house added to his alienation.

[13] Santería cannot be considered a religion of the poor. Among practitioners in general there is a large number of college-educated professionals, such as teachers, nurses, and social workers, as well as self-employed business people. There are also many artists, dancers and musicians who have traditionally been attracted to Santería and are largely responsible for its high visibility in New York City. Among second generation Hispanic and Black American practitioners, my impression is that persons of the middle class are disproportionately represented when compared with the general population. Many immigrant Cubans assert that practitioners in Cuba were of comparably diverse socioeconomic backgrounds.

During the 1970s and 1980s, however, the number of Black Americans in Fernando's house increased and so too did their ritual status and responsibilities. Black Americans were attracted to Fernando's house because of his reputation for orthodoxy, his disdain for Christianity, and his visible African descent. Now Bob is a key ritual specialist in the house and has participated in the initiation of both Black American and Hispanic practitioners. Hispanic and Black American practitioners in the house note that many of the racial and ethnic prejudices held by both groups have decreased over the years. To a large degree, these differences have been mitigated by the system of ritual kinship and by the collective participation of practitioners in the ceremonial affairs of the house. Bob noted, for example, that his position as elder within the house demanded the respect of less senior members; out of this respect emerged social relations of broader import.

Black American members of Fernando's house have learned sufficient Spanish to ensure their communication with non-English-speaking practitioners, while Hispanics have become sensitive to the communication problems caused by their exclusive use of Spanish. Bilingual persons have taken on the responsibility to act as translators during both religious and secular occasions. The kinship relations strengthened through the collective participation in tasks associated with maintaining the house and conducting its rituals also bind practitioners together in other areas of social life as well.

The network of social relations, cooperative labor arrangements, and various forms of social and spiritual support that develop through participation in a house of Ocha weigh heavily as factors involving both Hispanics and Black Americans in the religion. They are particularly important for persons from the Caribbean whose migration has reduced their face-to-face interaction with the full range of their immediate and extended kin. One Black American practitioner pointed out to me the important role that Santería plays in reconstituting the Black family.

Many illegal immigrants who do not have access to the subsidized institutional services available to citizens and permanent residents—such as health care, counseling, and other forms of social support—benefit from participation in these religious groups. Practitioners often assist their relations to find jobs and apartments, as well as to resolve legal, financial, and personal problems. In addition, houses of Ocha sometimes provide sanctuary for members who are avoiding immigration authorities (INS), for the temporarily homeless, or for those fleeing from a violent spouse. Fernando, for example, provided permanent accommodations for two of his godsons during the two-year period of my research, one of whom was a recent immigrant from the Mariel "boat lift."

Although many practitioners of Santería do not actively participate in the day-to-day activities of a house, the network of social relations that it both defines and structures often attains primary importance in their lives. Practitioners consider the relationship to their padrino or madrina, and to "godbrothers" and "godsisters" (persons sharing the same padrino or madrina), to be at least as important and binding as consanguineal relations, if not more so. As all ritual knowledge and spiritual power travel along these lines of ritual kinship, their maintenance is of critical concern to practitioners. For to offend one's padrino or madrina is to simultaneously offend the orisha who "rules the head."

As one's involvement in the religion increases, these social relations become more and more compelling. Conflicts sometimes arise between a practitioner and a spouse or parent who is not involved in the religion. A number of santeras have told me that their husbands oppose their participation in the religion, either because of jealousy over the attention they devote to the activities of their houses, or because of fear of the supernatural power they acquire. These and other potential areas of conflict and misunderstanding with nonpractitioners provide a strong incentive for making the house in particular, and the religious community in general, the focal point of one's social relations.

An increase in ritual knowledge carries with it an increase in responsibility not only to the orishas, but also to the social network through which the power of the orishas has been made manifest. Not only does the practitioner assume a greater role in ritual activities, but he or she also contributes to the education and training of novices. If the practitioner has been initiated as a santero/santera, he or she can then take on godchildren, thus creating a third generation in the house. This intimate relation between ritual status and assuming responsibility restrains the arbitrary exercise of power based on ritual status alone.

As a practitioner becomes more socially integrated into the house, he or she increasingly interprets the world according to the religion's cosmology. Social encounters, health issues, and everyday events are "read" (a term frequently used by practitioners) for their spiritual meaning. A chance meeting with a vagrant on the street, an argument with a co-worker, or a romantic relationship are not simply interactions between discrete individuals. Rather, they are encounters with spiritual forces and social contexts within which the orishas manifest their nature, communicate their will, or, more generally, reveal meanings of importance to the life of the practitioner.

One major factor in promoting this enculturation is the religious discourse that practitioners use among themselves to describe and analyze their experiences. To the outsider this discourse is obscure, since its referents are rooted in myth and in the complex symbolism associated with the orishas. Thus, a practitioner may read a meeting with a child at a traffic intersection as a meaningful encounter with the orisha Eleguá, who often appears as a child and is known as the "guardian" of the crossroads. The manner in which the child acted toward the practitioner plus other circumstances of the encounter are thought to provide valuable information to the practitioner concerning the status of his or her relationship with Eleguá or, by extension, with another orisha for whom Eleguá is acting as "messenger." If the encounter is deemed to be important, the practitioner will attempt to verify its meaning through divination. It is not uncommon for practitioners to change jobs, residences, or major aspects of behavior on the basis of such readings.

Possession, in particular, provides practitioners with a direct encounter and dialogue with the orishas. During possession this "sacred discourse" takes a dramatic form, involving all those present in deciphering the complex meanings being communicated by the person possessed by an orisha. Some-times an orisha will reprimand a practitioner for neglecting a ritual obliga-tion, or for having mistreated one of the orisha's "children," whether a spouse, friend, or casual acquaintance (such as the child encountered at the crossroads). More frequently, an orisha will warn a practitioner of an im-pending health condition, problematic social relationship, or behavioral trait that is "blocking" the person's spiritual development.

Often the family and friends of the person being addressed by the orisha will crowd around and listen attentively so as to gain insight into the issue being discussed, particularly if it affects their relationship with the person. In some cases, an orisha will explicitly direct a person to improve his or her relationship with a spouse or child; perhaps to be more patient, less jealous, or to resolve an area of conflict in the relationship. It is not uncommon for a family member, weeks after an orisha has spoken, to rhetorically ask the offending party, "Don't you remember what Yemayá said about your tem-per?" Few practitioners will take the advice or warning of an orisha lightly.

The above examples highlight the complex nature of the practitioners encounter with the sacred within both everyday and ritual contexts . Many practitioners point to this personal interaction with the orisha within a group-supported social context as one of the fundamental ways in which Santería differs from Christianity, Judaism, and Islam. They perceive Santería as having a more human and life-affirming set of beliefs and practices than the Judeo-Christian and Islamic traditions which are often identified as religions of conquest, colonialism, and slavery. Black American practitioners, in particular, emphasize these fundamental differences between African-de-rived religions and other religious groups such as the Nation of Islam, Rastafarians, and the various Protestant denominations which they assert "have nothing to do with Africa." One Black American, who has been a santero for over twenty years, observed :

> I think that Yoruba religion has helped people on an individual
> level to try to deal with their lives, or find meaning in their
> lives—meaning and purpose. That's a pragmatic thing . . . Most
> of the Christian religions don't approach that. Going through
> parochial school here, yes we heard about contemplation and
> meditation, but they never gave us the key to practicing it. There's
> a big difference. Had we gotten a methodology, many people

would never have converted [to Santería]. You see, Christianity is a religion that controls the masses—the clergy controls the masses. Yoruba religion is not about controlling the masses; it's about the individual and his self-realization.

However, the development of Santería in New York City has been affected by the dominant values, ideology, and institutions of American society. Many Cubans who were involved in the religion while in Cuba remark how it has changed in the United States, commenting in particular on its commercialization, on the competitiveness of its practitioners, and on the fact that some rituals are no longer performed correctly.

The high costs associated with sponsoring initiations and other ceremonies is an area of particular concern for most practitioners. To be initiated as a santero or santera, for example, can cost as much as $10,000. The high prices that must be paid for imported ritual materials and the greater emphasis placed on staging elaborate rituals by practitioners in the United States largely accounts for the seemingly exorbitant ceremonial costs.[14] One santera informed me that merchants in her neighborhood had inflated the price of goods (such as candles, cloth, and live animals) once they found out that they were being purchased by practitioners of Santería.

High real estate values also limit the amount of space available to practitioners for conducting rituals. Consequently, many santeros are forced to abstain from sponsoring important rituals and to refrain from accepting godchildren. This lack of space and the fluid residential patterns characteristic of New York City have mitigated against the establishment of permanent ceremonial centers that in Cuba, as in Africa, were supported by stable residential communities. Consequently, despite the disapproval associated with changing from one house to another, many practitioners do so.[15]

[14] Practitioners differentiate between two basic schools of Santería in Cuba: The Matanzas and the Havana Traditions. The Matanzas tradition is reputed to be closer to the religious practice of the *Lucumi,* more potent, and less refined with respect to ceremonial decor. The Havana tradition is associated with the more affluent and cosmopolitan residents of that city who, according to some practitioners, "cleaned-up" Santería and made it more acceptable to White, middle-class Cubans. As many of the early Cuban immigrants were from the middle classes, the Havana tradition became prevalent in the United States. Practitioners from the Mariel boat lift, being as a group less urban and affluent than the earlier wave of immigrants, are said to be closer to the Matanzas tradition in religious practice. Consequently, some practitioners assert that there is a power struggle at present between the two groups over which is the bearer of the authentic tradition.

[15] The fluidity of active participation in houses of Ocha makes it difficult to assess the continuity of practice among practitioners. During my field work, I have never heard of a case of a person actually leaving the religion once having been initiated, though persons do change from one house to another. Since there is no significant recruitment of practitioners, persons generally do not become initiated until they have already been involved in the religion for a number of years and have developed strong relations with the members of a particular house. Although there is no direct pressure to remain involved, for most practitioners, leaving the religion also means breaking the complex ties of ritual kinship that have become central in their lives.

The ritual sacrifice of animals has been a particularly problematic area for practitioners and one that has brought them into direct confrontation with the legal system. Raids by the police and ASPCA (the American Society for the Prevention of Cruelty of Animals) on houses of Ocha have greatly increased the secrecy surrounding the scheduling and conducting of rituals as well as practitioners' suspicion of outsiders. It is not uncommon for a person with personal grudges against a particular santero, or an entire house of Ocha, to "drop a dime" and phone the ASPCA to inform them that animals are about to be sacrificed.

Such intolerance on the part of state institutions has been further aggravated by sensationalist articles in the popular press, as well as by television broadcasts and films that perpetuate ethnocentric stereotypes of Santería and Vodoun among the population at large. Together, these ideological and institutional pressures have served to reinforce the posture of secrecy and resistance traditionally maintained by practitioners of Santería.

In recent years, some Hispanic and Black American practitioners are taking a more aggressive stance with respect to these issues. These practitioners maintain that African-derived religions are being suppressed in the United States as they had been in Cuba centuries before. Some have discussed testing statutes pertaining to animal sacrifice in a court of law as an issue of religious freedom.

There is also a trend among practitioners (particularly those who adopted the religion in the United States) to produce and disseminate literature on Santería and Yoruba religion. Many of these practitioners assert that it is essential for people in the religion to take an active role in documenting information as a means of both recovering and preserving the African cultural heritage in the New World. The Yoruba Theological Archministry, an organization directed by santeros, has played a key role in both producing and disseminating this information and in dispelling ethnocentric notions about African-derived religions.

This trend toward greater visibility and engagement with the institutions of American society among practitioners of Santería is but one manifestation of a broader-based recognition on the part of both Caribbean peoples and Black Americans of their common African cultural heritage. An interethnic sense of identity, grounded in both African culture and New World social history, has emerged from the encounter of Caribbean peoples and Black Americans in New York City.

This broadening sense of cultural identity has promoted direct religious contacts between santeros in the United States and African priests in Nigeria, thereby reproducing the intimate cultural relations that Afro-Brazilians have consistently maintained with Africa (Bastide, 1978). In addition, conferences in Nigeria and Brazil sponsored by the New York City Caribbean Cultural Center have brought together santeros from the United States, Brazil—*Can-*

domble priests, as well as Africa—Yoruba priests. The result has been a strengthening of traditional African-derived religious practices.

SUMMARY

It can be suggested that African-derived religions have played a role in New York City not unlike that which they had centuries before in Cuba and Haiti. By providing an alternative social and cultural framework for persons subject to economic, political, and social forms of domination, these religions have preserved in their followers a sense of cultural identity and served as a focal point for resisting the consequences of domination: the destruction of cultural identity, the decimation of kinship relations, and the negation of history.

For Cubans and other Caribbean immigrants, the practice of Santería has meant maintaining important cultural links with their pasts, as well as actively shaping their immigrant experiences.[16] For second-generation Hispanic practitioners and Black Americans, many young and college educated, the practice of Santería has meant asserting a distinct cultural identity, rooted in African culture. Moreover, this conversion has led them to appraise critically and restructure major aspects of their values, beliefs and social relations.

The development of Santería in New York City highlights many central issues concerning the shaping of immigrant identities and world views as they transfer and reconstitute aspects of their cultural heritage. Santería is a foci for the growth of an interethnic sense of cultural identity among Hispanic and Black American practitioners. Although the reasons for being initiated in houses of Ocha may differ, the common beliefs and ritual kin ties they acquire unite them in reproducing aspects of African culture in New York City.

BIBLIOGRAPHY

Archdiocese of New York
1982   *Hispanics in New York Religious, Cultural and Social Experiences* (2 vols.).New York: Office of Pastoral Research.

Barber, K.
1981   "Yoruba attitudes to their gods," *Africa*, 51(3):724–745.

---

[16] It is interesting to note that many Cuban practitioners visit relatives and friends in Cuba who are involved in Santería. Fernando, for example, has a son (biological) in Cuba who is a santero and an officer in the Cuban army. Ritual as well as biological kinship ties are thus maintained between the two countries. It is also said that all initiations that occur in the United States are recorded in a master register, maintained by santeros in Havana.

Bastide, R.
1978   *The African Religions of Brazil.* Baltimore: The Johns Hopkins University Press.

_____
1971   *African Civilizations in the New World.* New York: Harper and Row.

Cohn, S.
1973   "Ethnic Identity in New York City: The Yoruba Temple of Harlem." M.A. thesis, New York University.

Garrison, V.
1977   "Doctor, Espiritista, or Psychiatrist?: Health Seeking Behavior in a Puerto Rican Neighborhood of New York City," *Medical Anthropology,* 1(2):65–188. Spring.

Genovese, E.D.
1979   *From Rebellion to Revolution.* New York: Vintage Books.

González-Wippler, M.
1983   "Pancho Mora: Babalawo Supreme and Oracle of Orúnla," *Latin New York,* 6(9):27–28. Sept.

_____
1982   *The Santería Experience.* Englewood Cliffs, New Jersey: Prentice Hall, Inc.

_____
1973   *Santería.* New York: The Julian Press.

Gregory, S.
1986   "Santería in New York City: A Study in Cultural Resistance." Ph .D. dissertation, New York: New School for Social Research.

Halifax, J. and H.H. Weidman
1973   "Religion as a Mediating Institution in Acculturation." In *Religious Systems and Psychotherapy.* Edited by Richard Cox. Springfield, IL: Charles C. Thomas. Pp. 319–331.

Knight, F.W.
1970   *Slave Society in Cuba During the Nineteenth Century.* Madison: University of Wisconsin Press.

Koss, J.
1975   "Therapeutic Aspects of Puerto Rican Cult Practices." *Psychiatry,* 38(2):160–171. May.

Laguerre, M.S.
1984   *American Odyssey: Haitians in New York City.* Ithaca: Cornell University Press.

Lefever, A.G.
1977   "The Religion of the Poor: Escape or Creative Force?" *Journal for the Scientific Study of Religion,* 16(3):225–236. Sept.

Rodrigues, N.
1935   *O Animismo Fetichista dos Negros Bahianos.* Rio de Janeiro: Civilizaçao Brasileira.

Ruiz, P. and J. Langrod
1977   "The Ancient Art of Folk Healing: African Influence in a New York City Community Mental Health Center." In *Traditional Healing: New Science or New Colonialism?* Edited by Philip Singer. New York: Couch Magazine Company, Ltd. Pp. 80–95.

Sandoval, M.
1977   "Santería: Afro-Cuban Concepts of Disease and its Treatment in Miami," *Journal of Operational Psychiatry,* 8(2):52–63.

Taussig, M.
1979   "Black Religion and Resistance in Colombia: Three Centuries of Social Struggle in the Cauca Valley," *Marxist Perspectives,* 2(2):84–116. Summer.

Thompson, R.F.
1983   *Flash of the Spirit.* New York: Random House.

An Hispanic/Afro-Caribbean Comparison

THE PUERTO RICAN PARADE AND WEST INDIAN CARNIVAL:
Public Celebrations in New York City

PHILIP KASINITZ
New York University

JUDITH FREIDENBERG-HERBSTEIN
Mount Sinai School of Medicine, CUNY

The Puerto Rican Parade and the West Indian American Day Carnival are annual celebrations staged by Caribbean people living in New York.[1] Each asserts a distinctive sense of ethnicity reflecting the cultures and histories of these populations. At the same time each provides a dramatic forum in which competing ideologies of collective identity are put forward. These events not only reveal much about each group's sense of identity but also afford an opportunity to examine the respective modes of group mobilization and their linkages both to the nations of origin and to New York's social structure. This chapter compares these two cultural celebrations as collective rituals that carry para-political significance.

The peoples of the Hispanic and Afro-Creole Caribbean enter U.S. society with differing traditions of race and power relations stemming from different colonial histories (Mintz, 1974; Knight, 1978). Yet, today as "new immigrant" groups in New York, both Puerto Ricans and West Indians[2] find themselves in an ethnically and racially divided polity dominated by the children of earlier immigrants. They have entered a situation in which ethnic assertion has been a recognized basis for gaining social, economic and political power.

---

[1]   The original field work on the Puerto Rican Parade was conducted in 1974 and 1975 and that on the West Indian Carnival was conducted in 1983 and 1984. We wish to thank Constance Sutton, who originally suggested that we compare the two events and who has contributed extensive intellectual and editorial assistance in the writing of this paper. Antonio Lauría and Elsa Chaney also read and made helpful comments on several versions of the paper. Thanks are also due Professor Eric R. Wolf, to whom our analysis of the Puerto Rican parade is particularly indebted.

[2]   The term "West Indian," as used by the authors, refers to the inhabitants of the Anglophone Caribbean islands and the English-speaking, Afro-creole enclaves in predominately Hispanic Caribbean nations.

However, as "non-White" groups, this ethnic mode of mobilization is made problematic by the deeply embedded racial divisions of U.S. society. Thus the "new immigrants" are being incorporated not only into the United States but into a "Black America" and an "Hispanic America."

This distinction is not merely semantic. Historically, Blacks and Hispanics have been relatively excluded from the structures of opportunity in the United States. By contrast, "ethnic" groups, or to be more precise, those groups of European origin socially defined as "White ethnics," have long been considered at least potentially assimilable. In American political discourse the language of ethnicity has been largely a language of hope for collective upward socioeconomic mobility. While non-White groups have since the 1960s appropriated much of this language, they bring to U.S. politics a long history of exclusion from that process. Their situation also differs in that they have faced and continue to face unparalled exploitation and racial discrimination.

Today's Caribbean immigrants in New York City are well aware of the traditions of ethnic political activity established by earlier immigrant groups and of the exclusion of "non-Whites" from this process. They are also aware that their forms of ethnic assertion carry different political messages from those of earlier immigrant groups. The differences between Caribbean and past immigrants are further complicated by the changing economic and political structure of New York City and by the semicolonial relationship that exists between the United States and the countries from which the Caribbean immigrants come. Thus, the process of incorporating Caribbean immigrants into the mainstream of U.S. society coexists with the push of colonized peoples toward independence from the metropoles. Two differing responses to this complex political and cultural situation are ritually dramatized every year on the streets of New York in the form of the New York Puerto Rican Parade and the West Indian Carnival.

ETHNOGRAPHY OF THE TWO EVENTS

In contrast to the West Indian Carnival, the New York Puerto Rican Parade follows a pattern established by earlier immigrant groups in the city that have organized annual marches to assert their unity and pride to the American people and to themselves. With over one million Puerto Ricans, New York has long had the world's largest urban concentration of people from the Island (and is home to more than half of all Puerto Ricans living outside the Island). It is thus not surprising that the Parade is seen as an ethnic assertion by a group with the potential for real political power. An early Puerto Rican leader put it this way:

> The parade . . . should be an organization that demonstrates civic strength . . . that is the way the Jews organized themselves

into pressure groups, that is the way the Italians, the Irish, the Greeks, all showed strength at the beginning . . . Today, they have the power . . . (Presidential Report, 1963 Parade Campaign).

Almost twenty years later, Puerto Rican leaders asserted the same sentiment:

The best way for them (rank and file Puerto Ricans) to get their rights is to get involved in politics, not only today, but every day . . . to take a lesson from the Irish (Luis A. Olmedo, Grand Marshall, on occasion of the 1981 Puerto Rican Parade. *New York Times*, June 8, 1981)

This vision of Puerto Ricans as just one more tile to be fit into New York's ethnic mosaic is also espoused by leading members of the city's political establishment. For them the parade provides an important political platform.

This is the best parade in the city. Today I am proud to be Puerto Rican . . . In other parades I have been Greek, I have been Italian, I have been Irish, but today *yo soy boricua* (I am Puerto Rican) (Mayor Edward I. Koch, *El Diario-La Prensa*, June 10, 1985; our translation).

Yet many Puerto Ricans who participate in the Parade and others who don't, remain unconvinced that incorporation into U.S. society is either attainable or desirable. Puerto Rico's Commonwealth status in relation to the United States makes the notion of becoming "American" problematic to Puerto Ricans, both in New York and on the island. Thus, for much of its history, the Puerto Rican Parade has been a battleground between those who seek further integration into the contemporary U.S. political system and those who see such cultural events as part of the struggle for greater autonomy and independence. Yet, the parade is also an event in which these opposing views may be set aside for a symbolic display of Puerto Rican unity.

From its outset the Parade has been a self-conscious statement about "who we are," a statement that speaks both to New York's Puerto Rican communi and to the politically important others in New York and in Puerto Rico. a focus on portraying "what it means to be Puerto Rican," it has ine become a forum where competing political ideologies of ethnic ide projected. The mainstream political leaders of the Puerto Rican c who generally have dominated the organizing of the Parade, p vision of Puerto Rican economic and political integration into U.S. society while retaining a distinctive "cultural" identity through the use of Spanish and by continuing links to the island. Thus, the Parade is viewed

> . . . not simply [as] a legion of *boricuas* strolling along Fifth Avenue. It is much more than that . . . it is the honest desire to penetrate the heart of the great American people (*Este es mi Puerto Rico,* 1971:7–8).

This position is politically identified with acceptance of the present Commonwealth status for Puerto Rico and, for some, with moving toward eventual statehood. By contrast, the nationalists regard the struggle for Puerto Rican independence as a priority and thus oppose reformist ethnic organizations as well as the ideology of the Parade's leadership:

> We feel the Parade does not represent the reality of our people. While the problems of poor housing, education and poor jobs or no jobs at all beset our people, they cannot afford to join a parade which only benefits the *politiqueros* who dominate the event each year (*Claridad,* July 23, 1972).

Yet, rather than boycott the event, many nationalists attempt to use it as a forum to express their own ideology, as can be seen in banners such as "Parade One Day, Poverty Every Day!" Attempting to inject protest into the Parade, they emphasize the colonial and class dimensions of the Puerto Rican experience in the United States

During the early 1970s, there were unsuccessful attempts to bar the nationalists from participating in the Parade. However, with the growing concern for Puerto Rican unity, during the latter half of the decade the militants found themselves treated with condescending tolerance by even the most conservative Puerto Rican leaders:

> . . . they are good kids. Today they march with the Socialists. Next year they will march with us, when they open their eyes (Ramón S. Vélez, President 1976 Parade. *New York Times,* June 7, 1976).

~he mid-1970s a clique of right wing South Bronx politicians with a
for nepotism and misuse of funds have dominated the Parade's
~al structure. This has further distanced many nationalists, intel-

lectuals and middle-class Puerto Ricans from participating in the Parade. Nevertheless the Parade remains the one political event that unites the broad mass of New York Puerto Ricans in an expression of ethnic pride. For intellectuals and nationalists not to participate in such an event leaves them estranged from the proletarian majority. Therefore, many Puerto Ricans of various ideological stripes continue to participate despite their differences with the Parade leadership. Thus, the ritual of the Parade has become the arena where a bond of common identity is dramatized despite internal divisions.[3]

The immediate historical antecedent of the Puerto Rican Parade was the Hispanic Parade, founded in 1956 by the Federación de Sociedades Hispanas, Inc. to "demonstrate unity, discipline and civic strength" (*La Vox del Bronx*, June 2, 1974). Such unity, it was hoped, would emerge from the extension of the religious Fiesta de San Juan Bautista. As with its latter offshoot, the Puerto Rican Parade, the motivation to rework the religious festival into a political celebration was the desire to emulate those groups that had achieved upward mobility through ethnic mobilization. However, this Hispanic unity lasted only two years, for in 1958 a large Puerto Rican constituency broke with the broader group to found a solely Puerto Rican Parade. Leaders of this latter group felt that they could best be heard by the American authorities as Puerto Ricans and not as part of the larger Hispanic group. Since Puerto Ricans are U.S. citizens by birth, it was argued that they could more effectively struggle for their rights in the United States by disassociating themselves from non-Puerto Rican Hispanic organizations.

This separatist ideology, which was acclaimed in Puerto Rico as well as in New York City, had important implications for the organization of Puerto Ricans as an ethnic group. Early Puerto Rican migrants sought to identify with the wider and higher status Hispanic category, partially in an attempt to escape the stigma of being "non-White" (Mills, *et. al.*, 1950; Padilla, 1958; Estades, 1984). By the late 1950s, however, Puerto Ricans had begun to emerge as an independent political force, taking advantage of their unique political position in the United States. The Puerto Rican Parade was conceived as "the means to achieve the integral union of all Puerto Ricans so that they could then offer a hand to their "brothers of stock" (*see, Brief History of the Puerto Rican Parade* n.d.). Estades (*ibid.*) notes that from its inception, the Puerto Rican Parade featured more mass participation and was more explicitly oriented toward political mobilization than its more middle-class Hispanic predecessor. Yet the difference between "Hispanics" and "Puerto Ricans" was at that time more ideological than demographic since Puerto Ricans dominated the organizing committee of both the Hispanic and Puerto Rican Parades.[4]

[3] This definition of the situation is a victory for the mainstream leadership, for it helps to legitimize their claims to speak for all Puerto Ricans.

[4] The Hispanic Parade was immediately overshadowed by the founding of the Puerto Rican

Since 1958, the Puerto Rican Parade has been staged annually. Originally a conglomerate of grass roots organizations—primarily hometown associations—the Parade benefitted from the growth of state-funded Puerto Rican organizations during the late 1960s. By 1974, the Puerto Rican Parade included three quarters of all then existing Puerto Rican organizations in the city. These included hometown clubs, social clubs, political organizations, neighborhood and block associations, trade union groups, civic and service agencies, fraternities, masonic lodges, cultural and folkloric associations.[5] The Parade continues to represent a broad mix of organizations, although since the mid-1970s the hometown clubs have steadily declined in importance while commercial enterprises have become more prominent.

The Parade is financed by independently organized fundraising activities and by a number of businesses catering to a Puerto Rican market. In addition, the state provides a great deal of indirect support. Technically independent but substantially state-supported agencies contribute funds and the use of other resources (time, personnel, facilities, contacts) to the Parade planning effort. At the height of the "War on Poverty" programs, the Parade's structure was barely distinguishable from the web of the Office of Economic Opportunity (OEO) organizations that provided much of its support. For example, in 1974 the offices of the Parade were located in a large, federally-funded OEO agency. Several past presidents of the parade were on that agency's board of directors and employees of the agency were "urged" to participate in the activities in connection with the Parade. Of the agency's 100 subcontracting organizations, 78 were Parade sponsors and over half of the officers of the Parade corporation held full-time positions in the agency. The decline of antipoverty funding limited but by no means ended the political sponsorship of ethnic assertion. With the disappearance of OEO, political party-based groups have taken on a prominent role in the Parade's organizational structure, while the financial sponsorship of the event has largely shifted to commercial enterprises.

The entire week of the Parade is officially declared "Puerto Rican Week" by both the mayor and the governor. In addition to the Parade itself, other events are planned including a beauty contest, a competition of musical bands and a banquet that is the central annual event for the city's Puerto Rican politicians. It is attended by local and state officials as well as by representatives of the national Democratic Party and prominent political figures from the island.

---

parade. A separate Hispanic Parade was held in 1959. In 1960, it was merged with the Puerto Rican Parade, only to break off again and be held separately in 1961, after which it was disbanded. In the mid-1970s, following massive South American migration to New York, a new Hispanic Parade, held on Columbus Day, was established. A far more middle-class affair with little of the populist politics of the Puerto Rican event, this parade draws large numbers of Central and South Americans. Its cultural emphasis is on the common Spanish heritage of the many Latin American nationals in the city.

[5] For a detailed account of the 1974 Parade, *see*, Herbstein (1978).

The Parade can be viewed as an informal political institution that offers established and aspiring politicians an opportunity to advance their careers. As one past president states:

> I cannot refrain from recognizing that . . . presiding over the event had an immense value in my ambitions as a human being and as a community activist trying to advance in the city of New York (Puerto Rican Parade, Inc., 1974).

Moreover, Parade organizers are connected to each other in networks that serve to link the various Puerto Rican organizations. Through multiple position-holding these networks form a web that connects organization and individuals usually divided on questions of ideology and strategy.

As the very word "parade" implies, the event is a march based on the model of a military procession. Hierarchically organized, the parade requires election and appointment of various officials. Individuals with some visibility in a previous Parade are either nominated on a slate by their organizations or campaign for parade committee officers. There are usually two to four slates, headed by a candidate for president of the committee.[6] A slate is elected in a convention of Puerto Rican organizations that procedurally resemble an American major party presidential nomination. All officials serve in a voluntary capacity, ostensibly holding full-time jobs elsewhere. The actual planning of the event is done by an executive committee appointed by the elected president.

The second planning phase involves the selection of a grand marshal, a Puerto Rican with high visibility to both Puerto Ricans and other New Yorkers. This marshall leads the Parade, followed by representatives of the various participant organizations. They are identified by banners announcing their names, carried by nonuniformed but organized marchers. Contingents vary in size and splendor, some displaying musical bands, some floats, and some both. Among the largest contingents are those representing Puerto Rican workers in city agencies. Here the agencies' vehicles, including fire trucks, police cars, and most notably sanitation trucks, are proudly paraded in slow motion. Interestingly, the police contingent always receives a tremendous ovation from the crowd, even in years (such as 1985) when relations between the police and New York's minority communities are strained. The parade queen and her "princesses," white-gloved maidens who wave at the crowd from atop motorized carriages, are not associated with any particular

---

[6] The committee for the Puerto Rican Parade is composed of an executive committee (15) members, members-at-large (13), discipline officers (6) and a board of directors. The executive committee is comprised of a president, vice-president, general coordinator, subcoordinator, recording secretary, secretary for each of New York's five boroughs, an executive secretary, and public relations officer.

contingent. Rather, they represent the Parade itself as a community institution.

The Parade is traditionally held along Fifth Avenue from 37th Street to 86th Street on a Sunday in early June. Thus, it passes many of New York's most important cultural centers as well as some of its most expensive shopping and residential areas. It is an area where few Puerto Ricans live, yet it is of symbolic importance for New Yorkers of all ethnic backgrounds. Long associated with the city's "establishment," it is the site of many parades, notably the St. Patrick's Day Parade, the Labor Day Parade, and that most curious ethnic ceremony of New York's social elite, the Easter Parade.[7]

Several styles of parading can be observed. The contingents making a serious political statement (primarily left-wing and *independetista* organizations) march seriously. These do not display floats, bands, or other such frivolities but instead carry banners with political slogans such as *Obreros Unidos, Jamás Serán Vencidos* ("Workers United Will Never be Defeated"), and chant slogans such as *Qué Viva Puerto Rico Libre y Socialista* ("Long Live Puerto Rico, Free and Socialist"). Spectators tend to respond to these contingents with raised fists and the phrase *Qué Viva!* The participation of these groups varies from year to year.

Contingents that glorify hometowns are much less somber. They are accompanied by musical bands, floats and baton twirlers, and carry banners with announcements such as *Saludos de Boquerón* ("Greetings from Boquerón"). Often the mayor of the Puerto Rican town or members of its municipal assembly will fly to New York to lead the group. Their appearance in the parade is in turn broadcast on Puerto Rican television to the folks back home. Other contingents represent commercial enterprises. A few of these are Puerto Rican businesses but most are large corporations who do business with the Puerto Rican community. On elaborate floats they display banners such as: *Schaefer saluda a la comunidad puertorriqueña* ("Schaefer greets the Puerto Rican Community"), or *Estámos orgulloso de servir a la comunidad puertorriqueña* ("We are proud to serve the Puerto Rican community") as a float sponsored by Eastern Airlines.

Finally, community agencies and branches of municipal governments are well represented in the Parade. While they also carry banners and parade with baton twirlers and bands, their message is more directly political. They are champions of "ethnic assertion," but within the pluralist framework of New York City politics. Their banners urge the crowd to register to vote and their floats carry salutes to both local and Island political leaders who are present. These contingents are especially prominent during election years,

---

[7] Journalist José Rohaidy (1985:56) notes that in other cities where Puerto Rican parades are staged, they are generally held in the midst of Puerto Rican neighborhoods. Only in New York is "the Puerto Rican Parade held on a large avenue, rich and well lighted, prosperous and imposing. Here the participants march as if they are taking on this wealth and far from the misery, pain and discrimination in which they live."

particularly if a Puerto Rican is running for borough or city wide office. For example, they were out in full force in 1985 when the Parade's grand marshal, José Serrano, was a candidate for the Bronx Borough Presidency.

In addition to the tens of thousands of marchers there are hundreds of thousands of spectators who line Fifth Avenue cheering, waving flags and loudly applauding. They are divided into two strata: dignitaries seated in a *palacete* (literally the "small palace"—the podium) and the mass standing along the avenues, where some climb lampposts for a better view, and some sit on the curb. The dignitaries include not only leaders of New York's Puerto Rican community but also elected officials from Puerto Rico and New York State. National politicians as well as members of New York's political establishment including the Mayor are usually on hand. Police barricades and police officers mark a clear distinction between the marchers, the dignitaries and the spectators. Although the Parade is highly structured, the surrounding crowd spills over into Central Park where vendors sell Puerto Rican foods, flags and other ethnic paraphernalia throughout the day.

A central symbol in the Parade are the Puerto Rican flags, which during the weekend of the Parade can be seen throughout the city. At the Parade itself, Puerto Rican flags, carried by both marchers and spectators, fill the street. Also of political significance are the prominent double flags: the banners of both Puerto Rico and the United States bound together, and buttons on which both flags are represented. In Puerto Rico, this symbolizes a pride in the Island's connection to the United States, and is an anathema to those who advocate independence. In New York however, this symbol has taken on a new meaning. It proclaims the bearer to be a Puerto Rican of North American birth, a *Nuyorican*. This is a forceful statement that one's love of Puerto Rico is not diminished because one was born or grew up on the mainland. It is an assertion of one's continued tie to Puerto Rico, an assertion underscored by other buttons and pendants which proclaim "I Love Puerto Rico."

The entire Parade manifests a blend of cultural elements, both Puerto Rican and U.S.-based.[8] Together they constitute, as Lauría-Perricelli (1980) has noted, a generalized version of "what it means to be Puerto Rican." This transnational image of "Puerto Rican-ness," which the Parade reifies, has become increasingly important to the growing number of U.S.-born Puerto Ricans who may never have seen their "homeland." Their attachment to Puerto Rico expresses a sentiment beyond that expressed by most other

[8] A tradition of public celebrations, usually *fiestas patronales* (patron saint festivals), exists throughout the Island. In villages and towns, these celebrations involve processions, musical bands and, in an interesting variation on Marian iconography, the parading of local beauties selected to be festival "queens" and "princesses." As in New York these festivals are often sponsored by commercial enterprises. While the fiestas patronales exhibit distinct regional flavors, there are two national Puerto Rican parades that celebrate a vision of the nation as a whole: The Fourth of July and Constitution Day. Both of these are tellingly tied to Puerto Rico's semicolonial status, the latter marking the date of the initial U.S. occupation in 1898.

immigrant groups. They are saying, in effect, that being born in the United States makes you no less Puerto Rican.

That a parade held in New York should be the focus for recreating a concept of Puerto Rican culture as well as a venue for political mobilization is not surprising. With its demographic concentration of so many Puerto Ricans, New York has become as much a center of Puerto Rican life as San Juan. The bidirectional flow of people and ideas between these two centers is now part of the larger social field in which development in Puerto Rican culture and politics take place.

WEST INDIAN AMERICAN DAY CARNIVAL

;tival of the flesh that suspends normal social ιm, is a feature of many Christian cultures. In rope, it was often a period of ritual role reversal :ermed a "lampooning liberty" for the popular World by various Catholic plantocracies, it was taken over during the nineteenth century by newly emancipated Blacks who utilized this time of license to keep alive African traditions, to criticize (or at least satirize) the social order and to engage in what Reyes (1984:108) terms "ritualized resistance."

In Trinidad, Carnival developed into a "symbol of freedom for the broad mass of the population" (E. Hill, 1972:24). In the nineteenth and early twentieth centuries, it became marked by masquerades, the ritualized violence of calinda stick fighting and satiric calypso music. In the mid-twentieth century, highly competitive steel bands came to dominate the Carnival. By the 1950s, the Island's business elite sought to gain control of the event, sponsoring calypso and steel drum contests and repressing the more rebellious elements (Stewart n.d.). After independence in 1962, Carnival became a source of the symbols of nation-building (E. Hill, 1972), producing the paradox of a status conscious elite taking its cultural cues from the poor and converting their symbols of equality into expressions of national unity in an otherwise profoundly stratified society. Thus, the older tradition of Carnival as a leveling event became submerged though not eliminated.

West Indian migrants to the major metropoles of the English-speaking world have brought Carnival with them as a major annual festival and a rite of ethnic assertion. In London and Toronto, as well as in New York, it has become the symbol of West Indian unity and identity (Manning, 1982; Cohen, 1980, 1982).

Unlike the Puerto Rican Parade, Brooklyn's annual West Indian American Day Carnival is largely ignored by the city's press. Yet it is one of the largest

[9] This spirit of rebellion could not always be contained within the bounds of ritualized role reversal. More than once, Carnival was the occasion for mass violence and spontaneous rebellion. For a fascinating account of one such incident, *see,* Ladurie (1979).

regularly scheduled street events in North America. Held during the Labor Day weekend, the festival consists of four nights of concerts, steel band contests and children's pageants on the grounds of the Brooklyn Museum. On Labor Day, it climaxes with the huge Carnival procession on Eastern Parkway. These "official" Carnival events are accompanied by dozens of dances, concerts and parties in West Indian neighborhoods around the city. In 1982, 1983 and 1984, the police estimated the Labor Day crowd to be in excess of 800,000, while the West Indian community press put total attendance for all events at over one million.

Carnival was first celebrated in New York by migrants from Trinidad and neighboring islands in the 1920s. These celebrations were indoor, privately-sponsored dances. In 1947, immigrants from Trinidad organized a street Carnival that was held on Labor Day, a time of year more suitable for outdoor celebrations in New York than February. Scheduling the event on Labor Day also helped to break the always tenuous connection the pre-Lenten Carnival held to Catholicism.[10] New York's Carnival ran along Seventh Avenue through Harlem, then the heart of New York's Black community.

While based on the Trinidad model and dominated by Trinidadian organizers, this street Carnival was, from its inception, self-consciously pan-West Indian. West Indian unity, albeit on Trinidadian terms, has always been a central theme. The sheer numbers of people involved in such a highly visible event helped to promote a sense of group identity.

In 1964, following a small disturbance, the parade permit for Carnival in Harlem was revoked. Rufus Gorin, a Trinidad-born amateur band leader who had "played *mas*" (the West Indian term for masquerading in Carnival) in New York since 1947, attempted to organize a new Labor Day Carnival in Brooklyn, where a large number of West Indians had settled. The small ad hoc committee he headed initially met resistance from city officials, but in 1969 Gorin's successor, Carlos Lezama, obtained a permit to hold Carnival on Eastern Parkway, a wide boulevard that runs through the heart of Brooklyn's Black neighborhoods. Carnival has been held in this location ever since, and the committee, still headed by Lezama, is now a permanent organization known as the West Indian American Day Carnival Association (WIADCA).

Scheduling Carnival on Labor Day has had a number of unanticipated consequences. Many New York-based band leaders and costume makers attend Carnival in Trinidad in February, bringing back to New York's September event the latest in Carnival songs and fashions. Famous Caribbean entertainers also frequently spend Labor Day in New York. This continuous interplay between the New York and Trinidad Carnivals reflects the larger pattern of linkage between home and host societies that is a distinctive

[10] On the other hand, the New York City Carnival organizers avoided the more militant statement made by their counterparts in London and Toronto who scheduled their Carnival for the August Bank Holiday in order to correspond with the day on which Emancipation is commemorated in the English-speaking West Indies.

feature of the Caribbean Diaspora (Sutton and Makiesky-Barrow, this volume). The ties West Indians maintain with their home countries remain stronger than those most other ethnic groups have been able to manage. Another result of the Labor Day date was that it virtually guaranteed the event would be ignored outside the Black community. On Labor Day the New York press focuses its attention on the Labor Day Parade on Fifth Avenue, traditionally the occasion for assessing the state of the U.S. labor movement. While originally unconcerned by this lack of attention, the WIADCA leadership has lately become more interested in the potential for group recognition that Carnival offers. In recent years the WIADCA has made substantial major efforts to court favorable publicity, but with only limited success.

The location for holding Carnival has also been problematic. Many, including the tourist boards of several Caribbean nations, oppose the Eastern Parkway site because it is a "ghetto" location, and a move to Fifth Avenue is often suggested. In 1982, a group of West Indian businessmen attempted to mount a Caribbean festival in Manhattan on Labor Day weekend. While organizers insisted that the Manhattan festival would amend but not replace the Brooklyn event, it was soon perceived as a more "respectable" and "professional" rival to the WIADCA Carnival (Hall, 1982:14). The failure of this Manhattan festival was considered a victory for both Lezama and the Brooklyn site, which is both home to the largest concentration of West Indians in the city and rapidly becoming the center of New York's Black community.

In sharp contrast to the Puerto Rican Parade, the Carnival lacks a centralized structure. The WIADCA obtains the needed permit and deals with city officials, yet committee members are more coordinators than leaders. The other half of Carnival, the dozens of dances, shows and parties that go on throughout the city, are all run by individual promoters who operate independently of the WIADCA . The association receives most of its funds from small corporate, state and federal grants but compared to the Puerto Rican Parade committee it is a shoestring operation. The various steel bands and their accompanying retinues of elaborately costumed followers are all privately organized and their leaders are frequently at odds with the association over issues of scheduling, funding and organization.

These "bands"—some actually are steel drum bands while others are groups of costumed revelers that dance to recorded music in the Carnival procession—may each number from several dozen to several hundred persons. They are loosely organized around themes that emphasize fantasy ("Galactic Splendor" or "Party in Space"), ethnicity ("Caribbean Unite"), or current events ("Tribute to Bob Marley"). Their costumes are loosely coordinated but by no means uniform. In some bands all members are in costume, although in most only a few members wear elaborate outfits while most simply wear matching tee shirts. However, all bands feature at least two or three (and often a dozen) extremely complex and fantastic outfits that are not so much costumes as small, one-person floats.

Each band is organized around a flatbed truck that may carry a calypso group or a steel band, although in more recent years it is more likely to sport a huge sound system playing recorded music. The trucks display banners announcing the name of the bands' leaders, themes and sponsors (usually local businesses). The bands are completely independent of and in competition with each other. Unlike the organizations that march in the Puerto Rican Parade, most of the bands are organized explicitly for Carnival and do not represent ongoing political or social organizations. There is a striking absence of the numerous West Indian mutual aid organizations and high school alumni groups that are the functional equivalent of the Puerto Rican hometown clubs. Hence, while the Parade asserts an ethnic identity built on a web of organizations, Carnival suspends normal organizational life, creating the possibility of reformulating ethnic identity. This underscores the fact that Carnival is a special time when "normal" associations and boundaries do not necessarily apply.

A lack of central authority is evident in the Carnival procession itself. The procession starts with a collection of dignitaries, grand marshals (usually local business leaders, celebrities, and politicians) and city officials. They march, or rather saunter, down, the Parkway at about noon. However, at that time the main body of the Carnival may be a mile or even two miles behind them, so no one pays them any particular attention. They are usually followed (a full twenty minutes later in 1983) by a carload of West Indian American beauty contest winners. These young women, clad in bathing suits, are a striking contrast to the elegantly dressed "queen" and "princesses" of the Puerto Rican Parade. Like the dignitaries, the beauty contest winners are peripheral to the Carnival. The "action," the bands on flatbed trucks surrounded by masqueraders, may not make it down the parkway for hours. The huge crowds that line the Parkway eating, drinking, talking to friends, pay little attention to these "parade" elements that are grafted rather uneasily onto the Carnival structure.[11]

Long after the dignitaries and beauty queens have made their way down the Parkway the real Carnival begins. More than a dozen large bands and their retinues start down Eastern Parkway, theoretically in order. This structure breaks down almost immediately. Bands stop, change direction and take to the side streets. Most simply become bogged down in a dancing mass of humanity, in which the distinction between participant and spectator quickly disappears. In addition, groups of "devil-men," bands of nearly naked men (and in 1984 a few, slightly more modestly dressed women), their bodies blackened, wearing devil horns and tails, wander among the crowd

---

[11] Manning (1983) notes a similar lack of central force at the National Cricket Tournament in Bermuda. In that West Indian festival, the action on the sidelines, gambling and the display of the latest fashions, often "upstages" the cricket games themselves.

playing percussion instruments and generally moving against the flow of traffic. Many (in some years most) of the bands do not even finish the three-mile route in the allotted six hours. But as West Indians are quick to point out, it is not a race, it is a Carnival. As a dramatic event Carnival is strikingly leaderless. There are themes , a certain ebb and flow to the activity, but no particular center or head.

In contrast, the Puerto Rican Parade, based on a military metaphor, is largely about leadership. The dramatic structure of the Parade strives to intertwine the interests of the group with the careers of individual politicians. That is why aspiring leaders invest so much energy in obtaining parade offices and assuming visible positions in the event. The real political struggle takes place behind the scenes: Who will be president? Who will be grand marshal? Who will the huge drama serve to promote? What ideological image should predominate? The parade is intended to present a vision of a unified people marching behind their leader. Not surprisingly, many Parade leaders have used their positions as springboards for political careers.

The huge numbers involved in Carnival also draw those who seek recognition as community leaders. Yet the event itself subverts notions of leadership and presents instead a throng of autonomous individuals. The centerless nature of the Carnival leaves the politicians, and even the WIADCA officials, at something of a loss as to where to be. How does one "lead" an event without a head or even a very clear direction? The grand marshals are barely recognized by the crowd. Unlike the grand marshals of the Puerto Rican Parade, they are clearly not the focus of the event. Interestingly, neither of the two men who have dominated the WIADCA have used their positions to obtain political office.

Carnival is a leveling experience, symbolically obscuring the differences between high and low. Hence masks and masqueraders take on a tremendous importance. Rather than dramatizing existing rank and status differences in the manner of a parade, Carnival permits the masqueraders to take on new identities of their own creation. In the anonymous crowd, who one is becomes less important than who one can imagine one's self to be. Even the language of Carnival is participatory: one is not said to have watched a carnival or even marched in the Carnival. Rather one "plays mas" (i.e, masquerades) . This is an adult sort of play, in which one may take on the power, the beauty, the menace or sexual prowess of the costume. Yet, it remains "play," for tomorrow the dragon, the devil man, the fantasy queen will all resume their "normal time" roles and realities.

While the large bands all have themes, even they may be upstaged by individual masqueraders whose costumes represent outrageous satires on recent events. The vendors who line the route and the constant stream of people in both directions along the side of the Parkway further obscure any clear focus of attention. Near the Brooklyn Museum reviewing section, the police attempt to keep people out of the middle of the Parkway, maintaining some semblance of a distinction between those in the procession and those supposedly watching. Further up the Parkway they generally do not even try and, in any event, the distinction becomes meaningless as the day goes on.

Politically, Carnival is geared more toward group mobilization than toward any particular issue or individual. In 1983 and 1984, several groups took advantage of the opportunity to register voters and to urge legal residents of the United States to take out U.S. citizenship. Yet their pamphlets and posters stressed only that there are huge numbers of West Indians in New York (a fact made manifest by the Carnival setting), and that by participating in the United States these numbers could be converted into power. Their clear assumption was that West Indians constitute a political group with agreed-upon interests. The WIADCA in particular tries to get local political officials to show respect for the Carnival and, by extension, to view the West Indian community as an "ethnic" group. As Lezama writes:

To West Indians, as one of the many ethnic minorities in New York, the need for social collaboration, the introduction of a feeling of community and brotherhood are variables critical to us in maintaining our existence within the wide sphere of other ethnic groups (WIADCA, 1983).

A former Association officer puts it more directly:

We expect the powers that be to recognize Carnival as part of our culture, as the culture of any other group is recognized. We don't get that kind of recognition yet but we are working towards it.

The notion that West Indians are an ethnic minority like other ethnic minorities implies the presence of clearly recognized political leaders who may serve as brokers. The WIADCA attempts to present itself as such a group. To further that end, it works closely and visibly with city and state officials, holding fundraising events and garnering media attention. Yet, Carnival subverts these goals in its satirization of authority and hierarchy. Thus, in practice, Carnival tends to undermine the authority of both its origin organizers and the political officials from whom recognition is sought.

If Carnival, unlike the Puerto Rican Parade, does not create ethnopolitical leaders, it does assert group boundaries. More than any other event it visibly embodies the emerging pan-West Indian identity now evident in New York

(Sutton and Makiesky-Barrow, this volume). As Hill and Abramson (1979:83) note:

> Transplanted to Brooklyn, the great variety of dances seen in island performances has dwindled to two or three steps suitable for moving down Eastern Parkway in a huge crowd. In New York City the local villager has a new identity he or she is not just an islander, but a West Indian.

As Carnival draws on the common threads of Afro-Caribbean culture, it helps to form a conscious "West Indian" identity at a time when the politics of the Caribbean promotes differentiation between the islands. "Culture," one organizer notes, "can bring us together. Politics tends to separate us." The Mighty Sparrow expresses this sentiment in a 1976 calypso:

> You can be from St. Cleo, or from John John
> In New York, all that done,
> They haven't to know who is who,
> New York equalize you.
> Bajan, Grenadian, Jamaican, "toute monde,"
> Drinking they rum, beating they bottle and spoon.
> And no one who see me can honestly say,
> They don't like to be in Brooklyn on Labor Day!

> ("Mas in Brooklyn," Recording Artists Productions)

It is clear that in New York the old Carnival theme of "all of we is one" takes on a new meaning. To the symbolic reversal of class and caste differences is added the obscuring of island-of-origin differences. "New York equalize you!" Common themes are stressed, and national particularities are suppressed. Flags and symbols of national identity, so conspicuous at the Puerto Rican Parade are largely absent in the Carnival. Rather the central symbols are the mask and the costume, mediations between everyday reality and a fantasized world in which power, wonder, glamour and the terrible, reign.

Yet the fractious nature of the West Indies often breaks through the surface of this West Indian common identity, as Grenadian-born journalist Herman Hall (1982:17) notes:

Labor day weekend Carnival shows are becoming more specialized as nationals from each island do their own thing. Parties
organized by Guyanese are packed with Guyanese. The Haitians
have their own shows, as do the St. Lucians . . . each group has
its own fate . . .

To the extent that Trinidadian symbols have been the central themes of
the Carnival, the defining of this new West Indian identity takes place on
unequal terms. Although Carnival includes people from throughout the
Anglo-phone Caribbean and, more recently Haiti, Trinidadians and
Grenadians continue to dominate the WIADCA, the steel bands and the
costume-making workshops. Jamaicans, both the largest and fastest growing
West Indian population in New York, are particularly underrepresented in
Carnival organizations. In part this is because they lack a Carnival tradition.
It may also be because the Jamaican national musical form, reggae, is in many
ways a rival to the Trinidad-originated calypso that dominates the traditional
Carnival.[12] But whatever the reason, Carnival still masks divisions within the
community and, like the Puerto Rican Parade is able to present, on the
surface, a unified group identity.

In an attempt to include more Jamaicans, and more young people in
general, "reggae nights" were recently added to the festivities on the Thursday night preceding Labor Day. The reggae concert is both part of the
Carnival and at the same time distinctly separate from the weekend's other
events. Its inclusion represents a major, if tentative step, toward a broader
conception of Caribbean unity.

While the content of West Indian identity is still in flux, it is not surprising
that Carnival is the forum in which these issues are played out. The "special
time" nature of Carnival creates the social space for transitions in ethnic
identity. The major question hanging over the Carnival remains the West
Indian community's ambiguous relationship with the rest of Black America.
Despite frequent talk of Black unity and allusions to the common experience
of slavery, Carnival dramatizes a West Indian identity and thus distinguishes
Islanders from North American Blacks. The WIADCA leadership attempts to
project an image of West Indians as an ethnic group analogous to that of
European groups. Yet as Sutton and Makiesky-Barrow (this volume) point
out, the analogy is problematic. While some West Indians may see themselves
as "ethnics," in the United Statse they are largely regarded as part of the Black
community. As such, their status has been ascribed on the basis of race, not

---

[12] In Toronto, reggae has become an important feature of the Carnival and reggae events are
often among the best attended, a fact the Jamaican press reports with some pride (*Jamaica Weekly
Gleaner*, September 26, 1982). In London, the calypso/reggae split has divided Carnival along
generational lines. Cohen (1980) reports that since 1976, recorded reggae music has come to
dominate the event. Young West Indians seem to be mixing both Trinidad-originated masquerades
and Jamaican music.

cultural affiliation. While this means that as they become "Americanized" they become part of a low-status group; West Indian incorporation into Black America has also been the only viable route through which they have attained political effectiveness. In fact, West Indians have been disproportionately prominent among the city's Black political and economic leaders (see, Holder, 1980). The assertion of a West Indian identity in cultural rather than manifestly political terms allows their ambivalent political relationship with the rest of Black America to continue.

This contrasts markedly to the relationship between the Puerto Ric an and the larger Hispanic community. In the late 1950s, the Puerto Rican leadership believed that only separation from the rest of Hispanic New York would allow Puerto Ricans to come into their own politically. The majority of Spanish-speaking New Yorkers at the time, Puerto Ricans were also the most economically disadvantaged. They feared cultural and political domination by other Hispanic groups. Today, pan-Hispanic consciousness is growing, both in New York and throughout the nation. Yet the position of Puerto Ricans, now politically established but still the poorest segment of an increasingly diverse Hispanic population, has yet to be clearly worked out.

At the same time, Black America is also becoming more culturally diverse and many young West Indians, influenced by Rastafarianism, reject the ethnic model in favor of a more pan-Africanist vision that seeks to set aside differences within New World black communities. While this ideology is internationalist in content, it is nevertheless expressed in a form that is specifically Jamaican in origin. Not only does this signal important changes in the way many Black Americans and West Indians see themselves, but it underscores the fact that the process by which group self-definitions are constructed is a highly dynamic one.

CONCLUSIONS

While the ideology of cultural pluralism encourages ethnic assertion among contemporary immigrant groups, both Puerto Rican and West Indian New Yorkers confront the social reality of racial discrimination and the neo-colonial ties of their home nations to the United States. As Dominguez (1975:53) notes:

> Caribbean immigration is special because it is resulting in the formation of racial boundaries rather than ethnic ones . . . Geographical proximity, a recent history of colonialism and the current domestic situation of the U.S. contribute significantly to the trends and patterns of this migrant wave, but it is the generalized stigma of "non-whiteness" that distinguishes this massive immigration from previous ones to this country.

The two rituals we have explored express some of the contradictions that arise in this situation. Both dramatize a continued "ethnic" unity, and both are forums for competing ideas about group identity and political goals. Each represents not only the transfer of cultural traditions but statements about how each immigrant group seeks to relate to the wider polity.

The differences in these two public ceremonies are also instructive. Possessing a clear sense of nationhood, despite their long colonial history, Puerto Ricans parade up Fifth Avenue in a ceremony analogous to that of other New York ethnic groups. They express a unity that masks internal political differences behind a visible leadership. Yet the Puerto Rican sense of nationhood is embedded in a long history of dual struggle to obtain more rights from the colonial powers ruling Puerto Rico and to assert Puerto Rican independence from these powers. So, too, the Puerto Rican Parade. Staged by "Nuyoricans," it continues to project the struggle in a dual message. It calls attention to Puerto Ricans as an ethnopolitical constituency to be reckoned with by the New York City political establishment. Yet at the same time, it marks the Puerto Rican community's strong links to their home country where independence from the United States remains a live political issue. Emblematic of this conflict are the dual Puerto Rican and U.S. flags carried in the Parade.

In Carnival, West Indians make an ethnic statement within the larger framework of Black America, where West Indians have in the past gained prominence as Black political leaders but not as a distinct ethnic community. Their Carnival takes place within the black community and reaches an almost entirely black audience. Visible ethnic leadership, however, is not prominent in Carnival, for the colonial history of West Indian societies has not produced a strong sense of cultural and political nationhood. Instead it produced bipolar social structures within which populations display a conscious sense of social and cultural dualism often referred to as "double consciousness." After a long history of political and economic authority being concentrated in the hands of English and local white elites, the numerically predominant black population of the islands harbor a traditional suspicion of authority in general. This carries over into celebrations such as Carnival. Thus, rather than reify a sense of nation and politics in a flurry of flags, New York's West Indians play out their ritualized resistance to normal power relations in a festival of masks. In the Puerto Rican parade, group mobilization creates and reinforces status differences; in Carnival it obscures status differences. By donning outrageous masks in the midst of a dancing throng, anyone can be a "star" for the moment.

Both of the public rituals we have analyzed reflect the dynamics of Caribbean migration in the context of the contemporary world system. Within this system the politics and culture of home and host countries cannot be neatly separated; they are inextricably tied together by the migration of both capital and labor. The cultural traditions of the Caribbean nations, the ideological climate of the United States and the immediate political situation in New York City are all factors in the equation of how Caribbean immigrants respond to their sojourn in New York City. The symbolic realm of public celebrations crystallizes this dynamic process as immigrants transform their daily experiences and sentiments into a drama played out on the streets.

BIBLIOGRAPHY

Brief History of the Puerto Rican Parade
1984   NY: New York Puerto Rican Parade, Inc.

Claridad
1972   "Desfile un Día, Pobreza todos los Días," Claridad. July 23.

Cohen, A.
1982   "A Polyethnic London Carnival as a Contested Cultural Performance," Ethnic and Racial Studies 5(1):23–41. Jan.

————
1980   "Drama and Politics in the Development of a London Carnival." Man 15(1):65–86. March.

Dominguez, V.
1975   From Neighbor to Stranger: The Dilemma of Caribbean Peoples in the United States. New Haven: Yale University, Antilles Research Program. Occasional Papers No. 5.

El Diario-La Prensa
1985   "Poder Boricua Invade NY," El Diario-La Prensa. June 10.

Estades, R.
1984   "Symbolic Unity: The Puerto Rican Parade." In The Puerto Rican Struggle: Essays on Survival in the U.S. C. Rodríquez, V. Sánchez-Korrol, and J.O. Alers, eds. NY: Waterfront. Pp. 82–88.

Este es mi Puerto Rico
1971   "Historia del Desfile Puertorriqueño." San Juan, Puerto Rico: n.p.

Everybody's Magazine
1984   "Special Feature: Brooklyn Carnival '84," Everybody's Magazine 8(5):36–41. Aug.

Hall, H.
1982   "Inside Brooklyn's Carnival," Everybody's Magazine 6(7):12–24 . Nov.

Herbstein, J.F.
1978   "Rituals and Politics of the Puerto Rican 'Community' in New York City." Ph.D. dissertation, Graduate Center, City University of New York.

Hill, D.
1981   "New York's Caribbean Festival," Everybody's Magazine 5(6):33–37. Sept.

Hill, D. and R. Abramson
1979   "West Indian Carnival in Brooklyn," Natural History 88(7):72–85. Aug./Sept.

Hill, E.
1972   The Trinidad Carnival. Austin: University of Texas Press.

Hispanic Parade, Inc.
1956   Souvenir Journal.

Holder, C.
1980   "The Rise of the West Indian Politician in New York City: 1900–1952," Afro-Americans in New York Life and History, 4(1):45–57. Jan.

Jamaica Weekly Gleaner
1982   "Ethnic Festival in Toronto," *Jamaica Weekly Gleaner*, North American edition. Sept. 26.

Knight, F.W.
1978   *The Caribbean: The Genesis of a Fragmented Nationalism.* NY: Oxford University Press.

Ladurie, E. Le R.
1979   *Carnival in Romans.* NY: Braziller.

Lauría-Perricelli, A.
1980   "Reflexiones sobre la cuestión cultural y Puerto Rico." In *Crisis y Crítica de las Ciencias Sociales en Puerto Rico.* R. Ramírez and W. Serra Déliz, eds. Rio Piedras: Centro de Investigaciones Sociales. Editorial de la Univeridad de Puerto Rico. Pp. 295–310.

Manning, F.
1983   "Get Some Honey for Your Money: Gambling on the Wages of Sin." In *The Celebration of Society. Perspectives on Contemporary Cultural Performance.* F. Manning, ed. Bowling Green, OH: Popular Press, Bowling Green University. Pp. 80-99.

1982   "Carnival in Canada." Videotape.

Mills, C.W., C. Senior and R.K. Goldsen
1950   *Puerto Rican Journey.* NY: Columbia University Press.

Mintz, S.W.
1974   *Caribbean Transformations.* Chicago: Aldine.

New York Times
1981   "Puerto Ricans Parade in Cheer and Sun," *New York Times.* June 8.

1976   "Six Hour Puerto Rican Parade is Spirited," *New York Times*, June 7.

North American Congress on Latin America
1971   "El Parido Socialista Va; a New Stage in The Puerto Rican Struggle," *NACLA's Latin America and Empire Report*, 5(8):11–22. Dec .

Padilla, E.
1958   *Up From Puerto Rico.* NY: Harper and Row.

Puerto Rican Parade, Inc.
1974   Annual Report. NY: Puerto Rican Parade, Inc. Pp. 1–2.

Reyes, A.
1984   "Carnival: Ritual Dance of Past and Present in Earl Lovelace's The Dragon Can't Dance." *World Literature Written in English*, 24(1):107–120.

Rohaidy, J.
1985   "El Desfile de Nueva York fué la inspiración de los Demás." *Desfile Puertorriqueño '85.* NY: El Diaro-La Prensa. (Special Section, June 9, 1985):56.

Stewart, J.
n.d.   "The Changing Significance of Trinidad's Carnival." Unpublished manuscript.

Turner, V.
1983   "The Spirit of Celebration." In *The Celebration of Society: Perspectives on Contemporary Cultural Performance.* F. Manning, ed. Bowling Green, OH: Popular Press, Bowling Green University. Pp. 187–191.

La Voz del Bronx
1974   "La Historia del Desfile." *La Voz del Bronx.* June 2.

West Indian American Day Carnival Association
1983   *Souvenir Brochure.* NY: WIADCA.

Photographs

A Haitian at the Brooklyn public celebration of "Baby Doc" Duvalier's fall from power. (Photograph by Carl Andon. All rights reserved by the photographer.)

Puerto Rican Day Parade. (El Diario/La Prensa. Photographs by Vargas.)

Cooking pigs on the street in the South Bronx near Willis Avenue in New York. This vendor sets up shop every Friday afternoon. (Photograph by Ellan Young.)

West Indian Carnival, Brooklyn, September 1986. (Photograph by Philip Kasenitz.)

Mural in East Harlem. From "Nosotras Trabajamos en la Costura" slide show. Centro de Estudios de Puertorriqueño, Hunter College, CUNY. (Photograph by Max Colón.)

Street vendor selling Caribbean foods. From "Nosotras Trabajamos en la Costura" slide show. Centro de Estudios de Puertorriqueño, Hunter College, CUNY. (Photograph by Max Colón.)

A "family affair"—enterprising street vendor in the Bronx displays her wares under the old Third Avenue El, and solves the childcare problem by bringing her baby with her. (Photograph by Ellan Young.)

An international game—cat's cradle—is enjoyed by children of Colombian and Dominican migrants in Jackson Heights, Queens. (Photograph by Elsa Chaney.)

From "Nosotras Trabajamos en la Costura" slide show. Centro de Estudios de Puertorriqueño, Hunter College, CUNY.

Haitians celebrating the fall of "Baby Doc" Duvalier at Grand Army Plaza, Brooklyn, February 8, 1986.

About the Contributors

ABOUT THE CONTRIBUTORS

JOHN ATTINASI is associate professor and director of bilingual education at Indiana University, Northwest, in Gary. He has written several papers on Mexico, Puerto Rico, and Mayan language and culture and spent two years in field work in a contemporary Mayan village in Chiapas, Mexico.

LINDA BASCH is a Projects Director with the United Nations Institute for Training and Research. She has done extensive field work in Africa and the Caribbean and has also worked in Iran. Her research interests have included health care practices in Africa and Iran, race and ethnicity in the Caribbean, the implantation of transnational corporations in developing countries; and migration and development. More recently, she has explored and published on migrant women's organizations. She received her Ph.D. in anthropology from New York University and she has taught in the anthropology departments at New York University and St. John's University, and in the medical school at Pahlavi University in Iran.

UALTHAN BIGBY is a graduate student in geography at Indiana University, Bloomington. He received his B.A. from the University of the West Indies, Mona, Jamaica. His current interests include the study of economic development in the English-speaking Caribbean, especially Jamaica, and the impact of migration on that country.

ROY SIMÓN BRYCE-LAPORTE is the director of the Institute on Immigrant and Population Studies, City University of New York, CSI and Professor of Sociology at the College of Staten Island, New York. He received his Ph.D. in sociology from the University of California at Los Angeles, and has taught in several colleges and universities in the United States; he was the first director of the Yale University program in Afro-American studies. Dr. Bryce-Laporte was founding director of the Research Institute on Immigration and Ethnic Studies, the Smithsonian Institution, and has authored numerous works on Caribbean immigration to the United States and Central America.

MARIE LUCIE BRUTUS received her M.A. in anthropology from Hunter College, City University of New York in 1983, specializing in health. She did research in Haiti on medical belief systems and currently is enrolled in the doctoral program in health education in New York University.

ELSA M. CHANEY received her Ph.D. in political science from the University of Wisconsin in 1971. Since then, she has taught and carried out research on women in development, international migration and food and nutrition issues in Latin America and the Caribbean. She is a visiting scholar at Georgetown University, Washington, D.C., coordinating research in the Caribbean for the Center for Immigration Policy and Refugee Assistance.

CAROLLE CHARLES received an M.A in political science from the University of Quebec in 1978. She currently is teaching at Queens College, City University of New York, while working on her doctorate in sociology at Binghampton. She has done research on Caribbean women and migration, as well as on Haiti, her homeland.

DENNIS CONWAY received his Ph.D. in geography from the University of Texas at Austin. He is associate professor of geography and director of the Latin American and Caribbean Studies program at Indiana University. Current research interests include Caribbean migration, Trinidad's urbanization experience, and the Caribbean experience in New York City.

JOSH DeWIND received his Ph.D. in anthropology from Columbia University in 1978. He studied Peruvian miners for his doctoral thesis, and since has researched numerous aspects of international migration in the United States. Currently he is directing the Immigration Research Program at the Center for the Social Sciences, Columbia University.

JUAN FLORES is an associate professor of sociology at Queens College, City University of New York. He is a former director of research and currently an adjunct at the Centro de Estudios Puertorriqueños at Hunter College, CUNY. His published works include *Poetry in East Germany* (1971), *Proletarian Meditations: George Lukacs' Politics of Knowledge* (1972), and *Insularismo e ideología burguesa* (1980). His Ph.D. in sociology is from Yale University.

NANCY FONER is professor of anthropology at the State University of New York, Purchase. Her Publications include *Status and Power in Rural Jamaica: A Study of Educational and Political Change* (1973), *Jamaica Farewell: Jamaican Migrants in London* (1978), and *Ages in Conflict: A Cross-Cultural Perspective on Inequality between Old and Young* (1984). Dr. Foner received her Ph.D. from the University of Chicago.

GEORGES FOURON received his Ed.D. in language, literature and social studies from Teachers College, Columbia University, in 1984. His doctoral thesis was a study of Haitian immigrant adaptation to life in New York. He currently is an assistant professor in social and behavioral sciences at the State University of New York, Stony Brook.

JUDITH FREIDENBERG-HERBSTEIN originally from Argentina, received her Ph.D. in anthropology from the City University of New York in 1978 where her dissertation concerned political rituals in New York's Puerto Rican community. She is on the faculty of community medicine at the Mount Sinai School of Medicine/CUNY.

VIVIAN GARRISON received her Ph.D. in anthropology from Columbia University in 1972, and is senior research associate in the Institute for Urban and Minority Studies, Teacher's College, Columbia University. She is a visiting associate professor at the Charles F. Drew Postgraduate Medical School, Los Angeles. She has done extensive research, writing and teaching in medical settings on social networks, folk healing practices, and mental health in the Hispanic and Afro-American communities of the New York-New Jersey metropolitan region.

EUGENIA GEORGES received her Ph.D. in anthropology from Columbia University. She has researched Dominican migration in the United States and the Dominican Republic. Currently she is a research fellow at the University of Texas, Health Science Center, Houston.

NANCIE L. GONZÁLEZ has published extensively on the culture patterns of the Garifuna or Black Carib, with whom she has worked for 30 years. Recently, she did another year of field work in Guatemala, Belize, and Honduras, and is completing a book on ethnic diversity and development in the Atlantic lowlands of Central America.

STEVEN GREGORY received his Ph.D. from the New School for Social Research and is currently working as an urban development consultant for a number of community-based organizations in New York City. In addition to his field work on Santería in New York City, he has done research in Haiti and plans to conduct a study in that country on the political, economic and cultural impact of conservative evangelical Christianity. His research interests focus on problems of urban development, migration and culture change among Afro-American populations in the New World.

PHILIP KASINITZ a Ph.D. candidate in sociology at New York University, is currently doing research on West Indian ethnic politics in Brooklyn. He has taught at New York University, Fordham University, and the State University of New York, Old Westbury.

SUSAN MAKIESKY-BARROW is an anthropologist who has conducted research on social and political changes in Barbados. She currently is involved in studies of homelessness in New York City, where she is a research scientist at the New York State Psychiatric Institute. She holds a Ph.D. from Brandeis University.

PAULE MARSHALL is a second generation Barbadian-American writer whose novels and short stories reflect her West Indian background. Her works include *Brown Girl, Brownstones* (1959), *A Chosen Place, A Timeless People* (1969), and *Praisesong for the Widow* (1983).

PEDRO PEDRAZA, JR. is director of research, Language Policy Task Force, at the Centro de Estudios Puertorriqueños at Hunter College, City University of New York. He is the author of several reports and papers on language use and policy in the Puerto Rican community, including a study of inter-generational perspective on bilingualism. He holds an M.Phil. in sociology from Columbia University.

PATRICIA R. PESSAR is the Research director of the Center for Immigration Policy and Refugee Assistance, Georgetown University. She received her Ph.D. in anthropology from the University of Chicago in 1976, and has conducted research in Brazil, the Dominican Republic and the United States. She has published extensively on women and migration, and the role of the household in migration.

DAVID M. REIMERS received his Ph.D. from the University of Wisconsin. He is professor of history at New York University, where he teaches American history, including courses dealing with immigration to the United States. He is co-author of *Ethnic Americans: A History of Immigration and Assimilation* (Second Edition, 1982); his latest book is *Still the Golden Door: The Third World Comes to America* (1985).

SASKIA SASSEN-KOOB is an associate professor of economic development at the graduate School of Architecture and Planning, Columbia University. She is currently co-directing a study, "Hispanic Women in the Garment and Electonics Industries in New York, California, and Florida," and completing an investigation on the informal sector in New York City. Her forthcoming book is *The Foreign Investment Connection: Rethinking Immigration.*

NINA GLICK SCHILLER's doctoral dissertation in anthropology, Columbia University, traces the formation of Haitian ethnic identity in New York, 1969–1971. She has done research on women hospital workers and office workers, and on the mentally-ill homeless. She currently is a research associate at the Center for Social Sciences, Columbia University.

ISA MARÍA SOTO is a graduate student of anthropology at New York University. She has carried out research on regional migration in Trinidad and on international migration among West Indians in New York City. Her current interests include the study of social change and economic development in the Hispanic and English-speaking Caribbean.

SUSAN H.BUCHANAN STAFFORD is a program specialist for the Communit y Relations Service, U.S. Department of Justice, working in the Cuban-Haitian entrant program. She received her Ph.D. in anthropology from New York University, having conducted extensive research on the Haitian community in New York City, and she has published several articles based on this work.

CONSTANCE R. SUTTON is associate professor of anthropology at New York University, and associate of its Center for Latin American and Caribbean Studies, as well as president of the International Women 's Anthropological Conference. She received her Ph.D. from Columbia University and has carried out field research in Barbados and among the Yoruba of Nigeria. She has authored works on migration, gender, and collective action.

CAROL I. WEISS received a Ph.D. in sociomedical sciences from Columbia University. Her thesis involved field work with the networks of Dominican psychiatric patients in northern Manhattan. She now is a program evaluator with the New Jersey Division of Mental Health and Hospitals in Princeton.

INDEX